CR 767

[Stamp: OTDD 14 JUN 1993 TECHNICAL TRAINING WING]

D.0583704 9105867 388M 6/79 W.A.S.

M.O.D. Form 340 A

00347 -1
Accession No.

658.91
Classification No.

LIBRARY
(Command, Unit, Etc., Stamp)

E GREEN - G DRAKE - J SWEENEY
Author

This book must be returned on or before the last date stamped below

[Stamp: THE GILES STUDY CENTRE DO NOT REMOVE]

[Stamp: OTDD 14 JUN 1993 TECHNICAL TRAINING WING]

PROFITABLE FOOD AND BEVERAGE MANAGEMENT: PLANNING

PROFITABLE FOOD AND BEVERAGE MANAGEMENT: PLANNING

ERIC F. GREEN, GALEN G. DRAKE,
AND
F. JEROME SWEENEY

Harris, Kerr, Forster & Company

VNR VAN NOSTRAND REINHOLD
New York

Portions of this work originally appeared in *Profitable Food and Beverage Operation, Fourth Revised Edition*, edited by Joseph Brodner, Howard M. Carison, and Henry T. Maschal, also published by Hayden Book Company, Inc.

Copyright © 1951, 1955, 1959, 1962, and 1978 by Hayden Book Company, Inc.

Copyright © 1991 by Van Nostrand Reinhold

Library of Congress Catalog Card Number 77-25023
ISBN 0-442-00707-8

All rights reserved. No part of this work covered by the copyright hereon may be reproduced or used in any form or by any means—graphic, electronic, or mechanical, including photocopying, recording, taping, or information storage and retrieval systems—without written permission of the publisher.

Printed in the United States of America

Van Nostrand Reinhold
115 Fifth Avenue
New York, New York 10003

Chapman and Hall
2-6 Boundary Row
London SE1 8HN, England

Thomas Nelson Australia
102 Dodds Street
South Melbourne, Victoria 3205, Australia

Nelson Canada
1120 Birchmount Road
Scarborough, Ontario M1K 5G4, Canada

16 15 14 13 12 11 10 9 8 7 6 5 4 3 2 1

Library of Congress Cataloging in Publication Data

Green, Eric F
  Profitable food and beverage management: operations.

  (Ahrens series)
  Bibliography: p.
  Includes index.
  1. Food service management. I. Drake, Galen G.,
joint author. II. Sweeney, F. Jerome, joint author.
III. Title.
TX911.3.M27G73   658'.91'64795   77-25023
ISBN 0930745-02-7
ISBN 0-442-00707-8

Preface

Profitable Food and Beverage Operation was the title of an earlier text also edited by partners of Harris, Kerr, Forster & Company. That the present text is in two volumes—*Operations* and *Planning*—is one indication of the growth in the size of the food service industry and of its complications.

The growth itself was not exactly planned—it came about through dynamic changes in our economy: a growing work force, needing to eat away from home; nutritional mandates in our school systems; the restaurant meal as a tax deductible business expense to highly taxed businesses; new lifestyles of the younger and older generation. The growth has called forth new managerial ideas, new companies (many listed on the stock exchanges), and more need for managerial planning and control.

The growth of the industry has not gone unnoticed by consumer activists and both local and federal governments. Truth in advertising and in menu listings is required in addition to good food at fair prices in pleasant surroundings. Wage and hour laws, tip credits, uniform allowances, and increases in minimum wages require the restaurant operator to be ingenious and to understand well the laws that pertain to his business. Restaurant owners and managers must now expect to become political activists if their planning is to take place in reasonable stability. Familiarity with all the factors that relate to restaurant profitability is therefore essential.

The purpose of this volume is then to put into perspective those factors as we see they have been developed by owners and operators and that students and investors will want to be aware of.

New topics are covered that were not included in the earlier text. We are indebted to Mr. Gerard A. Navagh for the chapter on laws relating to the food service industry and to Mr. Richard Lorson for the chapter on energy control. For the illustrations of functional planning and kitchen planning we gratefully acknowledge the contributions of Cini-Grissom Associates, Inc., and Maurice B. Lafiteau, Inc. Automation poses a different problem in a book of this sort; the text may be out of date before it is printed. For that reason theory is discussed rather than specific applications.

We gratefully acknowledge the contributions of members of our staff and of the companies that have permitted us to use their material and illustrations.

The editors hope that the new volumes will supplement the earlier text and provide a sound basis for students and businessmen alike in making operations profitable.

Eric F. Green
Galen G. Drake
F. Jerome Sweeney

Contents

PART ONE: PLANNING FOR PROFITABILITY   *1*

  1. Introduction to the Food Service Industry   *2*
  2. Marketing Strategy   *19*
  3. Financial Strategy   *35*
  4. Conceptual Strategy   *67*
  5. The Feasibility Study   *72*
  6. Designing for Profits   *98*
  7. Kitchen and Cafeteria Design   *119*
  8. Pricing the Product   *148*

PART TWO: MANAGING THE BUSINESS   *163*

  9. Management   *164*
 10. Accounting Functions and Internal Controls   *185*
 11. Financial Statement Analysis   *199*
 12. Budgeting Procedures   *215*
 13. Automated Data Procedures   *227*
 14. Energy Management   *248*
 15. Advertising and Sales Promotion   *272*
 16. Laws Affecting Food and Beverage Operations   *297*
 17. Unions and Contract Negotiations   *311*
 18. Insurance   *319*

Bibliography   *326*

Index   *335*

PROFITABLE FOOD AND BEVERAGE MANAGEMENT: PLANNING

Part One

Planning for Profitability

1

INTRODUCTION TO THE FOOD SERVICE INDUSTRY

Providing food and drink for people away from home is a big business, one that plays an important part in the nation's economy. Businesses classified as "eating and drinking places" by the U.S. Department of Commerce employ almost 3 million people and account for over 25 percent of the total expenditure for food in the United States.* The U.S. Department of Commerce reported the sales of eating and drinking places to be $52.3 billion in 1976, making such businesses the fourth largest category of retail trade.

The food service market, however, is not limited to this one category. The National Restaurant Association (NRA) has classified more than 50 types of food services (see Fig. 1–1). Many of these are retail stores that operate food services as part of their selling operations. Others are nonretail businesses that frequently offer on-premises food and beverage service to employees, to passengers on planes, ships and railroads, to people in private clubs, camps, recreational centers, in schools, hospitals, institutions, in government office buildings and on military installations. The NRA estimated that the total sales of the food service industry in 1975 was $71 billion (see Fig. 1–1).

Structure of the Industry

According to 1969 Internal Revenue Service data from tax returns, about 75 percent of the eating and drinking places were single

---

*Eating and drinking places are defined by the U.S. Department of Commerce as follows:
Establishments primarily selling prepared foods and drinks for consumption on or near the premises; and lunch counters and refreshment stands selling prepared foods and drinks for immediate or take home consumption. Also included are caterers who sell prepared foods which are served elsewhere than at their place of business and in-plant food contractors. Eating and drinking places operated as leased concessions in theaters, hotels, motels, and places of amusement are included here.

The Foodservice Industry—Estimated Food and Drink Sales and Purchases

Number of Units	Type of Establishment	Estimated F&D Sales (000)	Percent of Total F&D Sales	Estimated F&D Purchases (000)	Percent of Total F&D Purchases	Source
	Group I—Commercial Feeding[1]					
113,582[2]	Restaurants, Lunchrooms	$23,584,728	33.49	$ 9,469,905	32.94	1,21,22,23
3,944	Social Caterers	930,091	1.32	382,175	1.33	1,22
8,222	Commercial Cafeterias	2,243,995	3.19	851,170	2.96	1,22,23
78,694	Limited Menu Restaurants (Refreshment Places)	12,767,350	18.13	4,592,415	15.97	1,21,22,23
5,506	Ice Cream, Frozen Custard Stands	487,978	0.69	165,912	0.58	1,21,22
44,112[3]	Bars and Taverns	5,923,911	8.41	362,425[4]	1.26	1,22
		$45,938,053[5]	65.23	$15,824,002	55.04	
5,836[6]	**Food Contractors**					
	Manufacturing & Indus. Plants	1,350,981	1.92	629,557	2.19	1,19,27
	Commercial & Office Bldgs.	351,788	0.50	163,933	0.57	1,27
	Hospitals and Nursing Homes	531,741	0.76	212,696	0.74	13
	Colleges & Universities	711,647	1.01	251,923	0.88	4
	Primary and Secondary Schools	430,524	0.61	202,347	0.70	3
	In-transit Feeding (Airlines)	267,985	0.38	128,632[7]	0.45	9
	Recreation & Sports Center	524,550	0.74	194,083	0.68	1,23,29
13,438	Hotel Restaurants	2,223,933	3.16	981,705	3.41	1,23,25,26
2,498	Motor Hotel Restaurants	556,506	0.79	190,042	0.66	1,23,25,26
13,551	Motel Restaurants	1,220,391	1.73	443,481	1.54	1,26

Fig. 1-1. Estimated food and drink sales and purchases in the food service industry for 1977. *(Courtesy of The National Restaurant Association)*

The Foodservice Industry—Estimated Food and Drink Sales and Purchases

Number of Units	Type of Establishment	Estimated F&D Sales (000)	Percent of Total F&D Sales	Estimated F&D Purchases (000)	Percent of Total F&D Purchases	Source
9,323	Drug & Prop. Store Restaurants	458,315	0.65	174,160	0.60	1
1,269	Gen. Merchandise Store Restaurants	35,658	0.05	13,550	0.05	1
3,882	Department Store Restaurants	725,642	1.03	290,266	1.01	1,30
6,509	Variety Store Restaurants	520,825	0.74	203,122	0.71	1
3,299	Food Stores ex. Grocery	146,102	0.21	49,675	0.17	1
9,579	Grocery Store Restaurants	312,682	0.44	115,692	0.40	1
7,738	Gasoline Service Stations	160,298	0.23	59,310	0.21	1
3,384	Drive-In Movies	98,634	0.14	32,549	0.11	1
3,622	Misc. Retailers (Liquor, Cigar, etc.)[8]	118,409	0.17	43,219	0.15	1
2,750	Vending & Nonstore Retailers[9]	1,403,861	1.99	477,314	1.66	1,19
	Mobile Caterers	268,515	0.38	93,980	0.33	1,2
3,828	Bowling Lanes	294,869	0.42	123,845	0.43	1
	Recreation and Sports Centers	393,477	0.56	145,586	0.51	1,24,29
	TOTAL GROUP I	$59,045,386	83.84	$21,044,669	73.20	

[1] Data are given only for establishments with payroll.
[2] Figures are latest Census Area Reports or Merchandise Line detail counts or updates when reliable data become available.
[3] Unit count includes only those establishments serving food; however, sales figure is for all bars and taverns with payroll.
[4] Food only. Cost of alcoholic beverages totaled $1,797,611,000.
[5] Food and drink sales for nonpayroll establishments totaled $2,236,364,000 with eating places accounting for $1,464,221,000 and drinking places $772,143,000.
[6] Individual businesses, not locations. Contract feeders are included in eating place totals in all Bureau of the Census publications although their sales volume figures for contract feeders are significantly understated.
[7] Food purchases only.
[8] Includes SIC 59, except 591 and 596.

Fig. 1-1. Estimated food and drink sales and purchases in the food service industry for 1977. (*Courtesy of The National Restaurant Association*) (Cont'd.)

The Foodservice Industry—Estimated Food and Drink Sales and Purchases

Number of Units	Type of Establishment	Estimated F&D Sales (000)	Percent of Total F&D Sales	Estimated F&D Purchases (000)	Percent of Total F&D Purchases	Source
	Group II—Institutional Feeding—Business, Educational, Government or Institutional Organizations Which Operate Their Own Foodservice					
	Employee Feeding					
4,000	Indus. & Comm. Organizations	891,570	1.27	445,356	1.55	20,27
532	Sea-going Ships (1,000+ Tons)	41,655	0.06	24,993	0.09	6
4,248	Inland Waterway Vessels	138,880	0.20	83,327	0.29	7
92,341	Public & Parochial Elementary & Secondary Schools (89,445 National School Lunch Program)[10]	1,686,782	2.40	2,227,932	7.75	3
	Colleges & Universities[11]					
971	Public	1,080,922	1.53	617,044	2.15	4
1,401	Private	415,818	0.59	237,627	0.83	4
	Transportation					
60	Passenger/Cargo Liners	64,157	0.09	35,286	0.12	8
28	Airlines	260,468	0.37	131,578	0.46	9
2	Railroads	22,806	0.03	15,022	0.05	10
10,310	Clubs	696,462	0.99	335,339	1.17	5
4,139	Voluntary & Proprietary Hospitals	2,940,680	4.18	1,176,272	4.09	13
1,840	State & Local Short-term Hospitals[12]	454,763	0.64	328,373	1.14	13
795	Long-term General, TB, Nervous & Mental Hospitals	746,542	1.06	298,617	1.04	13
382	Federal Hospitals[12]	203,679	0.29	180,189	0.63	13
26,672	Nursing Homes, Homes for Aged, Blind, Orphans, Mentally & Physically Handicapped[13]	1,457,821	2.07	936,302	3.26	14

Fig. 1-1. Estimated food and drink sales and purchases in the food service industry for 1977. *(Courtesy of The National Restaurant Association)* (Cont'd.)

The Foodservice Industry—Estimated Food and Drink Sales and Purchases

Number of Units	Type of Establishment	Estimated F&D Sales (000)	Percent of Total F&D Sales	Estimated F&D Purchases (000)	Percent of Total F&D Purchases	Source
3,165	Sporting & Recreational Camps	78,892	0.11	47,335	0.16	1,11
16,010	Community Centers	196,220	0.28	231,533	0.80	12
	Convents & Seminaries	...		105,791	0.37	17
	Penal Institutions					
337	Federal & State Prisons	...		134,951	0.47	15
3,921	Jails			110,956	0.38	16
	TOTAL GROUP II	$11,378,117	16.16	$ 7,703,823	26.80	
	TOTAL GROUPS I & II	$70,423,503	100.00	$28,748,492	100.00	
	Food Furnished Food Service Employees in Groups I and II			1,850,606		
	TOTAL GROUPS I and II and FSE	$70,423,503		$30,599,098		
	Group III—Military Feeding					
	Defense Personnel			754,343		18
967	Officers & NCO Clubs ("Open Mess")[14]	352,400		120,612		28
	Food Service—Military Exchanges[14]	190,600		83,864		28
	TOTAL GROUP III	543,000		958,819		
	GRAND TOTAL	$70,966,503		$31,557,917		

[9]Includes sales of hot food, sandwiches, pastries, coffee and other hot beverages.
[10]School lunch program commodities furnished in the calendar year 1975 under Sec. 6, 32,416, are worth $432,972,633. In addition, 2,217,728,144 half pints of milk worth $132,-460,828 were supplied to 82,555 outlets.
[11]Total number of colleges and universities which have foodservice whether contracted or not. Increase from 1974 due to recognition of branch campuses as entities for statistical purposes.
[12]Represents only sales or commercial equivalent to employees.
[13]Sales (commercial equivalent) calculated for Nursing Homes and Homes for Aged only. All others in this grouping make no charge for food served either in cash or in kind.
[14]Continental U.S. only.
[***]These institutions make no charge for food served either in cash or in kind.

Fig. 1-1. Estimated food and drink sales and purchases in the food service industry for 1977. (Courtesy of The National Restaurant Association) (Cont'd.)

proprietorships. These individual proprietorships accounted for only about 40 percent of the total business receipts, however. Corporations, which represented only about 17 percent of the businesses, accounted for more than half of the total revenue. By the 1972 census of business, single proprietorships had dropped to about 50 percent of the total.

The U.S. Department of Commerce reports that multiunit chains (those having 11 or more stores) accounted for only 7.7 percent of the eating and drinking place sales in 1974. When this figure is compared with other types of retailing (department store chains accounting for 87 percent of all department store sales, variety store chains accounting for 77 percent of variety store sales), it can be seen that the commercial food service industry is characterized by many small, individual operators.

There are big companies in the industry, however. Since 1964, *Institutions/Volume Feeding Magazine* has reported on the activities of the "Institutions 400," the 400 largest food service operators in the country. Since their list contains both commercial and noncommercial operations, it is not comparable to the Department of Commerce's eating and drinking place classification. *Institutions/Volume Feeding Magazine* estimated the total food service market in 1976 at $86.2 billion, of which the 400 larger organizations accounted for $36.8 billion, or about 43 percent. The 25 largest organizations accounted for almost $17.6 billion, or about 20 percent of the total market. These organizations are listed in Fig. 1–2.

In 1972 two of these top 25 food service organizations recorded sales of over $1 billion for the first time (McDonald's Corporation and Kentucky Fried Chicken). By 1976 McDonald's sales volume had exceeded $3 billion.

Franchising has long been a prime marketing and distribution method in the automotive, oil, and other industries (automobile dealers, gasoline stations, soft drink bottlers), but it is only in recent years that it has become of major significance in the food service industry. The Department of Commerce conducts periodic surveys of fast-food franchising in the United States. Sales of franchised fast-food operations (by both company-owned units and franchisee-owned units) amounted to about 26 percent of eating and drinking place sales in 1975.

The structure of the fast-food franchise industry is shown in Fig. 1–3. This tabulation shows that the industry is dominated by 18 firms that account for 64 percent of the franchised establishments and 68 percent of the franchise sales.

Trends in the Industry

In the 11 years from 1964 to 1975, eating and drinking place sales increased from $19.4 billion to $47.5 billion, an increase of over

	Rank	Food Service Volume ($ Millions)	Type of Business
1.	McDonald's Corp.	$ 3,063.0	Franchisor-Fast Food
2.	KFC Corp	1,600.0	Franchisor-Fast Food
3.	U.S. Dept of Agriculture - Food and Nutrition Service	1,279.6	School Foodservice
4.	Marriott Corp.	1,159.4	Diversified Lodging/Foodservice
5.	Burger King (Pillsbury Co.)	1,063.5	Franchisor-Fast Food
6.	Holiday Inns, Inc.	800.0	Diversified Lodging/Foodservice
7.	ARA Services, Inc.	783.0	Full Line Service Management Co.
8.	International Dairy Queen, Inc.	684.0	Franchisor-Fast Food
9.	U.S. Army	655.5 *	Military
10.	U.S. Navy	610.4 *	Military
11.	Canteen Corp.	539.0	Full-Line Services Management
12.	Pizza Hut	493.0	Franchisor
13.	Howard Johnson Co.	450.0	Diversified Foodservice/Lodging
14.	Saga Corp.	445.0	Foodservice Management
15.	Denny's, Inc.	420.9	Foodservice Management
16.	Servomation Corp.	404.0	Foodservice Management
17.	The Sheraton Corp.	400.0	Lodging Chain
18.	Army and Air Force Exchange	374.7 *	Military
19.	Foodmaker	372.4	Diversified Foodservice
20.	Ramada Inns, Inc.	353.4	Diversified Foodservice/Lodging
21.	Sambo's Restaurants	348.4	Franchisor-Restaurants
22.	Hilton Hotels Corp.	330.0	Lodging Chain
23.	Hardee's Food Systems	326.5	Franchisor-Fast Food
24.	U.S. Air Force	318.4 *	Military
25.	Tastee-Freeze International, Inc.	309.8	Franchisor-Restaurants

* Commercial Sales Equivalent

Fig.1-2. The top 25 food service organizations, 1976. *(Courtesy of Institutions/Volume Feeding)*

145 percent. In the same period, *Institutions/Volume Feeding Magazine* estimated an increase of over 168 percent in the total food service market and an increase of almost 285 percent in the sales of the 400 group. Within the 400 group, the top 25 had a growth of over 327 percent in sales, almost twice that of the total food service industry.

Profitability

Data from the Internal Revenue Service show that the average net income before income taxes for eating and drinking place corporations has been between 4 and 5 percent of sales. These figures include a wide range of operations of various sizes and types.

As in any industry, the profitability of any one firm can vary widely from industry averages depending on many factors, but profitability is heavily dependent on the quality of management. Profitability also varies with the economic structure of the particular type of business. Service restaurants tend to have a lower cost-of-goods-sold ratio because of the higher markup possible on liquor sales and because they tend to do more on-premises preparation, whereas

Size Groups	Franchising Companies Number	Establishments Number	Establishments Percent	Sales ($000)	Sales Percent
Total	293	42,983	100.0	12,261,964	100.0
1001 and Greater	7	19,646	45.7	5,613,962	45.8
501 - 1000	11	7,672	17.8	2,681,959	21.9
151 - 500	32	8,279	19.3	2,049,954	16.7
51 - 150	46	4,091	9.5	950,468	7.8
11 - 50	115	2,881	6.7	875,476	7.1
0 - 10	82	414	1.0	90,145	0.7

Source: Franchising in the Economy 1975-1977 — United States Department of Commerce.

Fig. 1-3. Fast-food restaurants (all types): Distribution by number of establishments, 1975-1977.

fast-food operations use a higher proportion of convenience food items. Labor costs, on the other hand, are higher in service restaurants because of the need for cooks and table service personnel. Selling and administrative expenses are slightly higher for fast-food operations, probably as a result of increased advertising and franchise royalties, whereas occupancy expenses in these operations indicate a need for costly high-traffic locations. For diversified companies, the proportions of the different types of services offered can affect profitability. Figures 1–4 shows the net profit percentages of several groups of food service companies, and Fig. 1–5 shows the variation within one of these groups.

Business Failures

The restaurant business has a high record of business failures, probably because the ease of entry into this business attracts a high proportion of entrepreneurs who are short on capital, or managerial capability, or both. Data on business failures, as compiled by Dun & Bradstreet, show that the failure rate is declining, presumably because of the increasing proportion of larger companies in the industry. These companies can usually attract financing and managerial capability not easily available to the individual entrepreneur. Average liability per failure has increased considerably, however.

The Growth of an Industry

The industry of feeding the public away from home has developed the way it has because the demand for its goods and

		(Net profit for each group as a percentage of total sales)		
			1976	1975
7	Franchise Holders		4.2%	4.3%
10	Larger Franchise Chains		8.7	7.8
6	Hotels/Motels		3.8	3.7
10	Larger Restaurant Chains		6.1	6.5
3	Food Management/Vending Co's.		2.8	2.7
11	Suppliers Distributors		3.8	3.1

Fig. 1-4. Comparative profitability, 1976 vs. 1975 (second quarter figures). *(Courtesy of Institutions/Volume Feeding Chain Reports)*

	1976	1975
Associated Hosts (Quarter to 6/26)	4.5%	4.0%
Cafeterias, Inc. (Quarter to 5/31)	7.4	6.7
Furr's Cafeterias (Quarter to 7/3)	4.5	6.0
Gino's (Quarter to 6/30)	3.0	3.9
Hamburger Hamlets (Quarter to 6/27)	7.0	5.9
Holly's (Quarter to 4/30)	2.3	2.4
Hungry Tiger (16 weeks to 6/4)	2.1	(1.2)
Hy's of Canada (Half to 3/31)	1.3	3.0
Kapok Tree Inns (16 weeks to 7/4)	9.8	12.1
Sambo's (Quarter to 6/30)	12.4	13.2

Fig. 1-5. Profitability of 10 larger restaurant chains. *(Courtesy of Institutions/Volume Feeding Chain Reports)*

services has grown. Several significant factors have contributed to this increased demand:

1. Absolute increases in the population, which have created increased demand for goods and services of all types. Changing proportions of young adults and older persons have also changed the nature of overall demand.
2. Rising standards of living and increased leisure time permit greater expenditures on luxuries such as pleasure travel, recreation, and dining out, as well as improved health care, education, business travel, and entertaining.
3. Changing social patterns such as urbanization and suburbanization and increased employment of women with families.
4. Increased availability of credit and use of credit cards.

The food service industry's most significant response to the increased demand has been the growth of large, publicly owned corporations. The large corporation can assemble the resources needed to deal with a rapid expansion of demand and a fast-changing technology; it can acquire the capital needed for investment; and it can attract skilled managerial talent. Having talent and capital, the large corporation can also invest in research and development of new products (and services). Therefore, it is able to adjust to changing market conditions and meet the new types of demand and competition.

Educational institutions have responded to the needs of the food service industry by establishing courses on hotel, restaurant, and institutional management in junior colleges, universities, and vocational schools. Continuing or adult education programs have also been developed by numerous trade associations, such as the National

Restaurant Association and the American Hotel & Motel Association. These schools and associations are working to fill an increasing need for trained workers at all levels of the industry. In addition, they are also engaging in industry research to aid the many small entrepreneurs and companies that are not able to invest in their own research and development programs.

The Outside Environment

No business or industry operates in a vacuum; rather, it must manufacture and sell its products and services in a "real world" situation where innumerable forces can affect it, both negatively and positively. The individual firm's responsiveness to such forces in its business environment can directly affect its profitability. The following are some of the external forces affecting food service operators today.

The Growth of Consumerism

There is a greatly increased public awareness of the need for good nutrition, wholesome food products, and good sanitation practices in public food services. Consumer groups, both nationally and on many local levels, have brought about new consumer protection legislation and increased enforcement of existing legislation. Much of the impact on the food service industry has been in enforcement of sanitation and health code requirements and, in a few instances, labeling and truth-in-advertising laws.

Environmental Concerns

In many cases, the rapidly growing fast-food business is facing community concern about the physical environment. Strip developments with brightly lit, garish signs, each competing for the local market, have been accused of visual pollution. Legislation has been enacted to control or eliminate signs from streets and highways, including the interstate highway system. In some rapidly growing residential sections, inadequate sewage disposal facilities have limited new construction and growth.

Air pollution from cooking exhausts and incineration of wastes has become a matter of concern. In some neighborhoods, complaints have been registered about noisy congregations of teenage patrons at local drive-in restaurants. Litter from disposable food packaging, excessive traffic, and exhaust fumes have also been held against fast-food restaurants.

Energy Shortages

Forecasts of shortages of gas, oil, and electricity have forced some utility companies to restrict supplies of utilities for new installations. Expansion and renovation of existing operations have also been affected. Shortages of gasoline may affect different types of food services favorably or unfavorably. Although the public may travel less, thus unfavorably affecting food service operators who cater to travelers and tourists, the patronage of local restaurants may be increased.

Suspicion of Big Business

Surveys have shown that among some sectors of the population big business is viewed with suspicion. These groups consider large corporations to be unresponsive to individual and public needs, especially those concerning the environment. It is in this setting that big business is just coming into its own in the food service business.

To avoid criticism and charges of unresponsiveness to public needs, some large firms such as McDonald's have instituted community action programs. Unit managers and franchise holders are encouraged to participate in local social action organizations, supporting such activities as athletic leagues for children, scholarships, parks, and playgrounds. Others contribute meals or money to worthy fund-raising activities. It should be noted that big business in the food service industry means franchise companies, and franchises are often locally owned.

Increasing Government Activities Affecting Food Services

Government activities with respect to antipollution and sanitation enforcement have already been mentioned. Among other activities of importance to the food service operator are minimum wage legislation, antidiscrimination legislation such as the Equal Employment Opportunity Act, and the Occupational Safety and Health Act of 1971.

Other programs directly affecting food service operations are the federal government's agricultural programs relating to farm prices and supply of foodstuffs. Originally, these programs were necessary to deal with surpluses. The National School Lunch Program was developed to help utilize surplus commodities; under the farm price support programs, surplus foods were purchased at predetermined prices to prevent an oversupply from diminishing returns to farmers. By the 1970s, food surpluses were much reduced and government again interceded in the market, this time with wage and price controls in the face of food shortages and rapid inflation.

Changing Food Consumption Patterns

Another variable facing food service operators is changing consumption patterns. Because of continuing changes in tastes and technological developments in food processing, the variety of foods available to the consumer is immense, and most of the new foods are in processed form. Acceptance of new products can be quite rapid since the public is accustomed to rapid technological change. There has been a decline in the use of fresh fruits and vegetables, dairy and cereal products, and eggs. Potato consumption has increased remarkably because of the availability of processed potatoes in a variety of forms. Beef and poultry consumption has increased, while consumption of pork, ham, veal, and lamb has declined.

The concern with ecology, the environment, and good nutrition has brought about a counter trend in a small but growing demand for "natural" or organic foods—that is, food crops grown without chemical fertilizers or pesticides and processed without chemical additives, and meat from livestock not fed with antibiotics. Although this trend has been receiving considerable publicity recently, it is doubtful that it will ever become a major force in the market. The health food industry has not yet overcome the poor image given it by faddists and quacks in the past. A much greater barrier is the difficulty of producing sufficient amounts of organic foods to achieve any widespread distribution.

The roles of various foods on the menu are also changing and therefore need to be recognized in food service marketing. Snack items, such as potato chips and soft drinks, and breakfast items such as pancakes are becoming meal components. Fruit juices have become popular snacks, and cheese is more popular as a snack than as the dessert course it once was.

Perhaps the major reason for these shifts in eating habits is the public's growing weight consciousness in its search for health and an active, youthful appearance. It is estimated that nearly 70 percent of all adult Americans today can be classed as weight watchers, compared with 40 percent in 1960. Prevalent meal skipping can lead to a consumption pattern of frequent snacking.

Business Cycles

Business conditions are seldom static. Although the long-term trend of the American economy has been one of growth, economic conditions fluctuate widely in the short run. Restaurants are particularly susceptible to fluctuations in the economy. During periods of economic growth and high employment, rising salaries and plentiful jobs encourage personal spending for dining out and other discretionary activities. Expense account spending is also high as businessmen compete in the higher levels of business activity. In times of recession, however, expense account spending is drastically curtailed, and consumers are more conservative about buying nonessential goods. In times of inflation, consumers may be forced by the shrinking value of the dollar to eat at more modestly priced restaurants than the ones formerly patronized.

New Products and Services to Meet New Market Demands

The traditional product of the food service industry is the table service restaurant meal. Although the sale of prepared meals was recorded in ancient times, the commercial restaurant traces its origin to the period following the French Revolution, when the development of a wealthy middle class permitted spending on lavish meals away from home. The companion volume to this text describes the history of the *à la carte* French menu and the *partie* system of kitchen operation. This type of restaurant operation has remained the model for hotels, private clubs, and elegant restaurants to this day, although economic and social conditions have forced many modifications. One major difficulty with this type of system in the United States is the lack of trained cooks and chefs.

Another type of food service organization developed in the field of dietetics, which is staffed predominantly by females, in contrast to the French kitchen, which is staffed almost entirely by males. Dietetics developed as a branch of home economics and endeavored to apply a scientific approach to the feeding of the sick. The field of dietetics today includes not only the study of normal and therapeutic nutrition but also the administration of food service departments in institutional situations. The scientific approach has been applied to research in quantity food production and service and many other aspects of institutional food service. One recent area of scientific exploration is the use of computers in menu planning and production control. Some of the management techniques that have come out of the field of dietetics are the standardized recipe, the cycle menu, and forecasting procedures. In the commercial restaurant business, companies such as Schrafft's and Stouffer's have operated with dietitians, using standardized recipes to eliminate the need for trained chefs and cooks.

Dietetics and the scientific approach to quantity food service developed early in the twentieth century. Two even more recent developments in quantity food service are the fast-food type of restaurant and the large diversified food service company.

"Fast food" is a general term that has been used to describe a multitude of short-order, limited menu food service operations, including take-out stores, lunch counters, ice cream parlors, snack bars, drive-ins, franchised hamburger, and other limited menu operations. Many coffee shops can also be classified as fast-food operations, depending on the type of menu offered.

Fast food originated from two very different sources. The sale of carbonated water by pharmacists in the mid-1880s eventually led to the drug store soda fountain. At first these fountains dispensed only carbonated beverages, but later ice cream was added. Then fountain operators added other desserts and cold sandwiches to their menus, and eventually they expanded to short-order cooking and limited offerings of prepared entrées.

The other side of fast food originated in the "free lunch" offered in saloons to bar patrons. It is said that it was at the free lunch counter that the sandwich came into its own, since the patron could hold his meat sandwich in one hand and his mug of beer in the other and not get his hands greasy. Eventually the free lunch become a paid lunch, but it may be considered as the forerunner of the stand-up self-service or cafeteria type of service.

Another development of the late 1800s and early 1900s was the snack stand or hot dog stand, such as Nathan's Famous at Coney Island, which was often found in places of entertainment. During the depression years of the 1930s, hot dog stands and five-cent hamburger chains such as White Castle flourished. Many of the large food service companies operating today had their beginnings in the low-priced, fast-service markets of the 1920s and 1930s. J. Willard Marriott started with an A & W rootbeer stand, and the Stouffer brothers sold buttermilk and their mother's apple pie from a snack stand in an office building.

Another innovation of the 1920s was the drive-in, although this type of restaurant did not really become widely established until the 1950s, when it became a part of the suburban, auto-oriented way of life. The early drive-ins had little or no inside seating, and patrons were served in their cars by carhops or carhostesses. Large, short-order coffee shop menus were offered, although some drive-ins (including McDonald's) adopted the low-priced, limited-menu type of operation developed by companies such as White Castle. This operating concept was well suited to the markets of the 1960s and was widely copied. Most of the fast-food companies operating today base their operations on some type of limited hamburger menu and self-service.

Fast Food Today

Although there is no hard and fast definition of "fast food" it generally means low prices, fast service, and convenience.

Convenience

To some patrons, convenience may be even more important than speed or price. For economic reasons, fast-food operations are usually located where they are physically convenient to large segments of the population in places where people congregate or in high-traffic areas. Since these restaurants are completely informal, there is no concern about how one is dressed or how the children are going to behave. Such operations offer a convenient meal, either to take home or to eat in the car or the restaurant.

Low Prices

To sell at low prices, the fast-food operator must maximize the productivity of all aspects of his business and tightly control costs. Menus are limited to high-volume items to avoid large inventories of many items and hence, spoilage. With these limited menus, it is possible to automate some of the preparation functions (both on-premises and in preprocessing), thus increasing labor productivity. Another technique to improve productivity is to transfer some of the work load to the customer through self-service. Tableware washing is eliminated through the use of disposable packaging. Although self-busing cannot be enforced in a public operation, operators in many areas have found that if they dispense the orders in a paper bag and station large waste cans at the exits, most patrons will put their waste back into the bag and deposit it in the waste can as they leave. This helps to reduce the amount of labor required to keep the seating area clean.

Fixed costs are minimized through standardization of construction and design, with layouts planned to make the maximum use of space and labor. Sites are carefully chosen to service the largest potential market for the size of the investment required. The fast-food units of the 1960s, for example, were very small structures with no on-premises seating. Changing market conditions and increased competition have forced most fast-food companies to add indoor seating and other amenities to their operations.

Speed of Service

To provide speedy service and minimize customer waiting time, all items must be ready for service on demand. Food is therefore prepared for inventory rather than to order. This is the crux of fast-food service and the difference between today's fast food and the traditional short-order method of preparation.

Diversified Food Service Management Companies

With the growth of large companies having a depth of specialized management personnel, diversification into noncommercial food service operations was almost inevitable. Companies such as Marriott, ARA, Servomation, and many others have large divisions that specialize in managing food services in hospitals and other health-related facilities, schools, industrial plants, and offices. Other avenues of diversification are in-flight catering, toll roads, stadiums and convention halls, amusement parks, and recreation areas.

The terms of the service agreements vary according to the economic structure of the operation. In some cases, the companies may operate as a purely commercial facility, paying rent and making a profit as in a regular restaurant operation. In others, restrictions on the market demand may require some sort of subsidy to be paid, as in an employee cafeteria. On the other hand, restrictions on competition, as on a toll road, may require that the operating company pay a premium in addition to a normal rent in return for the right to operate in an environment free from competition.

The management company brings its specialized expertise to a food service operation and relieves client management of day-to-day operating responsibility. It also provides food service in places or situations where it would not otherwise be possible. For instance, in public places such as parks, the company may operate a concession and provide service that the owning government body could not provide directly. Management companies may also provide subsidized service in privately owned facilities where a standard leasing situation would not be profitable but where the owner feels that some type of food service is necessary for the overall profitability of the project.

Another advantage offered by the food service management companies is economies of scale. One example is the benefits derived from large-scale purchasing power. Another can be seen in the economics of the in-flight catering operation. Occupation costs are a major consideration in the operation of a flight kitchen. Land values around major airports are among the highest in the country. Furthermore, once a flight kitchen is constructed, occupation costs represent fixed expenses that are incurred regardless of passenger loads or changes in routes or scheduled departures. The airline caterer is also faced with the same situation, but his risk is spread over many airlines, and his fixed costs are offset by higher volume. The same principle is now being applied by some companies to the production of school lunch meals, and some are reportedly investigating central production and assembly of hospital meals.

The basic human need for nourishment in a diversity of places and times is being satisfied more and more in a highly organized, businesslike way.

2
Marketing Strategy

What is marketing? The American Management Association has stated that marketing is ". . . the total function concerned with analyzing, creating, developing, packaging, pricing, distributing, selling, promoting, publicizing and advertising the goods or services of every enterprise. . . . Marketing is not only the key to sales success; it is the central function of a business to which all other functions are coordinate."*

The National Restaurant Association defined the marketing concept for restaurants as a "way of operating your food service organization so that all planning begins with the consumer and works backward into sales, service, production and purchasing . . . to fill the demands of the particular group or groups of people you want to serve."†

In both these definitions, the purpose of the marketing function is implied. In a commercial operation, this purpose is to maximize profits. In a noncommercial operation, such as an institutional food service, the purpose of the marketing function is to satisfy the needs of the persons served, within the economic structure of the organization.

In its earlier years, industry's task was to produce enough goods to satisfy the needs of a rapidly growing economy. More recently, advancing technology and rising levels of productivity have made it possible for industry to produce far more goods than can be sold. This abundance of goods, along with the rapid growth in consumer credit, gives the consumer independence in the market place. He now has many products and services on which to spend his disposable income.

Marketing as we know it today had its beginnings in the depression years of the early 1930s when, even though the economy was operating at levels far below maximum capacity, the amount of

---
*The Marketing Job, American Management Association, American Management Association, New York, 1961.
†"Marketing Management Guide," National Restaurant Association, 1968.

goods produced still greatly exceeded the demand. Today, shortages of materials and energy threaten jobs. Inflation reduces the buying power of disposable income while prices continue to rise. High interest rates discourage investment in home building and manufacturing plants and equipment. In periods of economic instability, marketing and particularly accurately assessing market demand are of great importance.

Consumer Buying Behavior

A marketing-oriented business determines the customers' needs and desires and then develops products or services that will satisfy those needs. Identifying customer needs and desires and predicting buying behavior are not easy tasks, but recent advances in social science research methods help marketers to study how consumers make buying decisions.

Psychologists have attempted to analyze and categorize the motives for human behavior. Abraham Maslow, for example, developed a hierarchy of human needs: physiological needs such as food and sleep, safety needs, belongingness and love needs, esteem and status needs, and self-actualization needs.

Others have developed lists of motives to try to explain human behavior in the market place. These are sometimes categorized as emotional motives such as satisfaction of the senses, preservation of the species, fear, rest and recreation, and so on. Economic motives include efficiency, durability, enhancement of earnings, and dependability of the product.

Social class values can have considerable impact on the consumer views of a particular product or service. Considerable research has been done on the effect of social class on behavior. When the idea of class structure was first developed in the 1930s, classes were defined by income, occupation, and neighborhood. These criteria have become blurred, however, by changing social values. The offspring of an "Old Guard" family may live in a tenement and work for a social service agency, whereas the blue-collar truck driver has a swimming pool and several automobiles parked outside his suburban ranch house. Social class is still defined largely in terms of occupation, but other factors must be included, such as tastes, values, expectations, and priorities.

Consumer buying behavior is also affected by availability of funds. "Disposable income" is the personal income available for spending after taxes are deducted. Out of disposable income, the family purchases what it considers to be necessities, such as food, housing, clothing, and medical care. Any funds left over are considered "discretionary income" and are available for the purchase of luxuries or for savings. The concept of discretionary income is much more difficult to define than that of disposable income, since one family's necessity may be another family's luxury.

Discretionary income is particularly significant in restaurant marketing because much of the spending for food away from home is discretionary. At low income levels, discretionary income is very small. It rises rapidly at higher income levels. Among multiple-earner families, discretionary income is considerably higher than in single-earner families.

Marketing and the Restaurant Industry

The growth of the publicly owned food service chain operations in the past decade has brought a growing awareness of the importance of the marketing approach to food services. During the 1950s, restaurant chains and some individual operators recognized the need for a more scientific approach to planning new operations. The growth of suburban areas presented new opportunities, and potentially profitable locations were available. Suburban life styles centered around the automobile, and drive-in restaurants sprang up to serve this new type of market.

Meanwhile, the "war baby" population boom of the 1940s became the "youth market" of the late 1950s and early 1960s. Restaurant operators discovered that teenagers as a market had a large proportion of discretionary income to spend. The low-priced, informal hamburger drive-in fulfilled their need for a place to hang out. Later, as the teenage market matured, married, and started raising families, the drive-ins (now called fast-food operations) adapted to offer attractions for children. The low-cost meals and the informality were still well suited to these young families. In the 1970s, this segment of the population is more mature, has more spending power, and is less restricted by the presence of small children at home. With time and money to develop more refined tastes, they look for restaurants that are more creative and more exciting but still informal. At the same time, their children are looking for excitement at the fast-food drive-in.

This vignette of one segment of the population demonstrates the need for a continuing market orientation. Markets are never static. Populations change both in size and characteristics; social patterns change; perceived wants and needs change; income levels change; attitudes and motives change.

The food service market is highly diversified, ranging from $100 dinners on an expense account to a cup of coffee at 2:00 A.M. for a trucker on the turnpike. The picture is further complicated by the fact that consumers can move from one segment or type of demand to another within a few hours. Consumer motivation can change rapidly as well. This leads to questions about the consumer's perception of what the product really is. A refrigerator is a refrigerator, but what is a restaurant meal? That it is a means of satisfying hunger is obvious, but this need can be satisfied by food prepared at home. The product may satisfy a desire for entertainment, sociability, or relaxation. A desire for a snack may be motivated by boredom or by a need for a short rest or change of pace during the day's activities. A desire for self-expression and individuality may motivate the search for imaginative and exotic restaurants, or restaurants serving ethnic foods. Salad bars and specialty foods such as fondues and hibachi items are a form of entertainment for the guest who participates in the preparation of the food. A desire for status may be a motive for a costly meal at a prestige restaurant.

The rapid growth of successful fast-food chains such as McDonald's and Kentucky Fried Chicken was not accidental. These companies perceived certain needs of one rapidly growing segment of the population and moved to fill those needs. Furthermore, as market conditions changed, the companies changed with them.

In spite of the obvious success of these mass market restaurants, there are still critics who deplore the passing of haute cuisine and the elegant French service, claiming that it is impossible to get a good restaurant meal any more. Some have proclaimed convenience foods "a fraud perpetrated on the public," and have even campaigned for "truth in menu" legislation which would require frozen prepared items to be identified on the menu. These critics have forgotten that the classic French restaurant from its beginnings catered to a very small group of very wealthy patrons and did so with a large staff of poorly paid workers. The wages paid to these workers, the hours they had to work, and the working conditions in the old restaurants would be unacceptable today. The modern French restaurant still caters only to a very small market, and the society in which it operates requires a very different economic structure. High menu prices are required in order to pay a living wage to the employees, and this makes the market for such a restaurant more restricted than ever. The classic French restaurant of the past cannot be compared with today's mass market restaurants. They are totally different businesses, serving different segments of a highly diversified market.

Market Research in the Food Service Industry

In spite of a rapidly increasing level of management capability, the restaurant industry in general still knows little about the customers it serves. Little research has been done to determine consumer attitudes and motivation concerning the purchase of food away from home. Until recently the only market research available was that done by a few of the major food manufacturing companies. In the last few years, the U.S. Department of Agriculture and the National Restaurant Association (NRA) have begun to gather market data for food service operations. Some large restaurant chains have also recognized the need for more meaningful and pertinent data. Figure 2–1 shows a summary of a consumer attitude survey conducted for the NRA in 1974. figure 2–2 shows demographic data developed from Bureau of Labor Statistics data.

A marketing approach is not limited to commercial restaurants; it has become an essential part of noncommercial and institutional food service operations. For many years, managers in such fields as college and employee feeding operations have acknowledged that customer relations is one of the most important aspects of their jobs.

Many contract feeding companies have developed techniques to determine the needs, wants, and preferences of their particular markets. The use of student opinion studies in some colleges, for example, has led to the introduction of health food menus, self-service salad bars, continuous serving hours, and a wide variety of meal contract arrangements. The military has converted some of its traditional mess operations into fast-food operations offering hamburgers, hot dogs, soft drinks, and beer. Troop preference studies are also made for use in planning menus for the more traditional mess operations.

Developing a Marketing Strategy

The first step in developing a marketing strategy is the selection of a target market and identification of that market's needs. Next, a plan is developed for meeting those needs. All factors that can be controlled by management are considered in this plan. Some marketing experts classify these factors as the "four Ps": product, promotion, place, and price. The total plan is a mix of these factors. A further consideration is the uncontrollable factors in the environment. The marketing strategy must be workable within this exterior environment.

Determining the Target Market

One technique the marketing manager may use to identify all potential customers is the market grid. A market grid for food service is shown in Fig. 2–3. Different types of food service operations can be seen as filling different types of needs. These needs are plotted along the horizontal axis. The characteristic of "accessibility" is plotted along the vertical axis, since if a particular type of food service is available only to certain groups or markets, all other groups are excluded. Accessibility may be restricted physically (as in an institution), economically (as by selling price), or by other means, such as membership requirements in private clubs.

MOST IMPORTANT FEATURES CONSIDERED WHEN SELECTING A SPECIFIC TYPE OF RESTAURANT

This Percent of the Respondents When Selecting This Type of Restaurant:

Gave These As The Most Important Features Considered:	Family Type %	Fast Food %	Atmosphere Specialty %	Cafeteria %	Coffee Shop %	Take Out %
Quality of food	72	61	67	69	59	69
Cleanliness of the restaurant	40	27	26	31	31	24
Speed of service including ordering, serving, getting check	31	59	13	27	45	60
Low prices	20	29	6	25	20	23
The selection and variety of food	20	12	28	45	15	15
Friendliness of waitress or waiter	15	8	17	5	17	5
Consistency of food (same every visit)	15	13	10	13	10	13
Children's portions at less cost	11	2	2	6	2	2
Atmosphere	10	2	35	4	4	1
Convenient location	9	17	3	11	15	19
Cleanliness of rest rooms	7	5	4	5	6	3
Have a salad bar	5	1	6	3	*	*
Adequate parking	4	18	4	6	7	17
Second cup of coffee free	4	1	2	4	16	1
A "no smoking" section	4	1	2	2	2	*
Personality of owner/manager	2	1	3	1	2	1
Good clientele	1	*	3	1	1	*
Handling of reservations	1	*	6	*	*	*
Continuous soft music	1	*	5	1	*	-
A relish tray served	1	*	1	*	*	*
Good wine list	*	*	3	*	*	*
(Number of Respondents)			(3,192)			

* Less than 0.5%

Note: Percentages may add to more than 100% because of multiple responses

Fig. 2-1. Most important features considered when selecting a specific type of restaurant. *(Courtesy of The National Restaurant Association)*

The market grid now contains numerous "boxes" identifying a number of markets. Each box can in turn be analyzed for submarkets. A subgrid for college feeding would include contract feeding of dormitory students, cash sales to commuting students, faculty and employee food services, snack bars and vending operations, and specialized services such as tray service and therapeutic diets for the

Characteristics	Annual Expenditure for Food Away from Home Per Family	Annual Expenditure for Food Away from Home Per Person	Total Annual Market Food Away From Home (Millions)	Share of Market
All Families				
Total Family Income (Before Taxes)				
Under $1,875	$145.60	$ 91.00	$ 931.4 *	3.0%
$1,875-3,399	178.36	93.87	1,141.0 *	3.8
$3,400-5,000	258.44	112.37	1,653.0 *	5.4
$5,001-6,899	313.56	120.60	2,003.6 *	6.6
$6,900-8,749	427.44	152.66	2,737.4 *	9.0
$8,750-10,549	479.44	154.65	3,064.6 *	10.1
$10,550-12,549	551.20	167.03	3,528.8 *	11.6
$12,550-15,199	618.80	176.80	3,957.2 *	13.0
$15,200-19,474	741.56	206.27	4,751.6 *	15.6
$19,475 and over	1,034.80	279.68	6,619.6 *	21.8
Occupation of Head of Household				
Self-employed	$577.20	$174.91	$3,092.1	8.9%
Professional, managers	724.88	226.53	10,096.1	29.2
Clerical, sales	569.40	219.00	4,507.9	13.0
Skilled worker	529.36	155.69	9,035.1	26.1
Laborer, service	430.04	143.35	3,597.7	10.4
Armed Forces	518.96	157.26	373.7	1.1
Retired	188.76	104.87	2,252.7	6.5
All other, NA	237.64	88.01	1,664.0	4.8
Education of Head of Household				
1-8 years	$262.08	$100.80	$3,837.6	11.0%
9-11 years	396.76	132.25	4,555.2	13.1
H.S. graduate	513.24	171.08	11,118.3	32.0
1-3 years college	620.88	221.74	6,641.6	19.1
4 years college	705.12	243.14	4,227.2	12.2
College graduate +	705.12	235.04	4,034.0	11.6
None, NA	157.04	60.40	328.5	.9
Family Size				
Single person	$343.72	$343.72	$5,997.6	17.3%
2 persons	424.84	212.42	8,676.9	25.0
3 persons	507.52	169.17	5,959.3	17.2
4 persons	635.96	158.99	6,815.6	19.6
5 persons	635.96	127.19	3,913.1	11.3
6 or more	581.36	84.25	3,376.5	9.7
Age of Family Head				
Under 25	$419.64	$209.82	$2,831.7	8.2%
25-35	560.04	169.71	8,187.8	23.4
35-44	644.28	149.83	7,407.3	21.3
45-54	616.72	186.88	8,240.6	23.7
55-64	429.00	186.52	4,944.7	14.2
65 and over	215.28	126.64	3,130.2	9.0

* Do not add up to total "all families" market because income not reported by some respondents.

Fig. 2-2. Consumer away-from-home food expenditures. *(Data calculated by Institutions/Volume Feeding Chain Reports, from the most recent data available from Consumer Expenditure Study by Bureau of Labor Statistics)*

	Physiological Needs – Hunger, Thirst	Health-Related Needs	Belonging and Love Needs Freedom from Rejection	Esteem, Status and Entertainment	Self-Actualization Needs
Restricted Matter	Institutions – prisons, homes, hospitals, etc. Military bases School lunch program Employee feeding College feeding (board contracts) Camps	Hospitals – patient food service	←——— Private Clubs ———→ Executive, luncheon, country, university, faculty, fraternal, military		
Partially Restricted	Hotel room service Transportation – Trains, planes, ships, highway operations Museums, concert halls, auditorium snack bars; arenas, stadiums	Spas Health clubs	Communes, half-way houses and certain rehabilitation communities	Luxury restaurants Resorts Nightclubs, supper clubs	Gourmet restaurants (highest quality, variety, originality of menu items, rarest wines, etc.) Conventions, business and educational meetings and seminars
Unrestricted Market	Coffee shops Department store and other retailing restaurants Snack bars Fast-food operations Take-out stores	Health food restaurants Juice bars Health food stores	Family restaurants Neighborhood taverns Singles' bars Teen hangouts and youth centers	Sports and recreation center restaurants "Occasion" type restaurants Amusement or theme parks Discotheques	Banquets and catering of social events Specialty ethnic restaurants Cooking schools, wine tastings

Fig. 2-3. Market grid for food services satisfaction of human needs.

infirmary, health-food operations, student union operation, and the catering of special functions. A food service company entering the college feeding market must be prepared to meet these needs. How the needs are met is determined by the marketing mix.

Two techniques for identifying the target market's needs have already been mentioned: preference and opinion surveys used in institutional feeding situations. In many cases, some wants and needs are self-evident. In commercial restaurant markets, observation of successful competing operations may reveal indirectly what the public prefers in restaurants. At present, these rather superficial techniques are the only ones used by food service marketers, and they provide little information about consumer buying behavior.

The Marketing Plan:
The Mix of the Four Ps

The marketing manager has in his control certain variables; product, promotion, place, and price. Decisions pertaining to each of these variables are what determine the nature of the goods and service the firm will offer to its customers, and they ultimately affect profitability. These variables are the basis of the marketing concept. In fact, almost all this book is concerned with some aspect of the four Ps and their effect on profitability.

Product. "Product" for the food service operator is not only the menu items to be offered but the particular recipes to be used, portion sizes, garniture, and presentation. The term also includes the decor, ambiance of the dining environment, service, and interpersonal contact involved in the whole dining experience. This concept of product is not limited to commercial food service operations; the importance of environment and interpersonal contact is being recognized in many institutional situations, particularly those concerned with the mental and physical health of the resident.

Promotion. "Promotion" includes not only advertising and sales techniques but also the creation of the image and identity of the business. Promotion can include elements of product development, such as in the merchandising and presentation of a menu item, and in the establishment of promotional or package prices.

Place. "Place" refers to the process by which products and services are made available to consumers at the appropriate time and location. In the restaurant business, place is primarily concerned with the selection of new sites and the reevaluation of present sites to ensure that the existing type of operation is still viable for the market it serves.

Location can have varying effects on the success of an operation, depending in part on the nature of the food sold and on the type of advertising and promotional policies. A restaurant in a prime location can be unsuccessful if the type of service is not what is required by the market at that location, or if the quality and price of the food and service are not acceptable. Conversely, well-merchandised, highly successful restaurants can be found in poor locations. In planning a new facility, however, it makes no sense to begin with a poor location.

One attribute of location that should be considered is that of the "trading area," the geographical area from which a business draws its patronage. The trading area for a particular site will vary according to the type of business located on the site, the quality and locations of its competition, and the presence of noncompeting businesses. A group of stores will usually draw customers from a wider area than any one store could draw alone.

Price. Determining selling prices, including promotional pricing, is an important tool in the marketing of a product, but in the food service business, very little sophistication has been achieved in the use of price as a marketing alternative. Price has a two-pronged effect on the success of the operation, being a factor both in influencing sales and in the cost/profit relationships. (See Chapter 8 for a discussion of menu pricing in food services.)

Other variables the marketing manager must consider are the capability of his own company and its objectives. Major marketing decisions, such as the development of a new operating concept, must take into consideration the company's strengths and weaknesses, including manpower position, availability of skills and creative talent, financial position, present geographical dispersion, size of operations, and market image.

The Uncontrollable Factors in the Business Environment

Decisions regarding the controllable factors discussed above must be made in consideration of an external environment over which the marketing manager has no control. Among these factors may be the following:

1. Legal, political, and governmental forces
2. Scientific and technological forces
3. Sociological, cultural, and ethical forces
4. Physical and environmental forces
5. Economic conditions

In Chapter 1, several factors were mentioned as stimulating the demand for food away from home: population growth in absolute numbers and the changing proportions of young adults and children in the population, shifts from rural to urban living, and the growth of suburbia. Other forces discussed were the rising levels of living, increasing leisure time and changing social patterns, including the increasing numbers of married women working outside the home. These trends will continue to affect the demand for food away from home, and no doubt new external forces will also influence demand. Effective marketing management requires that these trends be recognized and that marketing strategies be adapted to them.

Gathering Information for Marketing Decision Making

Effective decision making requires first the gathering of information. The marketing manager's concern with the collection of data is that the information be valid, that is, "true," giving a complete, unbiased picture of the situation. Furthermore, the information must pertain to the problem at hand, and third, the cost of collecting the information must be considered in relation to the value of the data collected. Marketing information may be of several types:

1. Data from within the company (where there is an existing business)
2. Secondary data—that is, information available from sources outside the organization
3. Primary data, developed through a special research project, with a particular purpose in mind

Data from Within the Organization

Information on sales patterns, check averages, and cover counts in an existing operation may already be available through daily sales reports. This information can be accumulated and analyzed for use in forecasting customer behavior and dining patterns in a new operation or in evaluating the performance of an existing operation. Figure 2–4 shows a form for collecting and evaluating data in an individual operation. Chain operators may require a more sophisticated format for analysis; some large organizations use computers for accumulating and analyzing data.

Secondary Data

There is a great deal of market information available either without charge or for a small fee. Data such as population census, retail sales patterns, census of business and industry, and other pertinent data can be obtained from various government agencies or from local chambers of commerce. Organizations such as trade associations or private market research companies are sources for more specific information. Generally, the more specific the information, the more it will cost.

▶ TO START...

    Think out and develop the best set of answers you can to this basic restaurant marketing question:

    "FOR WHOM...ARE WE TRYING TO DO WHAT...WITH FOOD AND BEVERAGE SERVICES?

    WHEN?   WHERE?   HOW?   WHY?

- FOR WHOM? (Describe types of people)
- WHAT? (Describe basic types of service)
- WHEN? (Days/hours/meal periods, etc.)
- WHERE? (Location description)
- HOW? (Describe basic menu mixes and methods of sales/delivery/consumption used)
- WHY? (Describe financial operation requirements, and/or profit and return-on-investment goals)

▶ NEXT...   IDENTIFY AND EXAMINE THE BASIC REVENUE OPERATING PERIODS AND CHARACTERISTICS. DO THIS FOR EACH OUTLET

Service Offered	Days and Hours of Operation	Average Number of Covers Served Daily	Who are These People - Where do They Come From?	Describe Typical Order Sold in This Service Type	Average Check and Average Daily Revenue	Average Daily Beer, Wine and Liquor Sales	How can we Increase Sales in This Period?
Breakfast or Brunch							
Coffee Break: AM/PM							
Luncheon							
Afternoon							
Dinner							
Late Supper							
Evening Snacks							
Special Functions (On-Premise and Off-Premise)							
Room Service (Hotel)							
Continuous Fast Food, Specialty Item, and/or Hamburger							
All Night Food Service							
Vended Food Business							

Fig. 2-4. Marketing analysis questionnaire. "For whom . . . are we trying to what . . . with food and beverage services?" *(Adapted from Marketing Management Guide, National Restaurant Association, 1968)*

Marketing Strategy 31

▶ LATER ON, AFTER COMPLETING YOUR MARKETING ANALYSIS...

 Now try to develop the best possible ideas and judgments you can in answer to these key questions below...

- ARE WE DOING A BASICALLY GOOD JOB OF TRYING TO SERVE OUR PRESENT MIX OF CUSTOMERS?

- WHAT ADDITIONAL TYPES OR NUMBERS OF PEOPLE SHOULD WE BE TRYING TO ATTRACT?

- WHAT IMPROVEMENTS OR ADDITIONS IN OUR BASIC SERVICES CAN WE MAKE TO HELP ATTRACT THEM?

- SHOULD WE SHORTEN/LENGHTEN/OTHERWISE CHANGE OUR OPERATING PERIODS IN ANY WAY?

- HOW CAN WE MAKE OUR LOCATION MORE APPEALING OR EASIER TO FIND AND USE?

- HOW CAN WE CHANGE/ADD TO/SIMPLIFY OUR BASIC MIX OF FOOD ITEMS, BEVERAGES AND SERVICES TO PROVIDE GREATER SATISFACTION?

- ARE WE ADVERTISING TO THE RIGHT GROUPS?

- WHAT WOULD BE THE FINANCIAL IMPACT OF VARIOUS MENU PRICING CHANGES...SALES-MAKING ACTIVITIES...OR MENU ADDITIONS OR SIMPLIFICATIONS?

Fig. 2-4. Marketing analysis questionnaire. "For whom . . . are we trying to what . . . with food and beverage services?" *(Adapted from Marketing Management Guide, National Restaurant Association, 1968)* (Cont'd.)

Research Projects

After all available data from within the organization and from secondary sources have been gathered and analyzed, management may decide that more specialized information is required and initiate a special research project. Retailers, for example, have developed numerous market research techniques, many of which can be applied to restaurant marketing studies. The following are three such techniques:

1. Customer surveys, which may be of several types:

    (a) The collection of factual data, such as frequency of visitation to restaurants generally or to specific restaurants in the area; distance traveled to the restaurant; and amount of money spent there
    (b) Attitude studies or motivation research, which concentrate on a smaller sample, using in-depth personal interviews to explore such questions as what influences buying decisions, or the business image in relation to that of competitors.
    (c) Product testing surveys, such as taste panels

2. Observation of customer buying habits, such as the pattern of traffic flowing past a restaurant entrance, the means of arrival, and likelihood of impulse sales.

3. Interviews with persons having inside information. For a restaurant market study, such sources might be institutional foods dealers or representatives of the local chamber of commerce

Since it is impossible and unnecessary to gather data from every potential restaurant guest, a sample group is usually selected for study. The size and composition of the sample must reflect the composition and characteristics of the total population if the research is to be valid. This is a highly technical field and is best left to specialists in the field of statistics and sampling.

Special Marketing Considerations

The Better Mousetrap

There are several types of restaurants that represent unique marketing situations. One can be considered a "better mousetrap," since the market literally beats a path to its door. This type of restaurant is a specialty or occasion-type operation, usually located in some out-of-the-way location. It is far from any visible source of patronage, yet the "better mousetrap" not only survives in its remote location, it actually flourishes.

In marketing terminology, this type of restaurant is a "generative" business, attracting patronage on the strength of its own market appeal. Closer observation of its source of patronage usually reveals that this type of restaurant actually has an extended trading area that includes parts of one or more metropolitan areas in a driving range of one to two hours. Furthermore, the restaurant probably has a long-established and well-deserved reputation for good food and service in attractive surroundings; and, because of a well-planned and executed merchandising program, it has a distinctive image in the eyes of its patrons. The trip and the meal are seen as an entertaining experience in themselves.

"Better mousetrap" operations are not limited to rural locations. They may be found in any area not usually frequented by restaurant-goers. Examples of such locations are heavy industrial areas, deserted downtown areas, piers, wharfs or warehouse districts, and other remote corners of the city. If the operation is of substantial size, it has probably grown to that size over a long period of time, while building a strong base of repeat patronage.

The success and appeal of an operation of this type can often encourage imitation. Unless the imitator is very skilled in restaurant operations and marketing, the venture has little chance of success. Such operations are subject to wide day-to-day fluctuations in patronage, depending on weather and driving conditions. Furthermore, they must be able to attract a work-force that will be available only when needed and not on a full-time basis. If the location is too far from a sizable labor market, staffing the operation could be a problem.

The Vanity Project

The vanity restaurant is almost always based on the classic French or continental operation. It is often built without regard for the size of the market or economic potential but rather to add prestige to a building project or as a hobby for the owners or investors. These individuals frequently have no experience in the food service business, except that they know and appreciate the finest foods, wines, service, and decor, and they wish to operate the finest restaurant in town. Sometimes the concept of the operation is closer to that of a club than a restaurant. Such objectives are laudable, but without a market sufficiently large to support a luxury restaurant, and without highly capable and experienced top management, restaurants of this nature usually operate at a loss.

Most of the successful luxury restaurants are small, owner-operated establishments. The owners are highly skilled entrepreneurs who are deeply committed to their restaurants and are willing to invest far more of themselves personally in the businesses than most hired managers would be willing to do. Since the restaurant is small, the owner–operator is able to oversee personally every detail of the operation and is not dependent on hired managers or supervisors. Furthermore, he can operate as he sees fit, without having to answer to others for his performance.

The objectives of a vanity restaurant are usually to provide prestige and pleasure for the owners and clientele. In all probability, these objectives will not be compatible with the economic objective of producing a profit. If the owners are willing to accept reduced profits, then a project that fulfills prestige motives still has merits.

Purchase of an Existing Operation

The purchase of an existing restaurant may be the fastest way to enter the restaurant business. The prospective buyer should determine why the business is available for sale. If it is because it is unprofitable, a careful analysis of the operation should be made to determine the cause of the unprofitability. Poor management practices can be corrected, but a lack of market cannot be corrected by a simple change of management.

The image of the restaurant in the eyes of the local market should also be determined. If the previous operation has a bad reputation, it may be necessary to make a substantial investment in renovating and redecorating the restaurant, and in advertising and promotion to overcome this reputation.

The foregoing examples show how marketing principles can be applied in evaluating the market and potential sales volume of a food service operation. Profitability is a primary objective of almost every commercial project, but without sales volume, there is little chance for profit.

3

FINANCIAL STRATEGY

Financial strategy goes hand in hand with market planning and with the third aspect of management strategy: conceptual planning (see Chapter 4). Financial planning must be done to ensure that the business has adequate amounts of capital available when needed to allow the firm to carry out its marketing and operational plans. The financial plan includes the amount of capital to be obtained, the sources of that capital and the related costs, and the time when the capital will be needed. The need for this type of planning is continuous in any ongoing business and is particularly important in a rapidly growing business. This chapter deals largely with financing new businesses and evaluating new investment opportunities. Financing of ongoing operations is discussed in Chapter 12.

Financial strategy goes beyond simply supplying adequate capital. The financial manager is also concerned with the uses of that capital and the results. He must allocate the available capital within the firm in order to obtain the greatest return on that capital over the long run. Three basic criteria are used in evaluating investment alternatives: (1) Can the proposed investment produce a profit?; (2) will this profit be sufficient to compensate the investor adequately for the risk he undertakes?; and (3) if debt financing is to be used, will the project provide sufficient cash flow to pay off the loan? Debt financing establishes a fixed cost (interest), which must be paid regardless of the profitability of the business or the amount of cash resulting from operations.

These three criteria—profitability, return on investment, and adequacy of cash flow—are basic measures used in the evaluation of a proposed investment, whether it be a whole new business or an additional investment in an existing operation. This chapter discusses these three concepts and how they are brought together in an overall financial strategy for a new business.

Sources and Types of Capital

Forms of Business Organization

The form of business organization used for a new business can affect the method of financing and the capital structure, and it has a number of legal implications as well. The three forms of organization most commonly found are the sole proprietorship, the partnership, and the corporation.

Sole Proprietorship. In a sole proprietorship, the business is owned by one individual, who has sole control of the business. If the venture is successful, he is the only recipient of the profits, but if it is unsuccessful, he alone bears the loss. Furthermore, the proprietor stands to lose not only the amount of his investment but also all his personal financial assets as well, since the law does not distinguish between the individual and his business; they are considered to be a single entity.

The single proprietorship is the most commonly used form of organization in the food service business, but proprietorships are rapidly losing ground to corporations. One reason is the extent of individual liability mentioned above. Another major difficulty with the single proprietorship is its instability and resulting difficulty in attracting debt capital. If the individual becomes unable to operate his business, the lenders have no guarantee that they will be able to recover their loans, since there is no guarantee of continuity of the business.

Partnership. The partnership is an association of two or more individuals who have agreed to conduct a business as co-owners and co-investors. The partnership permits a pooling of the equity capital of several investors, and profits are usually, although not necessarily, split in proportion to the amount each one has invested. Control of the business is also divided, and some division of authority and responsibility must be made among the partners.

Partnership offers a greater degree of continuity and stability than the single proprietorship and is seen as less risky by outside lenders. Like the sole proprietor, the individual partners are all personally liable for the debts of the business.

Corporation. Legally, the corporation is a separate entity apart from its ownership; the owners, the stockholders, are liable for the debts of the corporation only up to the amount that they have invested. Also, as a separate entity, the corporation has continuity and is not dependent on one person or a few individuals to continue in operation. Therefore, the corporation is able to obtain debt financing much more easily than a single proprietorship or a partnership.

One disadvantage of the corporate form of organization is that profits are taxed twice: the corporation pays taxes on its net income, and the stockholders pay personal taxes on the dividends they receive. Small, closely held corporations may be granted relief from this double taxation if they meet certain requirements.

The Capital Structure

Capital is the total amount invested in a business. It may be in the form of equity capital invested by the owners, or it may be debt provided by creditors. In the case of a going concern, equity capital may also be income earned in the past, which has been reinvested in the business instead of being paid out to the owners or shareholders.

The proportion of debt to equity in the capital structure is important both in the net profitability of the firm and in determining the investor's return on investment. A firm with a high proportion of debt to equity will have a high interest expense, and interest is a fixed cost. Therefore, the firm will have a high breakeven point, which means that it will have to maintain a high level of sales in order to maintain its profitability (see Chapter 11 for a discussion of breakeven analysis). Lenders will consider additional loans to be an increasing risk and will require increasingly higher rates of interest. On the other hand, investors, having contributed a relatively small proportion of the total capital, are in a position to earn a very high rate of return on that investment, since the profits are not diluted or spread out over a large amount of investment. Such a firm is said to be highly leveraged. Investors in such a business are assuming a relatively high risk and expect a high rate of return on their investment.

Taxes must also be considered in relation to the capital structure. Interest paid on debt is a business expense and therefore reduces the net taxable income. Dividends paid to stockholders under present law are not a business expense and therefore do not reduce the amount of net income on which taxes must be paid.

Financing a new or going business can be accomplished by capital from the owners (equity financing) or by loans from creditors (debt financing). In launching a new venture, a combination of both types of financing is generally used. In a going business, the type of financing used for additional funds is more dependent on factors such as the purpose of the funds, the profitability of the operation, the existing debt to equity ratio, and the cost of money.

Each type of financing has advantages and disadvantages. In equity financing, the owners of a business do not have to share the profits with lenders through interest payments. The business is not burdened with fixed payments (interest and amortization of principal), and operations are not hampered by restrictions imposed by creditors.

The primary disadvantage of equity financing is that not many individual entrepreneurs under present economic conditions have sufficient capital to meet the requirements of a new business venture. Those who do may not wish to risk it in an unproven venture.

Debt financing could be advantageous to an entrepreneur because it would not dilute his control of the business. Also, the earnings on the borrowed funds could be higher than the interest charged. Debt financing has several important disadvantages: This type of financing is difficult to obtain for a new company or for a company with a limited earning power; present borrowings can undermine ability to borrow in the future when the need is greater; interest must be paid irrespective of earnings levels; and creditors can make prior claim to income of the business and, at maturity of the loan, its assets.

Debt financing can be either on a short-, intermediate-, or long-term basis. Short-term usually refers to a loan of less than one year. Intermediate-term is generally considered to be up to 10 years, and long-term is a loan in excess of 10 years. The terms most commonly used to describe debt financing are *short-term* and *long-term*.

The use of short- or long-term debt financing should be governed by the intended use of the funds. Short-term financing is most often used for working capital purposes, that is, for financing the conversion cycle from cash spent for raw materials to cash collected from the sale of the finished product. Short-term financing is also used for short-period projects, or for the period during which arrangements are made to obtain longer-term funds from other sources.

Long-term financing is used most frequently for acquisition of fixed assets such as land, buildings, furniture, and equipment. Since the cost of these assets is substantial, a long time is required for earnings to generate sufficient cash funds to repay the loan.

Sources of Capital

The following are the more common sources of cash funds for financing a new business venture, as well as a going business:

1. Equity capital:

    a. For noncorporate organizations:
        Proprietor, partners, syndicates
    b. For corporate organizations:
        Sale of stock
        Retained earnings

2. Debt financing (short- and long-term):

a. Commercial banks
b. Life insurance companies
c. Pension funds
d. Finance companies
e. Bond offerings

Venture Capital. Private firms specialize in providing equity funds for new businesses. Since the failure rate for new restaurants is very high, the venture capital investor looks for a high rate of return on his capital. Venture capital funds are often used to finance the planning and development of a new enterprise until it has reached a point of stability where it will be more acceptable to conservative sources of financing.

Suppliers. In the food service industry, suppliers have traditionally been a source of financing for new operations. Equipment suppliers have been willing to accept notes in payment for furniture and equipment, and food purveyors have been willing to carry high balances in their new customers' accounts in anticipation of future business. In recent years, however, with higher interest rates and operating costs, suppliers have been less eager to finance new operators.

Government Agencies. State and local government agencies may make loans to new businesses in order to attract industry and jobs to a certain locale. The federal government is also involved in assisting businessmen with financing. The Small Business Administration (SBA) of the U.S. Department of Commerce regularly provides loans to small companies that are unable to obtain financing elsewhere. The SBA also participates with private lenders in providing loans and in guaranteeing lease payments of small businesses. In addition, the SBA licenses and regulates private companies that lend funds to small businesses. These are Small Business Investment Companies (SBICs) and Minority Enterprise Small Business Companies (MESBICs).

Leasing. Leasing may be considered as an alternative to financing. A bare building or a fully equipped "turnkey" operation may be leased instead of purchased. Leasing arrangements can also be made separately for specific pieces of equipment or furnishings. Many leasing arrangements provide for servicing and maintenance of the leased items, including replacement of obsolete models with new ones. The latter provision is an attractive feature when a piece of equipment is expected to have a short life span owing to rapid technological change. Some leasing arrangements are actually a form of installment sales agreement, in which ownership of the asset passes to the lessee at the end of a specified period.

Estimating Capital Requirements for a New Restaurant

To develop a financial strategy for a proposed restaurant, the total amount of capital required must be estimated. According to Dun and Bradstreet, lack of sufficient capital is a major cause of business failures. Therefore, it is important that all the costs of the project be included and that the estimates be made as accurately as possible. Some of these costs may be easily determined, whereas others must be based on general rules of thumb at this point in the planning.

To open a new restaurant, capital investment will be required in at least some of the following assets:

1. Land
2. Building
3. Leasehold improvements
4. Furnishings, fixtures, and equipment
5. Small equipment (china, glassware, silverware, and utensils)

Two other types of cost are associated with a new project, although they do not represent an investment in physical assets: organization costs and preopening expenses. In addition, the financing plan must provide for working capital—funds used in the day-to-day transaction of the business.

Land and Building

The decision to own or to lease land and buildings can have a major effect on profitability, cash flow, and investment strategy. Purchasing land and buildings outright with equity funds may increase the cash flow from operations but requires a substantial investment. Furthermore, the cost of the land cannot be depreciated for tax purposes, since land is assumed to have an infinite life. Therefore, one tax advantage is lost if land is owned outright. Leasing land and buildings establishes a fixed cost for the operation, but this cost is fully deductible for tax purposes, and the only investment required may be a small lease deposit.

Another alternative is to lease the land and erect a building. In this case, ground rent payments are deductible expenses for tax purposes, and the building is a "leasehold improvement" that is depreciated over the life of the ground lease (or the economic life of the building if it is shorter than the ground lease). At the termination of the ground lease, all remaining improvements become the property of the land owner. In this case, the initial investment must include the construction cost of the building.

An occasionally used strategy is the sale–leaseback. The company purchases the land and erects a building to its own specifications; the company then sells the land and building to an investor who leases it back to the company for a period of years. In this way the operating company gets a building constructed to its own specifications, and if it is one of a large chain, the company may be able to erect its own prototype building for lower cost than could an individual contractor. By selling the property, the company recovers its initial investment capital for use in further expansion and also gains the tax advantages of operating on leased land. Furthermore, the risk of loss or the benefits of growth in value of that parcel of land is transferred to another investor.

If a particular site is being considered, its purchase price or lease terms can usually be determined. If a building is to be erected, construction costs may be estimated on the basis of cost per square foot of recent comparable construction in the area. Architects and building contractors may be able to provide general figures for a particular area.

Leasehold Improvements

Any investment made in furnishings and equipment that are physically attached to rented premises is a leasehold improvement and cannot be depreciated over a period longer than the length of the lease unless there are renewal options. At the termination of the lease, any remaining improvements become the property of the owner of the premises. Examples of leasehold improvements include heating, ventilation and air conditioning systems, rest rooms, plumbing installations, structural additions or changes made by the lessee, and kitchen equipment that must be permanently installed.

The amount of investment required for leasehold improvements will depend on the condition of the premises when leased. For example, in a new shopping mall or office building, the space may be rented unfinished or "raw," meaning that the tenant must pay for all improvements in that space: decor and equipment; plumbing, electrical, and ventilation installations; and all finishes on walls, floors, and ceilings. Under such an arrangement, the tenant would want a long lease so that he could have a number of years to recover his investment.

Another type of lease agreement is the "turnkey," in which the owner has made all the investment and the tenant is ready to go into business simply by unlocking the doors. Turnkey rental agreements are common with franchised fast-food restaurants. Rental rates for a turnkey lease are, of course, much higher than for raw space, in order to give the landlord an adequate return on his investment.

Another frequent restaurant rental situation occurs when a restaurant tenant goes out of business and leaves the landlord with a vacant restaurant. Leasing such premises may be a very good way to get into business with a minimum of investment, but the location, design, and condition of the premises should be very carefully considered. Shorter leases are usually offered for such premises, and rents may be quite reasonable since the landlord may have difficulty finding a tenant for the space.

Furniture, Fixtures, and Equipment

Even if the premises are leased with the kitchen equipment installed, the restaurant operator probably will want to make some investment in dining room decor in order to project a unique market image. For a high quality restaurant, this could mean a substantial investment in antique furnishings, works of art, and fine carpets and draperies.

If kitchen equipment is to be purchased, design fees and installation costs will usually be incurred and must be included in the investment. Some equipment, such as coffee urns, ice cream freezers, and milk dispensers, may be furnished without charge by food purveyors.

The cost of interior finishing, furniture, and fixtures may be estimated on a square-foot or a per-seat basis. Companies that specialize in designing and installing food service equipment may be able to provide this information. Adequate provision must also be made for design fees and installation costs, which can add as much as 20 to 25 percent to the cost of the project. Furthermore, the cost of furnishings can vary widely depending on how elaborate the decor will be and how much kitchen equipment will be required. In a preliminary estimate considerable leeway should be allowed in estimating these costs.

Small Equipment

Small equipment includes china, glassware, silverware, kitchen utensils, pots, and pans. A supply of these items is purchased for opening stock, plus some reserve. This equipment may be considered par stock and is a fixed asset. Once in operation, the cost of replacement stock is usually included in expenses.

Small equipment costs, which include utensils and expendables, can be estimated on a per-seat basis. Such costs can vary widely, depending on the quality and amount of custom-designed tableware required.

Organization Costs and Preopening Expenses

Organization costs include legal fees and other expenses incurred in obtaining the corporate charter and raising initial capital. Preopening expenses are not directly a part of the cost of construction but are incurred during the planning and construction of a facility. These costs may include the following: salaries of those involved in planning the project; professional fees for financial, marketing, and legal services; comparison shopping of the competition; recipe development and product testing; development of the merchandising program, including logo and graphics as well as menu design; staff recruitment and training costs; and preopening advertising and promotion.

Because organization costs theoretically benefit the corporation throughout its life, they may be capitalized, that is, they may be treated as a deferred expense and amortized over a period of time. Preopening expenses may be amortized over a much shorter period.

Preopening expenses are difficult to estimate accurately, but a budget can be prepared, using all available information, including written proposals for professional services, license costs, projected salaries, and construction timetables. Costs such as advertising and promotion can also be budgeted. Organization costs can usually be estimated fairly accurately by the organization's lawyers.

Working Capital

Working capital requirements for a new business include cash for operating accounts, cashiers' change banks, lease deposits, and prepayments of expenses such as insurance, utility deposits, licenses, and fees. The purchase of opening inventories of food and supplies must also be considered, although the cash requirements for inventories may be reduced if the purveyors are willing to extend credit to the new operation.

When a high volume of charged sales is anticipated, working capital may also be required to finance accounts receivable. Many operations lose money initially and need sufficient working capital to carry payrolls and other operating expenses for a time.

Working capital requirements are usually estimated in proportion to the expected sales volume, plus an amount required to meet expenses during the initial operating period when losses may be anticipated from operations. Such losses can be estimated by preparing a cash flow calculation by months for the first year or two of operation.

The Sources and Costs of Management

One of the most important factors in the success of any business venture is the know-how that is brought to it, that is, the quality of the management. Although management is not often thought of as a potential cost, it is nevertheless an important cost to consider in determining a financial strategy. If management know-how is not provided internally (by the owners of the business), then it must be provided by outsiders, and the costs of those outsiders' services must be included in the financial planning. Management fees, franchise fees and royalties, and profit-sharing arrangements can have considerable impact on an operation's net results.

Management by the Owner

For the individual entrepreneur who operates his own restaurant, the obvious source of know-how is himself, and the cost of this talent is expressed in terms of the profits he draws from the operation over and above the reasonable return on his investment. Many individual entrepreneurs do not consider the double objectives of adequate personal income for their labors, plus a return on their investment. If they hired a manager instead of paying themselves, they would see that they were not getting a return on their investment.

In a company organization, managerial capability is provided by the unit manager, who receives a salary and perhaps a bonus based on the profitability of his operation. In multiunit operations, additional management costs may be generated by the company's central office staff. This includes the direct supervision of the operation and staff support, which often includes accounting and financial departments, purchasing, merchandising, advertising and promotion, production research, test kitchens, and planning and design services. The cost of all central office functions must be borne by the various profit centers or operating units, and this generally represents a cost beyond the control of the unit manager.

Theoretically, these central office expenses represent reductions of the costs of functions that, in the case of an individual operation, would be performed by individuals within that operation. However, by centralizing certain functions, economies are expected through more efficient use of labor and the ability to employ specialists. Also, through centralization of purchasing power, lower purchase prices can usually be obtained.

Management by Others

Many persons with specific interest in some type of food service business have no previous experience in this field and in many cases do not really wish to become involved in the day-to-day operations. Such persons may be administrators of institutions, real estate developers, or investors. They have their own areas of responsibility and expertise and prefer to leave food service operations to "food people." The food operation in such cases is usually secondary to some other primary activity. Finding the right food people and structuring the contractual arrangements are serious matters. There are a number of alternative methods. The following are the most common arrangements:

1. Hiring an individual to manage the food service
2. Engaging an operating company or contract feeding firm
3. Leasing the premises to an individual or a food service company
4. Purchasing a franchise

Hiring an Individual to Manage the Food Service Operation

Unless the selection of an individual manager is made carefully, it can be the least desirable arrangement. The advantage of this alternative is that the ownership or top management retains direct control over the operation, with the manager as an employee. One difficulty is in the selection of a capable individual. Ability in this field is extremely difficult to measure except by actual performance. There is a tendency to equate a managerial candidate's qualifications on the basis of his previous job title, salary, and the prestige or reputation of previous employers. Unfortunately, there is little standardization of job titles in this industry. Furthermore, it is an industry that is notorious for having a highly mobile work force. One labor expert in the field has made the observation that the hotel and food service industry is the only one he knows that rewards "job hoppers." An individual with a long list of past employers, particularly prestigious employers, is thought to have a great deal of experience; in another industry, such an employment history would be considered a sign of instability.

Another difficulty with hiring an individual is retaining a really capable person. If the individual is ambitious for a career, he may soon become frustrated if there is a lack of opportunity to advance in the organization. Other managers may be drawn toward remuneration and move on to the first job offering more money. Such an individual may be motivated to stay in a position by receiving a share of the profits as a part of his salary, making his income partially dependent on his performance.

A third and perhaps the most serious drawback to having an individual as the source of management know-how is that the employer must supervise and evaluate this manager's performance and must find a replacement for him if his performance is less than desired. Furthermore, in the manager's absence, day-to-day operating management needs may be neglected unless they can be assumed by the owner.

Engaging an Operating Company or Contract Feeding Firm

When an operating company is engaged, continuity of management becomes its responsibility, relieving the investor of the problem. A contract feeding company is also able to attract a higher caliber of career-oriented managers since it offers them opportunities for advancement in their chosen career field.

Another advantage offered by the contract feeding company is the availability of specialized services such as physical planning and design, labor counsel, large-scale purchasing power, and research and development in such areas as recipe development and equipment testing and design.

The agreement may provide that the staff will be on the contractor's payroll or on the client's. When the contractor's wage scales and fringe benefits are lower than those of the client, substantial savings can sometimes be effected in payroll costs by staffing the operation with the contractor's employees.

One negative aspect of contracting food service management is a fear on the part of the client management that it will lose control over the food service operation. Certainly, contracting will remove day-to-day decision making from the client management, which is not necessarily a disadvantage. Controls over major policy decisions do not have to be given up, but they must be specified in the contractual agreement.

Another concern of the client management is the cost of the management fee or operator's profit. The client management may fear that this fee or profit may be only an added cost to the operation, and this may be the case in some operations that are already being tightly run by the employer's own staff. Contracting companies also vary widely in the effectiveness of their systems, the capability of their personnel, the depth of their experience in different types of operations, and their purchasing power. Therefore, the contractor must be carefully selected.

There are several major factors that affect the success of a contracted operation, apart from the contractor's own capability. These are as follows:

1. The capability of the individual food service unit managers and their ability to carry out the contractor's systems
2. The employer–client's own policy or budgetary restrictions
3. The amount of support and cooperation given the contractor's manager by the employer–client management in such areas as interdepartmental relationships and employee relationships, particularly if the contractor must supervise the client's employees
4. The efficiency of the existing physical layout and condition of the equipment, and the contractor's ability to adapt his operating methods to this physical facility

The general operating goals and policies are spelled out in a contractual agreement and carried out by the contractor. The owner or a member of top management may monitor the contractor's performance but does not become directly involved with the operations.

There are several types of contract, as discussed below.

Fixed Management Fee. A fixed management fee may be a flat fee or an amount based on the number of meals served. A common arrangement is a flat base fee that covers the contractor's fixed costs at that operation and then a per-meal charge for meals served over an established amount.

Profit-and-Loss Agreement. Under the profit-and-loss type of agreement, the contractor's profit is the difference between sales and the operating expenses incurred. In situations in which sales are not made, such as in patient feeding in a hospital or in-flight catering, the contractor is paid a predetermined amount per meal out of which he must meet expenses and make his profit. Such operations are usually subsidized in a variety of ways, including free premises (no rent charged) or services provided by the owner. Such services may include maintenance and utilities, office services, and cleaning and trash removal services, all of which would normally be operating expenses for the contractor. Cash subsidies are also found as part of the agreement.

Profit and loss agreements are most effective when the population being served is not totally captive and has other mealtime options. In such cases, the contractor is forced by competition to try to satisfy his market and not try to reduce his operating costs at the expense of sales.

Cost-Plus Agreements. The cost-plus arrangement is more common in government contracts than in private industry. The contractor may receive a percentage of the total costs of the operation as his fee. Unless there are very stringent controls, the contractor's only motivation to minimize costs is his expectation of retaining the contract in the future.

Leasing

Real estate developers and managers lease out premises to individuals or operating companies who then install whatever type of operation they believe will be most profitable. Sometimes the lease restricts the type of merchandise to be sold, hours of operation, or exterior appearance and signs. Restrictions such as these are often found in leases of large complexes such as shopping centers where it is necessary to provide continuity and balance among all tenants in order to maximize the overall potential sales and profits of the group.

Purchasing a Franchise

For individual investors, purchasing a franchise may be an excellent way to obtain management know-how in the food service business. Franchising is one way the individual entrepreneur can exist and still compete with large companies. An established franchise company has a well-developed and proven operating system, and in most cases it places considerable emphasis on training the franchisees in the operation of their system. Franchise operators are assisted and supervised by company representatives to be sure that they are maintaining the standards established by the company.

Along with the license to operate under the franchisor's name and use his methods goes the franchisor's know-how that has been developed over a period of time. Services rendered by a franchisor may include site selection, construction, financing, merchandising techniques, accounting and cost control systems, research and development, and employee training. Participation in national and regional advertising programs developed by professionals permits the franchisee to compete with the expensive campaigns of larger competitors at a relatively small cost.

Most franchise companies require the payment of an initial franchise fee and a continuing royalty based on a percentage of sales. Some also require an additional percentage for national or regional advertising. In the past franchise companies required their franchisees to purchase all their foods and supplies from them and relied on markups on this merchandise to provide the parent company's margin of profit. The parent companies claimed that centralized control over purchases was necessary for quality control purposes to provide the public with the desired standards in products throughout the company. Agreements of this type have come under pressure in the courts, and many have been set aside as being in restraint of trade.

Many franchise companies will build and completely equip a facility, which is then leased to the franchisee. Some will also provide management for the units, either on a management fee or a share-of-profits basis.

Evaluating an Investment Opportunity

The three principal financial objectives of an operation—profitability, return on investment, and cash flow—are discussed in the following paragraphs.

Profitability

Profitability is the difference between total revenue and the costs and expenses incurred in producing that revenue. Profits are the primary concern of the manager, for without profits he cannot hope to remain in business for very long.

Generally speaking, costs can be classified into two types: operating costs and occupancy, or fixed, costs. Operating costs are those that vary in relation to sales and are usually controllable by the operating manager. This type of cost includes the cost of materials, labor, and overhead such as utilities, maintenance, advertising, and office expenses.

Fixed costs are those over which the operating manager has no control, and they are largely the costs of occupying premises. These costs may include rent or property taxes, or both; interest on a mortgage; insurance on the building and its contents; and depreciation on a building and equipment that are owned outright. These costs continue at a predetermined rate or amount, regardless of the level of sales volume.

Return on Investment

Dollars of profits alone are not a satisfactory measure of profit performance for investment purposes. The invstory or owner measures the amount of profit against the amount of investment required to produce that profit.

Two important aspects of return on investment are the degree of risk and the amount of income earned for undertaking that risk. The higher the risk, the higher will be the expected rate of return. For example, if the cash were deposited in a savings account (practically a no-risk investment), it would earn a certain rate of interest. Therefore, investors expect the rate of return on an investment in a business venture to be higher than the return on a low-risk investment such as a bank savings accounts.

Cash Flow

Cash flow is the primary concern of the lending institutions or creditors of a business. They want to be sure that the business will generate a sufficient amount of cash to meet the payrolls and pay the bills and still leave enough to pay the interest on the loan and repay the principal.

Cash flow and profits are not the same because businesses usually report their profits (or losses) on the basis of accrual accounting. This means that the operating results (profits or losses) for a period are determined by the income earned in that period, less the expenses incurred in earning that income. However, the collection of that income and the payment of the expenses may not have occurred in that period. For example, depreciation, although charged against income for a period, does not require any cash payments during that period. The cash outlay for the fixed assets that are being depreciated probably took place some time previously. Investment in inventory or accounts receivable affects cash flow adversely, whereas the receipt of advance deposits may improve it temporarily.

Cash flow planning is particularly important in the early stages of a new business, before the operation has fully developed its sales potential and before its staff is fully trained and operating at maximum efficiency. Later, as the business expands, cash is required for increased working capital, for larger inventories, and for refurbishing and replacing the original equipment and furnishings.

Pinpointing Profits: Comparing Different Types of Restaurant Investment

The following pages show representative operating statements of seven types of restaurant operations. Each model is based on an actual, successful, well-managed business. Some are independently owned; others are chain operations; and one, the fast-food model, is a franchise. Each model operation is located in a strong market area, but none is an unusual or monopoly situation. The models are used to show the sources of profitability, return on investment, and cash flow. Interest expense is not included because of the wide variations in financing methods.

Family Steak House

This chain operation (Fig. 3–1) offers the familiar limited steak and roast beef menu with self-service salad bar format. It has an informal, relaxed decor that emphasizes the theme of the operation. It operates every day for dinner only. There is a small cocktail lounge area with about 25 seats and a large dining area with 275 seats. The seat-turnover average is twice nightly most nights, and over three times nightly on Fridays and Saturdays, for an overall average of 2.1. The free-standing building contains about 7,000 square feet on a site of about one acre.

Beverage sales are not as high as management would like, probably because of the heavy amount of family business. A selection of moderately priced wines is promoted, which contributes to the above-average beverage cost. The average food check is about $7.00. The moderate menu prices coupled with the heavy emphasis on high-cost meat items produce a relatively high food cost of about 45 percent. Because of the partial self-service and the limited amount of on-premises preparation, however, labor cost, including fringe benefits and payroll taxes, is a low 20 percent.

The unit profit before occupancy costs is 26 percent. This figure does not include the cost of some functions, such as accounting, that are done in the company's headquarters office.

The company owns the land and building. It calculates depreciation on the building over a 25-year economic life. Furnishings and equipment are depreciated over eight years. After paying real estate taxes and insurance costs, the family steak house contributes $377,000

	Amount	Ratio
Sales		
Food	$1,470,000	85.0%
Beverages	230,000	15.0
Total sales	1,700,000	100.0
Cost of sales		
Food	662,000	45.0
Beverages	69,000	30.0
Total cost of sales	731,000	43.0
Gross profit		
Food	808,000	55.0
Beverages	161,000	70.0
Total gross profit	969,000	57.0
Operating expenses		
Payroll and related expenses	340,000	20.0
Advertising and promotion	34,000	2.0
Other operating expenses	153,000	9.0
Total operating expenses	527,000	31.0
Profit before occupancy costs	442,000	26.0
Occupancy costs		
Real estate taxes	17,000	1.0
Depreciation on building and equipment	42,000	2.5
Insurance	6,000	.3
Total occupancy costs	65,000	3.8
Profit before corporate overhead, interest and income taxes	$ 377,000	22.2%

Fig. 3-1. Statement of income of a family steak house for a typical year.

to the corporation. From this amount must be deducted this unit's share of the company overhead and taxes as well as any interest on debt financing.

The investment required for this type of restaurant might be as follows:

Land	$100,000
Building	430,000
Furnishings and equipment	200,000
	$730,000

A Downtown Coffee Shop

This independently owned operation (Fig. 3–2) is located in a central business district of a major metropolitan area. Because the area has little activity after business hours, the restaurant operates only from Monday through Friday, from 7:00 A.M. to 6:00 P.M.

	Amount	Ratio
Sales		
Coffee shop	$360,000	75.0%
Take-out	120,000	25.0
Total sales	480,000	100.0
Cost of sales	163,000	34.0
Gross profit	317,000	66.0
Operating expenses		
Payroll and related expenses	144,000	30.0
Advertising	2,000	.5
Paper supplies	6,000	1.3
Other operating expenses	43,000	8.9
Total operating expenses	195,000	40.7
Profit before occupancy costs	122,000	25.3
Occupancy costs		
Rent	72,000	15.0
Depreciation	19,000	3.9
Insurance	2,000	.4
Total occupancy costs	93,000	19.3
Profit before interest and taxes	$ 29,000	6.0%

Fig. 3-2. Statement of income of a downtown coffee shop for a typical year.

The restaurant occupies about 4,800 square feet on the ground floor of an office building. It has about 200 seats, 60 at counters and 140 at tables in the rear. The seat turnover is about three times at luncheon and an additional three times during the rest of the day. Waitress service is provided. The menu offers a wide selection of sandwiches, including "deli" sandwiches, grill items, and several hot platters. A few convenience items are used, mosty frozen pies and cakes, but rolls, danish, donuts, and other pastries are purchased daily from a commercial bakery. No alcoholic beverages are sold.

The average check is about $1.20, but this is a combination of luncheon business (which has an average check of about $1.80), breakfast, and coffee-break business. About 25 percent of the sales are take-out, which increases the operator's cost of paper goods and supplies. China service is used in the restaurant, with paper placemats and napkins.

This restaurant has an operating profit of over 25 percent before fixed costs. However, because of its location, it must pay a rather high rent of $15.00 per square foot. Depreciation is also fairly high because all investment in the equipment and leasehold improvements must be written off over a short period (eight years in this case). The very high occupancy costs leave a net profit of only $29,000 or 6 percent of sales before taxes.

At 1976 rates, it would take an estimated $150,000 to construct this coffee shop, assuming that heating, air conditioning and other utilities had already been installed by previous tenants.

A Full-Menu Cafeteria

This operation (Fig. 3–3), belonging to a well-known cafeteria chain, is located in a large suburban shopping center. It is open for lunch and dinner only, seven days a week. Lunch is served from 11:00 A.M. to 3:00 A.M. and dinner from 5:00 P.M. to 8:30 P.M.

The unit occupies about 10,000 square feet of space and has 300 seats that are divided among three attractively decorated dining areas. It has a straight-line layout of the serving area, and heavy emphasis is placed on merchandising the food displays.

The average check is only about $2.20, but the unit serves an average of 1,300 meals a day. It is very popular with young families in the area, and its large menu variety offers an alternative to the standard hamburger menus offered by the fast-food drive-ins nearby. It also attracts a large number of the employees of the shopping center. No liquor is served, although beer and wine are available.

Some of the menu items, including baked goods, are obtained from the company's central commissary, but most of the preparation is done on the premises. Labor costs are reduced somewhat by the use of part-time help, particularly high school students and housewives.

	Amount	Ratio
Sales	$1,030,000	100.0%
Cost of sales	391,000	38.0
Gross profit	639,000	62.0
Operating expenses		
Payroll and related expenses	371,000	36.0
Advertising and promotion	10,000	1.0
Other operating expenses	93,000	9.0
Total operating expenses	474,000	46.0
Profit before occupancy costs	165,000	16.0
Occupancy costs		
Rent	80,000	7.7
Depreciation	44,000	4.3
Insurance	4,000	.4
Total occupancy costs	128,000	12.4
Profit before corporate overhead, interest and income taxes	$ 37,000	3.6%

Fig. 3-3. Statement of income of a full-menu cafeteria for a typical year.

The cafeteria operation pays a total of $80,000 rent for its space in the shopping mall, or $8.00 per square foot. It also has a large depreciation expense, which contributes to a total occupancy cost of 12.4 percent of sales. This cost, combined with a low operating profit, produces a contribution to the company of only 3.6 percent of sales, or $37,000 before taxes and corporate overhead costs. An investment of $350,000 would be required to duplicate this operation at current costs.

A Franchised Fast-Food Restaurant

This franchised operation Fig. 3–4) is located in a suburban area of a small metropolis. It occupies a free-standing building located on a major thoroughfare. The owner, a local resident and his family, have several other units in the area, all franchises of a large, nationally known chain. This particular unit occupies about 25,000 square feet of land, with 140 feet of frontage on the main street. The building contains about 2,400 square feet, including a dining room of about 80 seats.

The restaurant is open from 10:00 A.M. to 11:00 P.M. five days a week and until 1:00 A.M. on Friday and Saturday. The average sale is around $1.70, and the owner estimates that about 60 percent of the sales are for take-out. All disposable tableware is used. The counter

	Amount	Ratio
Sales	$500,000	100.0%
Cost of sales		
Food	190,000	38.0
Paper supplies	20,000	4.0
	210,000	42.0
Gross profit	290,000	58.0
Operating expenses		
Payroll and related expenses		
(Including manager's salary)	95,000	19.0
Advertising (national and local)	15,000	3.0
Franchise fee	20,000	4.0
Other operating expenses	45,000	9.0
Total operating expenses	175,000	35.0
Profit before occupancy costs	115,000	23.0
Occupancy costs		
Rent (to franchise company)	40,000	8.0
Depreciation	11,000	2.2
Insurance	3,000	.6
Total occupancy costs	54,000	10.8
Profit before interest and income taxes	$ 61,000	12.2%

Fig. 3-4. Statement of income of a franchised fast-food restaurant for a typical year.

design has window pick-up points (as opposed to the cafeteria-type of layout), and the number of pick-up windows in operation varies according to the amount of business expected during each time period.

Under his franchise agreement, the operator pays 4 percent of his sales to the franchisor as a royalty fee and contributes another 3 percent for advertising. Part of this advertising contribution is used for the company's national campaign, and part is returned in the form of advertising in the local community. The franchise company owns both the land and building, but the local owner has invested in the equipment, inventories, and working capital (which is common practice under many franchise agreements.)

According to the franchisor's method of reporting costs, the cost of paper supplies and disposable tableware is considered to be a part of the cost of goods sold, rather than a separately stated operating expense. The payroll expense shown includes the salary of the unit manager, a relative of the owner.

Under the franchise agreement, a rent equal to 8 percent of sales is paid to the franchisor. The owner calculates his depreciation on an investment of $90,000 in furnishings and equipment with an eight-year life. In addition, he was required to invest an additional $40,000 in an initial franchise fee and working capital. The total occupancy cost is 10.8 percent of sales, leaving a pretax profit of $61,000, or 12.2 percent of sales.

A Large Specialty Restaurant

This very large restaurant (Fig. 3–5) has a well-deserved national reputation. It is located in a major metropolitan area and is heavily patronized by tourists, conventioneers, and visitors, as well as by the local residents and business community. Its reputation for good food and service, merchandising, and attractive, unusual decor account for a large amount of regular repeat business. In spite of its size (800 seats), the staff prides itself on giving personalized service.

The restaurant is family owned and has grown to its present size over a long period of time. The theme of the restaurant is historical, particularly local history and events. All service personnel are authentically costumed, and the menu is based on locally available foods and old-style recipes. Antiques and authentic artifacts of local interest are used to decorate the numerous dining rooms, and in fact, one section of the building dates from the time of the original settlement of the city. The building now contains a total of 28,000 square feet and occupies a site of about four acres.

The restaurant has 600 seats in various dining rooms, plus a total of 200 seats in several cocktail lounges. It averages 2.2 turnovers

	Amount	Ratio
Sales		
Food	$3,707,000	70.0%
Beverages	1,590,000	30.0
Total sales	5,297,000	100.0
Cost of sales		
Food	1,409,000	38.0
Beverages	366,000	23.0
Total cost of sales	1,775,000	33.5
Gross profit		
Food	2,298,000	62.0
Beverages	1,224,000	77.0
Total gross profit	3,522,000	66.5
Operating expenses		
Payroll and related expenses	1,801,000	34.0
Advertising	132,000	2.5
Other operating expenses	450,000	8.5
Total operating expenses	2,383,000	45.0
Profit before occupancy costs	1,139,000	21.5
Occupancy costs		
Real estate taxes	70,000	1.3
Depreciation	137,000	2.6
Insurance	14,000	.3
Total occupancy costs	221,000	4.2
Profit before interest and income taxes	$ 918,000	17.3%

Fig. 3-5. Statement of income of a large specialty restaurant for a typical year.

daily on the dining room seats and an average food check of $7.80. This is a combination of an average luncheon check of $5.00 and an average dinner check of $9.00. Luncheon business accounts for about 30 percent of the total covers served. The menu offers a selection of about 15 entrée items, plus a wide selection of appetizers, side dishes, and desserts. All baked goods are prepared on the premises.

All major credit cards are accepted, and commissions to the credit card companies amount to almost 1 percent of total sales. This cost is included in other operating expenses.

Through strong internal controls, good forecasting, and well-coordinated promotion to maintain the sales volume, this operation produces an operating profit of over 21 percent of sales.

In this example, depreciation is shown at $137,000, or 2.6 percent of sales. It is based on a building with a 40-year life, which would cost over $1.7 million to build today. Land value is estimated at $500,000, and the cost of equipment and furnishings at present rates is estimated at $745,000, depreciated over an eight-year life. In reality, a business such as this would probably have fully depreciated a large part of its building, because it has been in business in the same facilities for many years. These values are shown only to demonstrate what the operation might produce in profits if it were to be built today.

The profits shown do not include any interest charges. If this restaurant were built today, some or most of the investment would probably be supplied by debt capital, which could result in sizeable interest charges.

A Small Luxury Restaurant

This elegant French restaurant (Fig. 3–6) is jointly owned by two individuals who are both actively engaged in the day-to-day operation of their business. They also own the free-standing building in which it is located. The restaurant is located in a high-income residential area, but it is easily accessible to the city's business district. It has a high degree of repeat patronage from a rather small group of patrons. These individuals are well known to the staff, who make a special effort to cater to their desires. A large number of these patrons are top-level business executives who entertain clients at the restaurant; in fact, much of the luncheon business is from this source.

About 6,000 square feet of the building are devoted to the restaurant operations. There are 120 seats in several dining rooms and

	Amount	Ratio
Sales		
Food	$ 675,000	65.0%
Beverages	365,000	35.0
Total sales	1,040,000	100.0
Cost of sales		
Food	284,000	42.0
Beverages	120,000	33.0
Total cost of sales	404,000	38.9
Gross profit		
Food	391,000	58.0
Beverages	245,000	67.0
Total gross profit	636,000	61.1
Operating expenses		
Payroll and related expenses	395,000	38.0
Advertising and promotion	12,000	1.1
Other operating expenses	135,000	13.0
Total operating expenses	542,000	52.1
Profit before occupancy costs	94,000	9.0
Occupancy costs		
Real estate taxes	16,000	1.5
Depreciation	36,000	3.5
Insurance	5,000	.5
Total occupancy costs	57,000	5.5
Profit before interest and income taxes	$ 37,000	3.5%

Fig. 3-6. Statement of income of a small luxury restaurant for a typical year.

15 seats in a small lounge. Food is sometimes served in the lounge if the patron requests it. The restaurant is open for luncheon and dinner six days a week. It averages 1.25 turnovers daily on the dining room seats and an average food check of $15.00.

The *à la carte* French menu is extensive, and the staff will prepare any dish the patron requests, whether it is on the menu or not. Advance notice is required for some items. Beverage sales include a substantial amount of wine sales, which account for the relatively high beverage cost ratio. The payroll expenses include very modest salaries for the two owner–managers. The "other expense" category includes higher-than-average costs for table linens and laundry, for china and silver replacement, for commissions on credit card sales, and for fresh flowers and other costly decorations.

Profit before fixed costs in this operation is a low 9 percent of sales, primarily a result of the high labor costs. Fixed costs include insurance and real estate taxes, as well as depreciation on the building and contents.

In this case, the owners purchased a town house and allocated $125,000 of the purchase price to the restaurant, $40,000 to land, and $85,000 to the building to be depreciated over a 40-year life. The investment in furnishings, fixtures, and equipment amounted to $270,000, depreciated over eight years. Their net profit is only 3.5 percent of sales, or $37,000, but their cash flow amounts to $73,000 (net profit with depreciation added back).

A Traditional Table Service Restaurant

This independently owned restaurant (Fig. 3–7) is located in a well-established, upper-middle-income residential area. It draws its luncheon clientele from the professional men and merchants in the area and from a large population of retired couples and older women who frequently lunch out. These older persons are also the largest source of dinner business, although on weekends the restaurant does a good family business.

The restaurant offers a varied menu with about 20 entrées at dinner and a large selection of desserts. A feature is the bread tray, which is passed several times during the meal by a "roll girl." This tray includes a wide variety of breads and rolls including hard rolls, corn sticks, and sweet buns, all baked on the premises. Menus are written daily, and although a great deal of variety is included, the basic food products offered are not as varied as first appears.

The business is located in a group of store-front spaces in an older "strip" type shopping center. Contrary to the fate of many such areas, this particular center includes a number of high-quality shops that have been able to withstand pressures from the newer shopping malls. Nevertheless, parking is still sometimes a problem in the area,

	Amount	Ratio
Sales		
Food	$ 975,000	90.7%
Beverages	100,000	9.3
Total sales	1,075,000	100.0
Cost of sales		
Food	341,000	35.0
Beverages	28,000	28.0
Total cost of sales	369,000	34.3
Gross profit		
Food	634,000	65.0
Beverages	72,000	72.0
Total gross profit	706,000	65.7
Operating expenses		
Payroll and related expenses	414,000	38.5
Advertising and promotion	16,000	1.5
Other operating expenses	118,000	11.0
Total operating expenses	548,000	51.0
Profit before occupancy costs	158,000	14.7
Occupancy costs		
Rent	48,000	4.5
Depreciation	38,000	3.5
Insurance	3,000	.3
Total occupancy costs	89,000	8.3
Profit before interest and income taxes	$ 69,000	6.4%

Fig. 3-7. Statement of income of a traditional table-service restaurant for a typical year.

and the merchants' group has felt it necessary to reimburse their patrons for the cost of parking in the municipal parking lot.

The restaurant has 200 seats, all in dining rooms. In total, about 6,000 square feet of space are occupied in several storefronts and in the cellar. There is no cocktail lounge, but cocktails and wines are served. The dining rooms have a traditional decor. Table linen is used for dinner and on Sunday, but for weekday luncheons paper placemats and napkins are used. The average food check for lunch is $3.00 and for dinner, $6.00. The overall average is about $4.80. The restaurant is closed on Mondays, and on Sundays it offers dinner from noon to 8:00 P.M. Regular hours during the week are: luncheon, 12:00 to 2:30 P.M. and dinner, 5:30 to 9:00 P.M. On Sundays, the seat turnovers average about four times all day. On weekdays, turnover for luncheon is about 1.5 times, and it is slightly higher for dinners.

Food costs are maintained at about 35 percent by very careful management and heavy merchandising of low-cost, high-profit items such as chicken dishes and extended items. A complete meal is featured daily that includes this type of entrée, and because it is

	Family Steak House	Downtown Coffee Shop	Full Menu Cafeteria	Franchised Fast Food Restaurant	Large Specialty Restaurant	Small Luxury Restaurant	Traditional Table Service Restaurant
Sales							
Food	85.0%	100.0%	100.0%	100.0%	70.0%	65.0%	90.7%
Beverages	15.0	-	-	-	30.0	35.0	9.3
Total sales	100.0	100.0	100.0	100.0	100.0	100.0	100.0
Cost of sales							
Food	45.0	34.0	38.0	42.0 (1)	38.0	42.0	35.0
Beverages	30.0	-	-	-	23.0	33.0	28.0
Total cost of sales	43.0	34.0	38.0	42.0	33.5	38.9	34.3
Gross profit							
Food	55.0	66.0	62.0	58.0	62.0	58.0	65.0
Beverages	70.0	-	-	-	77.0	67.0	72.0
Total gross profit	57.0	66.0	62.0	58.0	66.5	61.1	65.7
Operating expenses							
Payroll and related expenses	20.0	30.0	36.0	19.0	34.0	38.0	38.5
Advertising and promotion	2.0	.5	1.0	3.0	2.5	1.1	1.5
Franchise fee	-	-	-	4.0	-	-	-
Other operating expenses	9.0	10.2(1)	9.0	9.0	8.5	13.0	11.0
Total operating expenses	31.0	40.7	46.0	35.0	45.0	52.1	51.0
Profit before occupancy costs	26.0	25.3	16.0	23.0	21.5	9.0	14.7
Occupancy costs							
Rent (2)	-	15.0	7.7	8.0	-	-	4.5
Real estate taxes (2)	1.0	-	-	-	1.3	1.5	-
Depreciation	2.5	3.9	4.3	2.2	2.6	3.5	3.5
Insurance	.3	.4	.4	.6	.3	.5	.3
Total occupancy costs	3.8	19.3	12.4	10.8	4.2	5.5	8.3
Profit before corporate overhead(2), interest and income taxes	22.2%	6.0%	3.6%	12.2%	17.3%	3.5%	6.4%

(1) Includes paper supplies.
(2) Where applicable.

Fig. 3-8. Comparison of profit ratios for a typical year.

moderately priced, it usually sells very well. The restaurant has also established a reputation for a chicken pie specialty item.

Payroll costs reflect the amount of on-premises preparation that is required for this type of operation. Management salaries are included for the owner–managers, but they are set at moderate rates.

Other operating expenses include the cost of parking reimbursement. No credit cards are accepted.

Profit before occupancy costs is 14.7 percent of sales. Rent and insurance amount to 4.8 percent, and depreciation is 3.5 percent of sales, based on an investment of $300,000 in furnishings, equipment, and leasehold improvements with an eight-year economic life. Profits before interest charges and income taxes amount to 6.4 percent of sales, or $69,000.

What Does the Comparison of These Models Mean?

What are the implications of these models for the individual who wants to invest in a restaurant operation? Figure 3–8 shows a comparison of profit ratios for these seven operations. In Fig. 3–9, statistical measures of profitability and return on investment are compared. Figure 3–10 deals with cash flow and related risk.

Operating Profitability

The cost of sales varies widely among the seven models—from a low of 33.5 percent in the large specialty restaurant to a high of 43 percent in the steak house (Fig. 3–8) This is due to the interrelationship of several factors—the amount of beverage sales in relation to food sales and the makeup of those beverage sales; the type of menu items being offered; the pricing structure and the buying habits of the particular market group being served. In the family steak house, beverage sales are low in relation to food, and there is a high proportion of wine sales to liquor sales. Liquor sales generally have a much lower cost ratio than do wine sales. Another factor in the steak house cost structure is the moderate price structure and the large proportion of sales of high-cost meat items in relation to lower-cost side dishes and dessert items. The large specialty restaurant, on the other hand, has a large proportion of sales in low cost ratio liquor sales. It also offers a large varied menu with numerous side dishes that have lower varying cost ratios than do the entrée items. Since the specialty restaurant caters to visitors and businessmen on expense accounts, there are more sales of these high-profit side items than in the steak house with its primary market of cost-conscious families.

The franchised fast-food restaurant includes paper supplies in its cost of sales, which results in a seemingly high food cost, and the luxury restaurant must carry a large inventory of items in order to offer its extensive classic menu.

Labor costs vary even more widely among the models than does the cost of sales. Both the family steak house and the fast-food restaurant have very low labor costs because there is limited on-premises preparation and the patron serves himself to all or part of the meal. The downtown coffee shop is able to achieve a labor cost lower than those of the other types of service restaurants because of its take-out business.

One industry rule of thumb is that food cost and labor cost together must be between 60 and 65 percent of sales. If the combined costs are greater than 65 percent, there probably will not be enough revenue left to meet fixed costs and produce a profit. If it is lower than 60 percent, in all probability the customer is not getting good value and the sales volume will not be maintained. Of these seven models, the cafeteria, the luxury restaurant and the traditional table service restaurant have combined ratios of over 70 percent. The specialty restaurant has a combined ratio of 67.5 percent. Although all these operations are still able to produce a profit, their return on investment is very low, as will be shown later.

The other elements of operating cost are small in relation to total sales, but advertising expense is significant in determining the total sales volume. The coffee shop, with its small trading area and restricted market, can minimize its advertising budget, but the large specialty restaurant must advertise extensively in order to maintain its high volume. The fast-food operation must also advertise widely because it is operating in a highly competitive market, with a product line that differs very little from its competitors' products.

Occupancy Costs

There are several statistical measures used to analyze the productivity of space occupied and the return for the occupancy dollar. One is sales per seat, and a related statistic is sales per square foot of space. Among the seven models, annual sales per seat range from a low of $2,400 in the coffee shop to a high of $7,704 in the luxury restaurant (Fig. 3–9). In both cases, these extremes of sales productivity are a function of the average food check and seat turnover. Using the measure of sales per square foot, the family steak house brings the highest return because it makes the most productive use of space, with only 23.3 square feet per seat. This type of operation can achieve this productivity because its limited menu operation requires minimal preparation and storage space. The downtown coffee shop and the cafeteria models have the lowest scale per square foot because of low average checks and limited serving hours. The fast-food restaurant has high sales per square foot, almost double that of the cafeteria, even though it has a lower average check and more square feet per seat. This is a result of the composition of the fast-food restaurant's business, with 60 percent of sales for off-premises consumption. This

Financial Strategy 63

	Family Steak House		Downtown Coffee Shop		Full Menu Cafeteria		Franchised Fast Food Restaurant		Large Specialty Restaurant		Small Luxury Restaurant		Traditional Table Service Restaurant	
	Amount	Ratio	Amount	Ratio	Amount	Ratio	Amount	Ratio	Amount	Ratio	Amount	Ratio	Amount	Ratio
Total sales ($000's)	$1,700	100.0%	$ 480	100.0%	$1,030	100.0%	$ 500	100.0%	$5,297	100.0%	$1,040	100.0%	$1,075	100.0%
Profit before occupancy costs ($000's)	442	26.0	122	25.3	165	16.0	115	23.0	1,139	21.5	94	9.0	158	14.7
Profit before interest and income taxes ($000's)	377	22.2%	29	6.0%	37	3.6%	61	12.2%	918	17.3%	37	3.5%	69	6.4%
Cash flow ($000's) available for interest, amortization and income taxes	$ 419*		$ 48		$ 81*		$ 72		$1,055		$ 73		$ 107	
Number of seats	300		200		300		80		800		135		200	
Building area (square feet)	7,000		4,800		10,000		2,400		28,000		6,000		6,000	
Average food check	$ 7.00		$ 1.20		$ 2.20		$ 1.70		$ 7.80		$15.00		$ 4.80	
Average daily seat turnovers	2.1		6		4.3		1.0		2.2		1.25		3.3	
Sales per seat	$5,666		$2,400		$3,433		$6,250		$6,621		$7,704		$5,375	
Sales per square foot	$ 243		$ 100		$ 103		$ 208		$ 189		$ 173		$ 179	
Square feet per seat	23.3		24.0		33.3		30.0		35.0		44.4		30.0	
Rent per square foot	$ -		$15.00		$ 8.00		$16.67		$ -		$ -		$ 8.00	
Total investment ($000's)	$ 730		$ 150		$ 350		$ 130		$2,985		$ 395		$ 300	
Return on investment before income taxes and interest	51.6%		19.3%		10.6%		46.9%		30.8%		9.4%		23.0%	
Ratio of total sales to investment	2.3		3.2		2.9		5.5		1.8		2.6		3.6	
Investment per seat - furnishings and equipment	$ 666		$ 750		$1,167		$1,125		$ 931		$2,000		$1,500	
Investment per seat - total	$2,433		$ 750		$1,167		$1,125		$3,131		$2,926		$1,500	
Years to recover investment (before income tax payments and interest)	1.7		3.1		4.3		1.3		2.8		5.4		2.8	

*Represents unit contribution to company overhead.

Fig. 3-9. Comparison of profitability and return on investment: Selected statistical data for a typical year.

	Family Steak House	Downtown Coffee Shop	Full Menu Cafeteria	Franchised Fast Food Restaurant	Large Specialty Restaurant	Small Luxury Restaurant	Traditional Table Service Restaurant
Cash Flow Available for Interest and Amortization of Debt and Income Taxes	$ 419	$ 48	$ 81	$ 72	$1,055	$ 73	$ 107
Annual Interest and Amortization in First Five Years (1)	76	27	65	24	301	59	55
Cash Flow before Income Taxes	$ 343	$ 21	$ 16	$ 48	$ 754	$ 14	$ 52
Sensitivity Analysis:							
Variable cost ratios							
Cost of sales	43.0%	34.0%	38.0%	42.0%	33.5%	38.9%	34.3%
One half of the operating expenses	15.5	20.4	23.0	17.5	22.5	26.1	25.5
Percentage rent	-	-	-	8.0	-	-	-
Total variable costs (percent)	58.5	54.4	61.0	67.5	56.0	65.0	59.8
Percentage of profit before fixed costs	41.5%	45.6%	39.0%	32.5%	44.0%	35.0%	40.2%
Fixed costs:							
Interest and amortization	$ 76	$ 27	$ 65	$ 24	$ 301	$ 59	$ 55
Occupancy costs (less depreciation and percentage rents)	23	74	84	3	84	21	51
One-half of the operating expenses	264	98	237	88	1,192	271	274
Total fixed costs	$ 363	$ 199	$ 386	$ 115	$1,577	$ 351	$ 380
Minimum sales volume to amortize debt	$ 875	$ 436	$ 990	$ 354	$3,584	$1,000	$ 945
Present level of sales	$1,700	$ 480	$1,030	$ 500	$5,279	$1,040	$1,075
Percent change before the business cannot amortize debt	-48.5%	-9.2%	- 3.9%	-29.2%	-32.1%	- 3.8%	-12.1%

(1) Based on a 20-year mortgage on land and building at 9% interest and a five-year loan for fixtures and equipment at 12% interest.

Fig. 3-10. Cash flow and sensitivity analysis for a typical year (in thousands of dollars).

requires larger storage and production facilities than an 80-seat operation would normally have. The coffee shop also has a take-out factor in its sales volume, but it is not large enough to have any significant impact on the overall productivity.

Profitability after occupancy costs varies from a low of 3.5 percent for the luxury restaurant to a high of over 22 percent for the family steak house. The latter is overstated in that it does not take into consideration the company's fixed overhead, some of which is allocable to this unit.

Return on Investment (ROI)

For illustrative and comparative purposes, investment is estimated at 1976 price levels. These investment figures cover several possible strategies that were discussed earlier—the purchase of a franchise as the source of management know-how and the leasing of a turnkey operation; the building of an operation in leased premises; and the totally owned business (land and building).

The luxury restaurant not only produces the lowest profit ratio; it also provides the lowest return on the owner's investment. This model also required the largest investment on a per-seat basis, since a fully equipped kitchen had to be installed to produce the extensive menu. A sizeable investment was also required for the elegant appointments and decor, and the total investment had to be recovered from sales generated by a smaller number of seats, since the luxury restaurant requires a greater amount of space per seat in the dining room and a smaller proportion of dining room or productive selling space to kitchen and back-of-the-house space.

The largest return on investment is in the franchised fast-food restaurant on the franchisee's investment of $130,000. This is the smallest investment required of any of the models and points up the popularity and rapid growth of fast-food operations.

These ROI calculations before interest expenses and income taxes show that the luxury restaurant, the cafeteria, and probably the coffee shop may not offer an adequate return on the investment for the amount of risk involved.

Cash Flow

The cash flow for each model is obtained by adding back the depreciation to the profit before taxes and interest. One use of cash flow is to measure the years needed to recover the investment. Again, it is seen that the luxury restaurant owners will need the longest time to recover their investment, and the fast-food franchisee will recover his investment the fastest.

Cash flow is also a major consideration in debt financing. Assume, for example, that in each model one third of the investment was provided by equity capital and two thirds by debt financing, and that land and buildings were mortgaged for 20 years, and equipment and furnishings for five years. Figure 3–10 shows the amounts of interest and amortization payments that would be required.

Sensitivity Analysis

One item a potential lender would ask about is the breakeven point or, in other words, "How low can the sales volume go and still produce enough cash flow to repay the debt?" This is a measure of the degree of risk involved in the project. Assuming the same operating profit levels (which may be an oversimplification), Fig. 3–10 shows a calculation of the minimum sales level required under the financing assumptions stated above. The calculation is made by applying the following formula:*

Sales (S) − Fixed Costs (F) − Variable or Operating Costs (V)
= 0, or breakeven.

It can easily be seen that sales minus variable costs is equal to the operating profit, and that operating profit minus fixed costs will equal zero at the breakeven point. The formula is:

$$\frac{\text{Fixed Costs}}{\text{Operating Profit Ratio}} = \text{Sales volume at breakeven point}$$

The difficulty in making this calculation sufficiently accurate to be of use is that many expenses are only semivariable. Even if no customers come and no sales are recorded, there will be some payroll and other operating expenses in the expectation that someone will come. Lights must be lit and heat provided. It is therefore unlikely that operating expenses can be reduced by more than half those of a typical year at a normal level of business. It is assumed in the illustration that half of the operating expenses are virtually fixed and the other half variable in direct ratio to sales. In practice, a more decisive measure would be made to assure greater accuracy.

Comparing the breakeven sales volume with the present level of sales gives a measure of the amount of decline in sales volume that would have to take place before the operation would be unable to carry its fixed costs and debt burden. It can be seen once again that the cafeteria, luxury restaurant, and the coffee shop could withstand very little loss of sales volume before they would be in difficulty, whereas the franchised operation, the family steak house, and the large specialty restaurant have very little risk associated with the proposed level of financing.

---

*Since percentage rent, such as the 8 percent rent of the franchisee, is not an absolute fixed amount, it is treated as a variable expense for the purpose of this calculation.

4

Conceptual Strategy

In the preceding chapter, seven financial models were presented. Each of these model restaurants was developed around a concept or idea. For example, the family steak house was planned around an idea of a menu limited to a few items of known appeal and a price structure attractive to a defined target market group. The family steak house has a merchandising theme that creates a distinctive image of the operation in the eyes of the public. It has established operating policies and procedures that enable it to meet operating cost goals, and its policy of constructing a standardized building on sites that meet certain criteria keeps occupancy costs within a prescribed range.

A concept may be defined as a plan that tells how the marketing strategy is to be carried out within the framework of the financial strategy. This plan is sometimes referred to as "the system," because it integrates all aspects of an operation. The "systems approach" is being used more frequently, not only in computer and information systems but also in the planning and management of large, complex projects and organizations (see Chap. 9). The systems approach emphasizes the flow and interrelationships among all the various parts of the entity. A systems approach to food service planning requires that all aspects of the operation be planned as a part of the whole, oriented to the needs of the target market, and aimed at operating within a specified financial objective, whether it be profit or return on investment for the commercial operator or budgetary constraints for the noncommercial operator.

Because conceptual planning is all-encompassing, it is difficult to develop a general list of procedures that apply to all projects. Nevertheless, the following key decision areas can be identified: the merchandising concept, the menu concept, the operating policies, and the location and real estate policies.

Developing the Merchandising Concept

Merchandising concepts include any aspect of the operation that makes it appear different from all its competitors. In marketing terminology, this is "product differentiation." It is particularly relevant in situations in which there is little difference between one company's product and another, as in some fast-food businesses. The merchandising plan must establish a unique identity for the product.

The merchandising plan for a restaurant includes the theme and decor of the operation. A heavy emphasis may be placed on a theme or unique atmosphere. In general, the most successful theme restaurants are those that carry out the theme in great detail throughout the operation, in the menu as well as in the decor and service. Some common themes are national or ethnic, or geographical or historical periods. Other popular themes include sports motifs, theater, transportation, or personality (real or fictional).

A theme must be selected with a great deal of care. It must have wide general appeal to the sector of the market that has been selected as the target. A personality theme must center on an individual who is well known and who has a strong positive appeal. A local theme may be suitable for a single operator but not for a corporation that may wish to expand beyond the local area.

Timeliness is another consideration. A theme commemorating a recent event or current fad may have limited appeal a few years hence. Timeliness may also be a problem with personalities such as entertainers or sports figures, who may fade from view in a short time. A concept may be planned to capitalize on a short-lived theme, but the investment must be structured so that the desired return is attainable within the expected life of the project.

Adaptability of a theme to restaurant operations should also be determined. Although many successful theme restaurants have themes that do not immediately suggest the service of food, some thought should be given to how the theme can be carried out in menu, decor, service, and advertising. For example, what kind of decor and menu can be built around a comic-strip character theme? Since a Western motif implies a heavy emphasis on beef, how can a roast beef and steak menu be adapted to the desired price structure? Are the foods indicated by an ethnic or regional theme generally available in the market? Is the public familiar with these dishes, and do the dishes have wide appeal?

Other merchandising aspects include the presentation of the food and drinks. Open-hearth display kitchens and self-service buffets are very popular in many areas. A wine cellar or display near the lobby can be part of the decor and can contribute to the overall image of the operation, as well as promoting wine sales.

A good merchandising plan does not necessarily require a special theme, but it should include some unity of style and a distinctive identity. Fast-food operators have become particularly skilled in developing distinctive types of buildings and logos or trademarks. The orange roofs of Howard Johnson's and the golden arches of McDonald's are examples. These symbols of identity are then used not only on the premises but also in all advertising and promotion.

Menu Concepts

Menu planning in the conceptual phase involves defining the basic menu structure and format, including the types of items to be offered. The menu concept must take into consideration the merchandising theme, if one is to be used, and also the desired price structure as defined by the market and the financial strategy.

The menu concept includes policies regarding the use of rotating or set menus and the extent and frequency of any menu changes. The number of different menus to be offered each day must also be decided, although this is usually dictated to a large extent by the defined hours of service. The menu formats should be established to define the number and types of item to be offered in each menu category.

If a special theme is to be used, time may be required to research and develop recipes for special dishes associated with that theme. Although detailed recipes are not required at this stage of planning, some preliminary work on the basic menu items and methods of preparation is usually needed in order to begin the development of the design program for the architects and designers. Many months of trial cooking and testing may eventually be required before recipes are perfected, purchasing specifications established, employees trained, and adequate sources of supply located. The testing may also indicate that a special piece of equipment is needed. Of more immediate concern is the need to test the overall pricing and materials cost structures against the marketing plan and the financial strategy to be sure that the concept is developing according to plan.

Operating Policies

Operating policies pertain to the systems and procedures for the preparation and service of food and beverages and for control of the related revenues and costs. Operating procedures include the use of standardized recipes, preparation methods, purchasing specifications, portion sizes, personnel training, staffing plans and schedules, and the establishment of standards of product quality and service.

The most basic operating policies pertain to the hours and days of operation. Although operating periods may vary according to the specific site selected, the nature of the target market will often determine when the facility should be open for business.

Another important operating decision is whether alcoholic beverages will be served. This is also largely a function of the market, since the availability of beer, wine, and liquor can significantly affect the nature of the operation and the financial structure. A decision to operate with a bar will require a site where a liquor license may be obtained; state or local laws may prohibit liquor service in certain places, such as near a school or church.

Food preparation and purchasing decisions are another area of operational policy. Production decisions usually involve "make-or-buy" decisions: what kinds of items will be produced on the premises and which will be purchased pre-prepared. A decision to develop a production system around convenience food items or short-order cooking will have considerable effect on how the kitchen is to be designed and the amount of space required. It will also affect the menu concept, the purchasing policies, and the payroll and staffing requirements. The financial operating results will also be affected by such a decision. Convenience foods are not the only instance of make-or-buy policies. Other operating alternatives restaurant planners often face involve centralized commissary operations versus on-premises cooking, butchering, meat aging, pastry and bread baking, laundry and linen rental, and in-house computers versus a service bureau. All these decisions affect both the investment and physical layout as well as the ongoing operating results.

Style of service is another important operating decision; a self-service operation has a different type of market image and price structure from a table service restaurant. French service may be appropriate in a luxury restaurant with a high average check, but a more moderate check average requires more seat turnovers and therefore a faster style of service.

The type of tableware to be used should be determined early in the planning. Fast-food operations usually use only disposable ware, although some may use a few pieces of china or glassware for their specialty items. For example, a chain that promotes its brand-name coffee uses china coffee mugs but serves everything else in disposable ware. One moderately priced table service restaurant uses only two sizes of plates, a coffee mug, and one size of glass, thereby reducing the costs of breakage and dishwashing. On the other hand, a luxury restaurant requires a very large stock of hollowware serving pieces, a variety of sizes and types of plates, ramekins and stemware, as well as a large selection of cocktail and wine glasses.

Staffing, recruitment, and personnel policies are another large area of operating decisions. Previous decisions regarding production policies, menu, and style of service will greatly affect the required staffing and payroll costs. Pay scales and fringe benefits will affect the ability of the operation to recruit in the local labor market. The types of employees sought will affect the payroll cost and can also affect the image of the restaurant. Policies of hiring young women, students, housewives, part-time workers, experienced professionals, or handicapped persons are all part of the overall concept of the operation.

Site or Location Policies

In the market research phase of the strategy planning, one or more target markets will be identified. These target markets may define the type of site to be sought. For example, a suburban shopper market identifies shopping centers as potential sites; office workers as a market are found in central business districts. For other types of market groups, a variety of types of sites may be suitable. Various types of restaurant sites are described in Chap. 5.

Another possible constraint on site choice is the financial and investment strategy. The amount and type of capital to be invested and the amount of income available for occupancy costs must be considered. If a minimum of capital is available, the firm may be limited to leasing existing operations, rather then constructing freestanding facilities to its own design on its own land.

Another consideration for the multiunit operator is the geographic dispersion of his units and the distances from any central commissary or source of supply. To facilitate overall control over operations, a company may concentrate its activities in a certain area. This area may be defined by a certain driving distance or time from the central office or from the firm's commissary or warehouse. By keeping units relatively close together, area managers spend less time traveling from one unit to another and have more time to supervise operations.

Concentrations also permit the chain to build a local market image and to utilize advertising and promotion budgets more effectively. When the chain determines that it has saturated its present market area, it may select a second area for development of a new regional group or cluster, with a central office and supervisory staff.

At the conclusion of the conceptual strategy phase, the project developer will have a basic plan for a food service operation that can meet the defined profit or cost objectives, but much detailed work must be done before the plan can be materialized.

5

THE FEASIBILITY STUDY

A feasibility study for a new restaurant operation may take one of the two basic approaches outlined in the flow charts shown in Fig. 5-1. In model A, an investor or entrepreneur has a particular site on which he wishes to establish a restaurant, but he has no particular concept in mind. In this case, the feasibility study must examine the market, determine what type of restaurant would generate the largest sales volume for that site, and then see if that sales volume would be sufficient to meet the fixed occupancy costs related to the site. Also, the study should include an estimate of the amount of investment required and some projection of the expected rate of return on that investment.

In model B, target markets are identified first, and a concept is developed to meet the needs of those target markets. The feasibility study must then be directed toward specific market areas (usually metropolitan areas) and must identify neighborhoods in those market areas and then specific sites where the operation could be located profitably. This is the approach used by the large chains and in the following discussion of the feasibility study.

Chain operators have a developed concept or prototype operation that they wish to extend to new areas. From their market development work and research in successful existing operations, they are usually able to identify a number of characteristics of their target markets. These characteristics are usually expressed in demographic terms—that is, statistical measures of population. The chain marketer then looks for new areas with similar characteristics when he seeks to expand his business. He may compare a number of general market areas in order to select the most promising.

The General Market Area

A study of the general market area includes gathering information about the population characteristics and spending habits, the economic bases of the area, labor supply and general wage structure,

SITE ORIENTED

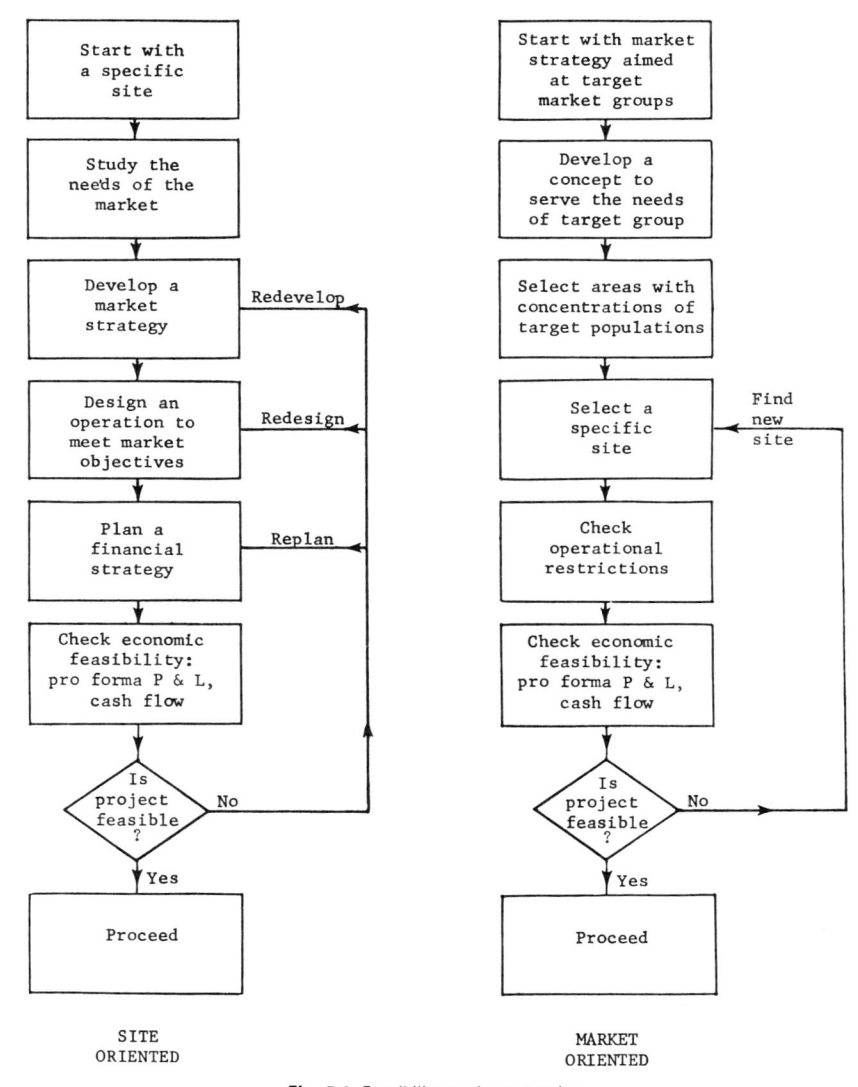

- Start with a specific site
- Study the needs of the market
- Develop a market strategy
- Design an operation to meet market objectives
- Plan a financial strategy
- Check economic feasibility: pro forma P & L, cash flow
- Is project feasible?
  - No → Redevelop / Redesign / Replan
  - Yes → Proceed

MARKET ORIENTED

- Start with market strategy aimed at target market groups
- Develop a concept to serve the needs of target group
- Select areas with concentrations of target populations
- Select a specific site
- Check operational restrictions
- Check economic feasibility: pro forma P & L, cash flow
- Is project feasible?
  - No → Find new site
  - Yes → Proceed

Fig. 5-1. Feasibility study approaches.

land uses and patterns of traffic flow, competition in the area, and any unusual business conditions that would affect a new business.

Population Characteristics

Population studies or demographics of an area include far more than just the numbers of people or families in an area. Population density and the distribution of the population into central city, suburban, and rural areas are noted, as well as the socioeconomic characteristics of the various neighborhoods. Family size and age factors are also determined, as well as racial and ethnic characteristics that may affect the demand for different kinds of food services.

Population trends and growth patterns are perhaps even more significant than a current situation. The following questions must be considered: Where are the areas with the fastest growth rates? Where are the areas available for future development? Are these areas served with utilities such as sewers, water mains, and power lines? Are transportation facilities such as highways and mass transit available or being planned, or are changes in existing facilities being considered? If these vital services are not available, development of the area may be delayed for many years. Evidence that such projects have been funded or are included in the capital budget of the local government body may still be inconclusive. Utility companies should be asked about their plans and schedules for expansion of services to such areas.

Older, developed neighborhoods can also be studied. Existing restaurant facilities there may no longer meet the needs of the market. Older neighborhoods may be going through a process of change because of public urban renewal projects or other reasons. New construction by private developers may lead to a significant change in the character of the neighborhood and in the needs of the market.

Area Economics

The economic bases of the market area must be determined. These are the sources of income for the area such as manufacturing, agriculture, trade, tourism, and recreation. Food service operations tend to be more successful in areas where income is derived from diversified sources and not subject to cyclical or seasonal fluctuations of one particular industry or a single employer. The types of economic activities determine the income patterns in the area. Manufacturing activities with a high level of productivity per employee may produce a high level of income per household. The future of the area's basic industries must also be considered. Are these growth industries, or are they well established and/or potentially declining? Is the area actively soliciting new industries?

Employment Levels and Wage Rates

The employment levels and prevailing wage rates must be determined. Wage rates are determined in part by the supply and demand for labor, partly by the productivity of the labor force and partly by the bargaining strength of the workers through their unions. High wage rates can indicate the presence of discretionary income that is available for spending in restaurants, but wage rates must be considered in light of the prevailing cost of living in the area.

Land Uses and Patterns of Traffic Flow

The general market survey should indicate major land uses such as the location of the central business district and other commercial areas, heavy manufacturing, light manufacturing, educational, transportation, recreational, agricultural, and residential areas. The characteristics of different residential areas are determined in the demographic survey. The flow of traffic to, from, and within these areas should be determined, along with any environmental factors that would hinder the flow of traffic. Natural barriers such as rivers and mountains, or man-made barriers such as a lack of entrances or exits on an expressway may hinder traffic flow. New highways can also drastically affect the pattern of traffic flow in an area. Local highway departments should be asked what new highway construction is planned.

Studies of land uses and traffic flows in the area may indicate sections or segments of land that should be more thoroughly considered for potential restaurant sites. Local and regional planning offices often have conducted in-depth studies of land use including long-range plans for future development. The general market study may also indicate a potential need for food services other than commercial restaurants, such as contract feeding in a new plant, office building, college, or transportation terminal.

Site Selection and Evaluation

Types of Restaurant Sites

Most restaurant locations fall into one of the following general categories:

Central Business District (CBD). The central business district, often referred to as "downtown," is usually characterized by a concentration of office buildings. In addition, there are usually a well-developed retail or shopping district, hotels, and sometimes an entertainment center. In many cities, the public food service market in the CBD consists of luncheon five days a week and dinner trade on the days when the stores are open late or when some entertainment or civic program is scheduled. Some operators have found that this demand is not sufficient to meet the high rents often found in the CBD. Furthermore, some CBD restaurants depend heavily on the expense account trade, a market segment that is sensitive to changes in the business climate.

Secondary Business or Shopping Districts. Secondary business or shopping districts are characterized as serving an older, well-developed portion of the city. They frequently had their beginnings as the center of a small town or village subsequently incorporated into the larger city or metropolitan area. These centers are usually "strip" centers, often at the intersections of major arteries, with stores fronting on the main and side streets and having parking lots in the rear. Inadequate parking and congested traffic can be problems in this type of location.

Highway. Free-standing highway restaurants can range from a franchised fast-food drive-in to a fine, specialty restaurant. Free-standing restaurants may be found in commercially zoned areas of the city, suburbs, or along major highways. They may also be found in the central business district, although high land values and real estate taxes usually preclude that sort of location for restaurants with limited land utilization.

Shopping Centers. With the exodus of the middle class from the city to the suburbs and the proliferation of automobiles, the development and growth of the shopping center as the major retailing avenue was inevitable.

Experts in the shopping center field foresee an even greater role for the shopping center of the future than as simply a retailing center. Consumers in suburbia are already looking to the shopping center not only as a source of goods and services but also for recreational, educational, cultural, and religious activities. It has become a place to meet one's friends and neighbors and the place in which to avoid loneliness and anonymity. Some researchers think that the shopping center will ultimately fulfill the same function in modern society as that of the town square in earlier times.

The Multiple-Use Complex. Another type of real estate development that has developed since about the mid-1960s is the multiple-use complex. From the large regional shopping center, it was a short step to the totally planned community. These new communities include residential development, office space, industrial parks, shopping centers, churches, schools, parks, and recreational and cultural facilities. Some communities are planned for retired people only, whereas others may be planned for young families with a wide range of income levels. Other multiple-use complexes have been developed around office building complexes such as the World Trade Center in New York City, around transportation hubs, or around entertainment centers such as Disney World.

Urban renewal projects are frequently multiuse projects, but they are not always planned as a unified entity. Different sites in the urban renewal area may be assigned to different developers. Often, too, an urban renewal project stimulates private investment in developing the surrounding area. Except for zoning laws, there is usually little coordination of this private investment with the planning of the renewal.

Other Types of Locations for Food Services. In addition to the locations described, public food service is often found as an adjunct of some other activity. Stores often provide snack bar or dining room service to keep the patrons in the store. Entertainment facilities such as bowling alleys, sports stadiums, and theaters may have some sort of food service provided through leased concessions. Mobile caterers and vending companies may provide snacks and meals to workers in many locations. Hotels and motels may operate their own food and beverage facilities or lease them out to others to operate.

Restaurant Sites in Planned Complexes

Real estate developers have not always considered restaurants and food service operations as the most desirable tenants. Restaurants often generate more litter and garbage than other retail establishments and may attract a type of clientele the developer (and other tenants) would prefer not to have. Furthermore, because of special utility requirements, restaurants must be designed early in the planning of the project, with designated floor drains, sewer lines, ventilation, and utility connections. Once the restaurant is installed, it is costly to relocate that kind of tenant or to convert his space to some other use later.

This view has changed, however, and most landlords recognize that restaurants are not only profitable tenants but also generate traffic for other tenants in the development. As with retail tenants, the types of food services and the locations and amounts of space devoted to each food outlet must fit the overall marketing program of the center.

Selecting the locations most suitable for food service in the larger complex takes particular skill. Developers must determine the combination of tenants and the optimum size and location for each tenant that will produce the best return to the total project. Because rents are usually based on a percentage of sales, it is to the landlord's advantage that the tenants be located where they can achieve the highest sales volume. If multiple restaurant outlets are contemplated for the complex, their physical relationships as well as their market relationships must be considered.

Site Evaluation

Once an area or neighborhood has been selected, consideration can be given to specific sites within that area. With the cost of land rising higher and higher, site selection must be based on more than intuition or counts of passing cars. Chain operators have developed a number of ways of evaluating sites using their existing operations as the basis for comparison. Some of the largest companies have developed computer programs that can analyze large masses of data very quickly and develop forecasts of sales volume and potential profitability of a number of sites under consideration. This enables the company to select sites that offer the greatest potential profit.

The Oklahoma Restaurant Association and the University of Oklahoma have developed a computerized site evaluation program to provide the same management tool for individual entrepreneurs and small firms. This program is available nationally through the various state restaurant associations. It was first developed in 1966 and is based on econometric models developed from in-depth study of 100 existing restaurants. These models have since been expanded and updated for changes in the economy. The various factors affecting sales volumes were isolated, and their relative impacts were measured and weighted. Information on a proposed site is submitted on a questionnaire provided by the association. This information is then entered into the computer, and a projection is made of the estimated annual sales volume.

In addition to the site evaluation program, the association also offers a simulation program that may be used in two ways: (1) to determine the effect of certain changes on the sales volume of an existing operation or (2) to determine what changes are required in order to achieve a certain desired level of sales.

Trading Area

The size of the trading area for a particular site will vary depending on the type of restaurant concept on that site. For a specialty or "occasion" type restaurant, the trading area may encompass an entire metropolitan area, whereas a snack bar in a transportation terminal may draw its business from an area measurable in feet.

The presence of other businesses near the site can influence the size of the trading area for that site. For example, a fast-food drive-in restaurant located adjacent to a regional shopping center would probably draw a large part of its business from shopping center patrons who may have traveled a considerable distance to the shopping center but who normally would not travel more than a mile or two solely for the purpose of visiting that type of restaurant.

Within the trading area, the sources of patronage must be determined and customer buying habits analyzed. Sources of patronage may include local residents, people employed in the area or attending a school there, shoppers, hotel guests, people visiting the neighborhood for business purposes, for sightseeing, or for a social visit, or attendees at sporting, cultural, or other types of entertainments. Each of these markets or sources of patronage must be studied separately to determine its size, growth potential, income levels, and other characteristics.

The Immediate Neighborhood. The neighborhood immediately surrounding the site should be studied. Is it a well-developed, stable neighborhood; is it still growing; or is it in the process of decline or decay? Are there demand generators in the neighborhood such as tourist attractions, theaters, or other entertainment facilities that attract potential restaurant customers into the area?

Is there new construction going on in the neighborhood? Construction can be a sign of a strong economic situation or of a changing neighborhood. An evaluation must be made of the effect that new buildings will have on the neighborhood and on the proposed food service operations. Schedules of completion and openings of the new buildings should be determined.

Are there undeveloped areas, indicating a potential for growth, and what is the expected growth? Are the local businesses prospering, or are there many vacant stores or housing units? What kind of businesses or activities will be the immediate neighbors of the proposed restaurant? Are they compatible with a restaurant? Some incompatible neighbors for the better kind of restaurant operations are cemeteries, funeral homes, garages, gas stations, playgrounds, industries (particularly those emitting smoke, dust, or disagreeable odors), old worn-out neighboring structures that may be fire hazards, and low-grade hotels or rooming houses that may house undesirable types of tenants. Good neighbors include luxury apartment complexes, theaters, auditoriums, arenas, office buildings, commercial, resort or residential hotels, and shopping districts.

Traffic Flow. Traffic studies must be made of both vehicular and pedestrian traffic. The numbers of people passing the site can be measured on a sampling basis at different times of the day. Peak hour and off-hour patterns must be determined. Characteristics of this traffic, such as age, sex, or direction and mode of travel, must also be observed. A sampling of pedestrians passing the site can be interviewed to determine their origin and destination, purpose of trip, occupation, and income level. Vehicular traffic patterns are not so easily determined, but traffic counts and origin–destination studies made by local highway or planning authorities may be available.

The vehicular traffic flow around the immediate area of the site is important and must be given careful consideration. How will cars enter and leave the site? Is there easy access? Are driveways and curbing determined by zoning laws? Is there sufficient parking space?

If parking is not contemplated on the site itself, is there sufficient parking space nearby for both customers' and employees' cars? What is the speed of traffic passing the site? On a high-speed highway, cars may be well past the site before the driver can slow down to turn off. On busy commercial streets or major arteries, the location of traffic lights, driveways, one-way streets, and divided highways should be noted. They may be an impediment to easy access to the proposed site.

Visibility of the site to passing traffic should be considered. If the site is near an expressway, is it visible to oncoming traffic? Is the exit from the highway near the site, or is the site visible only after the vehicle has passed the exit ramp? What restrictions or signs are there, if any?

Future plans for highway construction or relocation of city streets should be determined early in the study. City, county, and state highway departments can provide information on both the volume of vehicular traffic and any future road construction under consideration.

Competition. Close observation of competing restaurants is essential. Consideration must be given to the type of menu, the selling prices, the quality of food and service, the sales and promotional efforts, the type of clientele attracted to the operation, the hours of operation and flow of patrons, and the kinds of items being ordered. In many operations, the amount spent by the patrons can be estimated on a test basis by observing and averaging the sales being rung into the cash register.

Operators of existing restaurants in the neighborhood should be interviewed to try to determine their levels of sales. Even when research has indicated a strong market demand, too many restaurants can oversaturate an area.

The number and type of chain operations in the site area should be noted, along with their marketing strengths and weaknesses. The extent and impact of chain advertising should be considered. Chain operators receive much benefit from national advertising, and particularly from television, at a cost per unit far below that which an independent operator would incur to achieve the same exposure.

Customer surveys can be made to measure patron satisfaction with the existing restaurants in an area and to determine what kind of restaurant may be preferred.

The locations of primary competitors should be plotted on a map, along with the sources of patronage identified in the market study. Ideally, the site selected should be an interceptor—one that patrons come to before they reach the competitor's site.

Nonmarketing Factors in Site Selection

Factors other than market and site characteristics can affect the profitability of a proposed location. These factors include the availability of qualified workers and the prevailing wage rates, availability of sources of supply, site conditions, and legal considerations.

Labor Supply and Prevailing Wage Scales. In any proposed location, the availability of skilled and unskilled labor to staff the operation must be determined, along with the prevailing wage scales. The presence of schools with food service curricula should be noted as a potential source of skilled employees. Colleges and universities are also sources of part-time employees.

Wage scales for food service workers and for the general labor market should be ascertained. If the prevailing wage rates in the area are high, then food service employers will either have to meet those wage rates or accept the fact that they will be able to attract only marginal workers to staff the new operation.

Food service employers must also determine the following factors and their effect on payroll costs: the presence and strength of unions; local requirements regarding payroll taxes, unemployment insurance rates, and conditions of employment; and normally expected fringe benefits.

Another factor that can affect labor costs is the availability and cost of public transportation convenient to the proposed location, since low-income workers may not be able to afford the cost of maintaining a car. In some cases when the food service operation is located far from the source of the labor supply, transportation is provided by the employer, or, if public transportation is available, a travel allowance is paid in addition to the regular wages.

Site Conditions. The topography and status of the site must be determined. Is the property ready for construction, or must it be cleared of existing buildings, filled, or graded before work can start? Does the size and shape of the plot permit construction of a structure suitable to the planned operation? Are utilities such as sewer lines, water mains, gas, and electricity available? What sort of waste removal services are available, and what are the community's waste-handling requirements? Are there natural features in the landscape that would hinder or enhance the proposed operation? Are there any indications of possible site obstructions in the future that would be detrimental to the proposed operation? Is there provision for delivery trucks and a receiving area apart from the other activities on the site?

Sources of Supply and Supervision. Outside large metropolitan areas, availability of certain foods and supplies may be limited, and deliveries may be infrequent. If merchandise must be shipped a great distance, freight delivery charges can add to its cost. Proximity to the firm's own commissary or central distribution facility should be considered, as well as the distance that the firm's area management must travel to supervise the operation.

Legal Considerations. There are many legal considerations involved in the acquisition of a site. The following are the most important:

1. *Zoning:* There are several types of zoning controls: those that control the use of the property (such as residential, commercial, or light manufacturing) and those that pertain to the type of structure to be built. The law may specify the maximum building height or maximum percentage of the site that can be covered with a building. Front, side, and rear setbacks from the edge of the property may be required. The number of parking spaces and the entrances or exit from the property may be specified.

Zoning laws may also restrict the number of any one type of business that can be built in a given area and also control their location with respect to other similar businesses or to other types of activities, such as schools, churches, or hospitals. Signs and other exterior features may also be restricted.

Virtually all urban and suburban areas have some form of zoning restriction, and many states have or are enacting land use legislation. Although the absence of zoning or land use laws may permit greater latitude in the design of a particular project, in the long run, uncontrolled land development can lead to unsightly and destructive uses of land, with a negative effect on the environmental quality and the economy of the area.

2. *Building codes:* Building regulations include the type of materials to be used in construction, specifications for electrical and plumbing installations, and requirements as to numbers and locations of fire exits, numbers and locations of toilet facilities, and maximum numbers of persons permitted to occupy the premises at any one time.

3. *Clear title of purchase:* A good title shows that the seller has clear ownership of a property being considered for purchase. It also shows that no claims are outstanding against it. Deed restrictions may exist that limit the use, occupancy, rights of way, and easements or use of air rights as covenanted by previous owners.

4. *Lease restrictions on rented space:* The types of merchandise that may be sold, hours of operation, required membership in a merchants' association, and certain operating procedures may be specified in a lease. Major tenants in shopping centers may have the right to refuse subtenants if they do not fit into the merchandising image of the center.

5. *Licensing requirements:* The most important license for the table service restaurant is the liquor license. If liquor service is planned, the availability and cost of the license, as well as the conditions for obtaining such a license, should be ascertained early in the planning stages. Many states restrict the location of a licensed bar or restaurant, or the persons who may obtain a liquor license or be employed in a licensed operation. There may also be restrictions or conditions pertaining to the physical layout of the operation.

Other licenses may also affect the planning, such as permits for sidewalk cafes, licenses to serve specific types of products, or licenses for signs or exterior projections.

Pro Forma Estimate of Income and Expenses

If a site is found to meet the market, legal, and functional requirements, the next step is to estimate the sales and profitability possible for a restaurant on that site. An architect is usually engaged to prepare a preliminary plan and to determine the size of operation possible on the site within the prevailing zoning laws and building codes, and according to the conceptual guidelines provided by the operator. At the same time, the architect will require from the operator an estimate of the number of seats desired to serve the anticipated market. From this plan, an estimate is made of the number of seats actually possible for use in estimating the potential sales volume.

A preliminary estimate of income and expenses is made, using industry averages or rules of thumb. This estimate, or pro forma, shows the economic feasibility of the site—that is, whether or not the occupancy costs (rented or purchased) can be met by the proposed restaurant operation.

The pro forma should consist of an estimate of the results for an average or representative year of normal operating results, which is often not the first year or two of operation. In addition, since the early years of a new venture are critical, the operating results and cash flow should be projected for these early years in which additional startup costs are often incurred and sales have not yet reached the expected normal level.

In preparing the pro formas, the format of the Uniform System of Accounts for Restaurants should be used.* The Uniform System acts as a reminder of individual items of income and expense that must be considered. It also permits the use of certain industry operating ratios

---

*Published by the National Restaurant Association.

and other published guidelines since they are based on the same system.

Sales Forecasts—Food

An estimate is prepared, based on the market research data, of the number of persons, or "covers," that can reasonably be expected to be served at the proposed restaurant. Estimates are made for each meal period and for between-meal periods. These forecasts of patronage have an important bearing on the space requirements and physical design of the operation, as well as on the economic considerations.

Having determined that the space provided by the proposed site is adequate for the forecasted patronage, the sales revenue can be estimated.

The important factors in calculating food sales by meal period are the following:

1. The number of seats in the dining room
2. The expected seat turnover
3. The average receipt per cover, or the average check

Number of Covers to Be Served. The number of covers to be served is measured by the expected seat turnover and the number of available seats. The seat turnover will probably be different for each meal and for different days of the week. The average turnover for breakfast might be three or four times on working days, and less on weekends; between two and three times for lunch on weekdays; more or less on weekends depending on whether or not the operation is located in an area where the pedestrian traffic is heavier on weekends. For dinner the seat turnover could average up to two and a half times per period. Therefore, the number of covers to be served must be calculated for each meal period and for each day of the week.

The seat turnover will also vary depending on the location, the type of operation, the style of service, the menu, and many other factors. For example, a seat turnover in a coffee shop will be much higher than in a restaurant using classical French service. High-traffic locations will generate a higher turnover than the same type of operation in a low-traffic location.

Average Receipt per Cover or the Average Check. The average receipt per cover or the average check is a statistic used to compare and project sales volumes. In a going operation, average checks are determined by dividing sales revenue in each meal period by the number of covers served in that period.

In projecting revenue for a new operation, the average checks can be based on the experience of others in the area with similar operations, or, preferably, revenue can be based on a popularity forecast of menu items as described in *Profitable Food and Beverage Management: Operations.*

When using the popularity forecast method, the total menu and selling prices must be established. Since the desired result is an average by period, any base number of covers may be used. For convenience, sale of 100 covers may be assumed for each meal period; the breakdown is then by percentage of the total. The total revenue expected from the 100 covers is easily divided to show the average check.

The estimated food sales are determined by totaling the estimated sales for each meal period and each day of the week and multiplying by the appropriate number of days in the year for each type of day. These are the factors that must be considered:

1. Number of planned operating days and hours of operation (some restaurants close for vacation periods and certain holidays)
2. Holidays and their impact on patronage and average receipt per cover
3. Reduced patronage during vacation periods
4. Recurring special events in the area
5. Influence of climatic conditions on patronage (experience of the past can be used for this purpose)

Sales Forecasts—Beverages

Experience has shown that the ratio of alcoholic beverage sales to the combined food and beverage sales does not differ widely among operations of the same general class. The average ranges between 20 to 25 percent in most table service restaurants. Expressed another way, beverage sales usually range from a quarter to a third of food sales. This range holds true in areas where there are no restrictions on sales of alcoholic beverages other than sales to minors, for example. If food is incidental to liquor sales, as in most bar and cocktail lounge operations, the ratio of liquor sales to total sales will be much higher.

Before using any ratio for forecasting, the prospective investor should be sure that ratio is representative of the experience of other operators in the neighborhood. If, for one reason or another, this information is not available, then the ratio should be tested against the experience of operators in a larger area. This information is generally found in trade publications.

Another method used to project beverage sales is to estimate the percentage of patrons who will have one drink, two drinks, or more and/or wine. The estimate is made by meal period and multiplied by the anticipated selling price per drink. In addition, the number of *à la carte* or over-the-bar drinks is estimated on a per-day basis and is extended by the price and number of days the restaurant is open.

Cost of Food and Beverages Sold

An estimate of the cost of food sales can be based on an industry average for similar operations in the area or on the experience of other operators with similar menus and price structures. However, because the cost of food can be the largest individual item of cost in a food service operation, a more accurate method of estimating this cost is warranted than the use of averages experienced by others.

The forecast method using popularity of menu items can be used for forecasting the cost of food sold, as well as for forecasting sales. The cost of each menu item must first be determined. This is done by preparing a standard recipe for each item and applying actual costs to that recipe. Then the total cost of the forecasted sales is computed, using the same estimated sales mix by meal period as was used to obtain the average check. This total cost per 100 covers by meal period is then divided by the total sales revenue produced from the same 100 covers to obtain a potential food cost percentage by meal period. An allowance of one or two percentage points may be added for production waste. The operation should not neglect to consider the cost of bread, butter, salads, coffee, and other accompaniments in computing the cost of each meal. The resulting food cost percentage is then applied to the annual forecast food sales for each meal period to obtain the annual cost of food sold.

The same procedures used for estimating the cost of food sales can be used to determine the cost of beverage sales. The computation, however, is much less time consuming than the computation of cost of food sales. One source of the information for the mix of beverage sales (ratio of scotch, bourbon, gin, vodka, and so on to total sales) is beverage trade publications. It is also possible to use the cost-to-sales ratio experienced by others. However, the cost of beverages as an item of operating cost is significant and should be estimated on as accurate a basis as possible.

Payroll and Related Expenses

Payroll and related expenses represent the largest category of cost in many operations and the second largest category (after food cost) in others. For this reason, payroll and related tax and benefit costs must be carefully determined. The most accurate way to forecast payroll costs is to determine the number of employees required to staff each position on each shift, taking into consideration the need for coverage on weekends or days off and for seasonal fluctuations in sales volume as well as all other assumptions that went into the forecast of sales volume.

The number of employees in each job category is multiplied by the prevailing wage rate for that category, either on an hourly or weekly basis. The prevailing length of the work day and work week must be determined and the total weekly payroll cost computed. To allow for paid vacations and sick leave, the weekly payroll cost is often annualized on the basis of 54 or 55 weeks per year instead of 52. Whether this is done will depend on the fringe benefit program contemplated for the new operation and on the prevailing practice in the area.

Related payroll expenses include the mandatory employer's portion of payroll taxes, workman's compensation, and unemployment contributions. Then the cost of contemplated fringe benefit programs must be added. Such programs include life and health insurance programs or other benefits. The cost of employee meals should be included in the benefit cost category.

Other Controllable Expenses

Under the Uniform System of Accounts for Restaurants, other controllable expenses are categorized as direct operating expenses, music and entertainment, advertising and sales promotion, utilities, administrative and general expenses, and repairs and maintenance. Each classification is subdivided into a number of individual categories.

Direct operating expenses include laundry and linen, china, glassware, and silver, paper supplies, and licenses and permits. These expenses constitute a substantial expense category and should be considered carefully. Most of these direct expenses should vary with the number of covers served and therefore also with the sales revenues, but poor control, excessive breakage, and waste may cause other variations. Estimates calculated on a percentage basis are, however, usually adequate initially. Industry standards are available for use as a guide, but care must be exercised in using the grouped expense experience of others. It should be determined that the group is comprised of like expenses. For example, if the cost experience is taken from a restaurant using tablecloths, whereas the contemplated restaurant will not use table linen, then the cost of linens must be eliminated from the expense group in order to obtain a comparable cost ratio.

The experience of others cannot be used in estimating advertising and promotion expenses. A new venture requires a much higher expenditure for advertising in relation to sales than an operation that has an established reputation. There is no set formula for how much should be spent for advertising a new establishment. Some investors prudently seek professional advice on advertising budgets from advertising specialists.

In these days of significantly higher energy costs, it is especially important to use care in estimating the utilities expenses of any proposed new venture. This is best done in consultation with the architects and food facilities engineers engaged on the project, and with the assistance of local utilities. The architect and engineer should be able to prepare an accurate estimate of annual energy costs based on the volume assumptions provided by the operator.

Adequate expenditures for repairs and maintenance should also be included in the pro forma. These expenses are too often considered to be minor or are deferred in the event of a poor cash flow, thus compounding the operator's difficulties by presenting a bad public image or by running a less than efficient plant. Again, the architect and engineer can assist in estimating these costs.

Administrative and general expenses are defined in the Uniform System of Accounts for Restaurants and are usually relatively fixed in relation to sales. These expenses can be budgeted fairly accurately by taking into consideration each of the major categories and applying a whole dollar amount as an annual estimate. Credit card commissions and fees are included in this expense as part of the Uniform System, and if credit cards are to be accepted, the fee must be budgeted.

Occupation Costs

The pro forma must consider all the occupation costs associated with the proposed project. Such costs include rent, depreciation, interest, real estate taxes, fire and building insurance, and other taxes on the premises. No industry averages or shortcuts should be used in preparing the pro forma of these expenses. Actual costs should be estimated after consultation with landlords, real estate advisors, accountants, tax advisors, insurance men, and others equipped to provide expert advice. Again, many of these costs, with the possible exception of a rent based on sales, are not variable with sales and remain relatively fixed, even when business volume is low. Therefore, the pro forma must consider each of these expenses carefully in order to avoid the failure of the enterprise's ability to cover its fixed occupancy costs.

Pro Forma Statement for "The Example" Restaurant

As an illustration, the following design program has been developed for The Example Restaurant, a proposed operation in a midtown business and commercial district, with luxury apartment residences nearby.

Location: The restaurant will occupy the ground floor corner of a new high-rise office building, midtown location close to theaters, residences, and an entertainment complex.

Space: The restaurant will cover 6,300 square feet consisting of 2,200 square feet for a 150-seat dining room; 800 square feet for a 30-seat and 15-stool bar and lounge; 300 square feet for lobby, rest rooms and coat check; 2,000 square feet for kitchen; and 1,000 square feet for storeroom, lockers, and support facilities.

Type of Operation: A moderate price table service restaurant with a limited menu is planned.

Menu: The luncheon menu will offer carved meat sandwiches and grilled items with three daily specials. A limited number of salads and soups will also be offered. Popularity index estimate of the items to be offered indicates an expected average check (average receipt per cover served) of $3.50 at luncheon. The dinner menu will feature steaks, chops, and seafood. A different carved roast each night will be merchandised. Popularity index estimate of the items to be offered indicates an expected average check of $6.00 on Monday through Thursday, $7.00 on Friday, $7.50 on Saturday, $6.50 on Sunday, and $6.00 on holidays.

Hours of Operation: The Example Restaurant will be open for luncheon six days a week, except holidays. The restaurant will be open for dinner every day. The dining room will be open for luncheon from 11:30 A.M. to 3:30 P.M. Monday through Friday, and from 11:30 A.M. to 4:00 P.M. on Saturday. Dinner service will be from 5:30 P.M. to 11:00 P.M. on Sunday through Thursday and on holidays, and from 5:30 P.M. to 12:00 midnight on Fridays and Saturdays. The bar and lounge will be open from 11:30 A.M. to 1:00 A.M. on Monday through Thursday, from 5:30 P.M. to 12:00 midnight on Sundays and holidays. On Friday and Saturday nights, the bar and lounge will remain open until 2:00 A.M.

Organization: The partnership form of organization will be used.

Land and Building: Space will be leased at the higher of a minimum rent of $60,000 or 5 percent on food sales and 10 percent on beverage sales.

Equipment: Equipment will be purchased and paid in full at a cost of $312,000.

Estimate of Sales Revenue. Figure 5–2 shows the calculation of the Estimate of Sales Revenue for The Example Restaurant. A worksheet is prepared using the following column headings: Meal/Day, Turnover, Daily Covers, Days in Year, Annual Covers, Average Check, and Annual Sales.

90   *Profitable Food and Beverage Management: Planning*

Meal/Day	Turnover	Daily Covers	Days in Year	Annual Covers	Average Check	Annual Sales
Food						
Lunch						
Monday - Friday	2.5	375	250	93,750	$3.50	$ 328,125
Saturday	1.3	195	52	10,140	3.50	35,490
Sunday	-	-	52	-	-	-
Holidays	-	-	11	-	-	-
Total	-	-	365	103,890	3.50	363,615
Dinner						
Monday - Thursday	1.5	225	198	44,550	6.00	267,300
Friday	2.5	375	52	19,500	7.00	136,500
Saturday	2.5	375	52	19,500	7.50	146,250
Sunday	1.0	150	52	7,800	6.50	50,700
Holidays	2.0	300	11	3,300	6.00	19,800
	-	-	365	94,650	6.55	620,550
Total Food Sales						984,165
Beverage						
Lunch						
50% of lunch covers have one drink				51,945	1.25	64,930
15% of lunch covers have two drinks				15,585	1.25	19,480
10% of lunch covers have wine				10,390	1.00	10,390
50 drinks/day over the bar at lunch				15,100	1.25	18,875
Total				93,020	1.22	113,675
Dinner						
70% of dinner covers have one drink				66,255	1.25	82,820
20% of dinner covers have two drinks				18,930	1.25	23,660
15% of dinner covers have wine				14,200	2.00	28,400
100 drinks/day over the bar at dinner				36,500	1.25	45,625
				135,885	$1.33	180,505
Total Beverage Sales						294,180
Total Sales Revenue						$1,278,345
Food						77.0%
Beverage						23.0%

Fig. 5-2. The Example Restaurant. Estimate of sales revenue (150 seats).

The days of operation for each meal are then entered in the "Meal/Day" column. For food sales, the calculation is performed as follows:

Luncheon

1. *Monday through Friday:* The projected turnover (number of times each seat is expected to "turn over" or be occupied during the meal period, considering that not all seats are always occupied, as when a party of three sits at a table for four) is 2.5 times. This turnover of 2.5 multiplied by the number of seats (150) equals 375 covers. Insert this result in the column "Daily Covers." There will be 250 weekdays in the year excluding holidays that fall on weekdays. Multiply 250 days times 375 covers per day to get 93,750 covers per year. Multiply this by the anticipated average check of $3.50 to obtain annual sales from this meal period of $328,125.

2. *Saturday:* The projected turnover of 1.3 times multiplied by 150 seats equals 195 covers per Saturday, which multiplied by 52 Saturdays per year equals 10,140 covers per year, times $3.50 average check equals $35,490.

3. *Sundays and Holidays:* The restaurant is closed for luncheon on Sundays and holidays.

Therefore, total annual luncheon food sales equal $328,125 plus $35,490, or $363,615. This figure divided by total annual covers of 103,890 indicates an overall average luncheon check of $3.50.

Dinner

1. *Monday through Thursday:* The projected turnover of 1.5 times multiplied by 150 seats equals 225 covers per night, which multiplied by 198 nights per year equals 44,550 covers per year. These 44,550 covers times an average check of $6.00 equals annual sales of $267,300.

2. *Friday:* The projected turnover of 2.5 times 150 seats equals 375 covers each Friday, which times 52 Fridays per year equals 19,500 covers per year. These 19,500 covers times an average check of $7.00 on Fridays equals annual sales of $136,500.

3. *Saturdays:* Seat turns of 2.5 equals 375 covers per Saturday, times 52 Saturdays per year equals 19,500 annual covers. These 19,500 covers times an average check of $7.50 on Saturdays equals $146,250 in annual sales.

4. *Sundays:* The projected turnover of 1.0 equals 150 covers per Sunday, times 52 Sundays per year equals 7,800 annual covers. These 7,800 covers times an average check of $6.50 on Sundays equals annual sales of $50,700.

5. *Holidays:* The projected turnover of 2.0 times on holidays times 150 seats equals 300 covers per holiday, times 11 holidays per year, equals 3,300 annual covers. These 3,300 covers times an average check of $6.00 per holiday equals $19,800 in annual sales.

Total dinner food sales are then as follows:

Monday through Thursday	$267,300
Fridays	136,500
Saturdays	146,250
Sundays	50,700
Holidays	19,800
TOTAL	$620,550

This total of $620,550 divided by total annual covers of 94,650 reveals an overall average dinner check of $6.55.

Total food sales are then as follows:

Lunch	$363,615
Dinner	620,550
TOTAL	$984,165

For the purposes of this example, beverage sales were estimated using the percentage of customers who will buy beverages, and adding an estimated number of over-the-bar drinks served during each meal period.

The estimates were prepared using the experiences of similar restaurants in similar locations:

Luncheon

Fifty percent of luncheon covers have at least one drink. Therefore, total annual luncheon covers of 103,890 times 50 percent equals 51,945 drinks, and 51,945 times an average drink price of $1.25 equals annual sales of $64,930.

An additional 15 percent of luncheon covers will have a second drink. Therefore, 103,890 times 15 percent equals 15,585 drinks, times $1.25, equals annual sales of $19,480.

Ten percent of luncheon covers will order wine with luncheon, with an average price equaling $1.00 per cover. So, 103,890 times 10 percent equals 10,390 (rounded) times $1.00 equals annual sales of $10,390.

In addition, it is estimated that 50 drinks per day will be sold over the bar at luncheon time to patrons other than luncheon covers. The restaurant is open for luncheon 302 days per year, times 50 equals 15,100 drinks, times $1.25 equals $18,875.

Total beverage volume at luncheon is therefore $64,930 + 19,480 + 10,390 + 18,875 for a total of $113,675.

Dinner

Seventy percent of dinner covers will have at least one drink. Total dinner covers of 94,650 times 70 percent equals 66,255 drinks, times $1.25 equals $82,820 per year. An additional 20 percent of covers will have a second drink, or 18,930 drinks times $1.25, or $23,660 in volume.

Fifteen percent of dinner covers will have wine, at an average price of $2.00, or 14,200 × $2.00 equals $28,400.

In addition, it is estimated that 100 drinks per day will be sold over the bar during and after dinner to patrons other than dinner covers. This times 365 days equal 36,500 drinks per year which at $1.25 per drink results in $45,625 in volume.

Total beverage volume at luncheon is therefore $82,820 + 23,660 + 28,400 + 45,625 for a total of $180,505.

Total beverage sales are then as follows:

Lunch	$113,675
Dinner	180,505
TOTAL	$294,180

Total sales revenue for The Example is:

Food	$ 984,165	77.0%
Beverages	294,180	23.0%
TOTAL	$1,278,345	100.0%

These sales amounts are then posted to the pro forma annual Summary Profit and Loss Statement, shown as Fig. 5–3, and operating expenses are estimated.

Estimate of Operating Expenses. A worksheet is prepared using the Uniform System of Accounts for Restaurants, Summary Profit and Loss Statement as a format. Supporting schedules of itemized expense details are also prepared as needed according to the Uniform System, although this illustration includes only the Summary statement.

Cost of Sales

Food Cost is calculated on the basis of forecast popularity of menu items, as previously described. The unit cost of each menu item is multiplied times the estimated unit sales of that item, and a weighted average cost is produced. This cost is checked against industry averages for similar restaurants as a ratio of sales. The

	Amount	Percentage
Sales:		
Food	$ 984,165	77.0%
Beverages	294,180	23.0
Total food and beverage sales	1,278,345	100.0
Cost of Sales:		
Food	364,140	37.0
Beverages	73,545	25.0
Total cost of sales	437,685	34.2
Gross Profit:		
Food	620,025	63.0
Beverages	220,635	75.0
Total gross profit	840,660	65.8
Other Income	12,500	1.0
Total Income	853,160	66.7
Controllable Expenses:		
Payroll	365,000	28.5
Employee benefits	45,625	3.6
Employees' meals	9,125	.7
Direct operating expenses	74,000	5.8
Music and entertainment	9,000	.7
Advertising and sales promotion	25,000	2.0
Utilities	38,350	3.0
Administrative and general expenses	45,000	3.5
Repairs and maintenance	20,500	1.6
Total controllable expenses	631,600	49.4
Profit before Rent or Occupation Costs	221,560	17.3
Rent or Occupation Costs	78,625	6.1
Profit before Depreciation	142,935	11.2
Depreciation	31,200	2.4
Restaurant Profit	$ 111,735	8.7%

Note: Statistics rounded

Fig. 5-3. The Example Restaruant. Summary profit and loss statement (pro forma annual).

calculation for The Example Restaurant results in an average food cost equal to 37 percent of sales. This ratio is multiplied by the projected food sales of $984,165 to obtain the dollar food cost amount of $364,140.

Beverage cost is calculated as previously described, using the same estimated sales method. This calculation resulted in an average beverage cost of sales of 25 percent, which is checked against industry averages for table service restaurants with a similar sales volume. Beverage sales of $294,180 times 25 percent gives a beverage cost of $73,545.

Food cost of $364,140 + beverage cost of $73,545 equals a total cost of sales of $437,685. This amount is divided into total sales of $1,278,345 to indicate a cost of sales ratio of 34.2 percent overall.

Gross profit. Gross profit on both food and beverage sales is calculated by subtracting the cost of sales in each category from total sales in each category and dividing the result by sales to obtain the percentage ratio.

Other income. Other income for The Example Restaurant is estimated on actual anticipated revenues. Cigar stand sales of $2,500 less cost of sales of $1,500 gives income of $1,000; telephone commissions of $3,500; salvage and waste sales of $6,000; and cash discounts of $2,000 for a total of $12,500.

Total income. Total income is calculated by adding total gross profit to other income. The result is Total Income, which is divided into Total Sales to arrive at a percentage ratio.

Controllable Expenses

Controllable expenses constitute a major category of expense in restaurants and must be carefully estimated on a line-by-line basis:

Payroll. Payroll expense should be estimated by preparing an actual manning schedule for the restaurant. The staff required to prepare, serve, and clean up after the number of estimated covers must be determined in each job classification and department. Provision must be made for coverage on days off, for vacation relief, and for anticipated fluctuations in sales. After the total number of man hours in each department has been estimated by job classification, the total is extended by the average hourly rate for that category. The manning tables for The Example Restaurant indicate a total annual raw payroll cost of $365,000.

Employee benefits. An investigation of the cost of actual employee benefits should be prepared, including applicable payroll taxes and fringe benefit costs. For the purposes of a quick analysis, it is possible to apply a percentage ratio to raw payroll dollars to obtain this estimate. For The Example, a ratio of 12.5 percent of payroll dollars was used: $365,000 × 0.125 = $45,625.

Employee meals. The expense of employee meals can be estimated by calculating the anticipated cost per meal and multiplying it by the estimated number of employee meals that will be served each year. An alternate method, used for The Example, is to apply a percentage of raw payroll cost, in this case 2.5 percent of payroll: $365,000 × 0.025 = $9,125.

Direct operating expenses. The Direct Operating Expenses category of the Uniform System of Accounts for Restaurants includes 23 expense categories. Among these are uniforms, laundry, linen rental, china and glassware, silverware, kitchen fuel, cleaning supplies, menus and drink lists, and licenses and permits. A separate schedule of Direct Operating Expenses should be prepared, with careful thought given to each expense category. These estimates can be made on the basis of ratios to sales experienced by similar operations, or on actual projections of the costs to be incurred in dollars. Most are variable with sales to some extent, and therefore the ratio-to-sales method is useful. For The Example, total Direct Operating Expenses were estimated at 5.8 percent of sales, or $74,000.

Music and entertainment. This expense is based on an actual budget of anticipated entertainment programs for the pro forma year. No estimate based on a ratio to sales should be made, as this expense is entirely controllable by management policy. For The Example, a budget of $9,000 for music and entertainment was used.

Advertising and sales promotion. In this category, the experiences of other restaurants are not relevant because this expense is controlled by policy. In the early years of the operation, a somewhat higher expense for advertising and promotion should be assumed in order to develop new business. Once repeat business is built up by reputation and experience, advertising expenses may possibly be lowered. A budget of 2 percent of sales was established for The Example Restaurant, resulting in a dollar figure of $25,000 for advertising and promotion.

Utilities. As previously stated, the estimate for utility costs of gas, water, electricity, and similar expenses must be prepared carefully in association with the architects, engineers, and planners of the restaurant. For The Example, an amount of $38,350 annually was forecast for these expenses.

Administrative and general expenses. These relatively fixed costs were forecast on a line-by-line basis using the Uniform System's listing of some 23 account categories. In most cases, ratios to sales are not applicable, and the actual anticipated expenditure must be estimated. For The Example, the total expense is projected at $45,000 per year.

Repairs and maintenance. To provide for adequate maintenance, a budget of just over $20,000 was used for the restaurant. This includes the cost of preventive maintenance such as inspections and lubricants, and periodic overhauls of equipment. Any outside contracts for these services should be included in the budget. In this category, comparisons are of minimal relevance, since the frequency of repair, condition of equipment, and preventive maintenance programs for other restaurants are not necessarily acceptable.

The total controllable operating expense estimate for The Example, therefore, is $631,600, or 49.4 percent of sales. Of this total, $419,750, or 32.8 percent, involves payroll and related expenses, whereas $211,850, or 16.6 percent is for other controllable expenses.

Profit before Rent or Occupation Costs. This figure is calculated by subtracting Total Controllable Expenses from Total Income. The result is divided by total sales to determine the percentage ratio to sales. For The Example, Profit Before Rent or Occupation Costs is $221,560, or 17.3 percent of sales.

Rent or Occupation Costs. According to the terms of the lease described, The Example must pay a rental of the higher of a minimum rental of $60,000, or 5 percent of food sales and 10 percent of beverage sales. To determine which figure applies, the following calculation is made:

Food Sales $984,165 × 0.05 =	$49,208
Beverage Sales $294,180 × 0.10 =	29,418
TOTAL RENT	$78,626

(For the purposes of the pro forma, this amount was rounded to $78,625.) Because this amount is higher than the $60,000 minimum rent, the higher figure is used for the estimate.

Profit before Depreciation. This figure is calculated by subtracting Rent or Occupation Costs from Profit Before Rent or Occupation Costs.

Depreciation: The total investment in equipment was $312,000. The estimated useful life of this equipment is 10 years. For the purposes of the pro forma, a straight-line depreciation schedule is established, resulting in annual depreciation of $312,000 divided by 10 years, or $31,200.

Restaurant Profit. Restaurant profit is derived by subtracting Depreciation from Profit Before Depreciation. For The Example Restaurant, Restaurant Profit is $111,735 annually, or 8.7 percent of sales.

For this illustration, a partnership is used as the method of organization. Therefore, corporate income taxes are not applied as an expense. In a corporate organization, this expense would be shown on the Summary Profit and Loss Statement after Restaurant Profit.

The pro forma statement is then used to calculate return on investment against the goals of the investors to determine whether the proposed operation is economically feasible. Since the pro forma is based on certain sales projections, it is wise to test the impact of fluctuations in these sales on profits.

Once a determination is made that the potential earnings from the restaurant appear to be sufficient to justify the investment involved, plans may be made for design, construction, and opening. These functions are described in the following chapters of this text.

6

DESIGNING FOR PROFITS

When the market research is complete, the conceptual plan defined, and a financing plan formulated, design work for the specific project can begin. A new set of talents and skills is required in this next stage of project development. For a project needing a special-purpose building, such as a highway steak house, the architecture may seem to be the first consideration; if the project is to be included in an existing building, engineering may appear most important.

In recent years, however, design has been recognized as a controlling and coordinating function. In this chapter, the professional disciplines engaged in the design phase are described and a case study is given of a typical food service program development.

The Role of Specialists and Consultants in Food Services Planning

Depending on the complexity and scope of the proposed food service operation, the services of a number of outside specialists and consultants may be required. Their roles may vary, depending on the nature of the project, but in general their functions are as described in the following paragraphs.

Architect

In the construction of a new building or in an extensive renovation of an existing building, the services of an architect are usually required. The architect first must receive a program that defines the requirements of the building to be constructed. He then studies how the site can best be utilized in meeting those requirements, and he researches local codes, zoning, and any other ordinances that apply to that site. He then develops one or more preliminary designs for the building. He also prepares a site plan showing the location of the building on the site, a schematic diagram of the general areas within the building, elevations or flat views of each side of the building exterior, and perspectives—drawings showing more than one dimension to indicate depth. For an unusual or complex design, he may also construct a scale model of the building. He also prepares cost estimates for the proposed plan.

If the plans are acceptable to the client or owner, the architect then prepares the contract documents, draws up the working drawings and specifications, and solicits bids from construction companies. He advises on the awarding of the contract and supervises the construction of the building to ensure that the terms of the contract are being met.

During the planning and construction, the architect also acts as a coordinator of all other specialists who may be working on the project, such as the interior designer, food facilities engineer, and mechanical and electrical engineers.

Consulting Engineers

The architect is concerned with both the aesthetic and functional aspects of the building and the technical and engineering aspects of construction and operation. Large architectural offices usually have engineering capability on their staffs but may use consulting engineers for specialized applications such as structure, mechanical and electrical systems, air handling systems, and similar specialties.

Interior Designer or Interior Architect

The interior design may be developed by the building architect, or it may be undertaken by an interior designer or interior architect. This specialist starts with the building architect's plan for the shell of the building and works within the assigned spaces, coordinating his planning with the building architect and with the food facilities designer who is planning the kitchen and back-of-the-house areas. It is very important that these three persons—architect, interior designer, and food facilities designer—work closely together from the start of the project in order to avoid costly errors and omissions in more advanced stages of planning and construction.

The interior designer begins by preparing the functional plan of the public areas. He determines traffic flow, occupancy restrictions, and the locations of main entrances, fire exits, and so on. He develops a design plan, including specifications for all interior finishes—floors, wall coverings, ceilings—and for lighting and all furnishings and accessories. The interior architect may also handle the engineering aspects of the project—such as heating, ventilating, air conditioning, plumbing, and electrical requirements. He also works with the food facilities designer to integrate the service requirements such as side stands, kitchen entries, and dish-handling equipment into the overall plan.

He then prepares colored sketches or renderings of his plans and display cards showing samples of all materials to be used in each area of the plan, along with estimates of the costs. As the plans are accepted by the owner, the interior designer assists the owner in purchasing the items, or he may order them himself on the owner's account. He then supervises the installation to ensure that all specifications are met.

The interior designer may also develop logos and graphics to be used in promotional material or in interior design, and he may also offer menu design services. These services may also be subcontracted to specialized design firms.

Interior Decorator

The interior decorator's role is the most limited of the specialists, since it includes only the "decorations," or the embellishment of surfaces and things. This is in contrast with the interior designer, who deals with the total space, and the interior architect, who also handles the engineering aspects of the project.

When neither an interior designer nor an interior architect is employed, the interior decorator specifies furniture, floor, wall and ceiling treatment, lighting fixtures and lamps, window treatments, and accessories. For a restaurant, he also specifies the table appointments and uniforms for the service staff. He may also design the logo and graphics to be used in the interior decor, advertising and promotion materials, and the menus.

Food Facilities Consultant or Food Facilities Designer

The food facilities consultant's services may be limited to the design of the kitchen and back-of-the-house areas, or they may encompass the entire planning of the project from the market research stage through the design and installation. They may even include development and implementation of the operating procedures upon opening. In a large-scale project, a food facilities consultant may be employed either by the owner or the architect to develop the design program and to coordinate and supervise the activities of the other specialists involved.

In his more limited role, the food facilities consultant may provide plans only for the kitchen and related areas. In this capacity, he prepares the layout, determines the sizes or capacities and locations of the equipment required, and provides shop drawings for any pieces that must be fabricated. He calculates the load inputs for kitchen exhaust systems, water, waste, and electrical connections for use by the mechanical and electrical engineers. He also prepares specifications for all equipment to be purchased and an estimate of the equipment and installation costs for his plan. When the owner approves the kitchen plans, the consultant assists the owner in evaluating bids submitted by kitchen equipment suppliers. During the installation, the consultant supervises the work to see that all specifications are met.

As with the interior designer, it is important that the food facilities designer be involved in the project very early in the planning. Of the three principal roles described above—architect, interior designer, and food facilities engineer—the food facilities engineer may be the only specialist in the internal functioning of a restaurant or food service operation. His presence in the early stages of planning can avoid costly errors later on.

Several other types of specialist may be involved in the planning process, performing some of the functions described above plus some additional ones.

The Contract Furnishings House

Unlike the interior designer who may buy furnishings or contract for services in the name or on the account of his client, the contract house actually buys from primary sources (manufacturers) for resale to clients. The contract house operator maintains an inventory, and operates warehouses, showrooms, and delivery trucks. Although it may appear that the contract house is passing an additional markup on to its customers, its selling prices may still be competitive. The contract house usually pays the lowest possible price for its merchandise because it is buying directly from the manufacturer in large quantities.

Contract houses offer complete design services, and many have developed "packages," or stock decors, with all furnishings kept in stock. The contract house can also provide custom designs just as the interior designer does and will oversee installation. Some contract houses also offer kitchen design services. These houses, with their "packaged" designs, kitchen specialists, and installation services, can offer the owner a complete turnkey operation, ready for him to walk into and start operating. In addition, the contract house can finance the purchase or arrange for leasing, thus providing another way to finance a new venture.

It should be remembered that the contract house earns its income from its markup on the merchandise it carries in inventory. Its kitchen design and decorating services are offered only to support this selling effort.

The Kitchen Equipment Dealer

The kitchen equipment dealer fabricates all custom-designed equipment, either in his own shop or in that of a subcontractor. He assembles all equipment specified by the food facilities designer and installs it according to the plans. Like the contract furnishings house, the kitchen equipment dealer purchases merchandise from the manufacturers and maintains an inventory.

After the installation is completed, the equipment dealer tests all equipment to be sure it is operating correctly and makes any required adjustments. He then demonstrates how to operate each piece of the equipment to the owner and the employees who will be using it. He also explains normal servicing and maintenance procedures. The dealer should also assemble the various operating and servicing instructions and materials provided by the equipment manufacturers into a manual for the owner. Last, he should see to it that all guarantee or warranty registration cards are properly completed and filed.

Most kitchen equipment dealers have design departments and will design the kitchen and back-of-the-house areas. They do not usually charge a separate design fee but will build the cost of this service into the price of the job. If the owner is knowledgeable in kitchen operation and closely involved in the planning process, the use of the equipment dealer's design capability can often reduce the overall cost and expedite the planning process. If the owner is not involved, however, some dealers may be tempted to specify much more equipment than is necessary or attempt to "unload" some of their slow-moving inventory. Another disadvantage to using the dealer's designs is that the selection may be limited to the equipment lines handled by that dealer.

Equipment Manufacturers

Some equipment manufacturers provide design services for prospective customers. This is frequently the case if the design of the entire work station can significantly affect the efficiency of a particular piece of equipment, as with a dishwashing machine. Many dish machine manufacturers, for example, will design the entire dish room area, bringing a particularly specialized knowledge to this task.

Contract Food Service Companies

Many of the large contract feeding companies have layout and design specialists on their staffs. These companies can provide complete design services for their clients and also oversee the purchasing and installation of the equipment. The plans executed by a food service company will, of course, be most suited to that company's method of operating. Although this will permit the contractor to operate most efficiently, it may be a detriment if in the future another contractor is engaged who has a different method of operating.

The trend indicated by this description of the services of specialists is toward a broadening of services offered to the client. Architectural firms provide interior design services and may subcontract or even employ their own food facilities consultant. Interior design firms offer kitchen design services, and food facilities consultants may offer design services. Contract houses and kitchen equipment dealers are also moving toward full-line services.

Fees and Remuneration

As mentioned above, the contract furnishings house and the kitchen equipment dealer derive their income from the resale of merchandise from their inventories. Charges for design services (if any have been rendered) are usually included in the markup in the price of the merchandise.

The remuneration of the other specialists—architects, interior designers, and food facilities consultants—is in the form of professional fees, which are usually calculated in one of several ways:

1. A percentage of the total cost of the job
2. A fixed fee
3. A per diem or hourly rate
4. A combination of these

The difficulty with a percentage fee is that it provides no incentive for the designer to keep the costs down; in fact, a designer who makes an extra effort to keep the cost of the project low is actually penalized by a percentage fee, because his remuneration is also reduced. For this reason, some professionals are tending to move away from the percentage fee in favor of the per diem or hourly rate. This type of fee more closely relates the remuneration to the actual amount of work performed and reduces any potential conflict of interest.

Whatever method is used to determine the fee, all remuneration of professional designers is paid directly by the client. In fact, the various professional societies prohibit their members from receiving any remuneration from manufacturers or dealers whose products the designer may specify. In this way, the professional designer is free to represent the best interests of his client and is not influenced by manufacturers or dealers.

When stated separately in the form of professional fees (as opposed to being hidden in merchandise prices), design costs can appear to be a luxury. They may run as high as 20 percent of the total cost of the project, and the prospective restaurant owner may be tempted to eliminate this cost by being his own designer. This can be a "penny wise–pound foolish" decision. Professional designers bring to a project their specialized training, experience, and knowledge of the market place. They can assist the owner in obtaining the best value for his investment dollars, and they can avoid errors in decor and layout. Over the lifetime of the operation, such errors may cost many times the amount of the designer's fee in excess operating costs due to poor traffic flow, low productivity, and high maintenance costs.

Elements of Interior Design

The market goal and a merchandising theme developed to further that goal guide the designer. In carrying out the theme, the interior designer must create an atmosphere that is compatible with the needs of the target market and with the financial objectives of the operation. For example, the level of illumination, seating space, type of seating, and noise level are all factors that can influence the guest to leave quickly or to linger, thus affecting the seat turnovers and, perhaps, the average check. A general feeling of having had a pleasant experience in a restaurant may not be specifically attributable to the color of the walls or the style of a chair but rather to overall atmosphere that results from the combination of many elements.

The size and shape of the space is one such element. In some places, the designer may alter the shape of the space in order to create intimacy, to invite, or to stimulate. Areas may be emphasized and perspectives altered by lowering or raising the ceiling or creating different levels within the space. In some cases, accenting certain areas will draw attention to the patrons in those areas, making them a part of the attraction of the room. In another situation, privacy and intimacy may be preferred, requiring space to be divided into secluded little nooks and corners.

The level and type of illumination are other important design elements. Bright, cheerful lighting is used in restaurants with a fast seat turnover, whereas subdued lighting is preferred for more leisurely dining. Different types of lamps generate different wavelengths or colors and can affect the appearance of both objects and people. The appearance of food (and therefore its eye appeal) can be greatly affected by the type of lighting used.

The type of seating selected and the amount of space allowed per seat are essential design elements. In some operations, such as certain types of bars, crowding is desirable in order to create an atmosphere of conviviality and interaction among the patrons. A restaurant or club catering to business or professional people, however, requires a more spacious plan so that business can be conducted without being overheard. The type of seating used can influence the speed of the turnover. The seat turnover for booths is much slower than that for chairs, and counter stools generally have the fastest turnover rate. Some restaurant operators purposely avoid selecting dining room chairs that are too comfortable so that patrons do not linger too long at the table and the seat turnovers are increased. A careful balance must be achieved to result in both guest comfort and reasonable turnover.

The acoustics of a room can greatly affect its atmosphere and ambiance. The noise of conversation, entertainment or background music, the verbal communication of orders by the staff, the clanking of dishes and silverware can be deadened or amplified by the amount of sound-absorbing materials used in the room. Carpeting, draperies, table linens, and acoustical ceiling materials are all good sound absorbers, but too much deadening of sound can create an austere, formal atmosphere that may be forbidding rather than inviting.

The colors, textures, materials, furnishings, accessories, and other objects used in the decor are all part of the overall visual climate contributing to the desired atmosphere and ambiance. The materials selected must also be easily maintained and able to withstand heavy use.

The Design Process

To begin the designing process, the owner, manager, or the food service consultant prepares a preliminary design program to provide the designer or architect with as much information as possible about the proposed operation. The more information the designer has at the start, the better will be the resulting design. Furthermore, making changes or additions later may be very costly.

If the designer is not provided with a program, he must develop one himself, based on what he thinks the proposed operation requires and on his interpretation of what his client wants. This type of approach can lead to misunderstandings, costly delays, and subsequent change orders and still not produce a plan that satisfies either the designer or the client.

To prevent this problem, the preliminary design program should include as much of the following kinds of information as possible.

1. Days and hours of operation should be stated.
2. If multiple outlets are planned (such as in a hotel), the program should indicate the location of each and its relationship to the other parts of the program. In a large complex such as a convention hall or large airport, a separate study may be required just to select the best locations for food and beverage operations.
3. Estimates must be made of the numbers of meals to be served at each meal period and at the highest and lowest levels of business. For some types of operations, such as snack bars, these forecasts should be made on a per-hour basis as well as on a meal-period basis.

4. The proposed menu or menus, including the numbers and types of items to be offered, and the methods of preparation should be listed.
5. Operational policies and programs, such as the type and style of service, amount and nature of on-premises preparation, types of food to be bought or stored, speed-of-service goals, and how much preparation work service personnel will perform, should be indicated.
6. Special merchandising requirements, such as display cooking, self-service salad bars, lobster or fish tanks, or carving station, must be made known.
7. Estimates must be made of income and expenses, with supporting schedules of staffing.
8. The market to be served, the type of customers, and the marketing goals of the restaurant are necessary information.

In addition to the design program, the architect or designer must be provided with a plan of the premises. If the space is in an existing building, the plan should show entrances and exits, existing windows, columns and load-bearing walls, mechanical spaces, and any other obstructions that cannot be removed. If the program calls for a free-standing building to be built, a site plan must be provided.

Functional Relationships and Schematic Drawings

Working from the site plan and design program, the architect or designer begins by preparing preliminary plans or schematic drawings. For a free-standing building, the architect will first prepare a site plan showing the size and orientation of the building, public and service entrances, driveways, and parking areas. The purpose of these plans is to determine the optimal utilization of the site that will meet the local zoning and building codes. If the space is in an existing building, preliminary plans are still required to determine maximum capacities and exits required by fire laws and to analyze traffic flows and sources of patronage.

Next, the designer identifies all the elements of the program and analyzes each element to determine its functional relationship to every other element. For example, in a free-standing restaurant with one dining room and one cocktail lounge, the relationships of the various public elements—dining room, lounge, lobby, rest rooms, coat checking, guest entrance, and parking—will be studied from the standpoint of the traffic flows and control points.

In the back of the house, the flow of foods and other materials from receiving through storage and into preparation areas such as bake shop, butcher shop, preparation areas, main cooking areas, service areas and then finally into the dining room must be studied to determine proximity requirements. Dishwashing areas must be strategically located, whereas the location of potwashing is less strategic. Storerooms for extra china and silver stocks usually do not have to be near other areas and may be located wherever there is space available.

For an operation with multiple outlets, the designer must identify the elements of each outlet and determine how they fit into the overall plan. He then analyzes which elements can be combined to provide the most efficient layout to operate. A hotel is a good example of a multioutlet food service operation. A food and beverage department in a hotel may include a specialty dining room, one or more cocktail lounges and bars, coffee shop, ballroom and banquet rooms, and room service. The dining room, cocktail lounges, and coffee shops should be located where they can attract a high volume of business; the ballroom must be accessible to guests arriving in large numbers in a very short period of time; and the room service set-up area must be located near the service elevators. Each area must have access to the service areas in the back of the house. For the most efficient use of space and labor, back-of-the-house support functions should be combined when possible.

In making his functional analysis, the designer may prepare schematic drawings showing the various elements and their interrelationships.

Space Allocation

After the various functions have been defined and their general locations determined, the space requirements for each function are determined, and the available space is divided and allocated to the various functions. For general or preliminary planning purposes, space may be assigned to each function on the basis of the industry-wide averages or rules of thumb. Then, as planning becomes more advanced, a more detailed analysis is made.

For a public restaurant, the available space is first divided between front of the house and back of the house. Traditionally, 40 to 50 percent of the space is allocated to the front of the house for dining rooms, lobby, reception areas, check rooms, and public rest rooms. The remainder of the space is taken by the kitchen, receiving and storage, service areas, offices, and employee facilities. Many operators have found, however, that this small proportion of productive selling space does not generate enough revenue to meet high rents or land and construction costs and interest rates. Newer operations are designed to utilize available space much more productively. Some recently built table service restaurants have been able to utilize as much as 75 percent of their space for front-of-the-house functions. This increase in the productive use of space has been made possible through increased use of convenience foods, more limited menus, and more efficient arrangement of furniture and kitchen equipment. Using time and motion study techniques, kitchen designers have been able to plan more efficient work stations that eliminate unnecessary corridors and circulation space. This reduces not only the amount of unproductive space but also reduces the nonproductive time spent by employees in walking from one place to another to do their work.

Dining Room Seating

Because the number of seats and the expected turnovers are limiting factors on the potential sales volume, the designer's first consideration is the number of seats he can get into the given area. This is a factor of the required square feet per seat and the space available for dining. Figure 6-1 shows some general space requirements for different types of seating. These include allowances for service aisles and circulating space, but the actual number of seats that can be fitted into a particular space will depend on the types of seating and sizes of tables used, the number of columns or obstructions in the room, and the amount of space assigned to decor or architectural features.

When the number of meals to be served is predetermined, as with an institutional population, the designer will take the reverse approach to space planning. He will start with the number of meals and the expected length of the meal period and compute the number of seats required. Then, using the general guidelines, he calculates the square footage required for the dining and serving areas. The same approach is used in planning the back of the house.

Other Public Areas

Other public areas that may be included in the plan are the lobby, check rooms, and rest rooms. Local ordinances may specify the number of rest room fixtures required, or, if the planned operation is part of a larger complex, restrooms may be provided elsewhere. For a cafeteria operation, space must be provided for queuing, and the flow of traffic and queuing space must be very carefully planned.

A large ballroom requires an area for reception that should be as large as 40 percent of the ballroom space. This space is used for assembly, for reception and cocktails before a banquet, or for conference registration or coffee service if the room is used for meetings. In addition, a storage space equal to 10 to 15 percent of the ballroom space should be provided for storage of the different types of furniture and equipment required for varying uses of a ballroom, including

	Square Feet per Seat, Includes Aisles and Circulation Areas
Luxury Restaurants and Private Clubs*	18-22
Table Service - Moderate Price	15 18
Table Service - Coffee Shop	12-15
Counter Service, Including Service Area	18-20
	2 Linear Feet Per Seat
Cafeteria, Including Serving Area:	
Commercial	16-18
Industrial, Institutional	12-15
School Lunch Program	9-12
Cocktail Lounge, Including Bar	18-20
In a crowded bar with standees, allow three square feet minimum per standee	
Fast Food, Including Serving Area	16-20
Banquets - Large Ballroom	8- Long Tables
	10- Round Tables
Banquet Reception	40% of the size of the Ballroom

*Clubs catering to business people may require greater area per seat in order to provide privacy for the conduct of business conversations.

Fig. 6-1. Space requirements for various types of dining rooms.

different sizes and types of tables, extra chairs, platforms, lecterns, and the like.

Nonpublic Areas: Back of the House

Space allocations in the back of the house can vary considerably, depending on the operating program. A hotel with a large food and beverage department will require a very different space allocation from that of a limited menu steak house or an operation that uses a central commissary.

General guidelines exist for different functions, and these can be used in preliminary planning. For detailed planning, the space allocation must be developed to meet the requirements of the particular operation. One example is the planning of storage facilities. General rules of thumb may be used, but the actual size and configuration of the space is determined from the number of meals to be served, the size, weight, and nature of the items to be stored, and the frequency of delivery. The same type of analysis is used to determine the size of holding storage or in-process storage. The number of portions to be stored is determined; the size of the container or dish is decided; and the number of trays or pans required to hold the specified number of portions is calculated.

A Case Study in Functional Planning and Space Allocation

This section describes the steps taken by a design group in a typical planning project, from the development of the food service program, through the determination of area relationships, to the allocation of the available space to the various components of the plan.* The example is a 270-room motor hotel built in an affluent suburb of a large metropolitan area. The facility is located in a major business district and attracts patrons from the local area, as well as banquets and regional conventions. There are very few high-quality restaurants in the area. The following design program was developed by a consultant on the basis of market research done for the hotel. The program stated that the following types of operations should be included in the hotel:

1. A street-level coffee shop or moderately priced restaurant for breakfast for the hotel guests and for the heavy local luncheon business.
2. A street-level cocktail lounge to serve the local luncheon, afternoon, and evening trade and hotel guests.
3. A luxury restaurant or main dining room for both hotel guests and the entire suburban population. Because there was little high-quality competition in the area, accessibility and street visibility were not considered mandatory for this type of restaurant. The restaurant was to operate for lunch and dinner and offer modified French service.
4. Banquet facilities for functions of up to 500 persons divisible into several smaller areas. Direct access to the street and parking were required.
5. A separate kosher kitchen (completely self-contained, with separate ware, ware washing, and storage) located close to the banquet room.
6. A provision for room service.

These facilities were to be located on the street or lobby level and on the second floor of the hotel. Some additional space was available on a lower level for receiving, employee locker rooms, and small storage space.

The total street level space was 24,000 square feet, of which 5,000 were available for food and beverage facilities. The rest of the space on this floor was devoted to parking, elevators, lobby, and rental space for a retail shop. On the second floor, all the 22,000 square feet were available for the food and beverage operation except about 5,000

---

*Courtesy of Cini-Grissom Associates Inc., Rockville, Md.

square feet of core space taken up by elevators, stairwells, and toilet facilities. There were no window views from the second floor to influence the design of the public rooms on that level.

Working with these design criteria, the designer began to develop a preliminary plan. He determined the traffic flows of materials, guests, and employees, and he analyzed the functional nature of each part of the program to see which operations had to be located adjacent to one another.

The program required that the cocktail lounge and the coffee shop be located on the street level. The main dining room, banquet, rooms, and kitchens could be located either on the street level or on the second floor. Several options were considered:

1. Locating the main dining room and production kitchen on the first floor adjacent to the lobby and coffee shop, and the banquet rooms on the second floor with a separate banquet kitchen.
2. Locating the main dining room and production kitchen on the second floor along with the banquet rooms. Service to both the banquet rooms and the main dining room would be out of the production kitchen. A small service kitchen would be required on the street level for the coffee shop.
3. Locating the main dining room in a third area (one of the higher floors with a good view) and providing a separate kitchen and dishwashing facility in addition to a banquet kitchen on the second floor and the coffee shop kitchen on the street level. Main production would be on the high-level floor.

Since the street floor space was at a premium, option No. 1 was eliminated. Option No. 3 was also eliminated because the cost of constructing and operating three separate kitchens was found to be uneconomical. Option No. 2 was left, and it had several positive aspects. First, a combination of food production facilities on the second floor placed the heaviest food service load in one area. Second, since the coffee shop was programmed to operate only for breakfast and luncheon, only one kitchen would be operating in the evening, reducing the staffing requirements. The first floor kitchen could be limited to a short-order operation.

Concerning the other elements of the design program—the kosher kitchen and room service—the program specified that the kosher kitchen be located near the banquet rooms that were to be on the second floor. Room service had to be located in an area accessible to the elevators but could be either on the street level or the second floor. The designer decided to locate room service adjacent to the street-level coffee shop. He reasoned that, since most room service demand is for breakfast, operating room service out of the coffee shop kitchen would eliminate the need to staff the second floor kitchen at breakfast. The small amount of room service orders expected for dinner would be serviced out of the second floor kitchen, with room service tables and other equipment brought up from the street level as needed.

At this point, the program was restated as follows:

Street Level:

1. Cocktail lounge
2. Coffee shop
3. Coffee shop service kitchen, which could be serviced from the production kitchen on the second floor
4. Room service area, close to service elevator

Second Floor:

1. Main dining room (modified French cuisine)
2. Banquet room for up to 500, divisible into smaller rooms
3. Kosher kitchen adjacent to banquet room
4. Main production kitchen with serving areas for main dining room and for banquets
5. Access to street and parking for banquet guests

Allocation of Available Space

The task of allocating revenue-producing space was done jointly by the owner and the design consultant, using as a guideline the market study and the pro forma that had been prepared for the overall hotel project. On the street level, the owner wanted a flexible seating area that could be used for either breakfast service or lounge area. This made determinaton of space allocations on this floor relatively simple. A service kitchen for a coffee shop requires approximately half the amount of the seating space, assuming that storage, preparation, and bulk preparation are done elsewhere. Using this general rule of thumb, the designer allocated the space on the street level between lounge, coffee shop, and coffee shop kitchen by using some simple algebra:

Lounge space	$= x$
Coffee shop seating	$= x$
Coffee shop kitchen	$= \frac{1}{2}x$
Total space	$= 2\frac{1}{2}x$
Total available space	$= 5{,}000$ sq ft
$2\frac{1}{2}x$	$= 5{,}000$ sq ft
Therefore, x	$= 2{,}000$ sq ft

The resulting allocation was:

Lounge	= 2,000 sq ft
Coffee shop seating	= 2,000 sq ft
Coffee shop kitchen	= 1,000 sq ft
TOTAL	= 5,000 sq ft

Next, the designer calculated the number of seats that could be fitted into the lounge and coffee shop, using the general space guidelines (Fig. 6–1). At this point in the design process, he did not need to lay out each area in detail to find out how many seats were possible. In the lounge area, he used a figure of 20 square feet per seat, to allow for the bar and for some architectural or decorative features to be added. For coffee shop seating, he used 16 square feet per seat. The results of these calculations were:

Lounge (2,000 sq ft /20)   = 100 seats, including bar stools
Coffee shop (2,000/16)   = 125 seats

The designer and the owner compared this seating configuration with the results of the market study and the sales volumes for the lounge and coffee shop as projected in the pro forma. They determined that the coffee shop needed a maximum of about 150 seats for breakfast and luncheon and that the lounge could probably use about 150 seats during the cocktail hour. They decided that the idea of a flexible area was valid because the peak periods did not overlap and it was the only way to fit the required seating into the available space. The final allocation was:

Lounge	(75 seats)	= 1,700 sq ft
Coffee shop seating	(80 seats)	= 1,300 sq ft
Flexible seating	(65 seats)	= 1,000 sq ft
Coffee shop kitchen		= 1,000 sq ft
TOTAL		= 5,000 sq ft

Because of the flexible seating provision, the kitchen space might have been reduced. However, because of the room service requirement, the kitchen was left at 1,000 square feet.

Space allocation for the second floor was more complex and involved the following considerations:

1. Banquet space for 500 persons was required by the program. For a large ballroom, the general rule of 10 square feet per person was applied, producing a requirement of 5,000 square feet. However, for a function of this size, a reception area is usually

required, and an allowance of 40 percent of the size of the ballroom is a general rule. This added an additional 2,000 square feet, or a total of 7,000 square feet. The area was to be divisible into smaller rooms and have access from the kitchen for service.

2. The main dining room was to be a luxury restaurant serving a modified French menu. General rules of seating require 18 to 22 square feet per seat for luxury dining. The designer selected 22 square feet to provide sufficient space for the gueridons or carts and for elements of decor that might be included in the design of the room.

3. Main production kitchen had to be capable of serving the banquet room and the main restaurant and acting as support for the coffee shop.

4. The owner specified that the kosher kitchen should be capable of serving up to 40 percent of the capacity of the banquet room. Therefore, it had to provide service for an area of 2,800 square feet. The normal rule of thumb is that the preparation kitchen is 50 percent of the dining area, but this can be reduced for banquet production or luxury dining, which has a low density of seating. The designer allowed 40 percent, or 1,100 square feet. However, since the kosher kitchen was to be used only by an outside kosher catering firm that would bring in its own ware and partially prepared food, it was felt that a further reduction of the space was feasible, and the designer ultimately allowed only 750 square feet for the kosher kitchen, or approximately 75 percent of the standard-size kitchen.

To determine the space allocation between the main dining room and the kitchen, the designer went back to the algebraic technique he used for the street level.

Total space available	= 17,000 sq ft
Less: Kosher kitchen	= 750
Net available	= 16,250
Total seating	= x
Kitchen	= $0.4x$
Total space	= $1.4x$ = 16,250 sq ft
Total seating (16,250/1.4)	= 11,600 sq ft
Kitchen (16,250 × 0.4/1.4)	= 4,650 sq ft

Of the seating area, 7,000 square feet had been assigned to banquet space, leaving 4,600 square feet for the restaurant. On this basis, the total space allocation for the second floor was:

Banquet space (including reception area)	7,000
Main dining room	4,600

Kitchen space	4,650
Kosher kitchen	750
TOTAL	17,000 sq ft

Using his standard of 22 square feet per seat, the designer calculated that a total of about 210 seats would fit in the main dining room. This was a smaller number than was indicated by the market study and the hotel's pro formas. However, the designer felt that the most he could reduce the kitchen was 200 square feet. This amount was added to the main dining room, which produced a seating of almost 220 seats in 4,800 square feet. This was close to the original projection, and the owner accepted this configuration of space. The kitchen space was reduced to 4,450 square feet.

To test the total relationship between seating space and kitchen space, the designer added up the spaces in all areas (excluding the kosher kitchen):

	Seating	Kitchens
Coffee shop*	2,300 sq ft	1,000 sq ft
Banquets	7,000	
Main dining room	4,800	4,450
	14,100 sq ft	5,450 sq ft

The total kitchen space amounted to almost 39 percent of the seating space. If the flexible seating area is excluded, the ratio is 41 percent. This relationship was considered acceptable in view of the limited space available and the financial expectations.

The designer then divided the spaces in these proportions, considering the functional flows of people and materials and the proximity requirements. The final plans are shown in Figs. 6–2 and 6–3. The requirements of the design program and the pro forma were met, but some compromises were required. The coffee shop kitchen is located under the production kitchen, with a separate dumbwaiter to transport materials. The room service area is located in the end of the coffee shop kitchen, and the waiters must move the tables out through the coffee shop to the elevators, but this arrangement was felt to be less objectionable than a second floor operation that would require extra staffing every morning. The cocktail lounge has a street entrance as required by the program.

---

*Including flexible seating space.

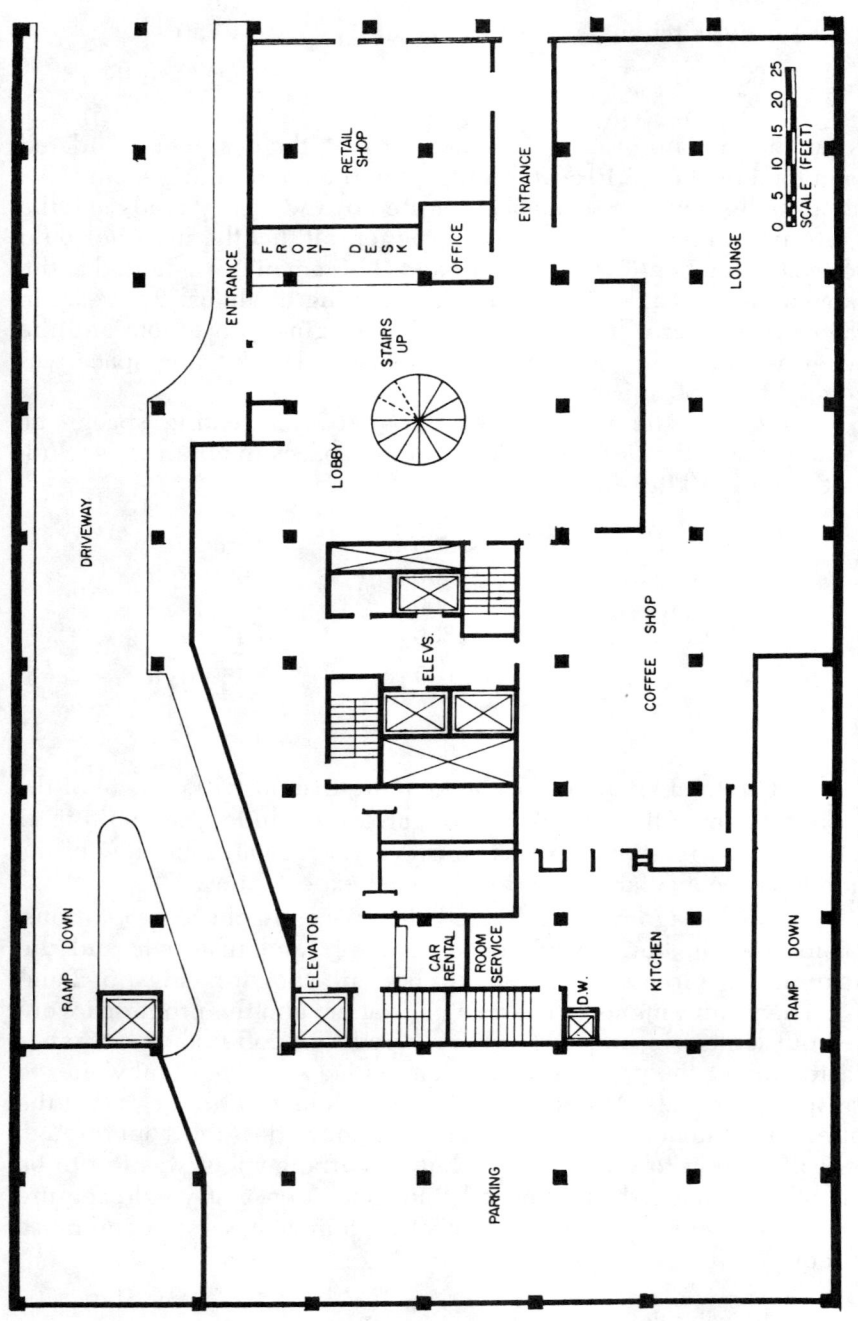

116 *Profitable Food and Beverage Management: Planning*

Fig. 6-2. A case study in functional planning: Final plan of the street floor. *(Courtesy of Cini-Grissom Associates)*

Designing for Profits 117

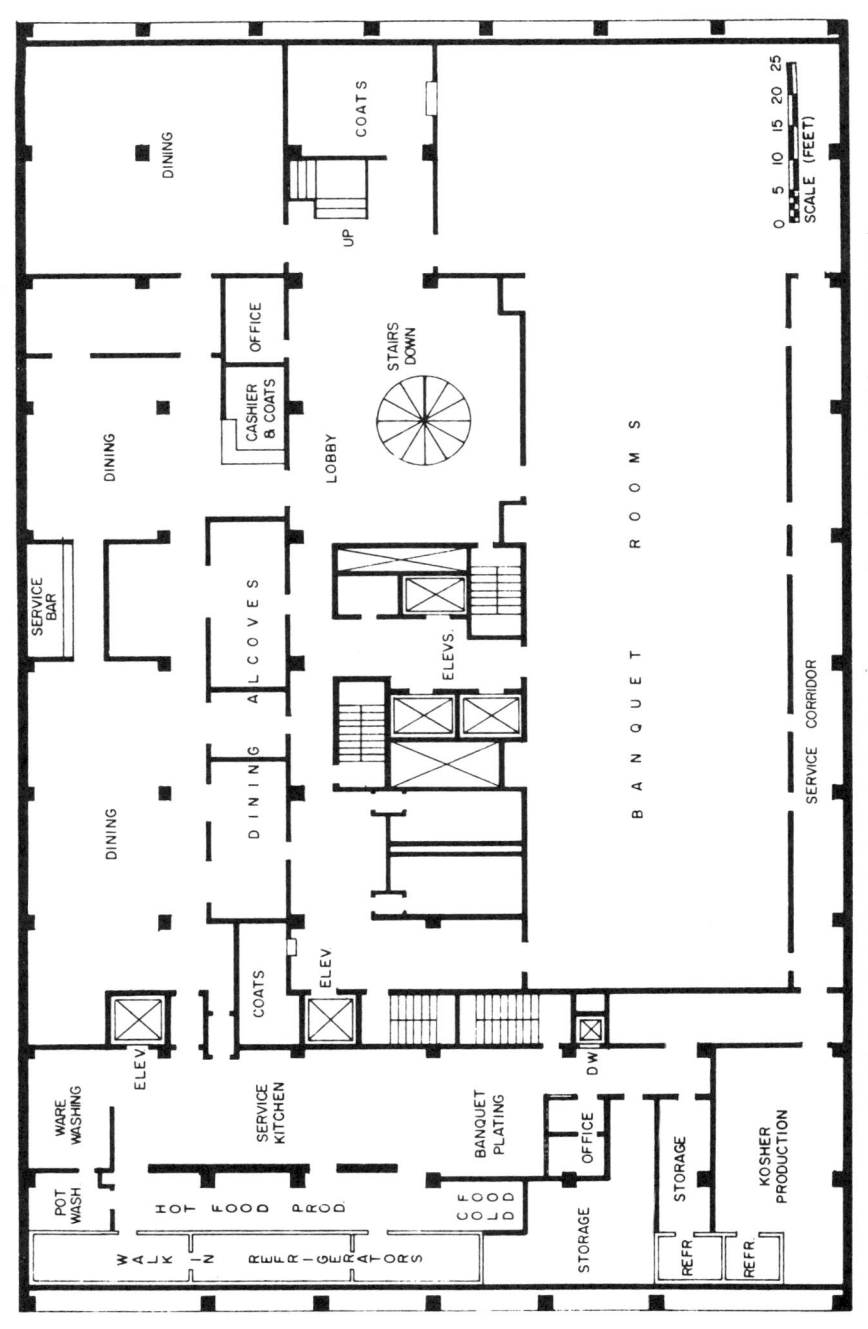

Fig. 6-3. A case study in functional planning: Final plan of the second floor. *(Courtesy of Cini-Grissom Associates)*

On the second floor, access to the main dining room and the banquet rooms is by means of a decorative circular stair from the lobby or a separate elevator (left end of the lobby). The banquet room is shown fully open on the plan, but it can be divided into smaller rooms. A corridor is provided for service to the various sections of the room. The main dining room area is also divided into smaller areas, both for intimacy in public dining and to permit the service of small groups if desired.

The main dining room is not quite as large as the owner wished, but it was felt that other areas on the floor should not be reduced in size in order to expand the dining room. A service elevator (upper left, Fig. 6–2) is used to supply the kitchen from receiving and bulk storage in the basement and to transport solid waste to a garbage area near the receiving dock. Unfortunately, this elevator does not service the street-level operation, and hence the need to build the dumbwaiter system at an added cost to the project.

Following the establishment of basic space allocations, the architect, designers, and food facilities engineers prepare preliminary designs based on the design program. These are reviewed in detail with the owners and operators to determine if the designs being prepared meet the needs of the market to be served, are within the financial guidelines established, and are in agreement with the overall project program. We have noted the importance of professional assistance in the food service design effort. In the following chapter, the elements of kitchen and cafeteria design are discussed.

7

KITCHEN AND CAFETERIA DESIGN

In planning the kitchen layout, the same sequence described in planning the overall layout is used: analysis of requirements, determination of materials flow and the physical relationships, and allocation of available space.

A kitchen consists of a series of work stations interspersed with temporary storage and holding areas. Each work station is designed to fulfill some specialized function. In a large hotel kitchen, work stations may include bake shop, butcher shop, soup station, range, *garde manger,* vegetable station, and cold pantry. Large centers may be divided into several work stations. The butcher shop may include separate areas for fish and poultry work as well as meat blocks or tables for several workers fabricating various meat products. The bake shop may be divided into areas for pastry work, cakes and puddings, bread baking, icing and finishing, and ice cream and frozen desserts.

A small restaurant with a limited menu, on the other hand, may have only two distinct preparation areas: a "hot" station with range, broiler, oven and steam table and a "cold" station for appetizers, salads, and desserts. A lunch counter operation will normally have a sandwich station, grill, and hot and cold beverage station.

The Importance of Menu Planning

The first step in the design of any kitchen facility is menu planning. As obvious as this rule may seem, too often new restaurants and other food service facilities are designed and built before the actual menu to be used is planned. This can lead to selection of improper equipment, poor layout, and enormous waste in both facilities investment and future operating costs.

The operator must plan the menu according to his marketing program, determining which items are most likely to sell and also which are most profitable. When this task is accomplished, the food facilities engineer and operator are in a position to decide which equipment is required to prepare the actual menu, how this equipment can be arranged into work stations, and the actual design of each work station. Naturally, future flexibility is desirable; the kitchen should be planned to allow reasonable future menu changes and additions and deletions of specific equipment in each work station. However, equipment selection and work station arrangement and design should be limited primarily to the servicing of the initial menu rather than an ability to prepare and serve a limitless variety of foods sometime in the future.

Work-Station Relationships

The relationships among the various work stations must be analyzed, just as the relationships among the various functions of the operation were studied. Some industrial engineers have made detailed studies of the interactions among work stations in existing operations. They observed the number of trips employees made among stations and the number of movements of merchandise. These trips and movements among work stations were tabulated and combinations ranked according to frequency. From this ranking, a schematic diagram or plan was developed showing the functional relationships among the various work stations. This plan was then adapted to the physical space available.

Another technique used in industrial engineering is flowcharting. The route of the materials is charted as they move through the production lines. The plant is then laid out so that the materials flow lines are as short and as straight as possible. In a commercial food service, the products generally do not go through a number of sequential processes, and the trend is toward elimination of as many processing steps as possible through the use of convenience and prepared foods.

This type of detailed research is possible only when a "laboratory" exists—an existing operation exactly like or comparable to the proposed operation. Unfortunately, a model is seldom available. Furthermore, such research is time consuming and expensive and does not necessarily take into consideration the need for flexibility to meet future changes. These studies do provide general guidelines, however, that can be adapted to the needs of similar operations.

Work-Station Design

According to the planning procedures outlined earlier, the next step in designing a kitchen is allocating the space to the various work stations. General guidelines do exist for assigning space within a kitchen, but the final allocation will depend on the number and dimensions of the equipment selected, the shape of the space, and the configuration of each station.

There are several types of work stations. One is a *specialized* station used by a number of people. Its major component is usually some specific piece of equipment. An example is a high-speed vertical cutter that may be used for preparing salad mixtures, vegetables for cooked mixtures, extended raw meat mixtures for meat loaves, and materials for cold sauces or salad dressings. The station includes the cutter, related floor drain and water source, a place to hold the ingredients being worked on, and a place for holding containers for the finished product. A cart may be used to transport the ingredients to the station and serve as a holding place both for the raw materials and the finished product. Therefore, space must be provided to maneuver a cart around the machine. This type of work station must be located where it can be used by workers from different areas without interrupting the activity of adjoining stations, and it must be within the general materials flow patterns. The station itself must be designed so that the major machine component can be used with optimum efficiency.

A second type of work station is the *general* station manned by one person. Here, the work comes to the worker, who does not go to the work center, as was the case with the specialized station. Examples of a general station are a sandwich counter or a broiler station. At each station the worker has the ingredients of a number of menu items, which he assembles or cooks according to the orders he receives. He must have space to store the raw materials and have easy access to them. He also must have a space to work on the ingredients (cut, chop, measure, weigh, inspect, assemble, portion, stir, or mix), a place to store the plates or other types of ware he needs for each item, and a place to hold the finished product until it is called for.

A third type of station is an *assembly line,* where a number of items are handled by a number of people, such as a hospital tray assembly or a machine dishwashing operation. The assembly line station is the most difficult to design because each component (man and machine) must be assigned an equal work load in order to obtain an even flow and minimize idle time.

Some general rules of work station design are as follows:

1. Locate materials, supplies, and (where applicable) service ware within the normal reach of an individual. The items most frequently used should be the most accessible.
2. Provide storage for utensils and machine attachments at the point of use.
3. Use leveling devices to keep materials at convenient work heights, to maximize productivity, and to reduce fatigue.

4. Store items that are frequently moved in mobile containers such as carts or dollies.
5. Provide work aisles sufficiently wide to allow for the passage of carts, where necessary, allow for door swings, and for equipment parts that may move beyond the base of the machine during operation.
6. Avoid using work aisles as main traffic aisles.

Principles of Equipment Selection

To select the best piece of equipment to do a task, the task must first be defined. What is the job that this equipment must do? Can this task be accomplished in any other way, or can it be combined with another task to simplify the work and eliminate the need for two separate pieces of equipment? Equipment needs must be established with consideration of the work to be done and a knowledge of the equipment available. Designers and equipment dealers can keep the food service operator informed of new developments in equipment design and enable him to select equipment that can improve the resulting product and reduce his operating costs. Once the task has been defined and available equipment ascertained, the following criteria can be applied in evaluating particular products:

1. Does the piece of equipment do the job required? If it does not, it is pointless to consider its other qualities.
2. Does the equipment do the job efficiently? How much manpower is required to operate it? Does it increase labor productivity? Is it efficient in the use of energy? How much floor space is required? Generally, the more specialized a piece of equipment is, the more efficient it will be at performing its special task but the less flexible it will be in performing other tasks. Specialization is warranted only when there is a large amount of the specialized task to be performed or the savings achieved by the specialized equipment are signifcant.
3. Does the equipment have the production capacity required? Overcapacity can be just as costly and inefficient as undercapacity. Designers use numerous formulas to calculate capacities required for different types of equipment, but all are based on the following general procedure:
    (a) Establish the item to be prepared and the type of equipment required.
    (b) Estimate the number of portions that will be sold in a given time period during normal and peak periods.
    (c) Calculate the amount to be produced, based on portion sizes and yield factors.

(d) Determine the capacities of the various equipment models available and their realistic "productivity" or output capability. This includes time to set up the machine and get ready, to load and unload the machine, and time for recovery of temperatures after a batch has been completed. Normal "down" time must also be considered.
(e) Select the model size indicated by the calculated production load.

Capacity should also be considered in terms of foreseeable future needs as well as present requirements. If expansion is expected, the estimated cost of increasing capacity in the future must be weighed against the cost of overequipping for present needs.
4. Does the equipment being considered fit in with the rest of the production system? Does it physically fit into the space? Does it require special sizes of containers that are not interchangeable with other equipment? Does it require special plumbing or utility connections or costly exhaust ducts?
5. Is the equipment safe to operate? The Occupational Safety and Health Act of 1971 makes many safety features mandatory, not only on new equipment but also on existing equipment. Chopping and cutting machines must have safety guards to shield the cutting edges. Electrical equipment must be grounded, with safety and overload cut-off devices. Hot surfaces must be shielded or insulated, and nontoxic materials must be used on surfaces that come in contact with food products.
6. Is the equipment easy to keep clean? It should carry the seal of the National Sanitation Foundation, indicating that it meets the standards and criteria of that organization.
7. Is the equipment well designed and easy to use? Are dials and indicators easy to read? Are controls readily accessible and located in such a way that they cannot be moved accidentally?
8. Can the equipment be easily replaced if production requirements change in the future or if a more efficient model becomes available? Is a complicated installation required?
9. Can the equipment be maintained easily? Does it require a great deal of servicing, and what is the manufacturer's program for servicing his products? What is his reputation for the reliability of his products?
10. The final criterion is that of cost. Cost includes not only the purchase price of the equipment but also the installation cost

and the cost of operating and maintaining it over its expected life. Additionally, the cost of the cash invested in the equipment—the potential interest on the capital—is also a part of the cost of that equipment.

All these costs should be weighed against the expected use or output of the various pieces of equipment being considered. Some may have features that add to the cost but that are not required for the particular tasks involved. With others, a standard model of equipment with slight modifications may serve the same purpose as a custom-designed piece being considered but at a substantially lower cost. On the other hand, a more expensive but more efficient model may save many times the amount of its extra cost during its lifetime. If it is anticipated that a much more efficient model of a particular machine may be available in a few years, it may be better to buy a low-priced model of the existing line or even a used machine rather than invest in an expensive heavy-duty model.

Lease or purchase of secondhand equipment may be alternatives to the purchase of new equipment. With certain types of equipment, such as ice cream freezers or coffee urns, food purveyors may provide the equipment without charge as a part of their dealer services to customers.

Designing for Safety and Cleanliness

The physical design and the materials used can contribute greatly to the ease of maintenance and the safety of the operation. The safety and sanitation considerations of equipment selection were discussed in the preceding section. In addition, the facilities should be designed so that the proper level of sanitation can be easily maintained. This includes not only the sanitation of the property but also the personal cleanliness of the employees.

Practically every area of the country has laws concerning public health and safety. Most of these laws are based on the U.S. Public Health Service's Food Service Sanitation Ordinance and Code. Owners, managers, and designers of new food service operations should be thoroughly familiar with the health codes that apply to their area.

The Public Health Service's model requires that:

1. *Floors, walls, and ceiling.* The floor surfaces in kitchens, in all other rooms and areas in which food is stored or prepared and in which utensils are washed, and in walk-in refrigerators, dressing or locker rooms, and toilet rooms, shall be of

smooth, nonabsorbent materials, and so constructed as to be easily cleanable.... Floor drains shall be provided in all rooms where floors are subjected to flooding-type cleaning or where normal operations release or discharge water or other liquid waste on the floor. All exterior areas where food is served shall be kept clean and properly drained, and surfaces in such areas shall be finished so as to facilitate maintenance and minimize dust.... All walls of rooms or areas in which food is prepared, or utensils or hands are washed, shall be easily cleanable, smooth, and light-colored, and shall have washable surfaces up to the highest level reached by splash or spray.

2. *Lighting.* All areas in which food is prepared or stored or utensils are washed, hand-washing areas, dressing or locker rooms, toilet rooms, and garbage and rubbish storage areas shall be well lighted.

3. *Ventilation.* All rooms in which food is prepared or served or utensils are washed, dressing or locker rooms, toilet rooms, and garbage and rubbish storage areas shall be well ventilated. Ventilation hoods and devices shall be designed to prevent grease or condensate from dripping into food or onto food-preparation surfaces. Filters, where used, shall be readily removable for cleaning or replacement. Ventilation systems shall comply with applicable State and local fire prevention requirements and shall, when vented to the outside air, discharge in such manner as not to create a nuisance.

4. *Dressing rooms and lockers.* Adequate facilities shall be provided for the orderly storage of employees' clothing and personal belongings. Where employees routinely change clothes within the establishment, one or more dressing rooms or designated areas shall be provided for this purpose. Such designated areas shall be located outside of the food-preparation, storage, and serving areas, and the utensil-washing and storage areas.... Designated areas shall be equipped with adequate lockers, and lockers or other suitable facilities shall be provided in dressing rooms.

Other sections of the code include requirements pertaining to the design, construction, and installation of equipment and utensils, materials to be used, methods and facilities for washing and sanitizing equipment and utensils (including dishwashing), water supply, plumbing and drains, toilet and hand-washing facilities, garbage and rubbish disposal, and vermin control.

The Occupational Safety and Health Act also contains requirements that must be considered in designing a new food service operation. Safety features on equipment have already been mentioned. In the design of the facility, the Act affects such considerations as lighting, noise levels, ventilation, means of egress from the building, toilet facilities, fire protection, working and walking surfaces, and electrical installations.

Most localities have codes or ordinances pertaining to fire protection. One common provision of the code stipulates maximum occupancy. Other provisions usually pertain to the kitchen exhaust system, since many restaurant fires originate in the ducts.

In older exhaust systems, grease is removed by passing the air through metal mesh filters. These filters trap the grease and hold it in the mesh until the filters are manually removed and washed. There are several disadvantages to this system. First, as grease builds up in the filters, air circulation is reduced. Second, instead of removing a fire hazard, the grease-soaked filters may actually present a hazard. A small flare-up of flames on the cooking surface can easily ignite them. Furthermore, as the filters become saturated, they permit grease particles to pass through into the ducts or flue. A fire started at the cooking surface that ignites grease in the filters is fueled in the ducts and can quickly travel to the roof. Additionally, if the flue is not properly installed and is in contact with combustible materials such as wood, heat from a fire in the flue can ignite the surrounding materials. Some protection can be obtained by installing sprinklers or other type of fire-extinguishing system in the ducts and at the cooking surface, but continual cleaning of the filters and periodic cleaning of the duct system are required for a safe operation.

Modern exhaust systems use a system of baffles instead of filters to remove grease from the air. These baffles force the air currents into swirling, cyclone-like movements, and the grease particles are forced out onto the walls of the extraction chambers by centrifugal force. These chambers are automatically flushed periodically with a solution of steam or hot water and detergent, so that the grease is dissolved and flushed away. There is no need for manual cleaning. Because there are no filters in the baffle system, the air circulation is not impeded, and smaller ducts and fans may be used. Furthermore, any fires that occur at the cooking surface cannot travel past the baffles into the ducts.

Additional fire protection is available through sprinklers or extinguishing systems installed over the cooking surfaces (Fig. 7–1).

Trends in Kitchen Design and Equipment

Until about 25 years ago, commercial kitchens were built and operated in the same manner as they had been for several centuries. It has been said that a cook from the eighteenth-century kitchen of

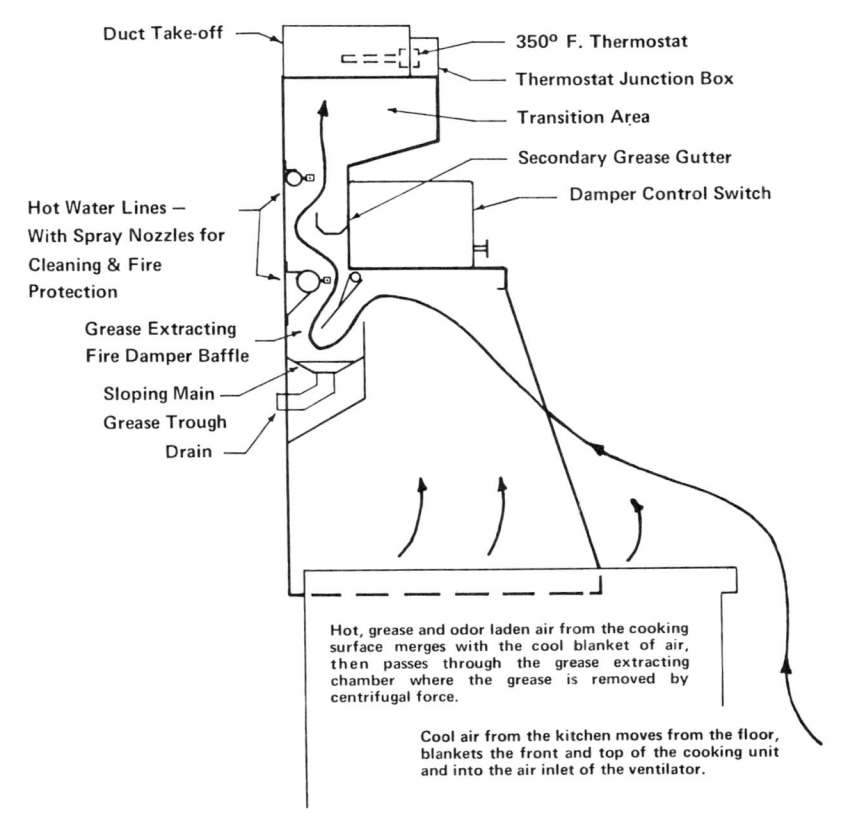

Fig. 7-1. Cross section of a Gaylord exhaust ventilator system. *(Courtesy of Gaylord Atlantic Corp.)*

Carême could have walked into a kitchen in the first half of the twentieth century and felt at home, since so little had been changed in kitchen equipment or operation. Had he walked into a commercial kitchen in the 1970s, however, he would have found much to puzzle over: entirely new ways of cooking (microwave ovens), warehandling (disposable ware), preservation of foods (freezing and freeze-drying), new ways of handling garbage and trash (disposers and compactors), and new ways to keep the accounts (computers).

Commercial cooking has changed from an art to a science, and the technology of this science is changing at an ever-increasing rate. Some of the most important trends that have emerged in the past 25 years are:

1. *Smaller kitchens.* The need to increase the productivity of space has been discussed. This trend goes hand in hand with the increasing productivity of labor. As fewer and fewer

workers are required to achieve the same level of output, less and less space is required for them to work in.
2. *Automated equipment.* The trend toward more highly automated equipment has been in response to the need for increasing labor productivity and also because of the shortage of skilled workers. Using automated equipment, the unskilled worker can produce what the skilled worker once produced by hand, and do it much faster.
3. *Quality control devices.* In conjunction with the automation of the work and the use of unskilled labor has come the need to monitor and control product quality.
4. *Ease of maintenance and sanitation.* Automated equipment requires maintenance, and the more moving parts and the greater the sensitivity of the control devices, the greater the need for maintenance. As a rule, the more complicated the machine, the harder it is to clean; hence, ease of cleaning has become an important factor in equipment design.

The next few years may be expected to bring an even more rapid rate of change as commercial applications of space age technology become available. Laser beams, electronic controls, and computers are examples. New types of ceramics and plastics will permit these materials to be used in many new ways. Cooking and reheating techniques will be developed to utilize energy far more efficiently. Preservation methods and packaging materials will be developed to permit food products to be stored at room temperature, reconstituted with a minimum of energy being applied, then served to the guest—all in the same package. The current trend toward off-premises preparation of food will continue. Because much of this new technology will require a large investment in highly specialized capital equipment, an investment of this size is feasible only when very large production quantities are possible.

Because of the rapid rate of technological change, a major requirement of new kitchen design should be flexibility. It is no longer necessary, or even practical, to build a kitchen that will last for 40 years. (Perhaps even the conventional 10-year life often used for depreciating kitchen equipment is too long.) Flexibility is achieved through the elimination of interior walls and curbing wherever possible and the use of modular equipment systems, mobile equipment, and overhead raceways and quick-disconnect couplings for utility connections.

Another trend in kitchen design is an increasing concern with improving the work environment. A pleasant work environment can not only improve worker productivity but also contribute to reduced labor turnover.

Some Special Types of Kitchen Layouts
Institutional Kitchens
Institutional kitchens must be equipped to prepare and serve a limited menu in large quantities. Therefore, the equipment in this type of kitchen must be sized to produce these large quantities in a short length of time. If the institution operates with a low food budget, the menu may lean heavily to dishes prepared in large steam-jacketed kettles or in the ovens. Institutions for the elderly may offer more plain roasted or broiled meals that are easily digested and few, if any, deep-fried items.

Some institutions have eliminated much on-premises food preparation in favor of purchasing preprocessed convenience foods. In such kitchen layouts, greater emphasis is placed on storage, particularly frozen storage, and on materials movement requirements than on preparation equipment. Reconstitution may be done in the central area, or, in the case of a hospital, in pantries on the patient floors.

Hospital Kitchens
The planning of a hospital dietary department is becoming an increasingly complex project. When planning a new hospital, the materials-handling and tray-delivery systems for patient food service should be integrated into the overall planning of the hospital from the beginning, because these systems are an integral part of the functioning of the total institution. Furthermore, by careful planning of the total operating systems, increased efficiencies can be built into the physical plant. For example, automated materials-handling systems can deliver fully loaded self-propelled trucks to preaddressed locations without any need for an attendant. These trucks are electronically programmed to follow circuitry embedded in the floors and to activate elevators on the way to a predetermined destination.

Even in less sophisticated systems, the relationships of central kitchen, floor pantries, subveyor or elevator requirements, receiving and storage areas, employee cafeteria and public visitor facilities, doctors' dining rooms, and other functions in the dietary department must be determined early in the planning process. The method of delivery of food to patients can affect the amount of service pantry space required on patient floors, the configuration of elevators or subveyors, and the amount of space and equipment needed for tray assembly in a centralized area.

Kosher Kitchens
A kosher kitchen is a requirement of an orthodox Jewish institution. Two separate kitchens are required, one for the preparation of meat meals and one for dairy meals. Separate sets of utensils,

separate potwashing areas, and separate facilities for washing and storing the separate sets of china and tableware are required.

Commissaries

The commissary is a food factory equipped for large "runs" or production quantities. Ideally, the product moves in a straight line from receiving entrance through holding, processing, staging or assembling of orders, and packing for shipment out through a shipping area onto trucks for delivery. Some commissary items may be processed for freezing, then transferred to a warehouse for future shipment. Thus production may be scheduled to meet daily orders or for inventory based on anticipated future orders. In some cases, the commissary itself does little or no preparation and simply functions as a centralized receiving and distribution center for a large company or institution.

Flight Kitchen

The flight kitchen is a type of commissary. Raw materials are received and processed, orders are assembled and the finished product is then shipped out to departing aircraft. An assembly line is used to set up trays with ware and cold items. Hot foods may be packed in a heated, chilled, or frozen state to be reconstituted on the plane. If the flight kitchen is operated by a caterer who services a number of different airlines, a wide range of menus and a corresponding number of types of service ware and equipment may be required. The warewashing and storage of the mobile "buffet" modules that are boarded on the aircraft can take a substantial proportion of the total floor space of a flight kitchen.

Evaluating a Plan

When the designers have completed their planning, they submit their drawings to the owner for approval. Following are some criteria that can be used for evaluating a proposed layout.

Traffic Flow

The various traffic flows can be traced through the plan: the flow of materials, employees, guests, and clean and soiled ware. The designer may provide a drawing with each flow indicated by a different colored line. There may be different traffic patterns at different times of day; each should be analyzed.

Ideally, there is no backtracking or cross traffic, and each line of flow is as short as possible. Areas where a number of lines converge indicate potential hazards or bottlenecks. These bottlenecks can often be avoided by providing an additional bypass route, such as another door or aisle. Other techniques include providing a wider corridor and eliminating work functions from main traffic aisles.

Materials Handling

Study the flows of materials and ware. Movement and storage of materials do not add value to the product and therefore should be reduced to a minimum. The route of the materials flow should be as straight and as short as possible. Multiple handling such as unpacking and repacking, stacking and restacking, transferring from one container or vehicle to another should be avoided. Container sizes should be standardized to fit into the various pieces of equipment involved. Wherever possible, mobile equipment should be provided, not only for ease of transport of goods but also for ease of sanitation.

Control

One very important aspect of control is visibility. Solid walls can prevent a supervisor from seeing what is happening in his department. Where solid walls cannot be avoided, windows or openings should be provided. Provision must be made for security, however, with lockable areas provided. Frequently, wire cages, half doors, or overhead gates can be used to provide both security and visibility. (They also provide the added advantage of improving the ventilation and air circulation that are important in food and beverage storerooms.)

The layout should not require nonfood service employees such as delivery men or employees of other departments to enter the kitchen or related areas. If an employees' cafeteria is provided (as in a hotel or institution), separate access should be provided.

Security and control should also be considered in the public area of the operation. Cashiers, rest rooms, and exits should be located so as to reduce the possibility of "walk-outs"—patrons who depart without paying their check. A secure area should be provided for counting cash, and preparing deposits and cashiers' banks.

Staffing

The number of employees required to staff the various stations at various times should be determined and this staffing compared against the payroll projection in the pro forma. The design should permit flexibility in staffing at different levels of business. Each station should be large enough for the number of employees required for peak levels of business and yet operable by a minimum number of employees at very low levels of business.

Flexibility

It must be determined if the plan permits flexibility. Would it be relatively easy to add an additional piece of equipment or to

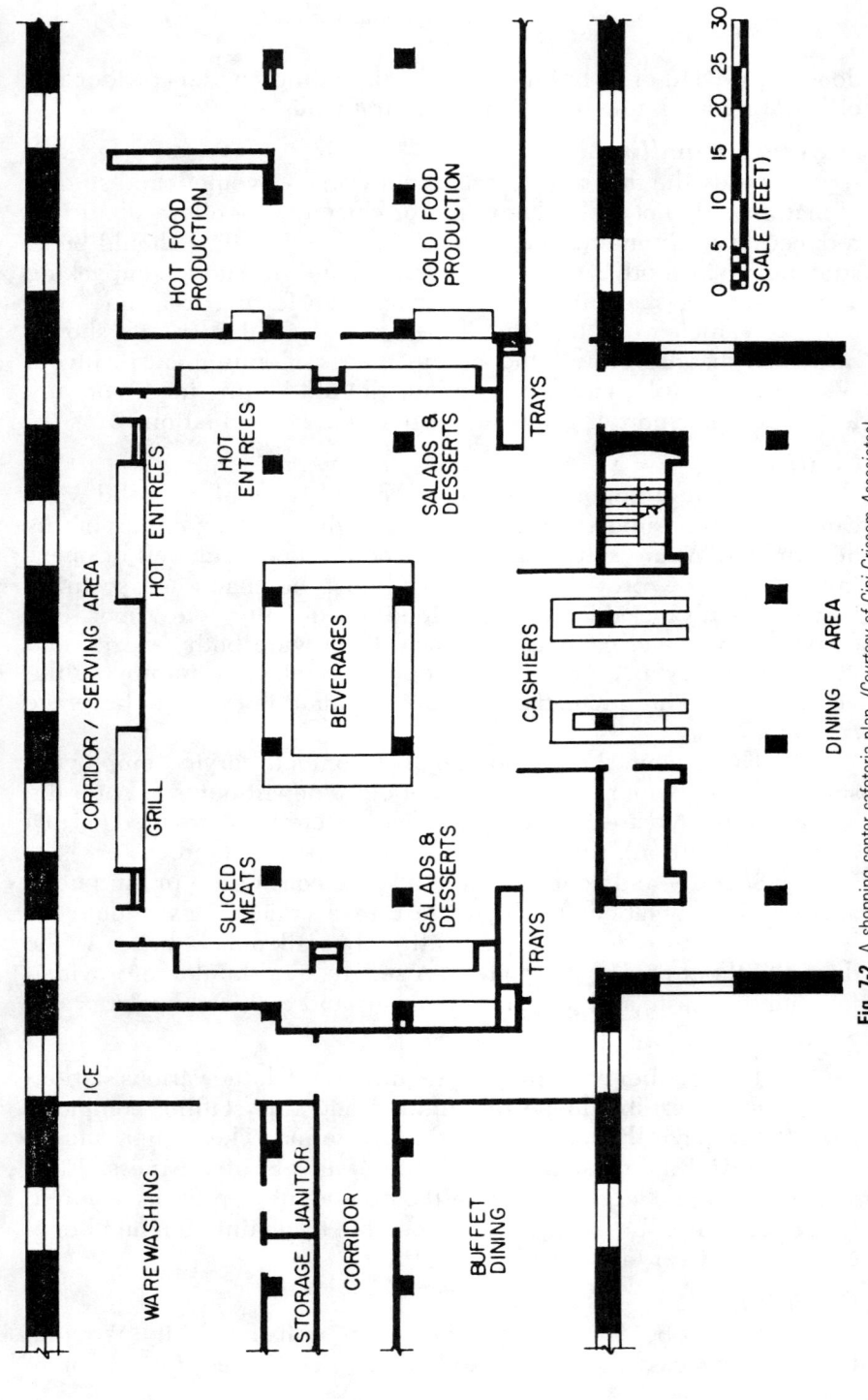

Fig. 7-2. A shopping center cafeteria plan. *(Courtesy of Cini-Grissom Associates)*

rearrange some areas if the nature of the operation changed? Would it be possible to expand the operation in the future? The size and location of exhaust hoods and walk-in refrigerators (particularly those with recessed pads) usually present the greatest limitations on future expansion or alterations because relocating them can require very costly major structural changes.

Structural features such as load-bearing walls, columns, or variations in floor level are usually beyond the kitchen designer's control, although sometimes the building's architect can accommodate a change. Mechanical spaces can sometimes be relocated if this will significantly improve the kitchen layout.

Work Station Design and Equipment Selection

Criteria for evaluating the layout of the work stations and the particular items of equipment have been presented in the preceding sections.

Cafeteria Layout and Design

There are two basic types of cafeteria layout. One is the single-line cafeteria where the customers must move in single file past all the serving counters on the line. Even though most line layouts provide enough space for one customer to pass another in the serving line, this type of layout may not lend itself to fast service or to high volumes.

The second basic type of layout is the "shopping center" or "scramble" cafeteria. Here the counters are separated into "islands" according to the type of items offered. The customer goes only to the islands offering the items he desires. This system often permits faster service. The customer does not have to select items in any given order as he does in the line system but can by-pass an area and return to it if he changes his mind.

The "shopping center" layout (Fig. 7–2) can serve large numbers of customers quickly, which makes it suitable for large industrial feeding operations. The alternative to the shopping center layout for high-volume operations is to build multiple single-line cafeterias, which require much more floor space, duplication of all equipment, and duplication of staff to operate them. The capacity of a "shopping center" layout can be increased by duplicating only those stations with the greatest demand.

Single-line layouts (Fig. 7–3) are preferred for smaller operations and for public commercial cafeterias. Public cafeteria operators maintain that single-line layouts result in higher check averages, because patrons are more likely to make impulse purchases than they would if they could by-pass certain counters. Also, speed is a lesser

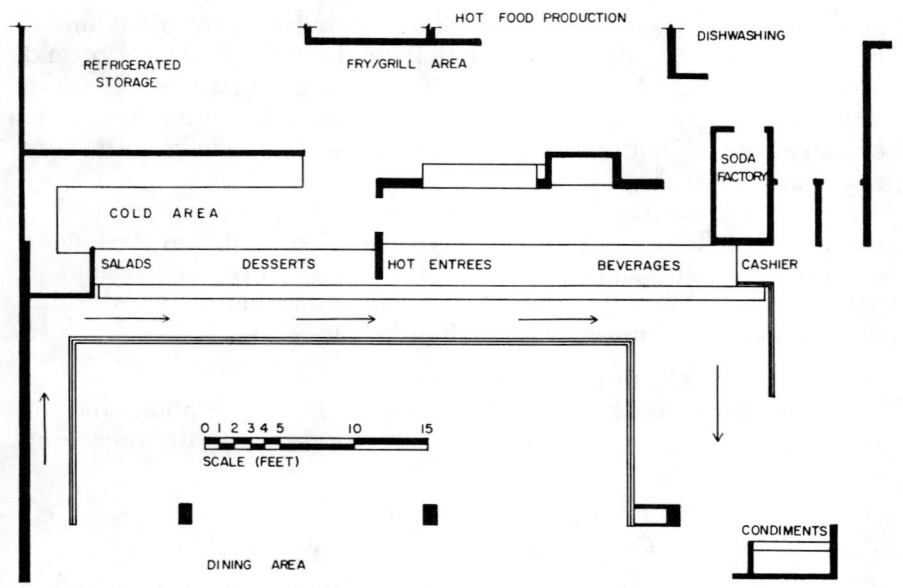

Fig. 7-3. A straight-line cafeteria plan. *(Courtesy of Cini-Grissom Associates)*

consideration in a public cafeteria than in an industrial operation. Since one person can easily service several stations at once, the single-line layout also requires less staff to operate in the slow periods than does the shopping center plan.

One other type of layout is occasionally found in cafeterias. This is the window or "hatch," where the customer picks up a complete meal or order at a single point. The assembling of the meal is done by the serving staff, either manually or by means of a small conveyor belt. This type of layout is limited to institutions offering a nonselective or very limited menu. It is also used in fast-food operations.

Counter Arrangement

The arrangement of the serving counters can affect both the sales volume and the traffic flow. In single-line cafeterias, salad and dessert counters are located at the beginning of the line because these items are often selected on impulse. If these items are placed at the end of the line, patrons may be inclined to pass them up, having already filled their trays. Beverage counters are usually placed at the end of the line because almost everyone will purchase a beverage and impulse is not involved.

The serving temperature of the food is also a factor in the arrangement of a serving counter. Another reason for locating the beverage station at the end of the line is that maintaining the serving temperature is more important for hot beverages than for any other menu item. Hot soups are second in importance, and hot entrées and vegetables are third. Desserts (except frozen desserts) are usually least critical as regards temperature and can safely be located at the beginning of the serving line.

In the single-line cafeteria, there is only one traffic flow—straight through the line. As a general rule, the longer and straighter the line, the faster will be the speed of the traffic flow. Turns, bends, and breaks in the line slow down the movement of the flow. Lengthening the line and expanding the amount of space devoted to each item permits several people to make their selection at the same time, which also speeds the traffic flow. The traffic aisle must be wide enough for one patron with a tray easily to pass another slower patron in the line. Separating the cashier stand from the rest of the line will also speed the movement of traffic, since space is provided for patrons to by-pass those who must stop to get out their money. The cashier should have an unrestricted view of oncoming trays so that the next patron's tray can be priced before the preceding patron has left the line.

In a "shopping center" layout, patrons are free to by-pass stations, but the general principles of the straight-line layout still apply. Dessert and salad counters are usually placed where they are highly visible to the patrons entering the serving area, and beverages are usually located just before the exit. Ice cream freezers with preportioned desserts and ice cream novelties are placed directly before the cashier stations so that patrons can select these items immediately before leaving the serving area, or they can easily return later for them.

Specialty stations, such as those for short-order items, the carving table, or made-to-order sandwiches, are more suited to the "shopping center" plan, queueing is not as critical as in the line layout items are to be offered in a line cafeteria, extra space must be provided for those patrons waiting for their orders.

Queueing

In a line cafeteria, space must be provided for queueing. Queueing space preferably is separated from the dining area so that persons standing in line do not disturb those already seated. In the "shopping center" plan, queuing is not as critical as in the line layout because the serving area can absorb a large number of patrons at once. When the "shopping center" cafeteria is subject to large, uncontrollable surges of customers, as in a school or college operation, space must be provided for a queue, and someone must control the number of persons entering the serving area. In an industrial feeding operation, this problem can frequently be solved by close scheduling of the lunch breaks. By scheduling the lunch periods at 10 or 15 minute intervals, the large peaks are evened out, and no employee has to spend more than a few minutes standing in line. Furthermore, better utilization of the dining room means that fewer seats (hence less space) are required.

Kitchen and Dishroom Layout

The kitchen layout should be determined by the counter locations, with the various preparation areas placed in direct relation to the serving counters they supply. One very efficient plan is to align each preparation station in the kitchen at a right angle to the serving counter that it supplies. Pass-through holding cabinets, either heated or refrigerated, are located between the serving area and the kitchen.

The shape of the available space occasionally presents limitations on the design. A serving counter layout that provides good traffic flows and merchandising opportunities should not be sacrificed for the sake of expediency in designing the kitchen.

In locating the dish room, the flow of soiled dishes from the dining room and the flow of clean dishes to the serving areas should be determined. If a self-busing program is to be instituted, the dish room planning must take this policy into consideration. Tray depositories (either conveyor belts or carts) must be located close to the dining room exits so that patrons do not have to walk out of their way to deposit their trays. (Other planning considerations are discussed in Chapter 6, Designing for Profits.)

Cashiering

Cashiering is the limiting factor in determining the speed of a cash cafeteria operation. A cashier can handle a maximum of six to eight transactions a minute in a peak period. If a checker is added to total the amounts, the capacity of the two together is increased to 10 to 12 transactions per minute. Therefore, the number of cashier stations required is determined by the desired capacity in the peak periods.

The location of the cashier stations is also of major importance. If the patron can gain access to the dining room without passing a cashier, some revenue may be lost. Some cafeteria operations use a checker at the end of the serving line and locate the cashier at the exit. The checker issues a check to the guest, who then pays his bill as he leaves the dining room after he has eaten. Under this system, the unscrupulous patron can reenter the serving line after he has eaten and purchase an inexpensive item such as a cup of coffee, receiving a second check from the checker. Upon leaving, he pays only the smaller check and receives a full meal for the price of a cup of coffee.

A Case Study in Kitchen Design

In the following case study, food service equipment consultant Maurice Lafiteau lists the considerations involved in planning a kitchen and describes how he handled them in the layout of a new private luncheon club:

There are many factors involved in designing a functional food and beverage operation. The most important—the ones affecting the final product—are:

- The menu
- The number of meals to be served
- The type of service
- The availability of supplies
- The utilities available and the sources of power
- Local and state health codes
- Length of lease, if the space is not owned
- Local union restrictions
- Method of disposing of garbage and refuse
- Cost factors
- Size and shape of the allocated space*

The Menu and Number of Meals to be Served

The menu to be served will determine the need for broilers, fryers, ovens, kettles, and steamers. The number and capacity of each appliance will be determined by the number of meals to be served. Supporting equipment, such as refrigerators, steam tables, plate warmers, food warmers, pot racks, and so on, is also part of the cooking arrangement, and all the pieces must be located so that time and motions are saved for the cooks.

In the case of the private luncheon club designed by Lafiteau, an *á la carte* menu was to be offered, featuring the finest quality food and beverage service. The club was being planned with seven private dining rooms, accommodating about 60 persons in total. The main dining room was to accommodate 175 and the bar about 50.

In luxury luncheon clubs of this type, there is usually only one sitting at each meal. This practice produces a seat turnover of about 0.8 times per meal. A high level of utilization was expected for the private dining rooms, but the occupancy of a room could be as few as two people, since its primary function was to provide a private place to conduct business over lunch and not to serve a social function. For this reason, Lafiteau estimated the seat turnover for the private room overall at 0.5 times per meal. No food service was planned for the bar.

---

*Maurice B. Lafiteau, Inc., Valley Stream, N.Y.

Therefore, the peak requirements were estimated at 140 regular dining room luncheons, plus an average of 30 in the private dining rooms, which could range up to a maximum of 60 at peak. In addition, it was expected that there would be some demand for special functions such as cocktail parties and receptions in the evenings.

Type of Service

The high quality *á la carte* menu requires fine French service in the dining room, which generally involves a captain who takes the order, a waiter or waitress who serves the food, and a busman who provides water, ice, bread, and butter and picks up the soiled dishes. As a rule, this type of service is supported by fine china, glassware, flatware, hollowware, and linen. A large number of pieces is required for each setting.

French service was required for the luncheon club. This told Lafiteau that extra space would be required in the kitchen, dish room, and waiters' service area for hollowware, underliners, side dishes and all the different types of flatware. In the dishwashing area, a silver burnisher large enough to take the big platters and bowls used for the private rooms and for the regular dining room serving pieces was also needed.

Availability of Supplies

In planning storage facilities—freezers, refrigerators, and storerooms—careful consideration must be given to weekend and holiday needs. If the operation is in a city, deliveries are generally excellent. In outlying areas where deliveries may be less frequent, the storeroom, refrigerators, and freezer must be bigger. The same consideration applies to laundry service deliveries and the size of the linen storage space.

The luncheon club was located in the middle of a large city, and it would not be open on weekends and holidays. Extra storage space was not required, therefore.

Available Sources of Power

The availability and relative costs of various sources of power have to be determined. The choices include electricity, steam, and gas (natural or bottled). Certain states now restrict the use of gas, and future costs and availability of supplies are uncertain. Electricity is billed to commercial customers on the basis of peak requirements as well as the total usage. Steam is usually available only in large cities, although sometimes it may be generated in the building, as in hospitals or institutions. When using steam in a small operation, it is best to use low pressures, because the law in most localities requires that a licensed engineer be on the premises if there is a high-pressure steam application.

Because energy for cooking, warming, and heating water is a major operating cost, it is of paramount importance that the equipment specified be well insulated and equipped with controls such as thermostats and timers to minimize the operating cost. The extra cost of these features will be more than paid for in reduced utility expenses over the long run.

The luncheon club was located on the top floor of a high-rise office building, so power was restricted to sources available in the building. Gas was chosen for cooking, a line of sufficient capacity having been supplied to that level of the building. Electricity was specified for dishwashing, hot water boosting, and warmers. If steam had been available, it would have been used instead of electricity.

Local and State Health Codes

It is imperative that the designer familiarize himself with the local and state health codes at the outset of the project. These codes vary throughout the country and in some areas involve not only the equipment but also the lighting, ventilation, plumbing, wall and floor finishes, and so on. Many health departments supplement NSF (National Sanitation Foundation) standards or even list specific model numbers of equipment they have approved. In most localities the board of health will furnish a form to be filled out with the submission of the kitchen plans and specifications. In many cases it has to be filled in jointly with the architects who specify floor finishes, ceiling, walls, and other architectural details.

Leased Premises Versus Owned Property

There is a difference in selecting equipment for a client who has a five-year lease and one who owns his property and is planning to be there for many years. The operator with the short-term lease will not make as great an investment in expensive equipment. Furthermore, if he decides to relocate his business later on, it will probably cost more to disconnect and remove the equipment than it is worth. On a long-term lease or under an ownership option, the equipment should be of a higher quality, since its expected operating life will be a lot longer.

The luncheon club was planned for leased premises, but it was expected that it would have a long life. The sponsors of the club were the building owner, who wanted a prestigious club to add to the luxury image of his building, and a long-term corporate lessee of a large part of the building. Therefore, the equipment chosen was of high quality.

Local Union Regulations

Union regulations can affect the design requirement of an operation. For example, some unions have contracted that all kitchen help be given their meals and that they have their own dining room and lounge. If this is a common practice in the area, then space must be provided for a cooks' dining room in a new plan.

Another common contract clause is a requirement that existing work stations must be staffed during meal periods. For example, if there is a kitchen service bar, some contracts require that it be staffed with a bartender even though service could be obtained from the main bar. Therefore, it is important that the designer not create built-in staffing requirements.

In the case of the luncheon club, the only requirements of the union local that affected the layout were that all employees be provided with their uniforms and meals. Provision had to be made for employee locker rooms for uniform storage, and for employee dining.

Disposal of Garbage and Refuse

The refuse room should be located so that trash and garbage can be removed without the refuse collector entering the premises. For security reasons, trash removal areas should be located away from employee entrances and exits whenever possible.

Refuse collection has become a very expensive item, especially in the cities. Since the cost of cartage is usually calculated on the cubic volume of waste, the designer should consider the following methods of reducing the volume of the waste that is generated:

- Garbage grinders or disposers (where local codes permit)
- Compactors, which vary from can size to trailer size
- Pulper systems such as Somat or Hobart. These reduce cubic volumes by as much as 10:1, but may require a significant investment.
- Incinerators (where codes permit)
- Can crushers
- Bottle crushers (a requirement in some states)

In some localities, the board of health may require a garbage refrigerator and/or can washer and can racks built to certain specifications. The luncheon club was provided with a garbage refrigerator in the basement of the building near the shipping department, as well as a refuse room with can-washing facilities. Garbage disposers were prohibited in the city in which the club was located.

Cost Factors

After a preliminary layout is made, a budget should be drawn up so that the client has an idea of the equipment costs.

All labor-saving devices that can justify their cost should be included, but the quality of the equipment should be uniform, that is, all of comparable life span and durability. The designer should not specify cheap hoods and expensive refrigerators. The level of quality and the number of "frills" will depend on the type of ownership as previously defined.

For the luncheon club, the sponsors specified that all equipment and furnishings were to be of the highest quality.

Allocated Space

It is always hoped that a generous amount of space will be allocated to the food operation, but that rarely happens. One may end up with cut-up, irregular walls and spaces full of columns, pipe chases, and ducts. Space is very expensive and the choice portions, of course, go to the dining rooms and public spaces that produce revenue. Kitchens, toilets, and so on do not share the same priority. If a pipe chase or duct must come through the space, you can be sure it will come through the kitchen. This is where time and effort pay off—with careful designing and choice of equipment, obstacles are overcome and a functional operation is developed.

In the case of the luncheon club, the spaces shown in Fig. 7-4 was allocated for all the back-of-the-house spaces, including storage, locker rooms and employee facilities, offices, dishwashing, preparation and a full *à la carte* kitchen, including a small pastry shop and butcher shop. The total space available amounted to 2,800 square feet.

One problem was evident immediately: All deliveries coming in and all refuse going out had to be taken across the public corridor to the service elevator. This was a situation that had to be lived with, however, since there was no other way to handle it. Prior to the club's opening, arrangements were made for morning deliveries.

The Designing Process

The designing process was started by listing all the departments that had to be included in the plan and then arranging them in a schematic diagram (Fig. 7-5). This diagram showed the traffic flows related to each department, and it also showed those departments that did not have to be directly related to the flows.

Next, the proportion of space to be assigned to each department was determined. Since there was a very limited amount of space to work with, the minimum amount of space possible for each department had to be calculated. It was very obvious that it would be impossible to fit everything into the available space. The client was able to find an additional 750 square feet of space in the cellar for liquor, china, glass, and utensil storage, a general storeroom, and waste holding space with a garbage refrigerator in the building receiving area. On the floor above, which was a mechanical floor, 650 square feet of space was also obtained. This space was assigned to employee locker rooms, silver storage, a small linen and uniform

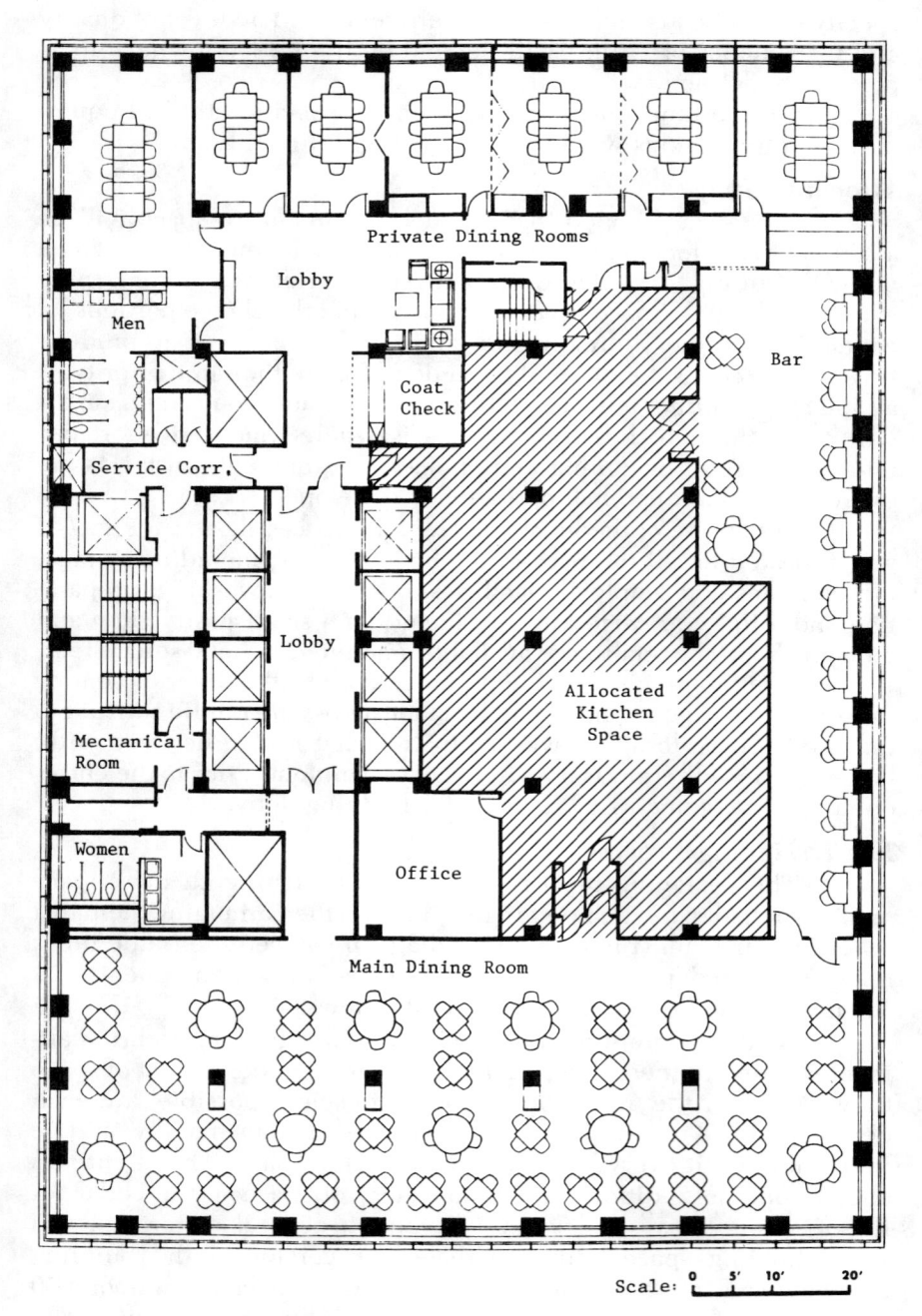

Fig. 7-4. Private luncheon club: Allocated kitchen space.

Kitchen and Cafeteria Design 143

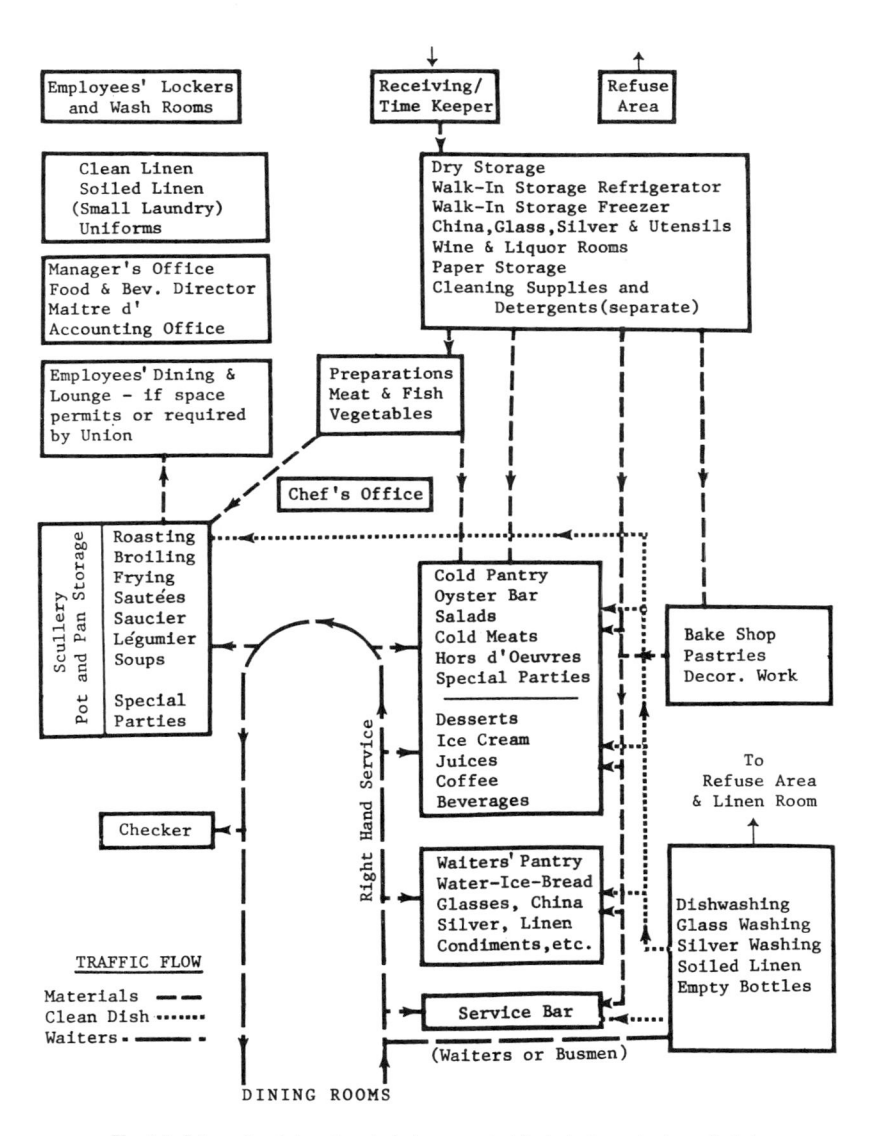

Fig. 7-5. Schematic of departments to be accounted for in laying out a large first-class *à la carte* club kitchen.

room, and mechanical refrigeration. The schematic plan was adjusted accordingly (Fig. 7–6).

With the general scheme determined, the layout for each station was started (Fig. 7–7). For the cooking battery, the menu that was planned was evaluated and the volumes required were computed.

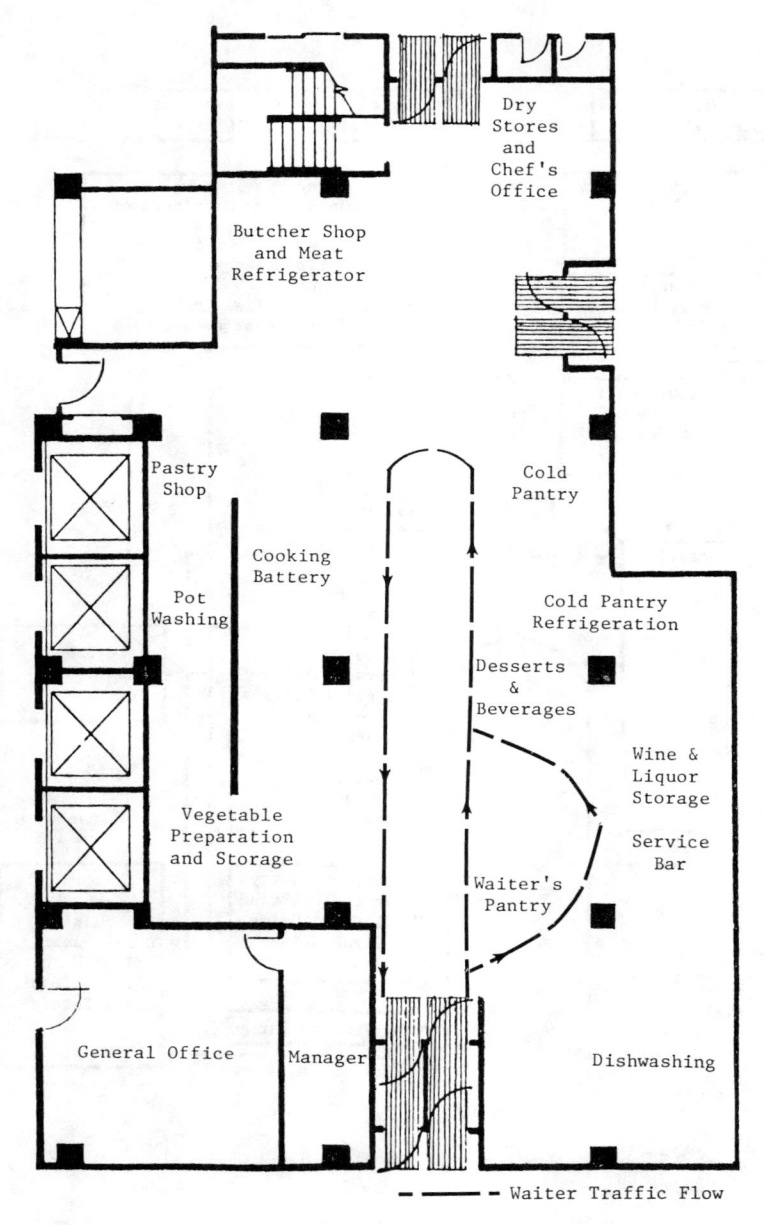

Fig. 7-6. General schematic of the luncheon club kitchen.

Kitchen and Cafeteria Design 145

Most of the items on an *à la carte* menu require top-of-the-range cooking or broiling. Of course, ovens for roasts, kettles for stock and *soupe du jour*, plus steamers for vegetables were added. A heavy use of fresh vegetables was planned; thus a preparation station was needed. The vegetable preparation station would preferably be located near the pot sink, since the pot washer often doubles as a prep person. The chef did not want a deep fat fryer, because he planned to use a *sauteuse* on the top of the stove, but a space was provided for a fryer if it were needed in the future. A small token pastry shop to be manned by one of the cooks on a part-time basis was included in the program and combined with the main cooking battery in order to keep it under the main exhaust hood. Undercounter refrigerators were put in the pastry shop and at the broiler station to provide work space on the top. A small butcher shop was provided next to the meat refrigerator.

The chef's office was combined with a small dry storeroom. The cold station was provided with a small oyster bar. A walk-in refrigerator was placed behind the oyster bar and combined with refrigeration for the service bar. Since most of the dessert pastries were to be served from a cart in the dining room, the dessert station requirements were very limited and were combined with the coffee station.

Considerable storage was provided for wines in conjunction with the service bar because the caliber of the club required a high-quality wine list.

The dish machine was sized to accommodate a large number of pieces per person and to move the ware through quickly. Since space was extremely limited, dishes could not be allowed to accumulate but had to be washed quickly and put back into service. Special glass racks were required to accommodate very tall stemware.

No space was available for employee dining facilities. The waiters' counters (items 63 and 64 in Fig. 7–7) were specially designed to permit the kitchen staff to use them for dining tables. The plan was to have the entire kitchen crew eat their meal at 11:00 A.M. The waiters, all part-time employees, were given a meal allowance that they could use in the sponsoring tenant's employee cafeteria.

This case study shows the results of careful analysis of the requirements of an operation and of selective trade-offs to obtain the most efficient layout possible in the available space. The luncheon club operation's overall plan maximizes the use of income-producing space for dining, and the kitchen design provides for a highly efficient operation in a small space. Each work station is compact, yet fully equipped for the items it must produce.

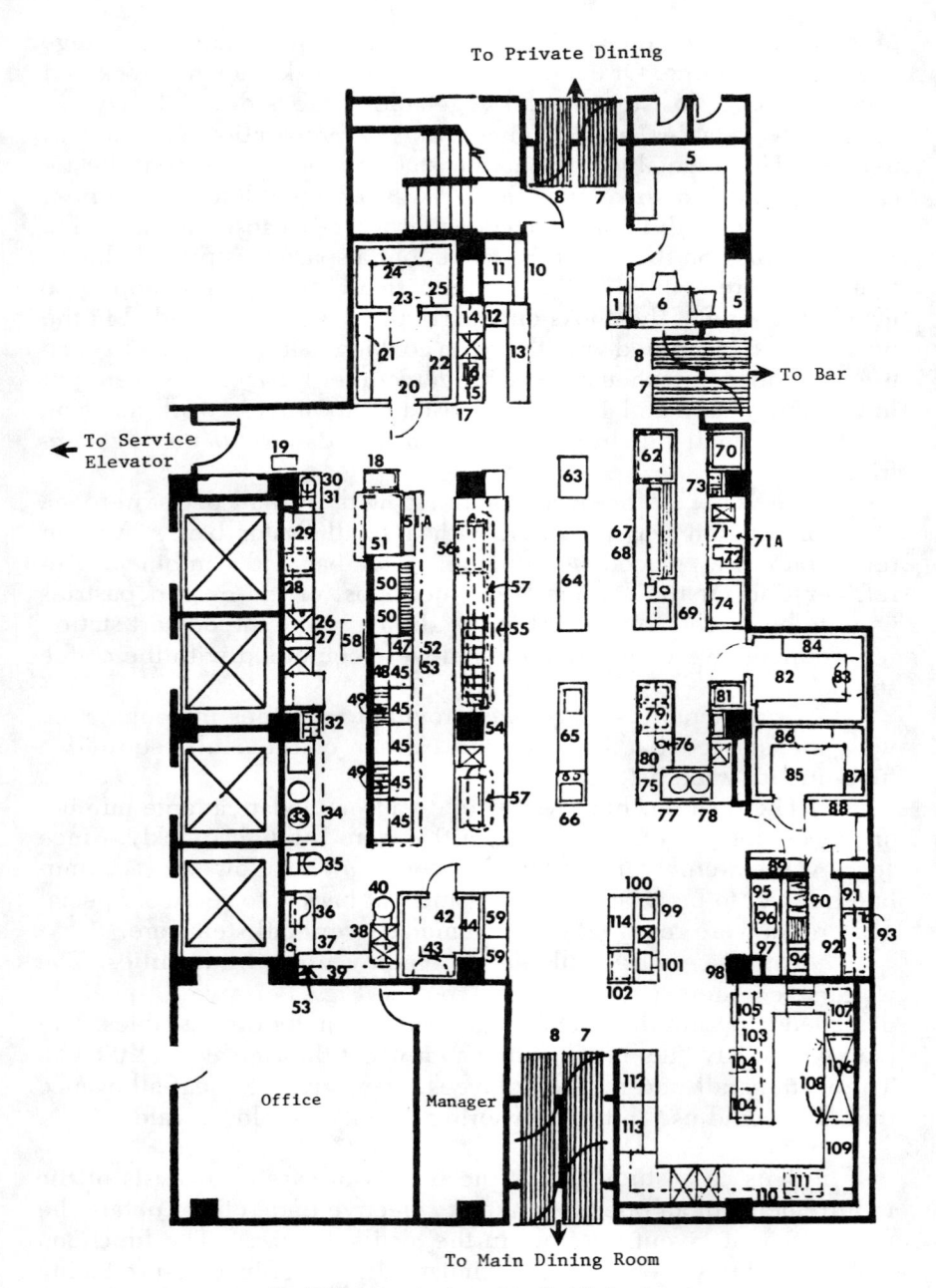

Fig. 7-7A. Private luncheon club: Final kitchen layout.

Kitchen and Cafeteria Design

EQUIPMENT SCHEDULE

Item #	Amount	Description	Item #	Amount	Description
1	1	Scale	62	1	Pass-through Overhead Refr.
5	1	Storeroom Shelving	63	1	Tray Rest and Dining Table
6	1	Office Furniture	64	1	Tray Rest and Dining Table
7	8	Door Operators	65	1	Tray Rest and Cold Pan
8	3 sets	Railings	66	1	Cup Disp. - Mobile
10	1	Ice Storage Bin	67	1	Cold Ctr., Ice Bins, Storage, Service Shelf
11	1	Flake Ice Maker			
12	1	Butcher Block	68	1	Overshelf
13	1	Worktable (Mobile)	69	1	Oyster Bar
14	1	Sink and Drainboard	70	1	Reach-in Refrigerator, Mobile
15	1	Table (Mobile)	71	1	Back Counter with Sink
16	1	Meat Chopper	71-A	2	Wall Shelves
17	2	Wall Shelves	72	1	Slicer
18	1	Pan Rack - Mobile	73	2	Toasters
19	1	Proof Cabinet - Mobile	74	1	Reach-in Refrig. - Mobile
20	1	Walk-in Refrigerator	75	1	Counter with Urn Stand
21	1	Mech. Refrig. for #20	76	1	Dipper Well
22	1 lot	Mobile Shelving	77	1	Coffee Urn
23	1	Walk-in Freezer	78	1	Exhaust Hood
24	1	Mech. Refrig. for #23	79	1	Ice Cream Cabinet
25	1 lot	Shelving for #23 (Mobile)	80	1	Service Shelf and Shield
26	1	Pot Sink and Drainboards	81	1	Reach-in Refrig. - Mobile
27	1	Electric Water Heater	82	1	Walk-in Refrigerator
28	2	Wall Shelves and Spice Bins	83	1	Mech. Refrigeration for #82
29	1	Baker's Table, Under-Counter Refrigerator	84	1 lot	Shelving for #82 - Mobile
			85	1	Walk-in Refrigerator
30	1	Mixer Stand - Mobile	86	1	Mech. Refrigeration for #85
31	1	Mixer - 20 qt.	87	1 lot	Shelving for #85 - Mobile
32	1	2-Burner Baker's Stove	88	1 lot	Storeroom Shelving
33	1	Kettle-Steamer Combination	89	1	Wine Rack
34	1	Exhaust Hood	90	3	Sinks
35	1	Mixer - 60 qt.	91	1	Back Counter
36	1	Food Chopper	92	1	Undercounter Refrigerator
37	1	Worktable	93	1	Wall Cabinet
38	1	Veg. Sink and Drainboard	94	1	Workboard and Cocktail Sta.
39	6	Wall Shelves	95	1	Service Bar Top
40	1	Vegetable Peeler	96	1	Counter and Ice Bin
42	1	Walk-in Refrigerator	97	1	Shutter
43	1	Mech. Refrig. for #42	98	1	Cleaning Station and Hose
44	1 lot	Shelving for #42 (Mobile)	99	1	Ctr. with Sink, Ice Bin
45	5	Ranges and Ovens	100		Overshelves
47	1	Expando Unit	101	1	Electric Conveyor Toaster
48	1 lot	Double Deck Shelves	102	1	Refrigerator - Mobile
49	2	Salamander Broilers	103	1	Soiled Dishtable
50	2	Upright Broilers	104	2	Soak Sink, Chute and Faucet
51	1	Bake and Roast Oven	105	1	Soiled Linen Hamper
51-A	1	Shelving Unit	106	1	Dishwasher and Sanitizer
52	1	Exhaust Hood	107	1	Hot Water Booster
53	1	Fire Protection System	108	2	Vent Risers
54	1	Cook's Table, Bain Marie	109	1	Clean Dishtable
55	1	Shelf and Warmers	110	2	Wall Shelves
56	1	Undercounter Refrig.	111	1	Silver Burnisher - Mobile
57	2	Sauce Pan Racks	112	1	Ice Storage Bin
58	1	Clean Pot Rack (Mobile)	113	2	Ice Cube Makers
59	2	Shelving and Tray Storage	114	1	Shelving Unit - Mobile

Fig. 7-7B. Key to layout on opposite page.

8

PRICING THE PRODUCT

Price is one of four variables that must be considered by the marketing manager. The others are product, promotion, and place. (See Chap. 2 for a definition of the marketing mix.) The price selected for a product must meet the objectives of the firm. The small, growth-oriented company may be more concerned with increasing its sales volume, whereas an established operator is more interested in maintaining net profits from a stabilized sales volume.

These two points of view—net profits versus a sales orientation—represent two basic pricing approaches: pricing based on the market and pricing based on product cost.

Pricing Based on Cost

The traditional way to establish a menu price has been to apply a markup to the base cost of the item. The difficulty with using cost as a basis for pricing is caused by the difference between fixed and variable costs.

Fixed costs are not related to output. They remain the same regardless of the level of production. Therefore, as the number of units produced increases, the fixed cost per unit decreases. Examples of fixed costs include rent and interest.

Variable costs are completely related to output. If there is no output, there is no variable cost. As output increases, variable cost increases proportionately. Examples of variable costs are materials and production labor cost. Some other costs, such as heating, service and clerical payroll, repairs, and administrative expenses, are semivariable or almost fixed and difficult to adjust quickly when sales volume changes. Advertising and promotional expenditures may have to be increased with declines in sales volumes.

Total cost per unit, then, is a combination of variable cost, semivariable cost, and fixed cost per unit of production and sale. How then does one determine a cost on which to base a selling price? One answer is to use average costs, and this method works well when output is relatively stable. If production can be maintained at an even pace, variations in unit costs are relatively small. The concept of average costs is not widely used in the restaurant industry, mainly because production levels are rarely stable.

Marginal cost is a concept that is occasionally used in pricing special promotions to stimulate sales when a business is operating at less-than-capacity levels. Marginal cost is defined as the change in total cost that results from producing one extra unit. Because, by definition, fixed costs do not vary with changes in production, marginal cost consists solely of variable costs. In a restaurant, the marginal cost to serve one more meal would include the cost of the food and the cost of the linen and supplies directly related to the service of that meal. As long as the marginal cost per unit is less than the marginal or added revenue obtained in the sale of the extra output, the operation will be improving its profitability.

Marginal cost and revenue analysis may be used to justify a reduced or promotional price if the normal recurring business is made to bear the burden of the fixed costs or overhead. This pricing philosophy is usually applicable only in short-term situations such as promotions to generate new sales that will not compete with the existing base of business.

Pricing Based on Market

The relationship of price and value is an important aspect of pricing, and value extends beyond just the cost of materials or the quality of the food served. The quality of the whole dining experience must be considered—the decor, style of service, ambiance, and merchandising.

Value is important whether the customer has only a few or many dollars to spend. It is a highly subjective judgment, however, and very difficult to assess. One method is to check which of the competitive operations are doing well because presumably their clientele believe these operations are giving good value.

In restaurants, a competitor's price structure can easily be determined from his menu. The problem arises in determining what the customer conceives the total product to be. The value placed on decor, sophistication of service, and the selection and quality of the food may be determined in a very subjective way by the customer.

New restaurant operators sometimes think they can obtain the same high prices as a successful competitor, without understanding all that the competitor gives the customer or what values the customer may be placing on the various aspects of the operation. Those unstated aspects may include personal recognition of the guest by the staff and memories of special meals enjoyed there in the past, as well as good food and service and an attractive decor.

Large marketers occasionally make consumer surveys in order to obtain objective data on customers' attitudes toward prices and perceived value. These surveys are sometimes done on a continuing basis in order to measure changes and trends. Unfortunately, the cost of this technique is usually beyond the reach of individual restaurant operators.

Market-oriented pricing may be equated with a what-the-market-will-bear policy. This term has a negative connotation of exploitation, but the philosophy is not unsound in a free, competitive market place. An operator who can find a market willing to pay a higher price for his particular product deserves the profits, for unless he is giving a better value at that price than his competitors, he will not retain that market.

The Nature of Demand

Numerous theories and concepts have been developed about consumers' behavior in the market place, some of which are particularly relevant to a discussion of pricing in restaurants. One is the concept of elasticity of demand.

Elasticity of Demand

Elasticity of demand is the sensitivity of sales volume to price changes. It reflects in part the strength of the customer's need for the product and the availability and ability of any other products to satisfy that need. A product or service may be said to have an elastic demand if a small decrease in the price will bring about a large increase in sales, or if a small increase in the price will result in a decrease in sales. For a product with an inelastic demand, a price reduction will not generate a large enough increase in the number of units sold to maintain the sales volume, and a price increase will not reduce the number of units sold. A product may have an inelastic demand within a certain price range and an elastic demand beyond that range.

Restaurant meals are an excellent example of a product with an elastic demand because most restaurant spending is discretionary, that is, the consumer has the choice of whether to spend or not. If the consumer does not feel that he will receive sufficient value at the prices charged, he always has the alternative of eating at home and using his available funds in some other way that will give him greater satisfaction. For this reason, an increase in menu prices can often result in reduced instead of increased sales.

Competition

The availability of alternatives was mentioned as affecting demand. For the individual firm, alternatives include competition. Some marketing experts consider competition to be as important as product cost and market demand in determining selling prices. In most locations, the restaurant business is highly competitive. Competition exists from both similar and dissimilar types of operation. For the luxury restaurant, competition comes not only from other luxury restaurants but also from private clubs. For business and personal entertaining, there is the additional alternative of entertaining at home. The choice of restaurants is wide, from inexpensive oriental to luxury, classic French. During a recession period, patrons of luxury restaurants may "trade down" to more moderately priced restaurants, whereas patrons of the moderately priced restaurants may switch to coffee shops and drive-ins for family meals.

In situations in which competition is very limited, some regulation may be imposed externally to protect the public. For example, operations serving such captive populations as toll-road travelers are usually controlled in their pricing to some extent by the operating government authority. In privately operated situations, management may exercise restraint in pricing as a general policy in order to present an overall market image. An example is a large amusement park.

Raising Prices

When management is faced with increased costs for merchandise, labor, and other expenses, the first reaction often is to raise prices. That may be the most convenient action to take, but it may or may not produce the desired effect. If the demand for the restaurant's products is elastic, higher prices may lead to declining sales, with even greater loss of profitability than if prices had been left unchanged. The number of covers served will start to decline as the customer looks for another restaurant that offers better value for his money. Meanwhile, the operating and fixed expenses remain at the same level, and the operation is started on a downward spiral.

Rising costs will ultimately require a price increase, but this approach should be taken with care, not as an initial reaction. The state of the economy must be considered to gauge the public's reactions to increases. It may be better strategy to cut costs by stringent control methods. Staffing levels should be reviewed. Food cost control procedures should be checked. Recipes and purchase specifications should be reviewed to see if less expensive ingredients can be substituted for the ones being used without lowering quality.

Portion sizes can be reduced if there is evidence that they are unnecessarily large. This can be determined by checking what food is left on the plates coming to the dish machine. All operating expenses should be analyzed for possible cost reductions.

The menu itself should be carefully studied. It may be possible to improve profitability by removing some high-cost or labor-heavy items. The number of listings may also be reduced, or the total format changed. An analysis of sales may reveal areas in which menu changes can be made to increase sales. Average checks in different time periods should be reviewed, as well as the range of sales per patron. A change in the pricing structure may produce an increase in the average check. A change of layout or other type of internal promotion may alter the sales mix by increasing sales of low-cost items. External promotion of low-cost specials, as previously discussed, may bring an increase in sales volume as new markets are tapped. It is important, however, that the existing base of business is not lost, because it is from this business that base costs are recovered.

If prices must be raised, it may be possible to do so without loss of customers. If portion sizes are reduced, prices may be reduced by a smaller proportion, so that the resulting cost ratio is improved. Combination prices may be altered in the same way to increase profitability. When the purchase price of an item has wide fluctuations, such as may be the case with lobsters, some restaurateurs do not establish a set menu price for that item but instead determine a daily or weekly price that is posted in the restaurant or communicated verbally by the server. Altering the product to reduce its cost for the purpose of maintaining the existing selling price is called *demand-backward* pricing.

Menu Pricing Techniques

Markup on Cost

The available literature on menu pricing mostly discusses the concept of markup on cost. *Cost* is generally defined as including the costs of all food and beverage components of the item being priced. Other cost bases are occasionally used, however. Fast-food take-out operations often include the cost of paper supplies in their cost base. Sometimes only the cost of the major ingredient is used. Another approach is the use of *prime cost,* which includes all food and beverage materials plus direct labor.

The concept of prime cost is taken from manufacturing cost accounting. It was introduced in the food service industry some years ago but until recently has had little application. Because of variations in the level of output, the determination of labor cost on a per-unit or per-portion basis can be difficult.

With the increasing use of convenience foods, the concept of prime cost is receiving much more attention now than when it was first introduced in the food service field. In menus using a combination of convenience items and items prepared entirely on the premises, a materials-only cost basis is not satisfactory because widely varying amounts of labor are included in the costs of the convenience items. The use of a prime cost for each item is required if the selling prices are to be determined on a uniform basis.

Determining the Markup. The markup is determined by taking the reciprocal of the desired food cost ratio. If the desired food cost ratio to sales is 40 percent, a markup of two and a half times the materials cost is required.

Once the cost of all the menu items has been determined, the markup factor can be applied to obtain the selling prices. Whatever factor is applied will largely determine the resulting food cost ratio. Theoretically, a three times markup on every item should produce a 33.3 percent food cost, but in practice production waste and unpriced items such as condiments will result in a higher cost ratio. One or two percentage points should be allowed for this. The problem with this method is that high-cost items are priced too high to sell, whereas low-cost items are underpriced and do not contribute enough to either the semivariable or fixed cost. The formula does not consider the value of the item or the competitive situation for the particular restaurant. A relatively low-cost item, prepared in an unusual, appealing manner and served graciously in a pleasant atmosphere, can command a high price in relation to the offerings of competitive restaurants. Similarly, a high-cost item may not yield the desired gross profit if the resulting price puts it out of the range of most customers' pocketbooks.

Therefore, prices determined only on the basis of a markup on cost must be adjusted up or down on the basis of the market demand and competition. Any pricing formula is only a guide, and the limitations of such formulas should be fully understood.

Base Cost Method

Using the markup method, prices are determined primarily on the basis of cost ratios. It is axiomatic, however, that percentages don't pay bills. What is missing is consideration of the total dollars. A $6.00 sale with a 40 percent food cost will produce more gross profit to meet the payroll and the overhead expenses than a $3.00 check with a 35 percent food cost—$1.65 more to be exact.

The base cost method takes into consideration not only the food cost but all costs of the operation, including the desired profit. It uses the concept of average cost, charging each customer with an equal

	Cost of Dinner	Markup	Selling Price	Cost Ratio	Gross Profit
Chicken (Half)	$1.00	3	$ 3.00	33.3%	$2.00
Steak (16 oz. Strip)	4.50	3	13.50	33.3	9.00
Roast Beef (10 oz. Rib)	2.35	3	7.05	33.3	4.70

Fig. 8-1. Markup on materials.

portion of all nonmaterials costs. A base cost per meal is determined by dividing the total cost of the operation including profit, but without materials, by the total number of meals served. These figures are preferably taken from carefully prepared budgets for the future, rather than from historical data that may be out of date.

To the base cost per meal is added the materials cost of the menu item being priced. This produces a menu price that still must be evaluated in terms of market acceptability. Under a base cost price structure, each meal sold contributes equally to labor and overhead costs and profits, while carrying its assigned cost of materials. Food cost ratios of each item will vary, as will the overall food cost ratio, depending on the sales mix.

A Simple Illustration

To illustrate the application and effects of these two pricing methods, assume a very simple menu consisting of chicken, steak, and roast beef. Figure 8–1 shows the pricing of these three items, using a markup of three times to produce an overall food cost of about 33 percent and a gross profit of 67 percent. Gross profit varies from $2.00 to $9.00 per cover.

In Fig. 8–2, a base cost has been determined, and a budget of $391 has been projected, including desired profit, but excluding food cost for each 100 covers to be served. Base cost is therefore $3.91 per cover.

One other factor that has not yet been considered can have a substantial effect on food cost and gross profit. That is the sales mix. Not every item will sell equally well. Under the standard markup method, the gross profit can vary substantially, depending on the sales mix. Under the base cost method, the food cost ratio can vary substantially, but the amount of gross profit will remain the same, regardless of the sales mix, as long as the total number of meals served remains the same. This is shown in Fig. 8–3. Under the base cost method, the amount of gross profit does not vary, but the food cost ratio changes from 39.7 to 44.3 percent when the sales mix shifts toward increased steak sales. Under the markup method, the food cost

	Cost of Dinner	+	Base Cost	=	Selling Price*	Cost Ratio	Gross Profit
Chicken (Half)	$1.00		$3.91		$4.91	20.4%	$3.91
Steak (16 oz. Strip)	4.50		3.91		8.41	53.5	3.91
Roast Beef (10 oz. Rib)	2.35		3.91		6.26	37.5	3.91

* before rounding.

Fig. 8-2. Markup on base cost.

ratio remains the same, but the gross profit increases from $523 to $631 with an increase in the proportion of steak sales.

The point that must be raised is whether it would be reasonable to expect to sell that proportion of steaks at that price. When the customers compare the price and value of the chicken dinner with that of the steak dinner, they may very well choose the chicken. Figure 8–3 shows the effect on the food cost ratio and gross profit of a shift to chicken sales. The intention of the menu price structure is not achieved.

Types of Menu Price Structure

Another factor affecting the total sales and gross profit is the number of courses ordered by the patron. This can be influenced by the type of pricing structure used. The number of extra items the customer orders can increase the gross profits and, depending on the pricing structure, can also affect the food cost ratio. Many operators regard such items as appetizers and desserts as extra sales and apply a marginal cost philosophy in pricing them. This practice ultimately produces a lower selling price for these items, which may increase both total sales volume and the food cost percentage.

There are two basic types of menus, *à la carte* and *table d'hôte*. Several variations of these types include the *prix fixe* and the package plan.

À la Carte

In the *à la carte* menu, every item is priced separately, including vegetables, beverage, and sometimes rolls and butter, in a cover charge. This kind of menu is usually featured in the more expensive clubs and restaurants that offer a wide selection. It is also found in a traditional cafeteria operation.

Table d'Hôte

A complete meal, including appetizer or soup (or both), entrée, dessert, and beverage, is offered at an all-inclusive price in the

	Number Sold	Total Cost(*)	Selling Price	Total Sales
Chicken	33	$ 33.00	$ 5.00	$165.00
Steak	33	148.50	8.50	280.50
Roast Beef	34	79.90	6.25	212.50
	100	$261.40		$658.00
	Food Cost Ratio = 39.7%		Gross Profit =	$396.60
Chicken	20	$ 20.00	$ 5.00	$100.00
Steak	50	225.00	8.50	425.00
Roast Beef	30	70.50	6.25	187.50
	100	$315.50		$712.50
	Food Cost Ratio = 44.3%		Gross Profit =	$397.00
Chicken	33	$ 33.00	$ 3.00	$ 99.00
Steak	33	148.50	13.50	445.50
Roast Beef	34	79.90	7.05	239.70
	100	$261.40		$784.20
	Food Cost Ratio = 33.3%		Gross Profit =	$522.80
Chicken	20	$ 20.00	$ 3.00	$ 60.00
Steak	50	225.00	13.50	675.00
Roast Beef	30	70.50	7.05	211.50
	100	$315.50		$946.50
	Food Cost Ratio = 33.3%		Gross Profit =	$631.00
Chicken	60	$ 60.00	$ 3.00	$180.00
Steak	10	45.00	13.50	135.00
Roast Beef	30	70.50	7.05	211.50
	100	$175.50		$526.50
	Food Cost Ratio = 33.3%		Gross Profit =	$351.00

*Based on costs per meal as shown in Figs. 8.1 and 8.2.

Fig. 8-3. Food cost ratios and gross profit with various price structures and sales mixes.

table d'hôte menu. Different entrées may carry different *table d'hôte* prices. A *table d'hôte* presentation also simplifies and speeds the ordering process, an important consideration in a fast-turnover operation. The club or *table d'hôte* breakfast is particularly important for fast breakfast service.

Prix Fixe (Fixed Price)

The fixed price menu, developed from the *table d'hôte* concept, allows the diner to select a complete meal from a variety of offerings, all at the same price. The entrée selections are usually limited to between five and ten. The advantage is that the guest knows exactly what his meal will cost. A disadvantage is that the menu rarely offers seven or eight items equal in popularity or cost. Thus there is a tendency for only a few of the items to sell well. Very careful sales and cost analysis is required to merchandise this type of menu successfully for any length of time. Some restaurants with a reputation for being expensive have found the fixed price menu to be a valuable device to broaden their market and increase patronage.

Package Plan

Following the lead of the airlines and resort hotels, some restaurateurs have successfully merchandised a package plan menu concept. This approach, a variation of the fixed price theme, usually combines a selection from a limited menu with one or more bonus features, such as "all the beer (or cocktails) you can drink," "all the salad you can eat," and so on. Depending on the price, the bonus features may also include entertainment. In some states, however, alcoholic beverages cannot be merchandised in that way, and special package prices must show a separate price for such beverages.

Variations and Combinations

Most restaurants feature variations or combinations of the *à la carte* and *table d'hôte* menus designed to appeal to their particular markets. Combination prices can be developed for a number of meal patterns. Some typical patterns are shown in Fig. 8–4. One very common pricing combination is to price the entrée to include vegetables, roll and butter, and sometimes salad, while pricing appetizers, soups, desserts, and beverages separately. Some restaurants, particularly *haute cuisine* operations, serve a larger portion for *à la carte* orders than for *table d'hôte* because of price differences. When a restaurant has such a policy, both the kitchen and dining room staffs must be trained to serve the proper portion size.

Whatever menu pattern is chosen, it should produce a selling price that is suited to the market and an average check that is suited to the economic structure of the restaurant.

Determining Table d'Hôte and Combination Prices

There are two ways to determine *table d'hôte* and combination prices: (1) using the item selling price as a basis, and (2) using cost as a basis. When item prices are shown on the menu both individually and in combination, it is best to use the selling price method because the customers may make comparisons on this basis.

Using the selling price method, the prices of each course are added and a predetermined amount is deducted to encourage the guest to order the combination or the full meal. Another approach is to use a "marginal cost" analysis, that is, determining how much more it would cost to serve a dessert or soup to a guest who is already in the restaurant. If the overhead costs are assumed to be borne by the entrée price, then the cost to sell additional courses consists primarily of the

A la Carte →					Table d'Hôte
DINNER					
Entree with garnishes only	Entree Two vegetables	Entree Two vegetables Salad	Entree Two vegetables Salad	Appetizer Entree Two vegetables Salad	Appetizer Soup Entree Two vegetables Salad
Roll and butter may be included	Roll and butter	Roll and butter	Roll and butter Dessert Beverage	Roll and butter Dessert Beverage	Roll and butter Dessert Beverage
LUNCHEON					
Entree only	Thick soup Roll and butter Salad	Entree Roll and butter Dessert Beverage	Entree Two vegetables Salad	Entree Vegetable Salad Roll and butter Dessert Beverage	Soup or appetizer Two vegetables Salad Roll and butter Dessert Beverage
			Soup Sandwich Beverage	Soup Entree Vegetable Roll and butter Beverage	
BREAKFAST					
Baked goods Beverage	Juice or fruit Baked goods Beverage	Juice or fruit Entree without meat Baked goods Beverage	Juice or fruit Entree with meat Baked goods Beverage	Juice or fruit Cereal Baked goods Beverage	Juice or fruit Cereal Entree without meat Baked goods Beverage
					Juice or fruit Cereal Entree with meat Baked goods Beverage

Fig. 8-4. Typical meal patterns.

material required to produce those items. Using the base-cost approach, the costs of the additional courses are simply added to the entrée selling price to arrive at a *table d'hôte* price. If the markup method is used, the markup is applied to the sum of the costs in the combination.

When a choice is permitted, as with appetizers or desserts, and there is a wide range of costs among the items, the high-cost items may be excluded from the combination price meals, or a premium may be placed on them, such as an *à la carte* shrimp cocktail for $1.50 and a charge of $1.00 extra for it on the complete dinner. When the cost range of a menu category is fairly narrow, a figure in the middle or upper third of the range should be used, depending on the sales mix. Items that are difficult to prepare in quantity may also have premium prices, not so much to recoup cost as to limit sales. An example of such an item is crepes suzettes. Premiums may also be placed on items with high labor costs.

Establishing Prices for Beverages

Bar pricing is usually not as complex as food pricing, and drink prices are frequently determined by the competition where there are similar types of operations. When prices must be established, the markup method is usually used. Calculating the cost of individual alcoholic drinks is a relatively simple matter. After drink sizes are established, the cost per bottle of liquor is divided by the number of drinks of the established size that the bottle will yield. When applicable, the cost of mineral waters is added.

The markup rate on the cost of beverages in operations other than those in resort areas generally ranges from three to five times cost, depending on the type of operation. In resort or night club operations, the markup rate may be much higher. Alcoholic beverages sold by the bottle are usually priced at a markup of two to two and a half times cost. Wines may be priced at a lower markup to promote sales that might otherwise be lost completely.

A study of the competitors' prices will indicate the price range acceptable to the market, but the other factors mentioned previously (value, ambiance, etc.) must be considered. Value in beverage prices, and particularly in wine prices, deserves special consideration. Some restaurants with extensive wine cellars have traditionally priced their wines solely on the basis of cost, but in times of rapidly rising wine prices cost is not necessarily the best base. An example of this is a luxury hotel that priced a 1964 Haut-Brion (A *premier cru* red Bordeaux) at $16.00 a bottle when the same wine was selling in liquor stores for over $20.00.

Special Pricing Considerations

Pricing to Discourage Sales

There are some occasions when a price may be established to discourage certain sales. One example has already been mentioned—the premium price on labor-heavy items in combination prices. Another example is the minimum charge. A coffee shop with a busy luncheon business may establish a minimum during the lunch hour to discourage patrons from taking up a seat for just a cup of coffee. Minimums may also be charged for certain seats, such as booths, where people tend to sit longer and reduce turnover. Such a minimum may be equal to the lowest priced entrée on the menu. Cocktail lounges with entertainment frequently establish minimums to discourage beer or soft drink orders and to generate sufficient revenue to pay for the entertainment.

Some restaurant menus are priced very high overall, not so much for the purpose of discouraging sales as for the purpose of limiting the clientele to those who are able to pay the price and thus to establish an image of exclusiveness. Such establishments must still offer value for the money in service, decor, and personalized attention to the guest.

The Loss Leader

Loss leaders are a retailing technique in which one or more items are offered at a very low price in order to attract patrons into the store. It is hoped that once the patrons are there, they will buy a number of other items at full price to enable the store to recoup the loss on the leader. Loss leaders usually do not work very well in restaurants because the patron does not buy enough additional items to recoup the profit lost on the "leader." Some instances in which loss leaders do work are the five-cent cup of coffee offered with the purchase of a full meal, or free or inexpensive food items offered in a bar to encourage liquor sales. Since liquor sales are, on a percentage basis, much more profitable than food, that kind of promotion is frequently quite justified.

Odd-Cent Pricing

Odd-cent pricing is also a retailing technique that is designed to make the patron think he is paying less than he really is. It is improbable that customers are fooled by it, but the practice remains. In food service, it may be used appropriately in price-conscious, highly competitive situations, but it is not in keeping with a better class restaurant or club in which prices are rounded to the nearest five cents. In some exclusive clubs, prices may even be rounded to the nearest 25 cents. The traditional odd cent used was the 9 cent, but some fast-food operators have been using other numbers such as the 7 cent or 3 cent, implying that costs are calculated very carefully and the patron is paying for a minimum of profit cushion.

Sales Tax Pricing

Sales taxes may influence pricing. If the operation has a high volume and fast turnover, the sales tax may be included in the selling price to speed transactions. If the sales can be in units of 25 cents or 50 cents, patrons frequently have exact change available. The principle is also applicable in high-volume bars and vending machines. Sales taxes paid are accounted for by applying a formula to the total sales. Since the guidelines vary in different states, local taxing authorities should be consulted when establishing tax-inclusive prices. Liquor authorities should also be consulted for bar pricing.

Another tax-related pricing situation arises when taxes on meals in restaurants are applied only on meals over $1.00. In those areas, offering a 99-cent meal is a good merchandising technique.

Resorts

A resort hotel may operate with several types of pricing arrangements for rooms and meals:

1. European plan (EP), in which the rate is for room only, and all meals are purchased separately.
2. American plan (AP), which includes all meals in the room rate.
3. Modified American plan (MAP), which includes breakfast and dinner in the room rate. It is the most prevalent practice in American resorts.
4. Continental plan or bed and breakfast (B&B) which includes breakfast in the price of the room. It is common in European hotels.

A resort hotel that offers several plans to house guests and attracts outside guests as well must consider all sources of dining room patronage when setting food prices. One approach is to offer an American plan dinner for a fixed price to outside or European plan guests. In effect, it is a *table d'hôte* pricing arrangement. Another approach is to permit American plan guests to order from a regular menu. High-cost items may be ordered but at a surcharge.

Subsidized Operations

Pricing policies for subsidized operations such as employee cafeterias are frequently determined by the subsidizer rather than by the food service management. Sales revenue may be expected to cover food cost only, food and labor costs, or food, labor, and operating expenses. When these goals are established, prices must be low enough to encourage participation but high enough to cover costs. In other situations, management alone or in conjunction with a union or representative group of the participants may set prices at a level at which the participants wish to pay, regardless of the economics of the operation. All costs not recovered by sales must then be subsidized.

Part Two

Managing the Business

9

MANAGEMENT

The food service business traditionally has been one of easy entry. No specialized training was required to go into the business, and one could open a restaurant with a minimum of investment capital. Managers had to learn their business on the job, often starting in a menial position at the bottom of the ladder, and the training they did receive was heavily oriented toward the technical aspects of cookery and table service rather than basic management skills. The few schools that offered training in the food service field were also technically oriented.

Thus food service managers in the past had little or no formal education in general management skills. They made their decisions intuitively, and they learned how to direct the work of others by trial and error. Their leadership styles were modeled on those of the managers under whom they had worked while learning their trade.

This "seat of the pants" approach to management is no longer adequate. Publicly held food service companies must compete with other industries for investment capital, and investors and lenders demand managerial competence that will ensure a good return on their capital investments and protect their loans. At the same time, the environment in which the food service company must operate is creating more and more demands on management. Consumer demands, shifting market patterns, growing union strength, shortages of supplies, rising costs, and increasing government control are creating complex demands on food service management. In fact, some observers of the food service industry feel that its greatest problem today is a lack of professional management.

The subject of this text and its companion volume is management or, to be more specific, the management of food service organizations. Although much of the knowledge required by food service managers is technical in nature, general management skill is also needed; the larger the organization and the higher one rises in it, the greater is the emphasis on general management skill and the lesser is the need for technical skills.

A Definition of Management

There are almost as many definitions of management as there are managers. Some common definitions are:

Management is getting work done through people.
Management is achieving results.
Management is directing or controlling activity.
Management is being in command.

A general definition of management usually contains the following elements:

1. The achievement of some definite objective or goal.
2. The use of resources in achieving that goal. These resources may be human, financial, capital such as plant and equipment, or intangible such as technical knowledge or general "know-how."
3. The active involvement by the manager in planning to achieve the goal and directing the use of the resources in implementing that plan.

A Brief History of Management Thought and Theory

In the 1880s, a philosophy of modern management began to develop to meet the needs of the large, complex industrial organizations that had begun to form during the latter part of the nineteenth century. Business history textbooks usually credit Frederick W. Taylor and his theory of scientific management as being the basis for much modern business philosophy.

Taylor (and others) held that work could be studied scientifically in controlled experimental situations. Conclusions could be reached through logical analysis of carefully collected data. Prior to this, managerial decision making had been based largely on general rules of thumb, intuitive reactions, or traditional patterns of response. The work of the Gilbreths in motion analysis, Henry L. Gantt in production scheduling, and others of this time are generally credited with giving birth to a discipline that is now called *industrial engineering*.

The scientific management approach included the establishment of a standard way to do a task, specialization of tasks, selection of workers best suited to perform specific tasks, and specialized training of the workers. The operator was viewed as an extension of the machine. Taylor held that by increasing the workers' productivity, higher wages could be achieved, thus satisfying the workers.

As a reaction to this idea of the human as an adjunct to the machine, the human relations approach to management began to develop in the 1920s and 1930s. Elton Mayo's studies in the Hawthorne plant of the Western Electric Company are usually cited as the pioneering work in this area, although initially they were not intended as such. The experiments were originally designed to determine the optimum lighting levels and other conditions for assembling telephone equipment. The workers, knowing they were subjects of the experiment and had the attention of top management, continued to increase their output even when undesirable working conditions were introduced experimentally. Researchers subsequently concluded that the *human* aspect of work had not been considered. Subsequent studies centered around the organization as a social system, and the dynamics of group behavior. The roles of motivation, status, role expectations, peer pressure, and styles of leadership were typical subjects for researchers in business.

During this period, a school of thought evolved that may be called "traditional" or "administrative" management. It attempted to define management in terms of functions, such as planning, organizing, implementing, controlling. Henri Fayol's model organization structure, which was arranged according to function (manufacturing, sales, finance, etc.), became the basic structure for the modern corporation. Alfred P. Sloan, Jr., added the concept of decentralization and internal competition when he planned a reorganization of General Motors around 1920.

In the 1960s and 1970s two additions have been made to the theory of management. These are the concept of management systems and operations research (also called management science, but not to be confused with the scientific management of Taylor). These concepts, along with the traditional approach, are described in the following sections.

The Traditional View of Management

Management is traditionally defined as a process involving certain functions, but there is no consensus as to what those functions include. They tend to fall into the general categories of planning, implementing, and controlling.

Planning

The establishment of goals or objectives is implied in planning. The goals or objectives of a business must be established by the ownership or top management; otherwise operations will drift haphazardly. Without goals, there are no guidelines by which to establish a course of action and no scale against which to measure accomplishment. Although the objectives of any business will vary according to the desires of ownership, the general or broad objectives certainly would include survival, growth, and profitability, and might also include community service or industry recognition.

The achievement of broad, long-range objectives requires the establishment of short-term, specific objectives such as profit goals, a desired rate of return on investment, attainment of a definite market position, stable employment and personal incentives, or achievement of environmental objectives.

Planning is the process of formulating a program for achieving these short- and long-term objectives. It is determining the means by which these goals are to be accomplished, including allocating resources such as manpower and capital, establishing time frames and priorities, and defining alternative methods. One commonly used planning tool is the budget or pro forma financial statement. Chapters 2, 3, 4, and 5 are all concerned with the planning aspect of management.

Implementation

Implementation involves putting the plan into action. One major aspect of implementation is organization. Organization structure and design are topics of great interest to business executives and researchers alike. Because of their importance in the functioning of the business, they will be discussed in greater detail later in this chapter.

Another aspect of implementation is policy formulation. Policies are general guidelines for the performance of a plan. They assist managers in dealing with matters that recur frequently. Policies provide a degree of predictability to executive decision making and reduce the possibility of a decision that may be in conflict with the overall organizational goals.

Directing is another function involved with implementation. Direction is usually defined as giving orders and instructions, supervising, motivating, and communicating. To give specific instructions and orders, the manager must be able to convert the general objectives of the overall plan into specific tasks and sequences of steps that must be carried out.

Control

In the control function, the manager evaluates the activity to determine whether the predetermined goals of the plan are being met; if not, he takes steps to correct the deviation. Evaluation may be made through observation, review of accounting records and reports, analysis of statistical data such as quality control checks, or signals of mechanical devices. Most of these techniques are reactive in nature in that they indicate a need to respond to some condition or event that has already occurred. More sophisticated control systems involve concurrent or preventive control to minimize or eliminate the possibility of undesirable occurrences. These systems include short-term planning for scheduling and forecasting, the training of workers, and special incentive programs for the employees.

The basis for most control systems, however, is the measurement of activity against some predetermined standard. This evaluation function is in turn related to the first function in the management process—planning and the establishment of goals and objectives for the organization. Realistic goal setting must be done in light of the organization's ability to perform.

Management Systems Theory

A system is defined as an orderly grouping of interdependent components that is intended to accomplish some purpose. A machine is a system, as is a physical organism. At its simplest level, a system involves some activity or process accompanied by an input and an output. A system may be an open system that is affected by the external environment or a closed system that is not responsive. The open system utilizes feedback to alter future response and output (Fig. 9–1).

The systems concept views the business organization as a system comprised of a number of subsystems. Because this concept stresses the interrelationship between these subsystems, it is particularly relevant to large, complex organizations with many fragmented, specialized departments and functions.

The connecting linkages between the subsystems of a business organization are information and communications flows. These flows are vital to management in performing the various functions of planning, implementing, and controlling. For this reason, there is a strong need to achieve maximum effectiveness in planning and controlling these flows. This is the task of the systems analyst.

Operations Research

Operations research (OR), sometimes referred to as management science, provides a quantitative approach to problem solving. It involves building mathematical models of an event or situation, using established scientific and statistical techniques. The large masses of data involved usually require a computer for the calculations.

One advantage of OR is that it requires the user carefully and objectively to identify and quantify goals or objectives and the

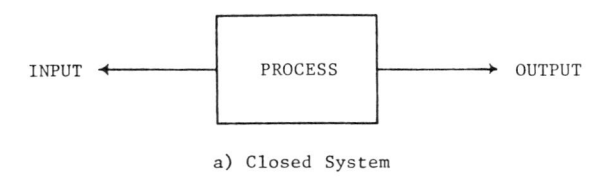

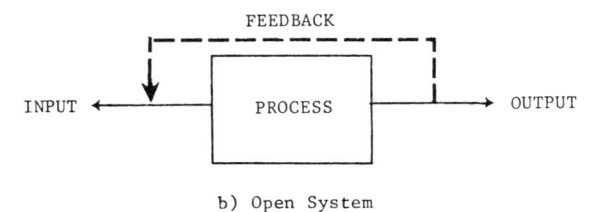

```
INPUT  ←————[ PROCESS ]————→  OUTPUT

         a) Closed System


                FEEDBACK
        ┌─ ─ ─ ─ ─ ─ ─ ─ ─┐
        ↓                 │
INPUT ←————[ PROCESS ]————→  OUTPUT

         b) Open System
```
Fig. 9-1. Open and closed systems.

controllable and noncontrollable variables in the problem. It also permits analysis in situations in which data are lacking or incomplete. This is done through application of statistical probabilities, and through simulation of the event using randomly chosen values. Other types of OR problems include scheduling and sequencing of production line activities, determining locations of plants and warehouses, Program Evaluation Review Technique (PERT), and critical path scheduling for coordinating large complex projects, econometric forecasting, inventory optimization, resource allocation, new investment decision analysis, and sampling for quality control.

Operations research is not intended as a total system of management because it can deal only with quantifiable data. It is one tool available to managers, who must use it in conjunction with their experience, knowledge, and intuition.

Mangement in the Food Service Industry

Although many managers have always applied the planning-implementation-controlling process, either consciously or intuitively, the application of scientific management principles to food service operations is quite new. Sophisticated, computerized operations research techniques, for example, are too costly for small firms. On the other hand, labor shortages and escalating wage rates, food costs, and energy costs provide a strong motivation to improve the level of management skills in the industry.

Organization

The need for organization arises from the fact that work must be divided into tasks that can be performed by individuals. The performance of these tasks must then be coordinated so that the desired objective, the completion of the work, is achieved.

An organization chart is a graphic description of a formal organization. It identifies the positions or departments, and it shows their relationships to one another and their places in the overall hierarchy of the organization. The positions are connected by lines showing authority and, sometimes, information flows.

Principles of Organization Design

How the various positions or departments are defined and the way their interrelationships are established can determine the effectiveness of the organization. Certain principles have been established to improve organizational effectiveness.

Specialization. It was discovered very early that by dividing tasks according to specialized functions, a group of workers can increase their output or productivity. Hence, specialization is a basic premise of organization design. One logical outcome of specialization is the assembly line. However, in recent years workers on highly automated assembly lines have begun to reject extremely specialized tasks as monotonous and tiring and to complain about the dehumanizing aspects of the work.

Authority. The most common definition of authority is the relationship between a superior and a subordinate. Authority involves the concept of power, such as the ability of the superior to command and require compliance by the subordinate. Implicit in this definition is the capacity to reward or punish. (Authority may also be defined as a right to make a decision or perform an act, such as the authority to sign a contract or to withdraw funds from the bank. In business organizations, both types of authority are found. However, in a discussion of organization characteristics, the first definition pertaining to interpersonal relationships is more relevant.)

In organizations authority is assumed to flow from the top down. That is, it is delegated by top-level managers to lower-level managers. In delegation the superior turns over to the subordinate certain aspects of his jurisdiction. The subordinate is given the right to make certain decisions and to act within certain limits without resorting to the superior.

Having authority does not guarantee that orders will be carried out. In fact, many scholars in the fields of management and organization behavior define the source of authority as the acceptance of a command by the subordinates. A general whose men do not obey has no command. In most business situations, however, authority is accepted as inherent in certain positions. Employees are culturally conditioned to accept direction from their supervisors and will reject or oppose direction from someone without the proper authority. Authority may also be based on demonstrated competence by the superior and, in a small business, on ownership of the firm.

Regardless of the source of authority, subordinates will not follow a directive if they find it unacceptable. For example, an order to perform a task that the worker is physically incapable of performing or that goes against his religious or moral values will not be obeyed. Therefore, the superior must be able to anticipate what directives will be rejected.

Span of Control and Levels of Hierarchy. *Span of control* refers to the number of subordinates or functions a manager can effectively supervise. This number will depend on the type of work being supervised and the degree of decentralization or delegation. At the operating level, where workers are performing relatively standardized tasks, a single supervisor can oversee a large staff. At higher levels of management, where the work is not standardized or routine and each subordinate is performing a different function, the effective span of control is much smaller.

The alternative to a wide span of control is a deeper hierarchy (see Fig. 9–2). By adding a layer of management, the span of each manager is reduced. The difficulty with adding layers of management is that it reduces the effectiveness of communication and requires greater coordination efforts.

In a food service operation, a labor-intensive business of small profit margins, the most suitable organization is not always easy to find. The tendency today is to return to the more horizontal structure. When lower-level employees are properly trained and motivated to perform well, the need for close supervision is reduced and the jobs are enriched and better paid. Expensive middle management costs can be reduced. Leadership is then the primary factor that assures the ongoing maintenance of efficiency and profitability.

Unity of Command. One basic principle of organization design has been that no employee should have more than one superior. In practice, however, it has been observed that individuals do, in fact, work successfully for more than one superior. Large, complex organizations probably could not function if each worker were responsible to only one supervisor. For this reason, the principle of unity of command now states that no employee should be responsible to more than one supervisor *on any single function.* Hence, a restaurant manager in

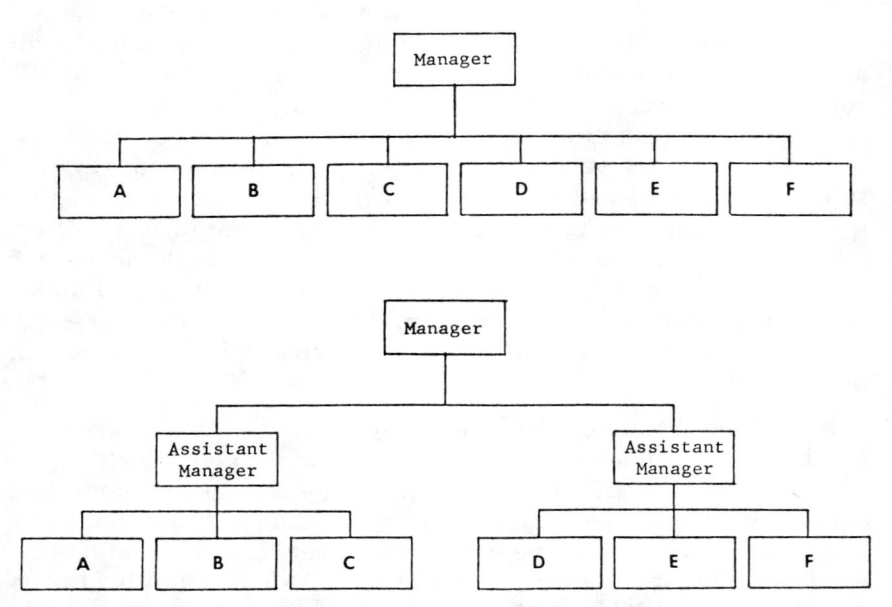

Fig. 9-2. Top: Wide span of control. Bottom: Hierarchal structure.

a chain operation may be responsible to his area supervisor on labor cost controls and to the company controller or chief financial officer on cash handling and reporting procedures.

Organization Structure

The simplest formal organization structure is the *line* organization, which is divided by function or specialty. A simple line organization chart is shown in Fig. 9–3.

As organizations grow more complex—larger and with more specialization—several staff functions are added, creating the *line and staff* organization structure. Figure 9–4 shows such an organization, with the staff functions of personnel, purchasing, and accounting. These departments do not directly exercise authority over the line departments. Rather, they serve a support and advisory function, relieving the line managers of certain tasks and ensuring that these functions are handled uniformly throughout the firm. Because of its specialized nature, the staff department can bring to the firm a much greater proficiency in its area than line managers can achieve.

Although the staff department operates in an advisory capacity, it may be delegated certain line authority by top management. In the case of the personnel department, policies to which line managers

Management 173

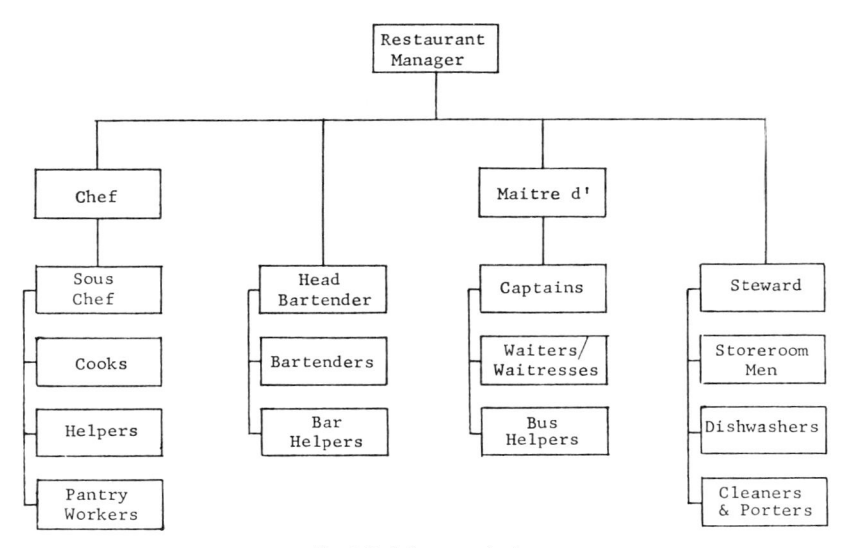

Fig. 9-3. A line organization.

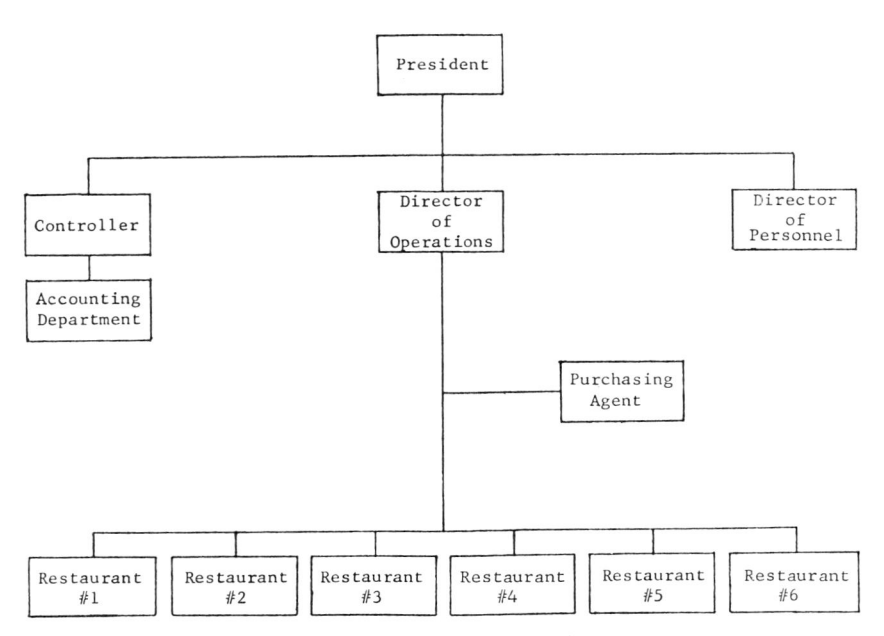

Fig. 9-4. Line and staff organization.

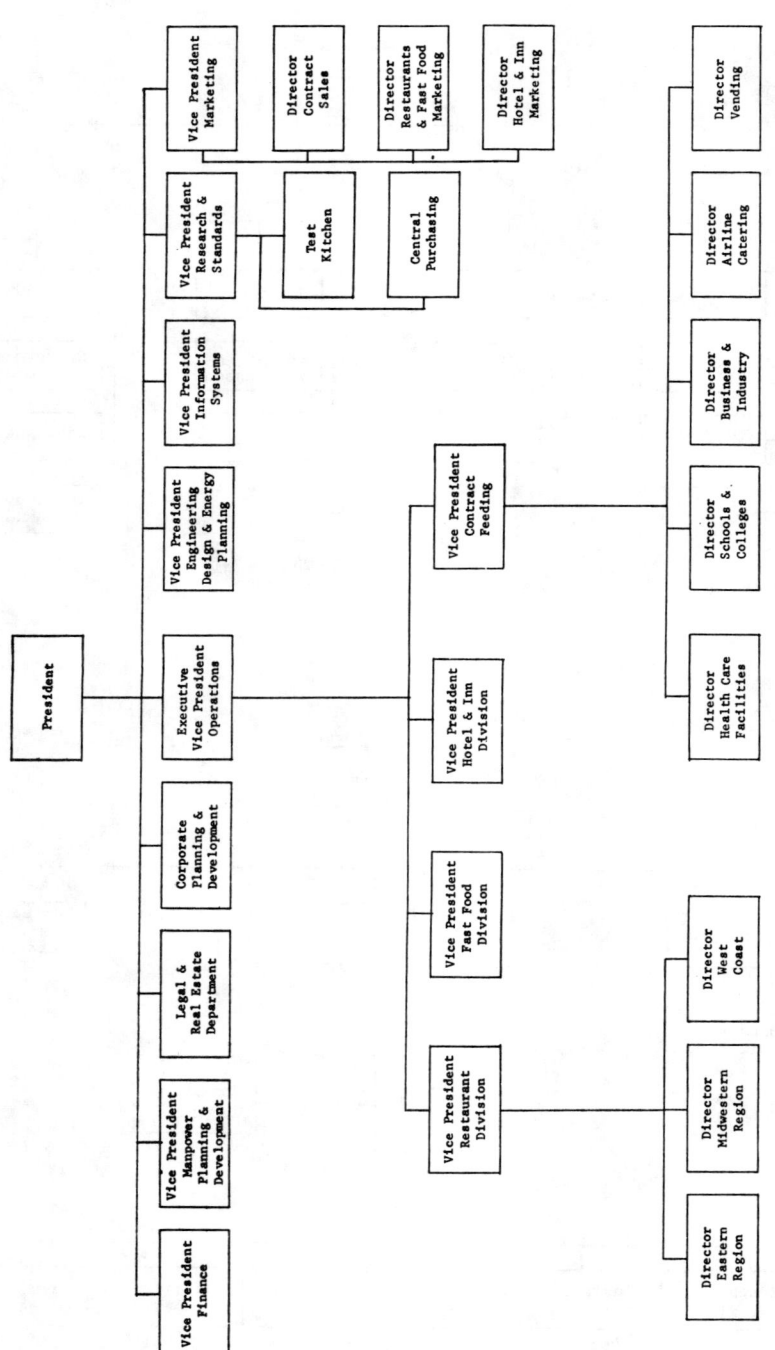

174   *Profitable Food and Beverage Management: Planning*

Fig. 9-5. Departmentalized organization.

must adhere may be developed pertaining to hiring and personnel record keeping. The personnel department is held responsible for seeing that these policies are carried out.

As the organization grows larger, greater division of work is required, and the various line and staff departments may be subdivided, forming a departmentalized organization structure (Fig. 9–5). These divisions may be on the basis of product line, geographical area, type of customer, or some other basis relative to the firm's operations.

The result is a greater complexity of line and staff relationships. For example, personnel departments may be established for the Eastern Region or for the Service Division, or for the Wholesale Division, all requiring coordination by the corporate personnel office and all having a close interrelationship with the line departments they serve. In a company operating in an international environment, the complexity is even greater because the requirements of the departments involved in foreign operations may differ substantially from departments with domestic operations.

This situation has led to a fourth type of organization structure—the grid or matrix. In this structure, the shape of the organization is no longer a pyramid but a box (Fig. 9–6). Communications flows are more likely to be lateral than up and down, as in the hierarchical structure, and managers may be responsible to a larger number of different individuals for different aspects of their jobs. Projects are frequently undertaken by teams of individuals from various departments, rather than by a manager and his subordinates in one department. This type of structure is found only in very large organizations.

The Informal Organization

In addition to the formalized organization structure represented by a neat chart of lines and boxes, every group has an informal organization. The importance of this informal organization in the functioning of the firm cannot be underestimated. The informal organization is built around the social values and beliefs of the group members. It establishes certain standards of behavior and provides for the satisfaction of certain social needs such as status, peer approval, and acceptance. Other functions of the informal organization include communications "through the grapevine." This communications network is often far more efficient and effective than the firm's formal information system.

The informal organization also provides peer leaders, individuals who are accepted as such by the members of the group because they embody the values commonly held by the group. Their position in the formal organization structure is usually immaterial. Their

176   *Profitable Food and Beverage Management: Planning*

Fig. 9-6. Grid or matrix organization.

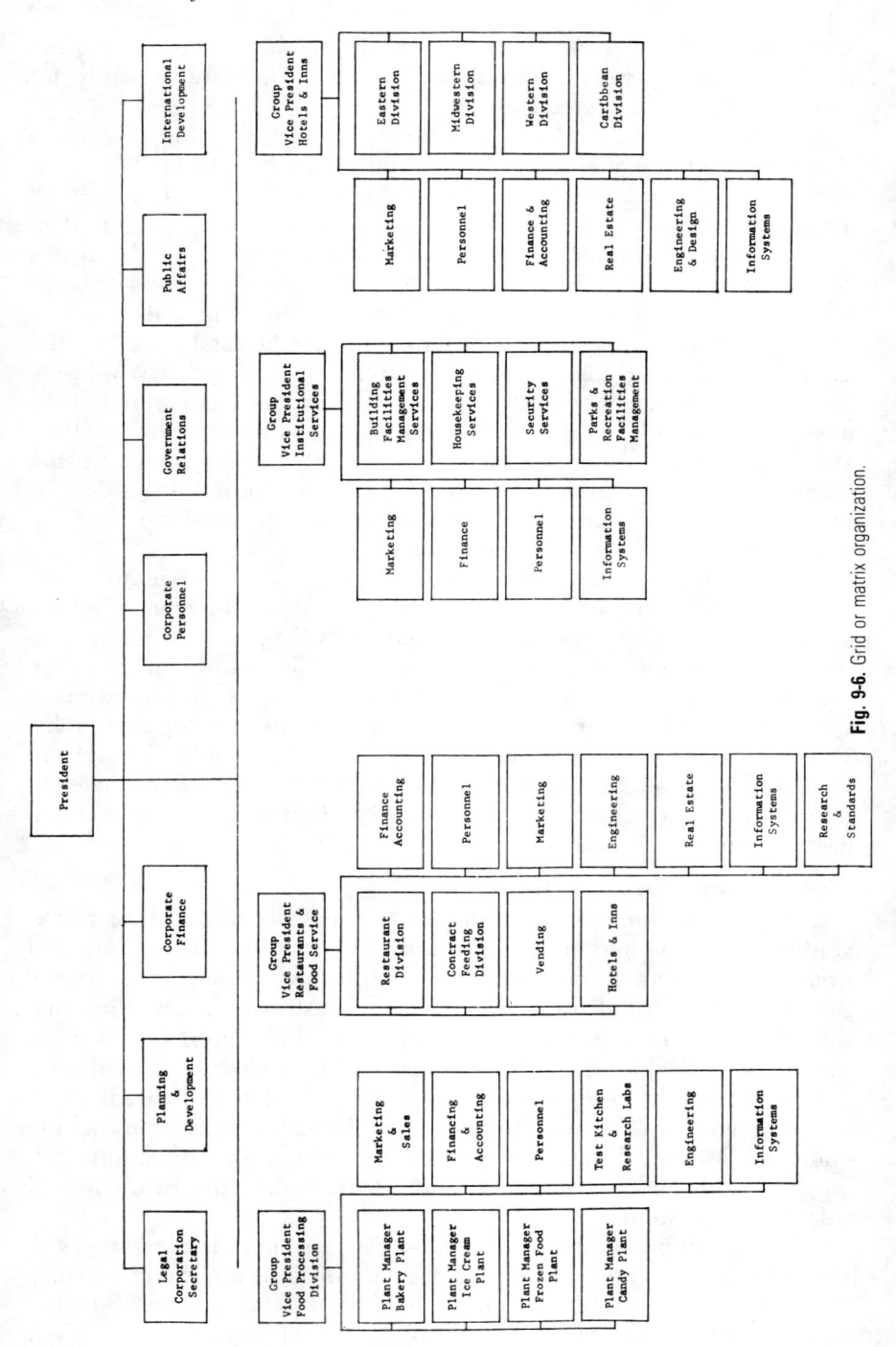

leadership position may be due to personality characteristics, skill level, age, or intelligence, in addition to their ability to communicate with the group members. They frequently function as sources of information to the members and as group spokesmen. The informal organization can work for or against the goals of the formal organization, and the peer leaders can be a major force in determining how the group will act.

How Managers Manage

Decision Making

Making decisions is a major part of the manager's job; in fact, some authorities consider decision making as one of the basic functions of management. All the traditionally defined functions—planning, implementing, controlling—involve decision making.

Rational decision making is a process involving several steps that are generally defined as:

1. Determining what the problem or objective is.
2. Establishing what the restrictions or constraints are on possible solutions, and determining priorities and criteria for evaluating solutions.
3. Seeking out alternative solutions, or information gathering.
4. Evaluating various alternatives.
5. Selecting the best alternative, or in some cases, the least undesirable alternative.

Although this procedure may appear to be quite cumbersome, it is a process that is used constantly in everyday decision making. Consider a simple example. You feel that none of your clothes are suitable to wear for an important occasion. Your decision making might proceed as follows:

- *Problem Definition.* Need new outfit.
- *Restrictions.* Cannot spend more than $100; must charge it; must be a style suitable for the special occasion and for work as well; must be available in proper size; prefer blue.
- *Information Seeking.* Look in newspaper ads for sales; go to stores that will accept credit cards; look at the selection available in the proper size, desired color, and price range.
- *Evaluate Alternatives.* Try on some outfits; ask advice of friend, spouse, salesperson; compare different outfits for appearance, quality of fabric and construction, fit, and style.
- *Selection.* Choose one that looks good on you, is within the desired price range, is well made, and can be charged to your credit card account.

Decision making in business usually involves much more than in the purchase of clothing. For this reason, a conscious effort is usually made to apply some logical and systematic approach.

Different types of managerial decisions are made at different levels in the organization. At the top level, management is engaged mostly in *strategic* decision making. Strategic decisions are those that pertain to the goals of the organization and involve determining the resources required to attain those goals, and the methods of acquiring, using, and disposing of those resources. Although management must consider the firm's present and future capabilities, much of the information required in strategic decision making will come from outside the firm and will pertain to changes in market conditions, the financial and economic climate, the actions of government and consumer groups, and changes in technologies.

At the middle level of management, tactical or administrative decision making is most prevalent. This involves translating the strategic decision made by top management into plans of operation for the firm and may involve preparing short-range plans, budgets, staffing, recruitment and training programs, sales programs, and production plans.

The lowest level of managerial decision making is *operational* —those decisions that ensure that the specific tasks of day-to-day operations are carried out in an effective and efficient manner. This type is largely the task of the line supervisor and lower level managers.

Styles of Leadership

Much has been written about styles of leadership and their effect on group performance. Four styles have been identified: autocratic, paternalistic, democratic, participative. A fifth style that is a lack of leadership is sometimes mentioned: the abdicative. The primary distinction made among these various styles is the way in which decisions are made and implemented.

The abdicative leader makes no decisions; in fact, he does not even attempt to identify any problems. His attitude is, "My people are all pros at their jobs. I let them operate as they see fit, since they know their jobs better than I do." Unfortunately, none of these "pros" is in a position to see and evaluate the overall situation. In times of change, leaderless groups are unable to adapt to new conditions.

At the opposite end of the spectrum is the autocratic leader. He makes all decisions himself and consults no one. His viewpoint is, "I am paid to make the decisions; the employees are paid to do what I tell them to do." He often fails to use the most important information source available—the people who will carry out his decisions.

The paternalistic leader is also an autocrat. The only difference is that the paternalist has the "best interests of the employees at heart." He wants the staff to be happy and therefore tries to "sell" them on the "goodness" of his decisions.

The democratic leader identifies problems and refers them to the group for solution. The solution favored by the majority constitutes the decision. The problem here is that the majority can be wrong, especially since it is made up of individuals, none of whom have access to or understanding of the total picture.

The participative leader is one who involves group members in decision making when the individuals are to be involved in the implementation of the decision. The leader establishes guidelines and objectives within which the individuals in the group are encouraged to make the necessary decisions in consultation with the leader. This style of leadership has received a great deal of attention in the business press. Management by Objectives (MBO) is one technique used by participative managements.

In MBO programs, individual managers and supervisors plan their own programs in conjunction with their immediate superiors. The superior provides general objectives and limitations within which the individuals must operate, and the superior determines that the resulting plan does not conflict with the company's overall objectives. Within this established framework, the individual establishes his own goals and objectives and his plan for implementation. Finally, he is evaluated by his supervisor on how well he met his own objectives.

Motivation

Worker motivation has been a subject of business research since the era of Taylor and Mayo. Taylor's hypothesis was that workers were motivated only by money. Subsequent research by behavioral scientists has shown that motivation is a much more complex subject than this.

Abraham Maslow's hierarchy of human needs (see Chap. 2) has been used to explain the motivation to work. At the lowest level is pay, which provides the means to purchase food, shelter, and clothing, thus satisfying biological needs. Next are security needs, satisfied by unionization, seniority plans, and so forth. At the third level are belonging needs, satisfied by formal and informal group acceptance. Next are esteem needs, which are satisfied by titles, status symbols, promotions, and recognition. At the top of Maslow's hierarchy are self-actualization needs, which are seldom met in work organizations, according to this analysis. (MBO is an attempt to overcome this lack.) Maslow also pointed out that once a need is satisfied, it no longer is a need, thus explaining why simply increasing wages does not always have the effect of increasing worker satisfaction or productivity.

Probably the best known treatise on worker motivation was written by Douglas McGregor in 1960. McGregor calls one set of generally held assumptions about human nature Theory X:

1. The average human being has an inherent dislike of work and will avoid it if he can.
2. Because of this human characteristic of dislike of work, most people must be coerced, controlled, directed, threatened with punishment to get them to put forth adequate effort toward the accomplishment of organizational objectives.
3. The average human being prefers to be directed, wishes to avoid responsibility, has relatively little ambition, wants security above all.*

In contrast to these assumptions, McGregor put forth his somewhat more positive Theory Y.

1. The expenditure of physical and mental effort in work is as natural as play or rest. The average human being does not inherently dislike work. Depending upon controllable conditions, work may be a source of satisfaction (and will be voluntarily performed) or a source of punishment (and will be avoided if possible).
2. External control and the threat of punishment are not the only means for bringing about effort toward organizational objectives. Man will exercise self-direction and self-control in the service of objectives to which he is committed.
3. Commitment to objectives is a function of the rewards associated with their achievement. The most significant of such rewards, e.g., the satisfaction of ego and self-actualization needs, can be direct products of effort directed toward organizational objectives.
4. The average human being learns, under proper conditions, not only to accept but to seek responsibility. Avoidance of responsibility, lack of ambition, and emphasis on security are generally consequences of experience, not inherent human characteristics.
5. The capacity to exercise a relatively high degree of imagination, ingenuity, and creativity in the solution of organizational

---

*From *The Human Side of Enterprise,* by Douglas McGregor. Copyright McGraw-Hill Book Company, 1960. Used with permission of McGraw-Hill Book Company.

problems is widely, not narrowly, distributed in the population.
6. Under the conditions of modern industrial life, the intellectual potentialities of the average human being are only partially utilized.*

Theory Y has many implications for managers who must motivate workers. It explains the recent popularity and success of participation management. It provides a means of satisfying the individual's need for self-actualization, by making the achievement of his personal goals the achievement of the company's goals as well.

The Management of Small Businesses

There are two types of small businesses. One is the ongoing business, often family owned. Its objective is to provide a stable income for the owners. This type of small business is often a retail operation or consumer service. It may be organized as a proprietorship, a partnership, or a Subchapter S corporation (in which the stock is held by a small number of stockholders).

The other type of small business is that of the entrepreneur, an individual who has developed a new product or service and is in the process of establishing and building a company. In contrast to the ongoing small business, the entrepreneur's objective is to grow and obtain a large share of the market for his product before competitors copy it. He may also have a second objective: to sell out at a strategic point. The entrepreneur is often a highly creative, imaginative individual who prefers to function on his own in a high-risk situation in which he can operate as he wants to, rather than accept the constraints and enjoy the stability of working for a large corporation.

Both the entrepreneur and the small business manager must deal with certain constraints not experienced by managers of large corporations, although they may deal with them in different ways. Some of these constraints are discussed below.

Difficulty in Raising Capital

The diffficulty of raising capital as a constraint on the small business was mentioned in Chap. 3. Individual proprietorships and partnerships do not provide the guarantee of long-term continuation and stability that most investors and lenders want. The entrepreneur's need for capital is much greater than that of the ongoing business because he must finance the development of his product and the start-up of his company, as well as provide for future growth. At the

---
*Ibid.

same time, the newness of the company and the high risk associated with an innovative product work to limit possible sources of capital.

Lack of In-Depth Specialized Knowledge

The manager of the ongoing business is usually a generalist with some knowledge in all areas of management as well as specialized knowledge about the technical aspects of his particular business.

The entrepreneur is frequently an individual with a technical background such as engineering or some other specialty such as marketing. This past training and experience provide the knowledge necessary to design a new product or to discover a new marketing opportunity. As his firm grows, the entrepreneur must provide new skills in management, marketing, and finance, either in himself or by hiring others to provide them. When the firm reaches a certain size, specialized managers are required. Sometimes the entrepreneur himself is unable to make the transition from running a small, one-man operation to coordinating the efforts of specialists, and his inability to adjust to the demands of managing the larger firm can actually hamper the firm's growth. It is at this point, when the firm outgrows its founder, that many entrepreneurs either sell their companies or turn over operating control to a professional management team.

Both the manager of the ongoing business and the entrepreneur in the small firm must utilize outsiders as a source of specialized knowledge until such time as the firm is large enough to employ specialists on a full-time basis. These outsiders include bankers, accountants, lawyers, management consultants, advertising agencies, and, often, suppliers.

Lack of Time

Because the small businessman is usually involved in all aspects of running his business, he seldom has enough time to devote to any specific area. Consequently, many of the refined management techniques usually found in large companies are often lacking in small firms. Installing a sophisticated cost control system, a forecasting and budgeting procedure, or a personnel training and development program often has a low priority when compared to getting today's production out or closing an important sale. To some extent, control and information requirements may be reduced by the owner's close personal involvement with his business, and many small businessmen have learned too late the value of good management information, internal control systems, forecasting and long-range planning.

Lack of Diversity and Resources

Large corporations usually have a wide range of product lines and a depth of resources (both financial and human) that provide a cushion against a poor year or a marketing mistake. The small businessman has neither the resources nor the diversity of products to protect him. The loss of one key employee, an investment in the development of a new product that does not pay off, or a downturn in the general economy can severely jeopardize the existence of the small firm.

Lack of Economies of Scale

Because the small businessman operates on a smaller scale than does the large corporation, he cannot achieve the efficiencies of large-scale operation. Therefore, his costs are usually higher, and he has difficulty competing with the large corporations on selling prices and on advertising and promotion budgets. Therefore, the small business must offer something extra in order to give the customer comparable value for the dollar and remain competitive. Often this "something extra" is personalized service or a high-quality specialty image.

Research and Development

In research and development, also, the small businessman cannot compete with the large corporation, simply because he does not have the resources to invest. He must, therefore, either be a follower, rather than a leader or innovator, or else he must take the high-risk route of the entrepreneur. For the operator of an ongoing family business, this would mean risking his family's present and future source of income.

Other Characteristics of the Family-Owned Business

In addition to dealing with the complexities mentioned above, the owner–managers of the family-owned business have several additional considerations. First is that of control. Internal power struggles between relatives can seriously weaken, if not destroy, an otherwise healthy business. Personal and family conflicts can also be a threat if they are permitted to spill over into the operation of the business. Another potential problem in the family-owned business is the involvement of unqualified individuals in decision making and the operating of the business. These individuals may either be involved directly or they may be in a position to exert considerable influence on those in direct control, such as spouses.

Paralleling the need to have competent members control the business is the need to plan for competent management in the future. This usually involves the training of sons and daughters, assuming that the children wish to enter the business, or it means selecting other relatives or nonfamily members to be developed for future management positions. Bringing a son or daughter into one's business can be the attainment of a parent's ultimate goal, or it can be a totally frustrating experience. The employer–employee relationship may be severely strained by parent–child relationships. The younger person (often college trained whereas the parent is self-educated) is full of eager, innovative ideas, but the parent may still perceive him as a child and greatly limit his participation in the business.

If the family decides to hire an outsider to manage the business, it may have difficulty attracting and keeping a qualified individual. Professionally trained managers tend to regard family-owned businesses as unstable employers with limited opportunity for advancement. The outside manager is always subject to the demands of the family–owners, demands that can create severe conflicts.

The need for estate planning is also a consideration for the individual proprietor and for the members of a partnership. Unless there is sufficient cash available to pay estate taxes or to permit a surviving partner to buy out the business, it may be necessary to sell the business. Dividing stock among surviving heirs can also create difficulties.

Small Business Management in the Food Service Industry

The food service business today is still dominated by small businesses although, as was shown in Chap. 1, larger chains are rapidly increasing their share of the market. Many of these chains are still small, young companies headed by youthful entrepreneurs. Another characteristic of the growth chains is the use of franchising as a means of expansion with limited capital. For the franchisee, the purchase of a franchise can help to overcome some of the disadvantages of a small business, since it provides managerial and technical know-how, reduced credit risks, access to specialists, the advantage of large volume purchasing, and marketing advantages in product identity and large-scale advertising campaigns.

10

ACCOUNTING FUNCTIONS AND INTERNAL CONTROLS

Accounting and Decision Making

The accounting department of a food service organization, just as that of any business, must maintain records and prepare reports providing information about the operations and the financial condition of the operation. This information must be maintained for both internal and external purposes.

Internally, management needs information for control purposes. Control, in a broad sense, includes decision making as well as the administering of operations. Effective managerial control requires both day-to-day and long-term information, the former for routine administration and the latter for planning and determination of policies.

The accounting department provides a number of other services to management. The controller or chief accountant ordinarily interprets accounting information for management and calls its attention to matters and activities requiring management action. He also assists in solving business problems, in calculating the cost of alternative plans of action, and in estimating the effect of a planned course of action on the operating statement. Because these financial considerations are always important in decision making, the controller occupies a key position in management, particularly in a larger organization.

Externally, the information requirements of federal, state, and local government agencies alone are burdensome, especially for a multiunit organization that extends across state lines. In addition, if its stock is publicly held, an organization must provide reports to stockholders and the general public.

Basic Financial Statements

The balance sheet and the income statement, the latter often referred to as the profit and loss statement, are most commonly used to evaluate the financial condition and progress of a firm. The balance sheet is a statement of assets, liabilities, and ownership at a specific date. The assets such as cash, accounts receivable, inventories, fixed assets, and so on are listed in order of liquidity to show the company's resources. The liabilities also are listed in order of liquidity and show the equities of various financial interests in the company, such as amounts owed to general creditors (represented by accounts payable—trade), to the government (taxes payable), and mortgage or bond holders (long-term obligations). The financial interests of the owners, if an organization is incorporated, are shown in a stockholder's equity section, which contains a summary of the capitalization consisting of the capital stock, retained earnings, and the like. In an unincorporated business, the interests of an individual owner or of partners are shown in an appropriately captioned section.

The income statement is a summary of all transactions related to the firm's operations during a specific period, such as a month or a year. Income statements of restaurants are comparable in format to those of other types of business and have sections for sales, cost of sales, and gross profit. There are also sections for controllable expenses and various fixed expenses, all of which when deducted from the gross profit leave a net profit (or loss). (Chapter 12 on budgeting contains several illustrations of operating statements.)

Comparative Statements and Ratio Indicators

The periodic income statement should show a comparison of the month's operation with that for the corresponding month of the preceding year, as well as with the current budget for the operation. It may also provide a comparison of the operation of the current fiscal year to date with that of the corresponding period of the preceding fiscal year. Review of these figures will indicate where further analysis and remedial steps may be necessary. Significant increases in expenditures or declines in revenue should be investigated.

A comparison of the month and year-to-date operations with an operating budget is preferable to a comparison with the prior year's results. When a realistic budget has been developed, this method of comparison provides much greater insight. Figures for the corresponding month or for the year-to-date of last year may not represent a satisfactory level of efficiency, and comparisons with them do not indicate how well an operation is doing in relation to its profit goals or potentials.

The use of ratios will disclose relationships among sales, costs, and expenses. Ratios are used extensively by food service operators in evaluating their financial results. An example of the use of ratios in the analysis of seven restaurant income statements is in Chap. 3. This procedure is known as *vertical analysis.*

On comparative statements (those showing two or more years' results), the increases or decreases in amounts for the current period as compared to last year may be shown as percentage changes. This practice facilitates a horizontal analysis for successive operating periods; it is a useful indication of trends developing in particular items, whether on the income statement or the balance sheet.

The prompt detection of changes in operations, as indicated by operating statements, is especially important in large multiunit organizations. A corporate executive, whether representing a division or the executive office, cannot be personally present at all operating units, which may be a considerable distance from one another, to observe, inspect, and direct the operations. The executive must rely on the adequacy of operating statements and routine reports to indicate any deficiencies or unsatisfactory operating results that may require follow-up for appropriate action. In Chap. 11 on financial statement analysis, identification of causes of unfavorable variances or trends is discussed, and certain actions are suggested to correct any unsatisfactory conditions.

To assist management further in the analysis of the balance sheet, certain additional relationships and ratios may be computed. Of the many indicators available to a businessman, the following are probably the most useful:

1. *Working capital.* Working capital represents the excess of current assets (cash, receivables, inventories, and prepaid expenses) over current liabilities (notes and accounts payable, wages and taxes payable). It is recognized that working capital requirements in the food industry are not as high as in many other industries because sales ordinarily are made for cash. Nevertheless, it is prudent to maintain an adequate level of working capital to make sure that the firm will be able to meet its current obligations.

2. *Current ratio.* The current ratio is computed by dividing the total current assets by the total current liabilities. It is another indicator of an organization's ability to meet its current obligations.

3. *Inventory turnover.* The inventory turnover ratio represents the rate of food inventory and beverage inventory turnovers when each is computed separately. The computation is made by dividing separately the cost of food sold (including the cost of employees' meals) and of beverages sold for a period (usually a

month) by the opening inventory of the respective commodity. The average inventory for the particular month may be used as a divisor if preferred. The result represents the number of times that the inventory is "turned over," or converted to cash (or a receivable). It may be more meaningful to compute the turnover on the basis of a class of commodity (e.g., meats, canned goods, baked goods, etc.) if the respective costs are available and separately accumulated. Like other ratios, a turnover ratio is more useful after experience over a period of time has been developed by an organization.

Perhaps a more easily understood alternative to a turnover rate is a computation in terms of the number of days that an inventory can be expected to last. To illustrate, the inventory of an item that turns over four times a month is sufficient for the needs of about seven days. If that is considered to be too much stock to have on hand because of the amount of cash tied up, the inventory should be reduced to meet more closely sales or usage requirements.

4. *Rate of return on investment.* Rate of return on investment is sometimes referred to as return on capital, or simply as the rate of return. The rate of return on total assets is considered to be an important indicator of an organization's earning power. The ratio may be computed on net income either before or after income taxes. It may be computed in several ways, such as:

(a) $$\frac{\text{Net income}}{\text{Average total assets (total investment)}}$$

(b) $$\frac{\text{Net income plus interest expense}}{\text{Average total assets}}$$

The use of a net income figure before interest deductions provides an earnings amount before any payments to creditors, which helps to eliminate rate variations resulting from changes in capital structure that may occur from year to year. Also, it permits a comparison of the ratios of two companies even though the sources of capital are of different types.

Of course, indicators must be used with care to avoid reaching erroneous conclusions. Underlying changes in business conditions may have occurred, such as changes in price levels. Another possibility is that nonrecurring or unusual transactions have taken place that affect percentages or ratios. Executives who use accounting information must consider all significant developments with the objective of maintaining favorable conditions and correcting any unfavorable trends.

Uniform Systems of Accounts

Basic accounting systems have been published for various types of food and beverage operations.*

The account classification for hotels (as an example) was formulated by joint committees of accounting and management representatives with the idea that if all hotels used the same classifications, comparisons could be made of operating costs and profits. The Uniform System devised by the committees includes a summary income statement showing revenues and direct expenses grouped by operating department in order to show an operating profit (or loss) for each department. The committee decided, however, that it would be impractical to devise any suitable method of allocating overhead on a uniform basis to each different department. Therefore, in a hotel only direct departmental costs are charged to the operation of each department. General overhead and fixed charges, such as rent, advertising, light, heat, water, and repairs, are grouped together as administrative or overhead classifications and deducted from the total of all departmental profits.

Although the Uniform System has permitted comparisons of the expenses of all hotels that use it and is helpful in accumulating statistical data, it is interesting to note that many hotel men still request that each department be charged with its share of the overhead expenses. Some have prepared supplementary statements providing for such an allocation. This practice facilitates a comparison with commercial restaurants whose food and beverage operations must naturally carry the overhead expenses as part of the total operational cost.

The Uniform System of Accounts for Restaurants is simpler because departmentalized statements are not usually required for individual restaurants. For multiunit restaurant operations, however, central office administration and financing expense is usually treated as overhead without allocation to operating units.

The adoption of individual uniform systems of accounts by restaurants, hospitals, and clubs has greatly helped them to gauge the efficiency of their operations by allowing them to compare their operating results with those of others.

---

*Uniform System of Accounts for Hotels (Hotel Association of New York City, Inc., Seventh Revised Edition, 1976). Uniform System of Accounts for Restaurants (National Restaurant Association, Fourth Revised Edition, 1968). Uniform System of Accounts for Clubs (Club Managers Association of America, Second Revised Edition, 1967).

Management Reports

In addition to the monthly financial statements, the accounting system should provide a series of supplementary reports pertaining to recurring analyses of sales, daily food and beverage costs, and payroll expenses. These reports should be designed to show clearly any inefficiencies in the operation. The reports should compare overall cost figures with some established norm, such as a budget. Comparisons with industry averages published by several of the national hotel accounting firms, trade publications, and local hotel and restaurant associations may also be used as a guide.

When the results off the current operation fail to meet the standards, more detailed reports or operational studies on the appropriate cost areas are required. The accounting system should be designed for both standardized reporting and fast and accurate retrieval of more detailed information when needed. The reports provided by the system should be designed to meet the requirements of both management and the controller. Those percentages and operating ratios should be incorporated that best furnish clues as to possible weaknesses in such areas as poor forecasting, scheduling, purchasing, or overpreparation. The design of such a system may require the professional assistance of an independent accountant.

Optimally, reports should be self-explanatory to a reader. If reports and statements could be made absolutely clear, the controller's function would become only that of an information gatherer and accumulator of figures, largely for income determination purposes. However, because of the human element, the dynamic nature of any viable business, and the variations in operating conditions that from time to time require monitoring and evaluating, a system of reports cannot become wholly repetitive and unresponsive to the needs of an organization. A controller needs to interpret key matters in his reports to management and solicit feedback on the data provided. Timely interpretations may prevent managers from making wrong decisions or taking inappropriate actions because they do not understand the reported cost behavior or the relevancy of particular figures to such actions.

Throughout this text, a number of special reports are presented and discussed. However, other types of financial reports may be necessary, depending on the type of business operation. For example, a food service operation that extends credit to its customers or accepts national credit cards may benefit from the preparation and use of an accounts receivable aging schedule. This schedule is a list and analysis of account balances according to the date of incurrence by a customer (e.g., current or 1 to 30 days, 30 to 60 days, 60 to 90 days, etc.). After an aging schedule has been prepared, it may be used as a basis for determining what provision must be made in the allowance for doubtful accounts. To illustrate, a decision may be made that the allowance account should be sufficient to cover 50 percent of the total amounts between 90 and 120 days past due and 100 percent of the total amount over 120 days past due.

Inventory turnover ratios alone will not identify particularly slow-moving or overstocked items. A periodic physical inventory, however, will provide an item-by-item record of stock levels that can be analyzed. Using the physical inventory record as a starting point, the date of last use and the quantities used in the past few months may be entered in columns by months for each item analyzed. The quantity on hand is divided by the average monthly usage to compute the number of month's supply on hand at the current level of use. This information can be particularly useful to the executive office or divisional management of a multiunit organization by serving as the basis for a possible transfer of supplies between units. It can also serve as the basis for menu changes designed to make use of overstocked items with a minimum of waste or loss. Also, such an analysis obviously may lead to a reassessment of the quantities of items purchased and the minimum and maximum inventory levels of various items.

Other Accounting Functions

Large, multiunit food service organizations usually have well-organized accounting and control functions that encompass specializations beyond the basic accounting work. Such large organizations have a need for specialists to handle systems and procedures, budgeting and cost accounting, automatic data processing, internal auditing, and tax accounting. Although needs vary for each organization, it is probably safe to say that such specialties are carried out to some degree by an employee in any organization even though the position or function may not be designated on the chart.

A particularly important function in a large organization is that of the systems and operations analyst. Systems and procedures must first be established and then monitored and controlled if they are to be effective. It is the responsibility of systems and operations analysts to ensure that the established procedures are followed, to detect and report variances from the desired results, and to report to management their findings and recommendations for securing adherence to procedures.

Internal Auditing and Controls

The internal auditor may assist in establishing adequate internal accounting and other procedural controls to ensure that loss and waste are avoided. More important, monitoring the internal control procedures must be assured in the day-to-day operations. In a small operation, managers themselves perform control of functions such as taking cash register readings, preparing receiving reports, handling cash receipts and disbursements, preparing payrolls, and performing on-the-spot observation. In larger organizations, top management's responsibility must be delegated, and more formal procedures and tests must be established than are necessary in smaller organizations.

The added cost incurred by delegating functions and, often, the added burden of paper work must not exceed the savings and satisfaction that can be derived. In practice, it is quite difficult to achieve a good balance.

Large organizations usually employ internal auditors whose job is to observe the degree of compliance with the company's policies and procedures and to make recommendations for improvements. The job requires an independence from line accounting responsibilities. The internal auditor should report to an executive on a high enough level to preclude any lack of objectivity in appraising and reporting on unsatisfactory conditions. In addition to the reassurance that management gets from a well-ordered internal audit, it may find that the time and expense of the outside audit is also reduced.

The features of internal controls have been considered extensively by public accountants. In 1973 The American Institute of Certified Public Accountants stated:

> Internal control comprises the plan of organization and all of the coordinate methods and measures adopted within a business to safeguard its assets, check the accuracy and reliability of its accounting data, promote operational efficiency, and encourage adherence to prescribed managerial policies. This definition possibly is broader than the meaning sometimes attributed to the term. It recognizes that a "system" of internal control extends beyond those matters which relate directly to the functions of the accounting and financial departments.*

The last two sentences in the statement are an important clarification of the original definition, which was issued by the American Institute of Certified Public Accountants in 1949.

Statement on Auditing Standards No. 1. The American Institute of Certified Public Accountants, 1973, p. 15.

The internal controls implicit in the definition can be characterized as those relating to accounting and those relating to administration. Accounting controls are concerned mainly with (1) the safeguarding of assets, and (2) the reliability of financial records. Administrative controls are concerned mainly with (1) operational efficiency, and (2) adherence to managerial policies.

In the restaurant and food service industry in general, controls of accounts receivable, accounts payable, payroll and other assets, liabilities, income, and expenses are similar to those found in other businesses. The reader is referred to standard texts for these topics. However, because control of revenue in food service operations differs from that in other retail businesses, some observations are required.

Restaurant Revenue Control Procedures

In a conventional restaurant, the guest check is the document presented to the guest for settlement, either by cash or charge. It may also serve as an ordering form and authorization for preparation and dispatch of the items ordered. Guest checks, therefore, provide a very strong method of internal control suitable for most operations from coffee shops to the most elegant table service restaurants.

Although income originates when a guest check is first used by a server, internal control procedures should start before this. Controls begin with the security of unused checks held in storage. Custody of these checks should be given to an employee whose responsibilities are not related to the control or recording of income. From this point, the following control procedures are followed:

1. All checks should be sequentially prenumbered. When books of checks are used, the books should be identified with a server's number or an alphanumeric designation.

2. Checks should be issued to the supervisor of a particular sales outlet and only in quantities sufficient for short periods (usually not in excess of one week's requirements). The shorter the period of supply, the faster will any loss of checks be detected. The issuance of the checks must be supported by a written requisition signed by the person receiving the checks. Checks must be issued strictly in sequence to facilitate detection of any missing checks.

3. The supervisor of a dining room should issue checks to servers in quantities sufficient to meet the requirements of not more than a day, and when practical, only for the meal period. At the close of a meal period or the day, all unused checks must be returned to the person in charge of the dining room or to a "drop box."

4. When unbound checks are used, the checks should be issued in sequence, preferably one at a time. The servers must sign for each individual check issued to them. This procedure requires a checker and is usually used only in operations with high average checks. When this procedure is not practical, checks bound in book form should be used. Each check should be numbered and each should be identified by a waiter number or identification. When books of checks are used, the server should be required to sign for the receipt of the checks and to record the number of the first check in the book. When going off duty, he records the number of the last check used. The signature forms—those used for the individual checks as well as for books of checks—are sent to the income controller at the close of the day.

5. When food checkers are employed—as at some hotels and clubs—the food is priced by the food checker on a machine similar to a cash register which accumulates the sales value of all food and beverages taken out of the kitchen for service to guests.

6. The check itself, or a duplicate prepared at the same writing, is used as an order form to the kitchen.

7. On completion of a meal, either the guest or the server—depending on the policy of the organization—takes the cash or the signed check to the cashier, who records it on the cash register as either a cash or a charge sale.

These procedures may be automated in various ways by the use of mechanical or electronic registering devices, but the essence of the system is always the same—to ensure that merchandise leaving the preparation area, either kitchen or bar, is recorded and accounted for as sales. The guest check system provides other advantages as well. A sales history of items sold may be abstracted readily and in great detail by hour, day, or other period for use in forecasting sales volume and menu planning; positive evidence of sales tax collections is available for tax examinations; and in the event of doubt about a charge account sale, details of the transaction are on record.

Fast-Food and Cafeteria Controls

The use of guest checks is often not practical or useful as a control procedure in operations where the server may also take payment or where speed in handling transactions is essential. Because preparation of a check takes time, its use may not be advisable for sales of small unit price, such as a cup of coffee or a soft drink. Therefore, a different plan is usually necessary. Cash registers with visual display of amounts recorded are frequently used to involve the customer in the control procedure and to enable supervisory personnel and outside "spotters" from agencies specializing in such work to observe whether sales are being properly recorded. Cash or charges must tally with amounts rung on the registers.

Cash registers may include elaborate features such as preset prices, item counters for a large number of menu items, and automatic tax calculators and change makers. The cash register sales-recording system does not, however, provide an independent control of merchandise issued, as does the restaurant check system. The expected sales yield from a given quantity of merchandise may therefore be used effectively. This method is discussed in detail in the bar and potential food cost chapters of *Profitable Food and Beverage Management: Operations*. If the sales yield is above or below that expected from the goods issued and consumed, under or overportioning, waste, and theft of goods or sales proceeds may be the cause. Supervisory procedures must then be used to correct the situation.

Bar Revenue Controls

The sale of beverages is settled in one of two ways: cash or charge. If the guest pays with cash, the transaction ends at that point. If the guest signs a check or if he uses a credit card, payment is received at a later date at another point.

Almost all bar operations use a cash register to record sales as well as the method of settlement. If cash is paid, the transaction is registered on a cash key. If it is charged, then the transaction is registered on a charge key. The combined total of the cash and charge keys must equal the total registered on the sale key. The cash receipts for the day must agree with the cash key reading, and the aggregate of the charge checks must agree with the charge key reading.

In a service bar operation (a bar used principally for preparation of drinks to be served in a dining room), there is no settlement for the drinks served so that the bartenders register only the drinks sold. The cash or charge settlement is made at some other point, usually that of the dining room cashier.

A public bar may be staffed with a cashier if the sales volume warrants one, but regardless of the staffing, the sale should be recorded on a guest check by means of a machine register for proper control purposes. An alternative to the use of checks is a register that produces a "throw check" or ticket showing the amount of each sale to provide evidence that the sale was recorded. At each bar a locked drop box should be provided in which all checks settled by cash are to be deposited. This procedure is imperative to prevent the same check from being used twice to collect cash payments. Reuse of charge checks is not possible because they include the signature of a guest.

In a cocktail lounge where bar waiters as well as bartenders may present checks to a cashier for payment, it is advisable to have a perforated stub, known as the waiter's receipt, attached to the check.

This portion should be torn from the main body of the check, initialed by the cashier, and handed to the waiter or bartender. In the event that a check is missing, this stub is the waiter's or bartender's proof of having submitted the check to the cashier.

When a bartender receives cash, a fixed routine to minimize check mishaps should be established. The bartender's procedures can be summarized as follows:

1. Obtains order from customer
2. Writes down order on check
3. Leaves check face up near guest
4. Mixes drink
5. Serves drink
6. Picks up check
7. Registers price on check
8. Returns check to customer
9. Collects from customer
10. Registers receipt of cash
11. Deposits paid check in locked box

It is not to be inferred that the bartender is to demand payment for each round of drinks. It is prudent, however, to require the bartender to close the cash drawer of the register after each transaction.

Banquet Revenue

The accounting control of banquets usually starts with a banquet contract agreed to by both parties, the seller and the purchaser of the services. A banquet contract shows in detail the services that are to be provided and the manner of payment. Advance deposits are frequently required and a guaranteed number of covers to be served is stipulated to protect the restaurant operator. It is the responsibility of the revenue controller to make sure that the terms of the contract are adhered to.

Food Service. Charges for banquet food are usually based on a stipulated price per person. To prepare the billing, a count must be made of the number of persons present at the function. The count may be made in one or two slightly different ways. The guests may be given tickets by the sponsor of the event on payment of the agreed price. The guests surrender the tickets at the entrance to the room or to the server. The final billing to the sponsor is then based on the number of tickets collected. If tickets are not used, a head count is made by captains or other supervisory personnel. In both cases, the count should be compared with kitchen records of the number of portions served. The number of guests served or the guaranteed number—whichever is greater—is billed to the sponsor.

Beverage Service. There are three types of arrangements for beverage service at banquets:

1. A specified number of individual drinks or bottled beverages is served at each table and billed at the unit price specified in the contractual agreements.
2. Stand-up bars dispense individual drinks during the time period specified in the agreement. Billing is predicated on actual consumption at an agreed price per opened bottle or per unit drinks of a specified ounce size.
3. Cash bars are operated at which the attendees purchase individual drinks at a stipulated price.

When the arrangements call for a stipulated number of drinks or bottles at each table, the captain prepares a beverage ticket for each table in his station. The waiter then surrenders this ticket at the bar and receives the number of drinks or bottles marked. At the conclusion of the beverage service, the bar supervisor or head bartender prepares a count of the number of bottles or drinks served at the banquet and submits it for billing.

When the arrangements call for a stand-up bar, the quantity of each brand of liquor issued to that bar is recorded . When service is completed, a count is made of the amounts left over. The consumption is then computed and priced at the agreed-on unit prices to arrive at the total amount to be billed. The unused inventory is usually figured on the number of unopened bottles, unless the agreement specifies that the billing is to be made on some other basis.

When cash bars are set up, a cashier is usually provided from whom the guests purchase tickets for individual drinks. On being served, the patron surrenders the ticket to the bartender, who drops it into a locked box to prevent its reuse. The amount of revenue turned in by the cashier should correspond to the number of tickets in the bartender's box and to the number of tickets issued. No billing is needed for this type of service unless arrangements have been made that the sponsor of the event will pay for the bartenders if sales do not reach a certain level.

Billing. Banquet checks are usually prepared in triplicate and serially controlled. At the conclusion of a function, the banquet manager prepares the check. It is then signed by a responsible representative of the sponsor. The check is distributed as follows:

198   Profitable Food and Beverage Management: Planning

  Original copy—Accounting department
  Duplicate—Banquet sponsor
  Triplicate—Banquet department records

  In a very large banquet department, such as in a convention hotel, data for billing have to be gathered from many sources. In this case, the billing is prepared in the accounting department on the basis of a charge sheet, which is used to assemble all the information (Fig. 10-1).

| HOURS OPENED ____ SET UP FOR ____ TIME FINISHED ____ PARTY LEFT ____ |
| GUARANTEED ____ SERVICE ____ SERVED ____ CHARGED ____ |

Room Rental			BROUGHT FORWARD		
Breakfasts					
Luncheons			SPECIAL GRATUITIES		
Reception & Teas					
Dinners			GRATUITIES		
Suppers					
Musicians' Meals			OTHER GRATUITIES		
Entertainers' Meals					
Special Cake			COAT ROOM FEES		
Hot Appetizers					
Cold Appetizers			TOTAL CHARGES		
Food Check #			SALES TAX		
			GRAND TOTAL		
Beverage Check #					
			REMARKS		
Corkage					
Bar & Bartender					
Cigars					
Cigarettes					
Flowers					
Corsages					
Boutonnieres					
Tags					
Menu Place Cards					
Escort Cards					
Candles			ITEMIZE BEVERAGES & CORKAGE		
Check Room					
Engineer					
Spotlight					
Amplification					
Photographer					
Motion Picture					
Security					
Cocktail Napkins					
Book Matches					
Miscellaneous					
TOTAL FORWARD					

Waiter to make all charges after function, complete all information and return this account immediately to Banquet Office

HEAD WAITER _____ CAPTAIN IN CHARGE _____
DIRECTOR OF CATERING _____ BANQUET REVENUE AUDITOR _____

Fig. 10-1. Banquet charge sheet.

11

Financial Statement Analysis

No businessman can long survive in today's economic climate unless he watches very closely the financial course of his business as it is shown by the financial statements. This chapter describes methods of analyzing and evaluating financial statements for use in future financial planning. The statements shown are taken from a hypothetical Avenue A Restaurant, a free-standing operation that is well managed and provides an extremely good return on the owner's investment.

Balance Sheet

Assets

Cash Position. The cash funds available for payment of the creditor's obligations, as shown on the balance sheet (Fig. 11-1), amount to $8,715, whereas the amount owing to creditors, employees, and the government amounts to more than $76,000. Clearly, the company is headed for some cash problems unless additional cash can be obtained shortly.

If surplus of cash funds had been indicated, the surplus would not have been permitted to lie idle. The recent rate of interest on certain short-term government obligations was then higher than the rate of return from operations. Although such favorable investment returns are not always available, surplus funds should at every opportunity be earning additional profits for the operation. No matter how low the rate of return is on a safe investment, it will add more to the profits from an operation than idle cash funds.

Too often the interest in a company's cash position, especially if it is favorable, ceases after it has been determined whether the available cash is sufficient to meet the trade creditor and other current obligations. The sufficiency or insufficiency of cash is only half the story. What is equally important is how and why the indicated cash position came into being.

	December 31	
ASSETS	19x4	19x3
Current assets		
Cash		
On hand	$ 1,000	$ 1,000
In bank	8,715	45,973
	9,715	46,973
Accounts receivable		
Customers	46,952	35,981
Credit cards	6,164	5,974
Total accounts receivable	53,116	41,955
Less allowance for doubtful accounts	941	750
Net accounts receivable	52,175	41,205
Inventories, at cost		
Food	16,634	10,958
Beverages	10,973	9,832
Supplies	1,750	1,000
	29,357	21,790
Prepaid expenses	5,716	10,754
Total current assets	96,963	120,722
Fixed assets, at cost		
Leasehold improvements	53,770	53,770
Less accumulated depreciation	20,508	17,820
	33,262	35,950
Furniture, fixtures and equipment	150,270	59,220
Less accumulated depreciation	66,539	54,104
	83,731	5,116
Net fixed assets	116,993	41,066
Total assets	$213,956	$161,788
LIABILITIES AND NET WORTH		
Current liabilities		
Accounts payable	$ 24,470	$ 4,496
Notes payable	38,750	29,000
Accrued expenses		
Payroll	9,850	8,321
Other	3,723	2,973
	13,573	11,294
Total current liabilities	76,793	44,790
Net worth		
Balance, beginning of year	116,998	101,455
Add profit for the year	70,165	55,543
Total	187,163	156,998
Less drawings	50,000	40,000
Balance, end of year	137,163	116,998
Total liabilities and net worth	$213,956	$161,788

Fig. 11-1. The Avenue A Restaurant's (a sole proprietorship) balance sheet.

The statement of changes in financial condition (Fig. 11-2) shows quite clearly that substantial amounts have been invested in improvements to the leased premises and in a major refurbishing. There will be no cash surplus until the new investment can be recovered from operations.

Accounts Receivable. The amount due from customers, as shown on the balance sheet, is $52,175 after deducting the allowance for

	Year Ended December 31	
	19x4	19x3
Source of working capital		
Operations		
Profit before income taxes	$ 70,165	$ 55,543
Add items not affecting working capital, depreciation and amortization	15,123	10,128
	85,288	65,671
Applications of working capital		
Additions to fixed assets		
Furniture, fixtures and equipment	91,050	-
Leasehold improvements	-	20,000
Proprietor's drawings	50,000	40,000
	141,050	60,000
Increase [decrease] in working capital	[55,762]	5,671
Increase [decrease] in components of working capital		
Cash	[37,258]	9,730
Accounts receivable	10,970	2,941
Inventories	7,567	1,973
Prepaid expenses	[5,038]	9,872
Accounts payable	[19,974]	2,431
Notes payable	[9,750]	[20,000]
Accrued expenses	[2,279]	[1,276]
Increase [decrease] in working capital	$[55,762]	$ 5,671

Fig. 11-2. The Avenue A Restaurant's statement of changes in financial condition.

doubtful accounts. Is this a reasonable amount of unpaid accounts when it is related to the sales volume?

In the previous year, management's analysis of the manner in which its patrons settled their food and beverage checks indicated that 15 percent used credit cards, 35 percent charged their accounts with the Avenue A Restaurant, and 50 percent paid by cash. If that ratio is still valid, the accounts receivable shown to be outstanding on the balance sheet represent the following average daily sales equivalents:

Type of Charge (After deduction of allowance for doubtful accounts)	Average Daily Sales Revenue	Accounts Receivable	Average Daily Sales Equivalents (Rounded Out)
Credit card	$411	$ 6,164	15 days
Regular	$960	$46,011	48 days

The foregoing computation indicates that the balance of outstanding accounts receivable in both categories is rather high.

Monthly and daily payments by credit card companies can be negotiated if cash needs are acute, as they are in this case.

The balances due from customers who have open accounts are also higher than desirable, as indicated by the number of revenue days represented by the outstanding balances. Because billings are made on a monthly basis for regular accounts and should be made as soon as possible after a banquet is served, a quicker turnover might be expected. Actually, however, the collection experience has improved; in the previous year there was an average of 55 days credit sales in the year-end outstanding balance. Perhaps the improvement in sales is also attributable to encouraging individual credit accounts. Such sales must be financed and can easily cause pressures on the cash position. Collection procedures might still be improved to alleviate the present problem.

Inventories. At the current cost of money, good business practice dictates that investment in inventories should be kept at a reasonable level unless circumstances such as existing or anticipated shortages of material dictate otherwise.

Is the investment in inventories shown on the balance sheet at a reasonable level? To an operator who has not made an investigation of this point, it would be difficult to make an evaluation as to its reasonableness. The following equation provides one method of determining inventory reasonableness:

$$\frac{\text{Cost of food consumed}}{\text{Average of cost of opening and closing inventories}} = \text{Rate of inventory turnover}$$

The cost of food consumed for the year amounted to $354,945. When it is divided by the average of the closing and opening food inventory of $13,796, a turnover of 25.7 times for the year is determined. An annual turnover of 25.7 times, expressed in another way, means that measured in dollars there is sufficient food merchandise in storage to service the requirements of about 14 days' operation. This ratio may be regarded as satisfactory.

The ideal turnover for a particular operation will depend on the style of operation, the availability of supplies, the menu structure, and the number and type of items that must be stocked. Other factors include the predictability of sales levels and the established purchasing policies of the operation. Management may determine, for example, that lower costs of infrequent, bulk deliveries (as opposed to frequent, small purchases) may offset the benefits of frequent inventory turnover. The interest on money tied up in inventory is sometimes overlooked in this evaluation.

Inventory turnover is of more value as a guide to an operator when it is computed on a monthly basis because the amount of inventory is more closely related to the seasonal fluctuations in sales volume. Also, any drop in the rate of turnover can be detected early and corrective measures, if needed, can be taken before there is a further accumulation of inventories.

The average beverage inventory during the year was worth $10,402, and the turnover was about 5.7 times. Because Avenue A is a modestly priced restaurant that does not need to carry an extensive variety of wine and liquors, it should be possible to reduce the amount of beverage inventory carried.

Fixed Assets. A glance at the fixed asset account shown on the balance sheet (Fig. 11-1) and at information given in the statement of changes in financial condition (Fig. 11–2) shows that a very substantial amount of money has been invested in the past two years in improving or expanding the leased premises and in refurbishing. An outlay of $101,050 for this purpose in the past two years appears to have been rewarded by a substantial increase in the sales volume from $662,391 in the previous year to over $1 million currently. The current annual sales of over $1 million are equal to almost 10 times the net book value of the fixed assets at the end of the fiscal year and to about five times the original cost of the improvements, furniture, fixtures, and equipment on the premises. These relationships are highly satisfactory and make it possible for the operation to make a high rate of return on the invested capital.

The total assets employed in the business at the end of the year had a book value of $213,956, on which a profit of $70,165 was earned, or over 33 percent in the year. In the case of the Avenue A Restaurant, this result is deceptive because no provision is made for the salary of the proprietor, who, it must be concluded, is expending a considerable amount of entrepreneurial energy in achieving such a good return. If a salary were included in the statements in respect of the time spent by the owner, the actual reported profit might be substantially reduced.

Liabilities

On the liabilities side of the balance sheet, the comparison between the two years tells the story of how the improvement program was financed. Because of the strain on the cash resources of the restaurant, money had to be borrowed either formally through bank borrowing (represented on the balance sheet as the entry "Notes payable") or through credit granted by trade purveyors. The statement of changes in financial condition shows that in the previous year $20,000 was raised in bank borrowing, probably to finance the leasehold improvements, but there does not appear to have been any specific borrowing to finance the large investment in furniture, fixtures, and equipment. Bank borrowing went up by only another $9,750, and the rest of the money came from creditors and the cash reserve that had been built up at the beginning of the year. In the circumstances, it looks as if rather astute financing has been used, unless the final expenditure on furniture, fixtures, and equipment was considerably over the original budget.

Net Worth

The net worth section of the balance sheet shows that the proprietor increased his drawings by $10,000 over the amount he drew in the previous year, perhaps because of the big improvement in the sales volume. This extra drawing, however, decreased the liquidity of the restaurant and is partly responsible for the poor cash position at the end of the year.

More insight into the nature of the operations at the restaurant is available in the statement of changes in financial condition. Cash that had been built up in previous years has been used up in financing the improvement program. At the same time, it appears that accounts receivable increased substantially during the year, as did the level of inventories. It may be concluded that these changes were necessary and probably helped to support the build-up in sales that occurred during the year. The increase in business required more working capital.

One may conclude from the balance sheet and the changes in working capital that the restaurant is probably going through a short period of working-capital shortage that should be corrected quickly from the higher profits being achieved from the increased level of business.

Statement of Income

In evaluating his operating results, an operator should not stop at the point of learning whether sales income exceeds expenses and therefore the operations result in a profit. What should be equally, if not more, important to him is whether the amount of profit is adequate, based on all the factors in the operation. When he begins to make a determination of the adequacy of the profit, he is beginning to evaluate. To make an evaluation, points of reference are needed for measurement.

The points of reference frequently used in an evaluation are as follows:

1. Operations of a prior period
2. Operations of another similar business

3. Industry experience
4. Predetermined standards

Each of these points has inherent deficiencies that must be kept in mind when making an evaluation. An evaluative comparison of the current period's operating results with those of a prior period may be misleading if the trend over a number of years is not considered. A substantial improvement in one year may still leave disappointing profits compared to the results of earlier years. For example, the Avenue A Restaurant may have produced the following results before taxes:

	Sales	Profit before Taxes	Profit Ratio to Sales	Percentage Change over Previous Year
1974	$1,001,539	$70,165	7.0%	26.3%
1973	662,391	55,543	8.4	[24.0]
1972	785,943	73,093	9.3	[6.4]
1971	773,219	78,095	10.1	

In spite of the 26.3 percent improvement in 1974, profits are still lower than in 1971 on higher sales volume.

The foregoing should not be interpreted to mean that evaluations based on prior results should not be made. If no other point of reference is available, this evaluation is better than merely accepting the current period's results just because they produced a profit. Furthermore, use of a prior period's operation for evaluation of certain of the component revenues and expenses such as sales, the sales mix, and entertainment will generate valuable information, as will be demonstrated later.

Evaluating operating results based on those of other, similar operations can be dangerous, especially if policies are established or corrective actions taken that are based on such a comparison. The use of this evaluation technique should be restricted to locating potential areas of improvement. The same is true of evaluations based on industry experience. Usually, industry experience is a composite of many operations ranging from those showing a loss to those showing exceptional profits, often owing to circumstances that cannot be duplicated elsewhere. Where the average for the industry group falls depends on the relative number of low-profit or loss operations to the number of good-profit and high-profit operations.

Unfortunately, the point of reference that will enable an operator to make a more valid evaluation is used infrequently in the food service industry, namely, predetermined standards. In those operations in which predetermined standards are in effect, their use is limited to cost of sales and payroll cost, probably because these two cost categories take by far the largest portion of the revenue dollar.

Year Ended December 31

	19x4 Amount	19x4 Percentage to Total Sales	19x4 Per Person Served	19x3 Amount	19x3 Percentage to Total Sales	19x3 Per Person Served
Sales						
Food	$ 801,231	80.0%	$ 2.61	$516,686	78.0%	$ 2.17
Beverages	200,308	20.0	.65	145,705	22.0	.61
Total sales	1,001,539	100.0	3.26	662,391	100.0	2.78
Cost of sales						
Cost of food consumed	354,945	44.3	1.15	212,358	41.1	.89
Less cost of employees' meals	35,254	4.4	.11	26,351	5.1	.11
Cost of food sold	319,691	39.9	1.04	186,007	36.0	.78
Cost of beverage sales	60,092	30.0	.20	40,797	28.0	.17
Combined cost of sales	379,783	37.9	1.24	226,804	34.2	.95
Gross profit	621,756	62.1	2.02	435,587	65.8	1.83
Controllable expenses						
Salaries and wages	271,417	27.1	.88	192,093	29.0	.81
Related payroll expenses	40,062	4.0	.13	27,820	4.2	.12
Total payroll and related expenses	311,479	31.1	1.01	219,913	33.2	.93
Direct operating expenses	51,643	5.2	.17	35,107	5.3	.15
Music and entertainment	6,150	.6	.02	3,312	.5	.01
Advertising and sales promotion	20,921	2.1	.07	14,573	2.2	.06
Utilities	20,115	2.0	.06	11,261	1.7	.05
Administrative and general	41,030	4.1	.13	29,145	4.4	.12
Repairs and maintenance	15,023	1.5	.05	7,949	1.2	.03
Total controllable expenses	466,361	46.6	1.51	321,260	48.5	1.35
Profit before occupancy costs	155,395	15.5	.51	114,327	17.3	.48
Occupancy costs						
Rent	60,092	6.0	.20	40,406	6.1	.17
Interest, insurance and municipal taxes	10,015	1.0	.03	8,250	1.2	.04
Depreciation and amortization	15,123	1.5	.05	10,128	1.6	.04
Total occupancy costs	85,230	8.5	.28	58,784	8.9	.25
Profit before income taxes	$ 70,165	7.0%	$ .23	$ 55,543	8.4%	$ .23

Fig. 11-3. The Avenue A Restaurant's statement of income.

(See *Profitable Food and Beverage Management: Operations*, Chaps. 7, 10, and 17, for the determination and use of food, beverage, and labor cost standards.) The use of standards can be extended to almost every item of cost and expense in an operation, however.

The measures most frequently used in evaluating a food and beverage operation are as follows:

1. Actual dollar amounts
2. Ratios of cost of expense to sales
3. Cost per cover or per person served

As will be illustrated later, all three measures are used in an evaluation, depending on which one most accurately measures a particular item of revenue or expense.

The comments in the following sections refer to the statement of profit and loss shown in Fig. 11–3 and the related statistical data shown in Fig. 11–4.

	Year Ended December 31			
	19x4		19x3	
	Amount	Percentage to Total Sales	Amount	Percentage to Total Sales
Composition of food sales				
Breakfast	$ 176,110	17.6%	$ 148,542	22.4%
Lunch	264,861	26.4	153,765	23.2
Dinner	216,140	21.6	84,725	12.8
Banquets	144,120	14.4	129,654	19.6
Total food sales	801,231	80.0	516,686	78.0
Beverage sales	200,308	20.0	145,705	22.0
	$1,001,539	100.0%	$ 662,391	100.0%

	Number	Average Receipt Per Person	Number	Average Receipt Per Person
Persons served				
Breakfast	161,500	$ 1.09	146,020	$ 1.02
Lunch	84,620	3.13	52,564	2.93
Dinner	36,986	5.84	15,542	5.45
Banquets	24,454	5.89	23,445	5.53
	307,560	$ 2.61	237,571	$ 2.17

	19x4	19x3
Average daily number of regular employees	89.7	73.2
Annual number of man-days worked	22,604	18,446
Number of persons served per man-day	13.6	12.9
Average wage per man-day (including fringe benefits)	$13.78	$11.92

Fig. 11-4. The Avenue A Restaurant's supplemental operating data.

Evaluation of Current Year's Profit Result

The profit before income taxes for the current year amounted to $70,165, or $14,622 higher than the $55,543 recorded for the preceding year. The rise in profit is equal to 26.3 percent. This performance appears to be an impressive achievement. But is it what it should have been when all factors are considered?

When the profit results are measured as a percentage of sales, it is found that this year's profit before income taxes was equal to 7.0 percent of sales whereas the profit last year was equal to 8.4 percent of sales, or a difference of 1.4 percentage points. How much does this difference represent in profit dollars? Applying the 1.4 percentage points to the combined food and beverage sales of $1,001,539, we find that it represents $14,022. This indicates that had the operations during the current year been conducted as economically as in the past year, the profit for the current year would have been $84,187, or 20 percent higher than the $70,165 profit shown.

Is this difference in profit sufficient motivation to probe into the operation to see if a higher profit could have been produced during the year? A decrease in the profit ratio should not be the only reason for an analysis of an operation. There are other benefits such as detection of changes in the market (sales mix), impact of price increases (patronages), and favorable or unfavorable trends in certain costs and expenses.

Sales

Combined food and beverage sales increased $339,148, or almost 51.2 percent above the sales level of the previous year. This is a substantial increase, and it was one of the major factors in the total increase in profit. What brought about this substantial increase in sales? It will be noted that both food and beverage sales were up over the previous year. Food sales increased 55 percent, and beverage sales rose 37 percent.

Food Sales. Management is aware that part of the increase in food sales was the result of a 10 percent increase in menu prices put into effect at the beginning of the year. The impact of this increase in menu prices can be very closely approximated by applying the average check per person for each meal period of last year to the number of persons served during the corresponding periods of this year. The following computation shows the approximate impact of the price increase.

Financial Statement Analysis 209

Meal Period	No. of Persons Served This Year	Average Receipt Per Cover Last Year	Sales Revenue
Breakfast	161,500	$1.02	$164,730
Lunch	84,620	2.93	247,936
Dinner	36,986	5.45	201,573
Banquet	24,454	5.53	135,231
Total			749,470
Actual Sales			801,231
Approximate impact			$ 51,761

The foregoing is only an approximation of the impact of the price increase because there is no way of knowing whether there has been any change in the sales mix since last year. Because different menu items carry different prices, a change in the sales mix of menu items will influence the impact shown in the above computation. Despite this, the computed impact will adequately serve as a guide for the purpose intended.

Reference to the statistical data indicates that the balance of the increase in food sales for the current year can be generally attributed to the greater patronage for all meal periods, particularly the patronage in the higher priced meal periods. It will be noted, for instance, that the patronage for the dinner meal period, where the average check was $5.84, more than doubled, whereas the patronage for the breakfast period, where the average check was $1.09, increased only 11 percent.

Beverage Sales. The increase in beverage sales for the current year was owing in part to an increase of 5 percent in drink prices. This increase contributed about 17.5 percent of the total beverage sales increase of $54,603 for the current period. The balance of the increase must be attributed to the greater number of persons patronizing the operation and the possibility that a greater proportion of higher priced beverages may have been sold during the current year. If the operator believes that the information as to the sales mix of high- and low-priced drinks is of importance to him, this information can be obtained from an analysis of the beverage purchases of the higher priced brands.

General Considerations

One of the objectives of the analysis of this year's operations is to determine the reason for the lower profit yield (7.0 percent of sales) of the current period as compared with the profit yield (8.4 percent) in the previous year. In this connection, it must be pointed out that an increase in sales will not always favorably influence the profit ratio.

For instance, a proportionately larger increase in food sales, where cost of sales and labor are appreciably higher than are those related to beverage sales, will reduce the overall profit ratio. This is not to be interpreted as meaning that an increase in food sales is undesirable. As long as food sales produce a profit, they should be promoted and encouraged because the more food sales there are, the more profit dollars there will be to take to the bank. The bank will not accept for deposit a higher statistical ratio. It should be remembered that the primary purpose of the analysis of the operation is to determine whether the operations were conducted as economically and efficiently this year as last year. To measure this, all factors that influence this statistical ratio (profit yield per dollar of sale) must be considered.

Other points present themselves as a result of the analysis of sales of the Avenue A Restaurant. They are as follows:

1. The increase in prices of food and beverages was not generally resisted because the number of persons served, after the price increase, rose more than 29 percent.
2. The increase in patronage was substantially higher in the higher priced meal periods, that is, dinner with a check average of $5.84 rose 138 percent; luncheon with a check average of $3.13 rose 61 percent; breakfast with an average of $1.09 rose only 11 percent.
3. Banquet service recorded the lowest increase in patronage, namely, 4 percent. However, an increase of 10 percent in prices produced an increase of 36 cents in the average check per person.

These changes are material, and they may be foreshowing a change in the nature of the restaurant's market, particularly in luncheon and dinner patronage. Because this hypothesis is a distinct possibility, the operator would be well advised to study the neighborhood as well as the market he caters to so as to prepare for future changes.

Cost of Sales

Many operators expect their total cost of sales to rise and fall in the same proportion as total sales, resulting in a constant cost-of-sales ratio. In theory, this is right, but unfortunately it doesn't work in practice. For the cost-of-sales ratio to remain constant, the following elements have to remain the same:

1. Sales mix of the menu as well as the relative proportions of food and beverage sales
2. Sales prices of items

3. Portion sizes and quality of the raw merchandise
4. Purchase prices
5. The amount of dollar loss from waste and over-preparation, and so on

We know that in practice these elements do change and with varying effects on the total sales volume, total cost of sales, and the resulting cost-of-sales ratio. Therefore, a simple comparison of ratios is not very meaningful. A preferable basis for evaluating the cost of sales is a comparison with a predetermined standard. This standard is the *potential cost of sales*. The preparation of potential costs takes into consideration changes from one period to another of (1) sales mix, (2) sales prices, (3) the quality of merchandise purchased, and (4) purchase prices.

The use of potential costs is described in *Profitable Food and Beverage Management: Operations*. The analysis technique used here to evaluate Avenue A's performance is the less effective, but often used, method of comparing this year's performance with last year's.

The combined cost of sales for the current period amounted to $379,783 as compared to $226,804 for last year, indicating a current increase of $152,979. This increase was almost 68 percent, whereas sales, as mentioned previously, increased only 51.2 percent. The higher increase in the cost of sales is a cause for the lower profit yield. The gross profit on sales for the current year was equal to 62.1 cents per dollar of sales, whereas last year it was equal to 65.8 cents per dollar of sale.

Although 3.7 cents decrease in gross profit per dollar of sale, when viewed only as a ratio, may not be startling, its conversion into dollars of lost profit is startling. The decrease, when applied to the combined sales of $1,001,539, is equal to $37,057, or more than 50 percent of the current year's profit of $70,165 before income taxes.

Reference to the income statement indicates that the higher combined cost of sales was due to a rise of almost four percentage points in the cost of food sold and two percentage points in the cost of beverages sold.

Food. It will be noted that the total cost of employees' meals has increased, as would be expected in view of the greater number of employees to be fed this year than last year. When measured on the basis of the number of persons served, the cost was equal to 11 cents per person, the same amount as last year. Although the cost was the same as last year, there actually was an improvement in this area because during the current year there was an increase of roundly 7 percent in the purchase price of food, according to market reports.

The cost of food sold during the current year was equal to 39.9 cents per dollar of sale, whereas it was 36.0 cents per dollar of sale in the previous year. This year's cost of food sales ratio, however, was affected by a 10 percent average increase in menu prices and a 7 percent average rise in the purchase cost of food.

If the current year's food sales are adjusted by the increased menu prices and the food cost is adjusted by the increase in prices of the food purchased, it shows that the food cost ratio for the current year would have been higher as shown below:

1. Sales revenue adjusted for menu price increases:

$$\frac{\text{Food sales of } \$801{,}231}{110\% \text{ (includes 10\% increase in prices)}} = \$728{,}392$$

2. Cost of sales adjusted for increase in purchase prices:

$$\frac{\text{Cost of food sales } \$319{,}691}{107\% \text{ (includes price increase)}} = \$298{,}777$$

3. Adjusted cost of sales ratio:

$$\frac{\text{Adjusted cost of sales of } \$298{,}777}{\text{Adjusted sales revenue of } \$728{,}392} = 41.0\%$$

That the cost-of-sales ratio was held to 39.9 percent of sales is due mainly to reduced waste, smaller portions, or a change in the mix of sales to include more lower cost items. The effect of changing sales mix on resulting food cost is discussed in Chap. 8.

In the case of the Avenue A operation, one can conclude that management was fairly successful in controlling food costs in a time of rising market prices.

Beverages. The cost of beverage sales rose 2 cents per dollar of sale when compared with the 28-cent cost performance of last year. Management estimated that the increase in purchase prices averaged 7 percent for the year. Taking into consideration the 5 percent increase in prices of the beverages sold and the increase of 7 percent in purchase cost, the cost of beverage sales should have been 29.4 cents per dollar of sale. For the current year it was 30 cents per dollar of sale, or a difference of 0.6 cents on each dollar of sale. A difference in the sales mix between this year and last year could account for the 0.6-cent increase. This cost performance should be considered satisfactory.

Salaries, Wages, and Related Expenses

After the cost of sales, the largest share of the revenue dollar is consumed by salaries and wages and their related costs (payroll taxes, fringe benefits, employee meals, etc.). In the Avenue A Restaurant, salaries and wages and related expenses this year increased approximately $92,000. An increase should be expected in this expense category because of the greater number of persons served. The measure used to evaluate labor cost is not cost per dollar of sale but rather the number of persons served. This measure is preferable because it is not influenced by the increase in food and beverage sales prices during the year. In the example, salaries, wages, and related expenses took 31.1 percent of total sales this year, or 2.1 percentage points less than last year. It is not known from the use of this measure (ratio to sales) whether the lower rate was due to higher menu prices or a more efficient operation.

Although the labor cost percentage declined, the total dollar cost increased, as noted above. The question that must be asked is whether this overall increase was reasonable, taking into consideration the fact that during this year, management estimates that there was an average increase of about 15 percent in the rates paid to employees.

The statistics relating to labor, its productivity, and the rate per man-day will enable the operator to ascertain whether the higher payroll cost was reasonable. These statistics show that although there were 16.5 more employees than last year, the productivity per employee man-day was better this year. This year, one man-day was required for 13.6 patrons served, whereas last year one employee serviced 12.9 patrons. Had the output this year been the same as last year, the number of employees required to handle this year's higher volume would have been 94.6 as compared to the 89.7 employed.

The question now arises why there is a higher labor cost per patron this year in view of the improved productivity. The higher per-patron cost this year is the direct result of the increase in wage rates mentioned previously. The following computation shows that if the same payroll cost per man-day prevailed this year as last year ($11.92), the cost per patron served this year would have been roundly 88 cents, or 5 cents per patron lower than the 93-cent cost of last year.

22,604 man-days × $11.92 = $269,440, hypothetical payroll cost

269, 440/307,560 number of persons served = $0.88 per person

Lacking information as to whether the staffing was proper and the workers performed at optimum efficiency, it must be concluded from the information available in the statement of income that the labor cost performance this year was satisfactory when compared with the performance of last year.

Other Operating Expenses

The remaining expenses, higher by about $54,000 this year than last year, show a higher cost of 8 cents per patron for this year. Some of the expense increases such as music and entertainment were probably planned, whereas others such as utilities were largely beyond the control of management. The total increase in this classification, however, amounts to over 50 percent of the previous year's expenses, an extraordinarily high ratio of increase for semivariable expenses, even though as a percentage of sales the expenses rose only slightly. Very careful attention should be paid to each item of such expenses to keep them under better control.

Fixed Charges

Fixed charges are those expenses that are fixed, either in amount, such as interest and leasehold amortization, or in the measure for payment, such as rent (which is at a rate of 5 percent of food sales and 10 percent of beverage sales). There is not much that management can do about such expenses except to keep the amount of the operating profit before deductions at a sufficient level to cover them and still produce a net profit, which, after income taxes, will provide to the owners a reasonable return on their investment.

12

BUDGETING PROCEDURES

Types of Budgets

A budget is management's basic profit plan for operating an entire company or a subdivision. The several types of budgets in common use may be characterized according to purpose as follows:

1. *Operating budget.* A forecast of revenues and an estimate of expenses prepared by management as a profit plan. The objective is to provide guidelines for attaining desired profit and perhaps growth goals.
2. *Capital budget.* A plan showing the estimated expenditures and the timing for the replacement or acquisition of assets such as buildings, equipment, furniture, and fixtures.
3. *Cash budgets.* A projection of cash receipts and disbursements prepared in order to have a basis for determining the cash that will be available or required to meet business needs such as regular payroll, debt retirements, and capital expenditures.

There is a very close relationship among the budgets listed above. For example, the pressure to reduce payroll cost tends to increase the need for labor-saving devices to increase the efficiency and productivity of employees. To give another example, the projected level of earnings is important in determining the availability of cash, the need for working capital, and the selection of a source or form of financing for capital improvements. Preparation of both operating and capital budgets must be completed before preparation of the cash budget, in which cash inflow and outflow will be estimated.

Basic Budgeting

Any business should be able to improve its performance by using a budget as a management tool for planning and control purposes. A large multiunit restaurant organization should have a complete budgeting program, including the types of budgets just mentioned, together with projected financial statements. A smaller business will find it advantageous to have at least an operating budget.

An established restaurant (or any other type of food service operation) should have historical data available as to the number of covers (meals) that have been served in each meal period during an operating period (day, week, or month), as well as the average receipt per cover for each meal period. This is the basic material for the preparation of a sound sales forecast for an operating budget. It can be used to estimate the number of covers that will be served in the period covered by the budget. Likewise, historical information on expenses can be used to budget future expenses. These projections can be summarized in an income statement to provide an estimate of profit. If the expected profit is unsatisfactory, changes in operating policies and procedures may be required.*

Planning and budgeting may be undertaken for either long-term or short-term purposes. Most basic budgets are prepared for a projected single level of activity. In this chapter, the structure, preparation, and utilization of an operating budget for a short-term period of one year or less are explained.

The period of the budget must coincide with the period of the firm's operating statments for the effectiveness of budgetary control to be fully realized. Furthermore, such statements must show a comparison of the actual revenues and expenditures with budgeted amounts. Differences, often referred to as variances, must be evaluated by department or division in a large organization. Unjustified variances, either over or under the budget, should also receive management attention for appropriate action. The objective of budgetary management, after all, is to correct unfavorable performance or to improve operating conditions in order to attain the planned profit.

Prerequisites to Sound Budgeting

Organization and System

If a budget is to be a sound working tool, it must be carefully planned, organized, implemented, and utilized; otherwise the variances developed, as subsequently discussed, will be meaningless for control purposes. The essential prerequisites to an effective budget are as follows:

---

*For a further discussion of budgeting and profit planning, see Clifford T. Fay, Jr., Richard C. Rhoads, and Robert L. Rosenblatt, *Managerial Accounting for the Hospitality Service Industries* (Dubuque, Iowa: Wm. C. Brown Company, 1971).

1. A well-defined organization structure with definite lines of authority and responsibility established for department or function heads.
2. An accounting system designed to meet the organization's needs. The Uniform System of Accounts for Restaurants provides adequate accounting systems suitable for use in many food service organizations.
3. Established policies, standards, and procedures to be followed by all personnel so that the organization will attain the end results expected by management.

Participatory Budgeting

In the preparation of a budget, it is vital to involve all executive employees in determining the estimated costs and expenses for their respective areas of activity. Without participation in and commitment to a budget by the executive employees, there tends to be less interest in the achievement of the budgetary goals set by someone else and in the correction of indicated variances from the budget figures. On the other hand, having accepted a budget as feasible and attainable, participants may be held responsible for the accomplishment of the planned projections. Moreover, there is greater self-motivation to achieve end results that one has personally forecast.

For a large or multiunit restaurant organization, budget preparation can be facilitated by establishing a budget committee to develop and coordinate the goals and efforts of all participants. For example, in a multiunit operation, the committee may be composed of an executive from the operations department, the finance or accounting department, and the marketing department. Divisional or functional employees whose participation is deemed desirable can also be included. The committee establishes budgetary policies and procedures and a budget calendar. Detailed instructions and forms are prepared, ordinarily under the direction of the controller or a budget manager.

During the budget preparation process, either the committee or the budget manager, as authorized, reviews the proposed departmental budgets. Differences and inconsistencies are resolved and any revisions may be made that are consistent with profitability objectives.

The Operating Budget

Structure and Statements

Forms are usually designed on which budgeting information can be submitted by each department head. These forms provide for recording projections of operating information (revenues, expenses, unit work loads, labor man-hours, etc.) applicable to each department's operations. The use of standardized forms permits accumulation of budgeted and actual expenditures and allows comparison and computation of variances from budgeted amounts for each department and for the organization as a whole. The format of schedules and income statements, either as presented in the Uniform System of Accounts for Restaurants or as modified to fit particular requirements, can be adapted for this purpose.

	Period Ending	
Current Month	**Particulars**	**Year-to-Date**

This Year (Actual $/%, Budget $/%) — Last Year (Actual $/%)	Sales:
	  Food
	  Beverages
	  Total Food and Beverage Sales
	Cost of Sales:
	  Food
	  Beverages
	    Total cost of sales
	Gross Profit:
	  Food
	  Beverages
	  Total Gross Profit
	  Other Income
	  Total Income
	Controllable Expenses:
	  Payroll
	  Employee benefits
	  Employees' meals
	  Direct operating expenses
	  Music and entertainment
	  Advertising and sales promotion
	  Utilities
	  Administrative and general
	  Repairs and maintenance
	    Total controllable expenses
	Profit before Rent, etc. (Operating Profit)
	Rent or Occupation Costs
	Profit before Depreciation
	Depreciation
	Restaurant Profit
	Additions to/or Deductions from Restaurant Profit
	Net Profit before Income Taxes
	Income Taxes
	Net Profit
		This Year (Actual $/%, Budget $/%) — Last Year (Actual $/%)

Fig. 12-1. Free-standing restaurant monthly operating statement.

Figure 12.1 shows a monthly operating statement commonly used in a free-standing restaurant. This statement is a summary of income and expense information well suited to the needs of top management. It provides comparisons of actual results for the current period with those for the preceding period and, more important, with the budget.

Figure 12.2 shows a statement for a food and beverage department operation that is part of a hotel or club. Additional columns

	Actual			Budget		
	Total	Food	Beverages	Total	Food	Beverages
Gross Sales:						
Dining rooms*	$	$	$	$	$	$
Room service						
Banquets						
Total gross sales						
Allowances						
Net Sales						
Cost of Sales:						
Cost of merchandise consumed						
Less: Cost of empl. meals						
Cost of sales						
Gross Profit						
Other Income:						
Cover charges						
Sundry banquet income						
Miscellaneous						
Total Revenue						
Departmental Expenses:						
Salaries and wages						
Related payroll expenses						
Employees' meals						
Uniforms						
Music and entertainment						
Laundry						
Kitchen fuel						
Linen						
China, glassware, silver						
Utensils						
Cleaning supplies						
Dry cleaning						
Contract cleaning						
Guest and paper supplies						
Menus and beverage lists						
Printing and stationery						
Decorations						
Banquet expenses						
Licenses and taxes						
Bar expenses						
Miscellaneous						
Total expenses						
Departmental Profit [or Loss]	$	$	$	$	$	$

* List each room separately, such as dining room, grill, cafe, bar(s), etc.

Fig. 12-2. Food and beverage departmental operations.

for amounts and percentages may be added as desired to show budgetary variances. Separate statements should be prepared for the month and for the year to date.

Preparation of the Budget

Before a department head can prepare his department's budget he must have certain information, such as the departmental budget and actual figures for the preceding period. Department heads must also be advised of management's overall sales projections and operating plans, such as proposed menu, price changes, expected monthly or seasonal variations, and shutdowns for renovations. Information must also be furnished about any proposed or anticipated wage salary adjustments and supply or expense trends to the extent that these can be predicted. Questions such as "How tight should the budget be?" should be dealt with so that department heads have a clear understanding of budget policy and how it will be applied to the subsequent execution of plans.

Using the information pertaining to prior periods and any other guidelines provided by management, each department head can budget the payroll and expense items applicable to his department. The mechanics are explained in the illustrations included in this chapter. After departmental income and expense budgets have been prepared, they are submitted to the budget committee or to a designated budget coordinator for such revisions as may be required. After all segments of the overall budget have been approved, a combined budget is prepared and issued, along with departmental budgets.

Conditions may change during a budget period, and if the consequences are expected to be major, budget revisions may be required. It is unrealistic to make comparisons of actual results with initial budgeted amounts that are no longer applicable. For example, changes in operating policies and conditions or prolonged weather conditions that affect sales are just two developments that could adversely affect operating results and cause a variance from budgetary goals. The budget would have to be revised to reflect them. If the concept of operations were changed from that of a high-priced exclusive operation to that of a lower priced, general public type of operation, then the budget would have to be recast in its entirety.

Larger, well-established organizations can afford the use of data-processing equipment for budget preparation and revision, thus eliminating much clerical effort. For example, historical data for the desired months, quarters, or years may be entered into a computer, which will quickly produce a trend analysis or statistical forecast. After review of the output from this type of analysis, management can modify the calculations based on future plans as appropriate to achieve profit objectives. After a budget has been prepared and stored in a computer's memory, it is feasible to introduce alternatives (e.g., price changes, menu changes, volume or cost revisions, etc.) into the computer for the purpose of generating their probable impact on the end results. Projected statements may be prepared in minutes by the computer for use by management in determining which, if any, of the alternatives should be adopted.

Budgetary Control

Not all expenses are controllable. Certain expenses, however, are subject to varying degrees of control, the degree depending on factors such as patronage and sales volume. Fixed expenses such as depreciation, rent, licenses, taxes, and contractual expenses are not controllable by supervisory personnel. Certain fixed expenses may be controllable by top management but only at the time they are incurred. For example, depreciation expense is determined (usually) at the time a piece of equipment is purchased. In addition to the fixed category of expenses, there are those classified as semivariable and variable. Semivariable expenses are those that are influenced only by substantial fluctuations in number of patrons or in sales volume. As an example, the need for a second cashier or an additional dishwasher is dictated by a substantial increase in patronage, whereas a variable expense such as that for linen or paper supplies is affected by each meal sold.

In exercising control, management must be careful to avoid certain pitfalls in budgeting. For example, a department may be operating within its budget and yet have the potential for additional improvement. Some budget estimates may be unrealistic owing to changes in operating conditions. For example, menu changes resulting in more bulk preparation and less individual item preparation may call for a revision in budgeted payroll and food costs. In sum, a budget does not relieve management of the responsibility for utilizing sound management techniques.

Benefits of Budgeting

In the foregoing sections, some of the benefits of budgeting have been mentioned and some are self-evident. To be valid, of course, the benefits must exceed the cost and effort required to control a business by budgeting. There is no point in having a dollar of cost chasing a dime of savings. To avoid such a situation, it is required that a value analysis of the cost of budgetary controls be compared with the estimated value of the benefits.

The more important benefits of budgeting may be summarized as follows:

1. *Planning.* Since an integral part of budget preparation is a forecast of sales volume, it becomes essential to determine

future policy as it relates to hours of operation, expansion plans, menu structuring, and so forth. Since much of this type of forecasting requires a subjective evaluation of the market and changing market conditions, budget development offers an opportunity for management to become somewhat introspective and evaluate itself, its policies, and its operation.

2. *Control.* A budget provides a valuable management tool for evaluating actual performance and cost. A comparison of current results with the results of a prior period may not be valid because of changed conditions, changes in personnel, past inefficiencies, and the like. A basic cause of a difference may be simply that the number of days in the current period was not the same as in the corresponding period a year ago.

When department heads participate in budget development, they become aware not only of what their responsibilities are but of the performance required and the expense limitations that must be imposed on them in order to attain the company's established profit goal. Subsequently, if it appears that a budget item will be exceeded, the staff knows the alternatives; there does not have to be any confusion or misunderstanding. If an overexpenditure is anticipated or is unavoidable, management's advance approval may be obtained or alternative actions discussed and decisions made as to the action to be taken.

An Illustration of Budget Preparation

The basic procedure outlined below emphasizes use of a unit-cost or percentage approach in budget preparation:

Step 1. Sales Forecast. The use of historical sales volume adjusted by an estimated growth factor, inflation, and other known conditions is a common method of forecasting sales. If carefully prepared, the forecast, even for a long period (a year or more), can be quite accurate. To be adequate for control purposes over a short period, however, forecasts must give consideration to seasonality, holidays, and any special events or trends.

Preferably, unit sales of prior periods should be reviewed and adjusted for holidays and any upcoming events that are likely to have a significantly favorable or unfavorable effect on business. Unit sales or cover counts by meal periods (breakfast, lunch, and dinner) should be compiled from available information in order to study trends in sales patterns. Unless the study of trends dictates otherwise, unit sales may be analyzed for a four-week period, instead of an entire year, and the results annualized. The four-week period reviewed might consist either of one week from each season or of a peak-volume week, two average-volume weeks, and one low-volume week. Sales for each outlet, however, must be analyzed separately and the figures recapped into quarterly and annual summaries as required. Figure 12–3 shows a simple form for completing a sales analysis.

The amount of the average check or receipt per cover has to be forecast separately for each meal period included in the summary and then multiplied by the number of covers served of the applicable meal in order to compute the forecast of total sales.

For budget purposes, beverage sales can be forecast in one of two ways. The total number of covers served (breakfast covers should be eliminated if there is a material fluctuation in these covers from period to period) is divided into the beverage sales so as to arrive at the average dollar amount of sales per cover. That average, after adjustment for any contemplated price changes, can be applied to the forecasted covers to forecast the dollar amount of beverage sales for the budget period.

If cover statistics are not available, then a ratio of beverage sales to food sales can be used for the forecast. This method has proved very satisfactory in operations where the ratio of beverage sales to food sales has remained constant from one year to another.

Step 2. Direct operating costs. This group of cost items has been defined previously. The cost of salaries and wages can be budgeted by applying expected wage rates to each job classification as delineated in the staffing guides (the procedure is explained in Chap. 16 on staff planning in *Profitable Food and Beverage Management: Operations*). From the staffing guides the fixed staff can be determined. Variable staff requirements are determined by the number of covers forecast and the expected levels of productivity. Vacation pay and other fringe benefits are projected in accordance with historical relationships to payroll costs and adjusted for any planned changes.

Music, entertainment, and all other fixed expenses can be projected by analyzing each one individually, based on current policy and arrangements. For example, the expense of contract cleaning may be budgeted in accordance with contract terms. The expense of music and entertainment may be budgeted in accordance with the entertainment policy of the operation.

Other expenses in this group may be budgeted by developing ratios of items directly related to one another. For example uniforms expense may be projected by analyzing past trends in terms of expense per employee, laundry expense may be projected in terms of a cost per cover served, and so on.

Step 3. Fixed operating expenses. This group of expense items has been defined previously. It must be recognized that a category such as "administrative and general" is essentially a responsibility cost center

Detail of Food Covers Served
Period _____

		SUN.	MON.	TUE.	WED.	THU.	FRI.	SAT.	TOTAL
	FACILITY _____								
Meal _____									
	Week Ended								
	Week Ended								
	Week Ended								
	Week Ended								
	Total								
	Average								
Meal _____									
	Week Ended								
	Week Ended								
	Week Ended								
	Week Ended								
	Total								
	Average								
Meal _____									
	Week Ended								
	Week Ended								
	Week Ended								
	Week Ended								
	Total								
	Average								
TOTAL									
AVERAGE									

Fig. 12-3. Sales forecast.

that covers many expenses, some of which are variable and others that are fixed. Each expense has to be analyzed and projected, giving consideration to planned changes. Certain expenses such as commissions on credit cards may fluctuate in relation to sales and should be projected accordingly, whereas others such as the manager's salary are fixed and are not subject to change because of sales volume changes.

Step 4. Capital expenses. Capital expenses relate to the financial structure of ownership and to the manner in which the business is set up rather than its operation. Included are such items as rent, depreciation, insurance on the building and contents, taxes, etc. Generally, these expenses are relatively fixed and simply budgeted in accordance with historical data and known plans.

A budget developed on the basis of expected sales volume and expenses under current operating conditions may result in an estimated net profit that neither meets profit objectives nor provides an adequate return on investment. Although projection of an inadequate end result may be realistic, it probably indicates a need to reevaluate business policies and operations and to consider alternatives.

The Capital Budget

In the preparation of a capital budget, proposed expenditures for capital items such as additional facilities and long-term equipment are itemized for a budget period. The final budget generally is a summary that shows the estimated cost and acquisition date for each type of capital item or project.

In large organizations, a capital asset summary form generally provides also for showing procurement reasons, approval signatures, and accounting information. This practice facilitates the budgeting process, which ordinarily begins with department supervisors submitting proposals in writing for needed items. These proposals are evaluated by management, which takes into consideration financing requirements, sales trends, long-range plans and the like. Management then establishes priorities for the items it approves for procurement.

Dissemination of approved budget summaries to the department manager, purchasing agent, controller, and interested executives facilitates control over implementation. It also facilitates a subsequent comparison of the actual results and benefits of expenditures with the advantages and justifications predicted in the proposal.

An important aspect of an effective capital asset program is the evaluation by management of proposals for major projects in order to select the most profitable projects for implementation. There are various methods by which to evaluate these proposals. One of the more commonly used is the return on, or rate of recovery of, an investment. For example, the payback or accounting method measures the time required for savings or cash inflow to recover the cash outlay for an investment in a project. Because this method does not measure the profitability of a project or consider the time value of money, it is not as good as the discounted cash flow method, which is gaining in use. Discussion of these methods is beyond the scope of this textbook; the reader is referred to texts dealing with capital investment analysis.

The Cash Budget

Most small restaurants do not need a cash budget, largely because they are operated on a strictly cash basis. Restaurants that accept national credit cards usually get their cash from credit card sales very quickly. Consequently, in the restaurant field, a lack of cash for product purchases and for payrolls is not as great a problem for a profitable operation as might be the case in other fields.

A large restaurant organization, especially one with several units, needs a cash budget to assist management in planning for major expenditures such as advertising and sales promotion campaigns, equipment purchases, capital improvements, or business expansion and possibly short- or long-term borrowing requirements. A multiunit operator should have a cash transfer procedure in effect to provide transfers of cash to central bank accounts on which disbursement checks are drawn.

During a given period, many items flow from the operating budget into the cash budget. Care must be exercised in the preparation of a cash budget to exclude noncash items such as depreciation and to show disbursements according to payment date rather than the period covered by the obligation to pay.

A common budget format shows the beginning cash balance, plus cash receipts, less cash disbursements, and then the ending cash balance. Any special or financing transactions, such as borrowings or repayments, or minimum cash balances required to be maintained in banks, are shown separately. The period covered by a cash budget may range from a week to a year or more, with breakdowns by months or quarters as desired by management.

It is necessary to forecast the collections on any receivables as well as the payments required by suppliers' invoice terms, government tax regulations, payroll pay days, and so on. A completed cash budget statement finally shows the excess or deficiency of cash for the period(s) covered. With this information, management can plan its financing needs or cash disposition as applicable.

13

Automated Data Procedures

The highly personalized nature of food and beverage service is such that automation of any kind has not always seemed compatible with it. At one time even cash registers were not acceptable in many restaurants where it was felt that a hand-written bill was more personal.

Public acceptance of a high degree of automation in almost all services offered has changed that attitude, while new automated technology in preparation and controls has made it possible to provide a better product at lower manpower cost. In the highly competitive food service industry, automatic data processing can play a major role in controlling costs and expenses and in releasing manpower that would otherwise be expended in clerical or low-productivity jobs for more personal and productive uses.

In this chapter, Automated Data Processing (ADP) as it serves all the functions of food and beverage management is discussed. The computer can serve and aid almost any function considered in the other chapters of this book. In the food service industry, however, it has proved difficult until recently to design a cost effective system to take advantage of the computer. Essentially, the cost to process items of small unit value and sales price may consume too much of the profit margin for ADP to be economically feasible. The potential saving may well be lower than the cost of securing the information. With the advent of minicomputers and well-developed software packages, the situation has changed rapidly and will certainly continue to change in the future.

Data Processing Applications

The data processing applications that have proved to be of most value to the food service industry are the following:

1. Management Information Systems:
    a. Inventory control
    b. Purchasing

      c. Sales analysis
      d. Labor productivity analysis and control
      e. Financial management reporting—profit analysis
  2. Accounting Functions:
      a. General ledger and financial statement preparation
      b. Accounts receivable and payable
      c. Cash flow projections and cash management
      d. Payroll preparation and tax reporting

Management Information Systems

A good example of a comprehensive restaurant management system is one distributed by the National Cash Register (NCR) Corporation using the name Restaurant Evaluation of Cost and Inventory by Product and Employee or Recipe. This system utilizes data captured on an electronic cash register unit at the time the guest check is settled. It can also gather data from a prechecking device at the time the kitchen order is placed by the server. The system from the data captured produces three groups of reports.

  1. Sales Analysis
      a. The Daily Analysis Report—This report shows sales by specific menu item. It includes the description of menu items, the menu price, the number of units served for the period, total dollar sales, percentage of gross sales represented by each menu item, the item cost, the total cost, the cost percentage, the sales cost to-date, the percentage of gross sales to-date, the sales year to-date, and the percentage of gross sales to-date. The report enables management to measure sales performance of food and beverage items in units and dollar sales.
      b. The Waiter/Waitress Reports—This report shows by server number the amount of tips paid, the amount sold, and the perentage of gross sales represented by those sales. This report is a comprehensive analysis of the sales productivity of individual waiters and waitresses relating to certain selected menu items.
  2. Inventory Control
      a. Month to-date Inventory Report—This report shows the inventory purchases, inventory issues, the shrinkage, and the amount on hand.
      b. A Below Minimum Report—This is an exception report that shows a minimum figure established in inventory for each food and beverage item and which items are below that minimum and the date of the last purchase, the

last price paid, current quantity on hand, and description of the item.
3. Cost Evaluation Report
   a. Month to-date Cost Analysis—This is a report that shows by menu item the menu price, number of units served, total dollar sales of the items, percentage of gross sales, the planned unit cost, the planned cost, the planned cost percentage then the actual unit cost, actual cost and actual cost percentage, and a variance percentage. Gross profit for each menu item and percentage of the overall menu profit can also be reported.
   b. Menu Explosion Report—This report takes the cost analysis one step further and shows the cost of each food or beverage item of the menu and shows the cost of the individual ingredients within that item.

The reports that may be generated by this system are used as illustrations in this chapter.

Inventory Control. The strongest feature of a computerized system is its ability to store, retrieve, and print out large volumes of data in a timely, efficient manner. Inventory control is one of the best uses the food and beverage service industry can make of this capability.

The important fact to be understood in terms of computerizing the inventory is that the more data included in the data base, the more reporting functions can be performed. If the data base includes purchases, receipts, issues, recipes, menu sales by item, and daily forecasts, the management reporting capability will be greatly enhanced.

Many food service operations could probably benefit from computerized inventory management. In the absence of a computer, the procedure of physical inventory counting, extension and valuation, review, analysis, and reordering can take a great deal of time and is subject to various inaccuracies. Computerizing the procedure has many advantages, one of which is reduction of inventory. With manual systems, biweekly or weekly calculations are impractical to obtain. The computerized system will allow weekly or even daily calculations. Food service managers may then monitor inventory levels and avoid excessive investments in food, beverage, supplies, utensils, and so on.

A reduction in inventory normally produces at least two direct monetary benefits. First, money that was locked up in inventory can be used in another part of the operation. Second, smaller inventories mean lower storage costs. These two areas of cost savings can amount to a significant percentage of total inventory value. It is currently

230 Profitable Food and Beverage Management: Planning

DATE 02/04/7-
PAGE 01

INV NO	DESCRIPTION	LOC	UNIT OF MEAS	USEAGE QUANTITY DOLLAR	AVE COST DAY USE	MTD PURCHASES QUANTITY DOLLAR	INVENTORY REPORT PRICE LAST AVERAGE	VARIANCE	SHRINKAGE QUANTITY DOLLAR	AVERAGE	MINIMUM QUANTITY	ON HAND QUANTITY DOLLAR	AVE COST DAYS ON HAND
1010 0	BRANDY	0001	FLOZ	117.50 / 22.94	0.19 / 29.37	281.60 / 55.12	0.20 / 0.19	0.01	13.30 / 2.60	0.19	25.60	176.40 / 34.58	0.19 / 6.00
1020 0	CREME DE COCOA	0001	FLOZ	258.00 / 34.76	0.13 / 64.50	256.00 / 34.50	0.13 / 0.13	0.00	7.80 / 1.05	0.13	25.60	15.80 / 2.14	0.13 / 0.24
1021 0	CREME DE MENTHE	0001	FLOZ	283.50 / 38.20	0.13 / 70.87	537.60 / 72.84	0.15 / 0.13	0.02	10.00 / 1.36	0.13	25.60	269.70 / 36.73	0.13 / 3.80
1030 0	GIN	0001	FLOZ	292.00 / 47.33	0.16 / 73.00	537.60 / 86.84	0.15 / 0.15	0.01*	9.60 / 1.54	0.16	25.60	261.60 / 42.12	0.16 / 3.58
1040 0	RUM - DARK	0001	FLOZ	134.00 / 32.45	0.24 / 33.50	281.60 / 67.63	0.16 / 0.21	0.03*	0.00 / 0.00	0.00	25.60	173.20 / 41.38	0.23 / 5.17
1041 0	RUM - LIGHT	0001	FLOZ	134.00 / 23.55	0.17 / 33.50	281.60 / 49.09	0.21 / 0.15	0.02*	25.60 / 4.44	0.17	25.60	147.60 / 25.60	0.17 / 4.40
1100 0	VERMOUTH	0001	FLOZ	36.50 / 2.89	0.07 / 9.12	352.00 / 27.96	0.08 / 0.07	0.01	16.00 / 1.27	0.07	32.00	331.50 / 26.34	0.07 / 36.34
1110 0	TEQUILA	0001	FLOZ	147.50 / 31.68	0.21 / 36.87	281.60 / 61.34	0.22 / 0.21	0.01	6.80 / 1.49	0.21	25.60	152.90 / 33.67	0.22 / 4.14
1120 0	TREPLE SEC	0001	FLOZ	29.50 / 4.37	0.14 / 7.37	281.60 / 41.32	0.12 / 0.14	0.02*	15.00 / 2.20	0.14	25.60	262.70 / 38.55	0.14 / 35.64
1500 0	WHITE WINE	0001	GAL	0.91 / 4.27	4.69 / 0.22	15.00 / 70.75	4.75 / 4.7:	0.04	1.50 / 7.07	4.71	1.00	13.59 / 64.11	4.71 / 61.77
1510 9	TOTAL ALCOHOL			1,433.41 / 242.44		3,106.20 / 567.39			105.60 / 23.02			1,804.99 / 345.22	
2000 0	ARTICHOKE	0001	EACH	37.00 / 23.31	0.63 / 9.25	264.00 / 166.80	0.65 / 0.63	0.02	15.00 / 9.47	0.63	24.00	236.00 / 149.14	0.63 / 25.51
2010 0	CABBAGE	0001	LB	10.96 / 1.75	0.15 / 2.74	550.00 / 89.00	0.18 / 0.16	0.02	8.00 / 1.29	0.16	50.00	581.04 / 93.96	0.16 / 212.05
2020 0	CARROTS	0001	LB	50.96 / 6.11	0.11 / 12.74	50.00 / 6.00	0.16 / 0.12	0.00	5.00 / 0.60	0.12	50.00	44.04 / 5.29	0.12 / 3.45
2030 0	CELERY	0001	LB	10.96 / 1.64	0.14 / 2.74	550.00 / 84.00	0.18 / 0.15	0.03	0 / 0				
2040 0	POTATOES	0001	LB	18.28 / 2.88	0.15 / 4.57	550.00 / 86.00	0.15 / 0.14	0.01*	7 / 5				
2500 0	ALMONDS	0001	LB	3.98 / 8.31	2.08 / 0.99	60.00 / 128.10	2.18 / 2.13	0.05	11 / 1				
2510 0	APPLES	0001	LB	55.86 / 9.49	0.16 / 13.96	150.00 / 24.00	0.16 / 0.14	0.02*	8 / 1				
2520 0	CANTALOUPES	0001	EACH	47.50 / 35.62	0.74 / 11.87	110.00 / 82.20	0.72 / 0.74	0.01	6 / 4				
2530 0	LEMONS	0001	EACH	315.75 / 13.61	0.04 / 78.93	500.00 / 22.50	0.05 / 0.04	0.01	7 / 26				
2540 0	LEMON SLICES	0001	EACH	16.08 / 0.70	0.04 / 4.02	250.00 / 11.25	0.05 / 0.04	0.01					
2550 0	LETTUCE	0001	EACH	243.64 / 65.98	0.27 / 60.91	288.00 / 78.70	0.30 / 0.27	0.03	13.00 / 3.65	0.28	24.00	55.36 / 15.57	0.28 / 0.90
2551 0	LETTUCE - LEAF	0001	EACH	10.74 / 69.81	6.50 / 2.68	10.00 / 65.00	6.50 / 6.50	0.00	0.00 / 0.00	0.00	1.00	0.26 / 1.69	6.50 / 0.09

INVENTORY REPORT

Inventory Report indicates the current status of each inventory item on either a month-to-date or year-to-date basis and includes a detailed analysis of item usage, purchases, and shrinkage.

- Shows quantity, dollar value and average and current purchase prices as well as days-on-hand
- Figures showing average day usage assist management in enforcing strict inventory control through more efficient re-ordering procedures.
- Report can be based on either month-to-date or year-to-date history.

Fig. 13-1. Bar/restaurant sales analysis.

estimated that if inventory can be reduced by $10,000, costs of computer service will be paid for in less than a year.

An analogy can be drawn between the storeroom of the food service operation and a supermarket. If every food, liquor, or supply item that is taken from the storeroom can be recorded or checked out as it would be when purchased at the supermarket for use at home, complete inventory control would exist. The computer not only makes it possible to record every item withdrawn from inventory, but the computer can charge the item to various production or service departments, remind the purchasing agent when stock is low, project trends for future requirements, and perform many other functions discussed in this chapter, all of which stem from control of inventory. The computer has made inventory control and related controls of costs easier and faster and has made real control of costs feasible even in small operations.

Figure 13-1 illustrates a computerized inventory print-out in one of a variety of formats that can be tailored to the individual operator's needs.

Purchasing. A computer can perform the *purchasing* function by automatically generating purchase orders for items that have dropped below a par stock. The system can generate a purchasing report that will show these needs and the last price paid as a guideline for the purchasing department. The same report can show the amount in number of units that was last purchased and the elapsed time between the receipt of the goods and the request for reorder. These functions can be provided on a daily basis to the purchasing department; all the data needed to produce these reports and the purchase orders can be maintained on magnetic files. The amount of file space and clerical staff needed to provide the same information manually can be replaced, along with the errors indigenous to the manual method (Fig. 13-2).

LOC	NO	CD	DESCRIPTION	U/M	MINIMUM	LAST PUR	LAST PRICE	ON/HAND	
1	1020		CREME DE COCOA	4	25.60	73176	0.13	15.80	BELOW MINIMUM
1	2020		CARROTS	3	50.00	73176	0.12	44.04	BELOW MINIMUM
1	2551		LETTUCE - LEAF	1	1.00	73176	6.50	.26	BELOW MINIMUM
1	3002		BUTTER - LEMON	3	1.00	100176	1.20	.80	BELOW MINIMUM
1	4401		SNAIL SHELLS	1	1152.00	100176	0.03	842.00	BELOW MINIMUM
1	5005		BREAD CRUMBS	3	1.00	100176	1.00	1.00	BELOW MINIMUM
1	7020		CHERRIES	1	96.00	73176	0.04	66.00	BELOW MINIMUM
1	8010		CLUB SODA - LARGE	6	1.00	73176	0.35	.90	BELOW MINIMUM

Fig. 13-2. Below-minimum report, which is produced as a by-product of inventory update and lists those items that fall below a preestablished minimum. This report shows minimum figure established for each food/beverage item, indicates date of last purchase and purchase price per measure, shows current status of inventory on hand, and identifies with numerical coding unit of measure used in stocking each item.

232   Profitable Food and Beverage Management: Planning

DATE 02/04/7-   MTD COST ANALYSIS   PAGE 1

ITEM NO	DESCRIPTION	MENU PRICE	UNITS SERVED	TOTAL SALES	% OF SALES	PLANNED UNIT COST	PLANNED COST	PLANNED COST %	ACTUAL 1 UNIT COST	ACTUAL COST	ACTUAL COST %	VARIANCE	GROSS PROFIT	% OF PROFIT
L 1 P	SHRIMP COCKTAIL SHRIMP - JUMBO COCKTAIL SAUCE LETTUCE	2.75	240 6.00 2.00 0.07	660.00 EACH FL-OZ EACH	1.88	1.83	439.20	66.54	1.8396 1.7532 0.0668 0.0196	441.50	66.89	2.30	218.50	33.10
L 2 P	SNAILS SNAILS SNAIL SHELLS BUTTER - GARLIC WHITE WINE	2.75	342 6.00 6.00 3.00 1.00	940.50 EACH EACH OUNCES FL-OZ	2.68	1.27	434.34	46.18	1.4773 0.6822 0.4830 0.2754 0.0367	505.23	53.71	70.89	435.27	46.28
L 3 P	OYSTERS / HLF SHELL OYSTERS COCKTAIL SAUCE HORSE RADISH CRACKERS - OYSTER	2.10	174 6.00 2.50 2.50 1.00	365.40 EACH FL-OZ FL-OZ EACH	1.04	0.92	160.08	43.80	0.9114 0.6942 0.0836 0.0920 0.0416	158.58	43.39	1.50	206.82	56.60
L 4 P	CRABMEAT BIARRITZ CRABMEAT ARTICHOKE MAYONNAISE CREAM - WHIPPING CAPERS CAVIAR LEMONS	4.25	240 3.00 1.00 1.50 0.50 0.12 0.06 0.50	1,020.00 OUNCES EACH FL-OZ OUNCES OUNCES OUNCES EACH	2.91	2.02	484.80	47.52	2.0217 0.8908 0.6319 0.0436 0.0257 0.0199 0.3871 0.0227	485.20	47.56	0.40	534.80	52.43
L 5 P	PROSCIUTTO W/MELON PROSCIUTTO MELONS LETTUCE - LEAF	2.40	144 3.00 0.50 0.03	345.60 OUNCES EACH EACH	0.98	1.08	155.52	45.00	1.1012 0.6339 0.2723 0.1950	158.57	45.88	3.05	187.03	54.11
P	TOTAL APPETIZERS		1,140	3,331.50	9.50		1,673.94	50.24						
P 1 P	SOFT SHELL CRAB SOFT SHELL CRAB BREAD - TOAST ALMONDS FLOUR MILK LEMONS LETTUCE DRESSING - SALAD BREAD BUTTER	7.25	360 3.00 1.50 0.75 0.50 0.50 0.25 0.50 2.00 2.00 0.07	2,610.00 EACH EACH OUNCES OUNCES FL-OZ EACH EACH FL-OZ EACH POUNDS	7.44	2.60	936.00	35.86	2.6332 2.1549 0.0424 0.0992 0.0050 0.0050 0.0227 0.0703 0.0629 0.0950 0.0758					
P 2 P	SURF & TURF FILET MIGNON LOBSTER TAIL BREAD - TOAST BUTTER - LEMON	10.95	480 5.50 4.50 1.00 2.00	5,256.00 OUNCES OUNCES EACH OUNCES	14.99	4.25	2,040.00	38.81	4.2087 1.7688 1.9326 0.0283 0.1750	2,020.17	38.43	19.83	3,235.83	61.56

COST ANALYSIS REPORT MENU EXPLOSION FEATURE
The unique Menu Explosion Feature of the Cost Analysis Report breaks down the cost of each food or beverage item and shows the cost of the individual ingredients within that item.
• Aids in analyzing degree of item profitability.
• Alerts management to take corrective action based on the cost, sales, and profit data relating to each item.

Fig. 13-3. Bar-restaurant sales analysis.

From the same data base, the computer can assist the menu-pricing and recipe-planning functions by providing up-to-date information on current prices being paid for ingredients. If the recipes themselves are included in the computer files, the system will "cost" the recipes as the prices change and provide exception reporting on menu items that should be discontinued or whose prices should be raised (Fig. 13–3).

The capability of computers to calculate costs swiftly makes it possible to precost a proposed menu and to make sensitivity tests of various sales mixes. This feature is commented on in Chapter 2, *Profitable Food and Beverage Management: Operations.*

Purchasing and purchasing cost control functions as implemented by several users achieve a rather complex level. At one firm, the purchasing application physically prepares the purchase orders based on bulk orders from the outlets. The outlet does not necessarily know the vendor of each item. In the preparation of the outlet's order, one standard form is used by all outlets. These are consolidated on the computer at the home office.

With automated files containing the current prices issued by its vendors, plus data on historical sales trends, management can take full advantage of economic order, quantity techniques, and seasonal price fluctuation. In addition, effective automation permits easy detection of overordering by outlets.

Sales Analysis. One of the major problems in any food service operation is caused by the difficulty of forecasting future sales. A computerized information system, which provides output immediately and accurately, can pointout patterns that will aid management in spotting eating trends, thus enabling the operator to change present purchasing and production procedures and schedules before they fall behind the trend and result in waste.

Sales analysis is used by some operations to extract inventory data. The reported units sold by menu item are extended by ingredients called for in the standard recipe.

If the operation adheres to standards, the end product of this report indicates inventory consumption. Discrepancies detected in periodic physical inventories reveal the degree of adherence to company standards.

If the actual inventory flow is higher than the sales analysis projection of inventory flow, one or more conditions requiring management attention might exist. These include wastage, unreported sales, poor portion control, and inventory shrinkage.

If the actual inventory consumption is lower than the projection, there may be other conditions that require management atten-

234 Profitable Food and Beverage Management: Planning

DATE 02/04/7—   PAGE 1

DAILY ANALYSIS

ITEM NUMBER	DESCRIPTION	MENU PRICE	UNITS SERVED	TOTAL SALES	% OF SALES	ITEM COST	COST TOTAL	COST %	SALES MTD	SALES %	SALES YTD	SALES %
L 1	P SHRIMP COCKTAIL	2.75	52	143.00	1.70	1.83	95.16	66.54	803.00	1.84	6,875.00	1.78
L 2	P SNAILS	2.75	67	184.25	2.20	1.27	85.09	46.18	1,124.75	2.59	9,308.75	2.42
L 3	P OYSTERS / HLF SHELL	2.10	48	100.80	1.20	0.92	44.16	43.80	466.20	1.07	4,347.00	1.13
L 4	P CRABMEAT BIARRITZ	4.25	37	157.25	1.87	2.02	74.74	47.52	1,177.25	2.71	9,031.25	2.34
L 5	P PROSJUTTO W/MELON	2.40	58	139.20	1.66	1.08	62.64	45.00	484.80	1.11	5,208.00	1.35
	TOTAL APPETIZERS		262	724.50	8.66		361.79	49.93	4,056.00	9.34	34,770.00	9.04
P 1	P SOFT SHELL CRAB	7.25	85	616.25	7.36	2.60	221.00	35.86	3,226.25	7.43	28,456.25	7.40
P 2	P SURF & TURF	10.95	74	810.30	9.68	4.25	314.50	38.81	6,066.30	13.97	46,537.50	12.10
P 3	P BREAST OF CHICKEN	7.75	88	682.00	8.15	1.41	124.08	18.19	3,937.00	9.07	33,325.00	8.67
P 4	P FILET MIGNON PERIG	10.25	70	717.50	8.57	5.52	386.40	53.85	3,792.50	8.73	33,312.50	8.66
P 5	P RAINBOW TROUT	7.75	80	620.00	7.41	2.23	178.40	28.77	2,480.00	5.71	24,800.00	6.45
P 6	P POACHED ENGL TURBOT	9.45	67	633.15	7.56	5.21	349.07	55.13	4,602.15	10.60	35,673.75	9.28
	TOTAL DINNER ENTREE		464	4,079.20	48.76		1,573.45	38.57	24,104.20	55.53	202,105.90	52.58
A 1	A CHEESE OMELET	3.35	124	415.40	4.96	0.81	100.44	24.17	2,425.40	5.58	20,435.00	5.31
A 2	A CHICKEN CORDON BLEU	3.75	136	510.00	6.09	1.33	180.88	35.46	2,535.00	5.84	22,875.00	5.95
A 3	A BRISKET OF BEEF	3.50	117	409.50	4.89	0.90	105.30	25.71	2,089.50	4.81	18,637.50	4.84
A 4	A SAUTEED SCALLOPS	3.85	119	458.15	5.47	1.45	172.55	37.66	2,075.15	4.78	19,538.75	5.08
	TOTAL LUNCH ENTREES		496	1,793.05	21.43		559.17	31.18	9,125.05	21.02	81,486.25	21.20
P 59	P CHOCOLATE PARFAIT	1.25	154	192.50	2.30	0.20	30.80	16.00	717.50	1.65	7,437.50	1.93
P 58	P SPONGE CAKE	0.45	77	34.65	0.41	0.12	9.24	26.66	169.65	0.39	1,541.25	0.40
P 57	P APPLE PIE	0.75	133	99.75	1.19	0.10	13.30	13.33	504.75	1.16	4,518.75	1.17
P 56	P MELON W/ICE CREAM	0.95	95	90.25	1.07	0.46	43.70	48.42	204.25	0.47	2,826.25	0.73
	TOTAL DESERTS		459	417.15	4.98		97.04	23.26	1,596.15	3.67	16,323.75	4.24
P 50	P COFFEE	0.40	253	101.20	1.20	0.16	40.48	40.00				
P 51	P TEA	0.40	135	54.00	0.64	0.05	6.75	12.50				
P 52	P LEMONADE	0.75	122	91.50	1.09	0.20	24.40	26.66				
P 53	P TOMATO JUICE	0.60	101	60.60	0.72	0.17	17.17	28.33				
P 54	P FRUIT PUNCH	0.50	82	41.00	0.49	0.14	11.48	28.00				
	TOTAL BEVERAGES		693	348.30	4.16		100.28	28.79				
P 41	P MARTINI	1.35	146	197.10	2.35	0.37	54.02	27.40				
P 42	P GRASS HOPPER	1.65	142	234.30	2.80	0.44	62.48	26.66				
P 43	P PLANTERS PUNCH	1.65	134	221.10	2.64	0.54	72.36	32.72				
P 44	P STINGER	1.65	94	155.10	1.85	0.34	31.96	20.60				
P 45	P MARGARITA	1.65	118	194.70	2.32	0.35	41.30	21.21				
	TOTAL ALCOHOLIC BEV		634	1,002.30	11.98		262.12	26.15				
C. 1—												
RECORD COUNT.. 35												
C.01-NEW VOLUME												
	TOTAL		3,008	8,364.50			2,953.85	35.31	43,406.00		384,320.00	

DAILY ANALYSIS REPORT
Daily Analysis Report enables management to measure sales performance of food and beverage items in units and dollar sales.
- Provides sales comparison by menu items for today, month-to-date, and year-to-date.
- Shows relation of each item sold in terms of percentage of total sales for day, month-to-date, and year-to-date.
- Enables management to compare percentage of sales and planned food cost percentage by menu item or category.
- Report can be printed in random sequence with group totals as desired.
- Each menu item can be "exploded" into as many as 20 inventory items by portion and unit of measure.

Fig. 13-4A. Bar/restaurant sales analysis.

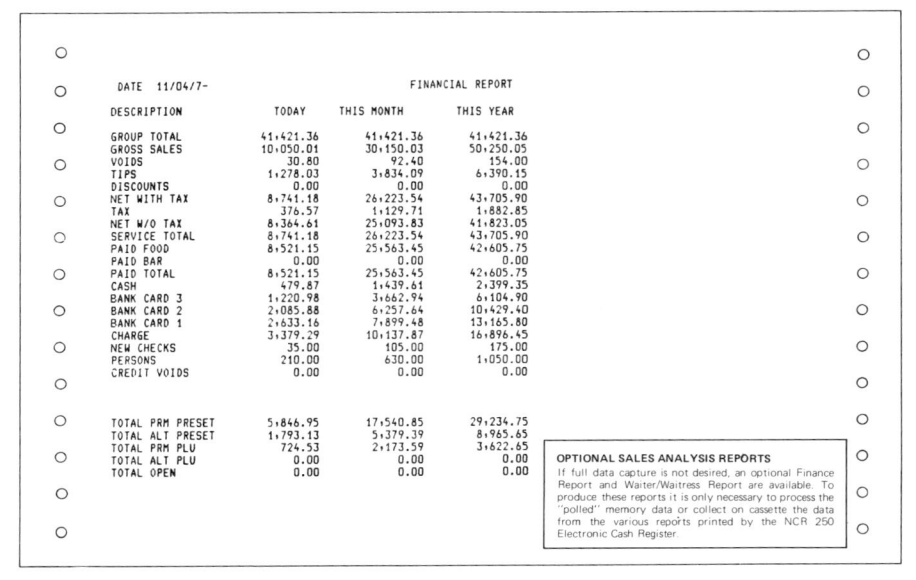

```
DATE 11/04/7-                    FINANCIAL REPORT
DESCRIPTION          TODAY       THIS MONTH      THIS YEAR

GROUP TOTAL         41,421.36     41,421.36      41,421.36
GROSS SALES         10,050.01     30,150.03      50,250.05
VOIDS                   30.80         92.40         154.00
TIPS                 1,278.03      3,834.09       6,390.15
DISCOUNTS                0.00          0.00           0.00
NET WITH TAX         8,741.18     26,223.54      43,705.90
TAX                    376.57      1,129.71       1,882.85
NET W/O TAX          8,364.61     25,093.83      41,823.05
SERVICE TOTAL        8,741.18     26,223.54      43,705.90
PAID FOOD            8,521.15     25,563.45      42,605.75
PAID BAR                 0.00          0.00           0.00
PAID TOTAL           8,521.15     25,563.45      42,605.75
CASH                   479.87      1,439.61       2,399.35
BANK CARD 3          1,220.98      3,662.94       6,104.90
BANK CARD 2          2,085.88      6,257.64      10,429.40
BANK CARD 1          2,633.16      7,899.48      13,165.80
CHARGE               3,379.29     10,137.87      16,896.45
NEW CHECKS              35.00        105.00         175.00
PERSONS                210.00        630.00       1,050.00
CREDIT VOIDS             0.00          0.00           0.00


TOTAL PRM PRESET     5,846.95     17,540.85      29,234.75
TOTAL ALT PRESET     1,793.13      5,379.39       8,965.65
TOTAL PRM PLU          724.53      2,173.59       3,622.65
TOTAL ALT PLU            0.00          0.00           0.00
TOTAL OPEN               0.00          0.00           0.00
```

OPTIONAL SALES ANALYSIS REPORTS
If full data capture is not desired, an optional Finance Report and Waiter/Waitress Report are available. To produce these reports it is only necessary to process the "polled" memory data or collect on cassette the data from the various reports printed by the NCR 250 Electronic Cash Register.

Fig. 13-4. Bar/restaurant sales analysis.

tion. Unauthorized and unreported purchases and improper portion control are possibilities.

Several data processing departments, particularly in limited-menu fast-food operations, derive sales analysis from inventory control. Based on standards for product preparation at each outlet, potential sales are computed by establishing a sales dollar value for a specific quantity of a specific food item.

When the sales analysis is derived from the inventory flow and then compared with the actual sales at each outlet, a fairly accurate control indicator is developed.

In a few operations, the sales analysis is developed from inventory movement of packaging material rather than from the food product. A prerequisite to the use of this technique is that each menu item have a unique packaging material associated with it. Over a longer period of time, the food product movement is compared with the packaging product movement to establish an element of quality portion control.

Several fine food restaurants capture sales analysis by menu item (Figs. 13–A and 13–B). Periodically a new item is added to the menu. If the new item does not provide a sufficient percentage of total sales within a relatively short period of time, the item is dropped. Its replacement goes through the same procedure. Similarly, if an item of long standing on the menu shows consistently declining sales, it is dropped and replaced.

One chain records cost trends and projects them into the future, using these data to project menu pricing. The menu planning function at this chain is limited owing to a relatively consistent menu. In another chain with a slightly more variable menu, the variations in the menu are based on the combination of anticipated food costs and historical sales analysis.

Labor Productivity. The use of a computer for routine tasks frees employees for more productive activity. For instance, when a cashier is relieved from the drudgery of manual calculations, another function such as telephone order taking might be added without harming customer service. But perhaps the greatest increase in productivity will come at the management level. Managers can spend more time in their true function, which will result in greater operating efficiencies.

In some instances, certain applications are logical extensions of combinations of other applications. For example, with payroll and sales analysis automated, a few users have developed "productivity" standards by relating sales dollars to payroll expenses within job classifications. This type of reporting is particularly applicable to multiple outlet operations, permitting management to gain experience in establishing standards and thereafter to compare the ratios from one outlet to another. This makes possible detecting of over- and under-staffing conditions.

The payroll system on the computer can automatically gather gratuity information by employee from the electronic cash register (ECR) to facilitate the payment/checking process. For example, a food service operation may decide to pay out all gratuities included in checks at the end of the work day. This method ensures greater accuracy in disbursing the cash. The computer can easily provide a report of the tips to be disbursed by waiter and, if necessary, a check-by-check breakdown for audit purposes (Fig. 13–5).

The information is used by management to gauge the efficiency of the staffing at various outlets. In addition, it serves as a source of quality control information. (If the staff is too small in relation to sales, it is possible that there is insufficient service to customers.) An illustration is shown in Fig. 13–6.

The relationship of sales to payroll expense is an arithmetic ratio of the hours and dollars for various job classifications (server, cashier, busboy, etc.) to sales. The sales may be expressed in gross dollars and/or detail menu item count.

One chain using such a reporting system flags as exceptions those locations that deviate from established standards. The chain

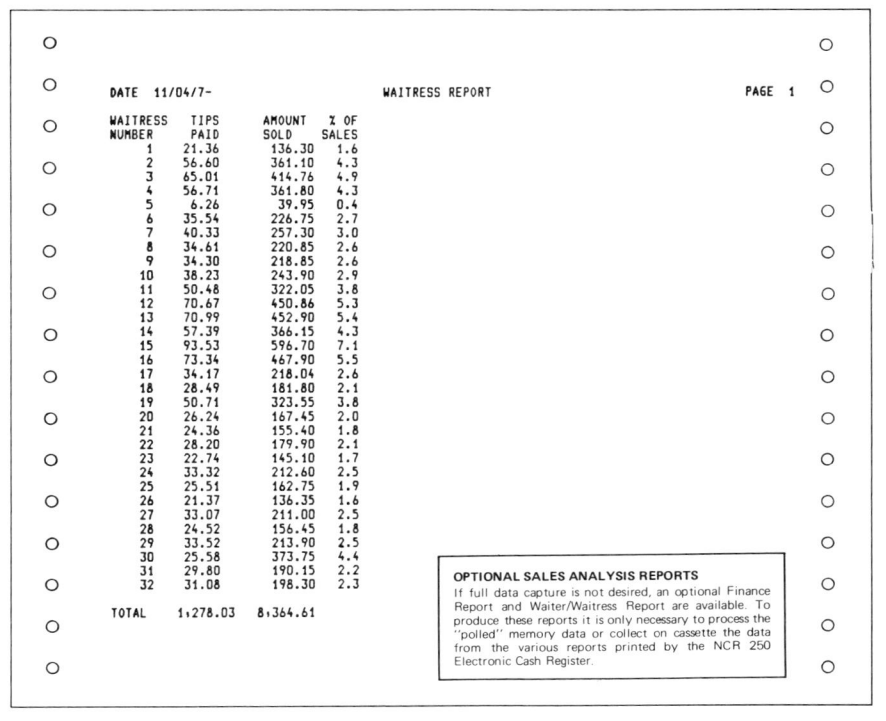

```
DATE 11/04/7-                WAITRESS REPORT                    PAGE 1

WAITRESS   TIPS      AMOUNT    % OF
NUMBER     PAID      SOLD      SALES
   1       21.36     136.30    1.6
   2       56.60     361.10    4.3
   3       65.01     414.76    4.9
   4       56.71     361.80    4.3
   5        6.26      39.95    0.4
   6       35.54     226.75    2.7
   7       40.33     257.30    3.0
   8       34.61     220.85    2.6
   9       34.30     218.85    2.6
  10       38.23     243.90    2.9
  11       50.48     322.05    3.8
  12       70.67     450.86    5.3
  13       70.99     452.90    5.4
  14       57.39     366.15    4.3
  15       93.53     596.70    7.1
  16       73.34     467.90    5.5
  17       34.17     218.04    2.6
  18       28.49     181.80    2.1
  19       50.71     323.55    3.8
  20       26.24     167.45    2.0
  21       24.36     155.40    1.8
  22       28.20     179.90    2.1
  23       22.74     145.10    1.7
  24       33.32     212.60    2.5
  25       25.51     162.75    1.9
  26       21.37     136.35    1.6
  27       33.07     211.00    2.5
  28       24.52     156.45    1.8
  29       33.52     213.90    2.5
  30       25.58     373.75    4.4
  31       29.80     190.15    2.2
  32       31.08     198.30    2.3

 TOTAL   1,278.03   8,364.61
```

OPTIONAL SALES ANALYSIS REPORTS
If full data capture is not desired, an optional Finance Report and Waiter/Waitress Report are available. To produce these reports it is only necessary to process the "polled" memory data or collect on cassette the data from the various reports printed by the NCR 250 Electronic Cash Register.

Fig. 13-5. Bar-restaurant sales analysis.

places such emphasis on its standards that outlet managers are paid bonuses based on adherence to standards, with no bonus if the ratio is too far *above* or *below* the standard.

Financial Management Reporting. Profit analysis and cost control by menu item may be used to good advantage (Fig. 13–7). Although a valid promotional effort in a restaurant may use a low-profit item as a loss leader, unless management is well informed about the actual profitability of its menu item, a wrong decision may be made. With good information a more profitable promotion might be made with a high-profit item.

The profit analysis by menu items plays another important part in management of the food establishment; it assists in menu construction. Sales analysis alone can provide minimal data or decision making. The data are basically sales units. By adding profit analysis, management is given greater insight into the construction of a profitable menu. In addition, the menu designer can use placement to promote the higher profit items.

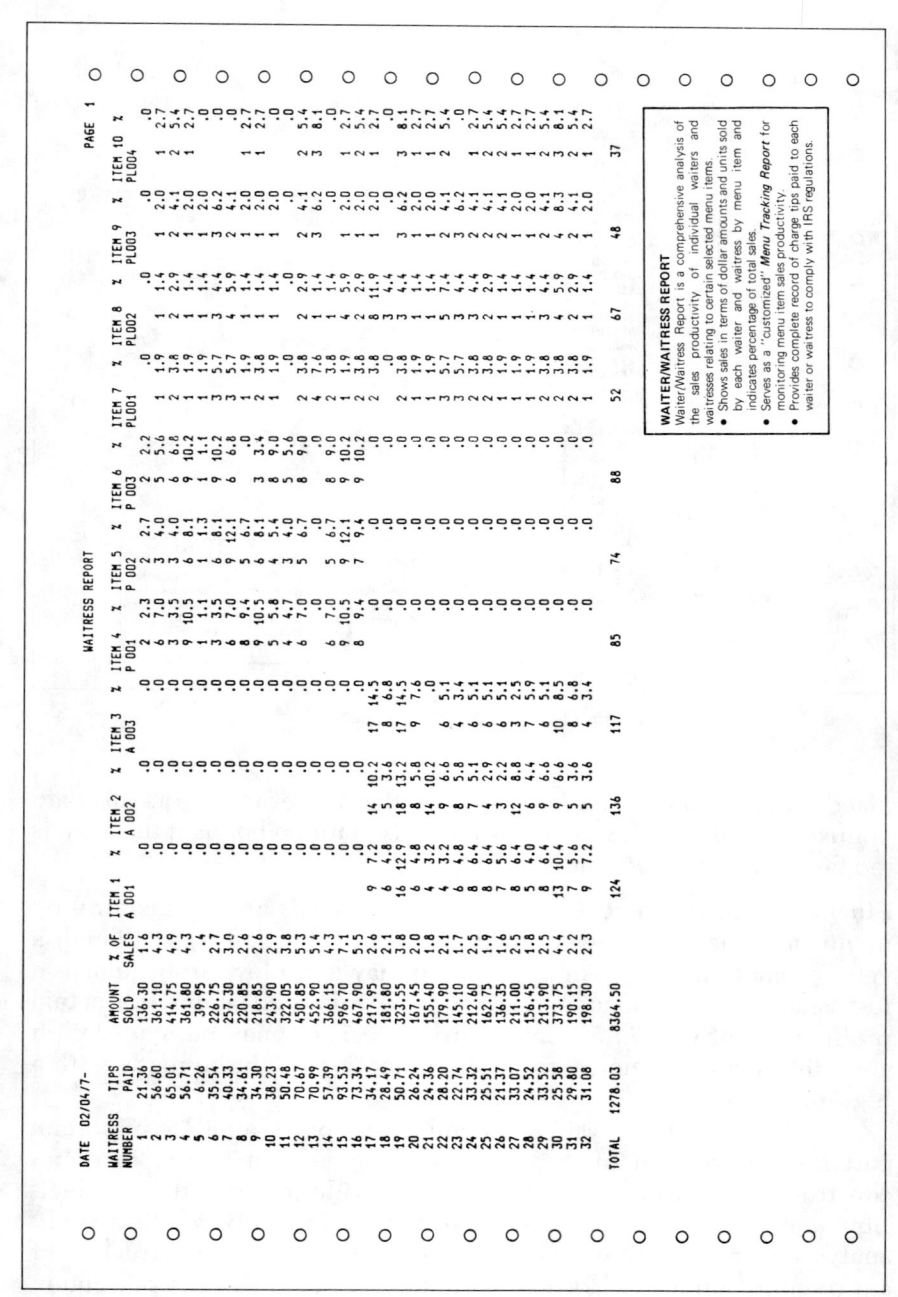

238   Profitable Food and Beverage Management: Planning

Fig. 13-6. Bar/restaurant sales analysis.

Automated Data Procedures   239

ITEM NO		DESCRIPTION	MENU PRICE	UNITS SERVED	TOTAL SALES	% OF SALES	PLANNED UNIT COST	PLANNED COST	PLANNED COST %	ACTUAL 1 UNIT COST	ACTUAL COST	ACTUAL COST %	VARIANCE	GROSS PROFIT	% OF PROFIT
1	L P	SHRIMP COCKTAIL	2.75	240	660.00	1.88	1.83	439.20	66.54	1.8396	441.50	66.89	2.30	218.50	33.10
2	L P	SNAILS	2.75	342	940.50	2.68	1.27	434.34	46.18	1.4773	505.23	53.71	70.89	435.27	46.28
3	L P	OYSTERS / HLF SHELL	2.10	174	365.40	1.04	0.92	160.08	43.80	0.9114	158.58	43.39	1.50*	206.82	56.60
4	L P	CRABMEAT BIARRITZ	4.25	240	1,020.00	2.91	2.02	484.80	47.52	2.0217	485.20	47.56	0.40	534.80	52.43
5	L P	PROSIUTTO W/MELON	2.40	144	345.60	0.98	1.08	155.52	45.00	1.1012	158.57	45.88	3.05	187.03	54.11
	P	TOTAL APPETIZERS		1,140	3,331.50	9.50		1,673.94	50.24		1,749.08	52.50	75.14	1,582.42	47.49
1	P P	SOFT SHELL CRAB	7.25	360	2,610.00	7.44	2.60	936.00	35.86	2.6332	947.95	36.31	11.95	1,662.05	63.68
2	P P	SURF & TURF	10.95	480	5,256.00	14.99	4.25	2,040.00	38.81	4.2087	2,020.17	38.43	19.83*	3,235.83	61.56
3	P P	BREAST OF CHICKEN	7.75	420	3,255.00	9.28	1.41	592.20	18.19	1.4096	592.03	18.18	0.17*	2,662.97	81.81
4	P P	FILET MIGNON PERIG	10.25	300	3,075.00	8.77	5.52	1,656.00	53.85	5.4704	1,641.12	53.36	14.88*	1,433.88	46.63
5	P P	RAINBOW TROUT	7.75	240	1,860.00	5.30	2.23	535.20	28.77	2.2189	532.53	28.63	2.67*	1,327.47	71.36
6	P P	POACHED ENGL TURBOT	9.45	420	3,969.00	11.32	5.21	2,188.20	55.13	5.1893	2,179.50	54.91	8.70*	1,789.50	45.08
	P	TOTAL DINNER ENTREE		2,220	20,025.00	57.14		7,947.60	39.68		7,913.30	39.51	34.30*	12,111.70	60.48
1	A P	CHEESE OMELET	3.35	600	2,010.00	5.73	0.81	486.00	24.17	0.7911	474.66	23.61	11.34*	1,535.34	76.38
2	A P	CHICKEN CORDON BLEU	3.75	540	2,025.00	5.77	1.33	718.20	35.46	1.3188	712.15	35.16	6.05*	1,312.85	64.83
3	A P	BRISKET OF BEEF	3.50	480	1,680.00	4.79	0.90	432.00	25.71	0.8597	412.65	24.56	19.35*	1,267.35	75.43
4	A P	SAUTEED SCALLOPS	3.85	420	1,617.00	4.61	1.45	609.00	37.66	1.3406	563.05	34.82	45.95*	1,053.95	65.17
	A	TOTAL LUNCH ENTREES		2,040	7,332.00	20.92		2,245.20	30.62		2,162.51	29.49	82.69*	5,169.49	70.50
59	P P	CHOCOLATE PARFAIT	1.25	420	525.00	1.49	0.20	84.00	16.00	0.3595	150.99	28.76	66.99	374.01	71.24
58	P P	SPONGE CAKE	0.45	300	135.00	0.38	0.12	36.00	26.66	0.1198	35.94	26.62	0.06*	99.06	73.37
57	P P	APPLE PIE	0.75	540	405.00	1.15	0.10	54.00	13.33	0.3371	182.03	44.94	128.03	222.97	55.05
56	P P	MELON W/ICE CREAM	0.95	120	114.00	0.32	0.46	55.20	48.42	0.4523					
	P	TOTAL DESERTS		1,380	1,179.00	3.36		229.20	19.44						
50	P P	COFFEE	0.40	660	264.00	0.75	0.16	105.60	40.00	0.1309					
51	P P	TEA	0.40	330	132.00	0.37	0.05	16.50	12.50	0.0491					
52	P P	LEMONADE	0.75	432	324.00	0.92	0.20	86.40	26.66	0.2052					
53	P P	TOMATO JUICE	0.60	546	327.60	0.93	0.17	92.82	28.33	0.1781					
54	P P	FRUIT PUNCH	0.50	408	204.00	0.58	0.14	57.12	28.00	0.1363					
	P	TOTAL BEVERAGES		2,376	1,251.60	3.57		358.44	28.63						
41	P P	MARTINI	1.35	324	437.40	1.24	0.37	119.88	27.40	0.3676					
42	P P	GRASS HOPPER	1.65	216	356.40	1.01	0.44	95.04	26.66	0.4442					
43	P P	PLANTERS PUNCH	1.65	174	287.10	0.81	0.54	93.96	32.72	0.5332					
44	P P	STINGER	1.65	222	366.30	1.04	0.34	75.48	20.60	0.3470					
45	P P	MARGUARITA	1.65	288	475.20	1.35	0.35	100.80	21.21	0.3343					
	P	TOTAL ALCHOLIC BEV		1,224	1,922.40	5.48		485.16	25.23						
		GRAND TOTAL		10,380	35,041.50			12,939.54	36.92		13,073.31	37.30	133.77	21,968.19	62.69

COST ANALYSIS Report enables management to determine profitability of each item by comparing planned costs with actual costs calculated by the system.

Through use of "operator lead-through" the NCR 499 operator is able to instruct the system to compute actual unit cost on the average on-hand, average purchase, last purchase, or average usage price as desired.

- Report indicates the variance between planned and actual cost.
- Gross profit and percentage of profit are shown for each item.
- Total sales, units served, and percentage of sales are shown for each item.
- Report can be produced on a month-to-date or year-to-date basis.
- Each item can be "exploded" to show cost of individual ingredients within each item.

Fig. 13-7. Bar/restaurant sales analysis.

Accounting Functions

Computers have traditionally performed accounting functions in every industry. For many years, restaurants have used computers to handle accounts receivable and payable, payroll preparation, and general ledger and financial statement generation. These applications are frequently fragmented and handled by different service bureaus or other vendors of data processing services. Increasingly, they can be handled by minicomputers, computer time sharing, and as additions to the management information systems described previously.

The various accounting applications are so well known that there is little need to elaborate on them in this text. Food service operators should be aware of the benefits to be derived from uniform accounting and plan the chart of accounts and financial statement format to conform closely to the Uniform System of Accounts for Restaurants. Together with purely financial results, the reporting system should include statistics on such matters as number of covers sold, sales per man-hour, average receipt per cover sold, and budgetary variations, as well as ratios of expenses to sales. Some service bureaus have developed specific software packages to produce financial statements in an approved format.

Payrolls. The computerization of food service payrolls is of particular value because of the reporting complexities surrounding the treatment of tips and the tip credit, employee meal benefits, union benefits, and overtime that are peculiar to the industry. A few firms have developed specialized computer programs for this purpose.

Ideally, the data collected for use in the accounting functions should be integrated into the total management information systems previously discussed. It is becoming more feasible to achieve this goal through the use of equipment and programs now available or in advanced planning stage.

Computer Equipment

Traditionally, the basic equipment from which sales information is gathered in any food service operation has been the cash register. The computer, connected to specialized cash registers, can give the operator far more information than was ever available from a simple cash register.

Point-of-Sale-Devices

The traditional mechanical cash register for guest check settlement has in recent years been replaced in many locations by the ECR. This unit provides the same cash control and cash audit services of its predecessor in addition to several data-gathering capabilities.

The ECR can record sales by menu item, including number of covers, and can provide a daily report by meal period and/or server number of the detailed menu sales. The ECR can price a restaurant check and clearly print the menu name of the item on the restaurant check. The result of those features has been to reduce discrepancies with the customer and to completely eliminate arithmetic errors on the checks. The ECR can also provide a missing check report at the end of the work day for accounting of checks that have been issued and entered to the unit.

Precheck and Ordering

The ECR has been adapted to the kitchen ordering process by eliminating the cash features and adding preset keys. A preset key on an ECR permits a server to place a blank restaurant check on the printing bed of the ECR, press a key that describes the menu item to be ordered, and thereby prepare a preprinted, prepriced check. A duplicate copy of the check becomes the order for the kitchen. The ECR can now provide a control of the kitchen orders placed and compare that with the checks settled to eliminate losses or cheating. The data gathered by this method can also be exploded back to the ingredients of the menu items to provide an estimated food cost for comparison to actual cost.

The data collected by point-of-sale equipment must be combined with data generated by the purchasing, payroll, and accounting departments to give a total data base. The handling of the data base to provide all the output needed for reports is the job of the systems designer who, today, has a wide variety of computer hardware with which to work.

Hardware

Hardware is the physical unit, the computer itself. Computers are defined in three general categories:

- Macrocomputers or full-scale general purpose systems
- Minicomputers ("mini" refers more to size than power)
- Microcomputers, which are a recent innovation primarily responsible for the pocket calculators and video games so popular today.

Software

To make a computer perform a task requires software, which is usually in the form of computer programs designed and written to fulfill a specific purpose.

Software also is defined from the user perspective as falling into two major categories:

- *Packages*—refers to software that is bought preprogrammed to perform a specific function, thereby requiring no in-house development effort.
- *User-developed application*—refers to software designed and written in-house by a company's data processing staff, taking into consideration any special or unique requirements of the user's operations.

The data processing vendors are increasingly marketing turnkey systems rather than hardware or software. The term *turnkey systems* refers to a computer and preprogrammed software package marketed to serve a particular function in a specific industry. This approach is based on the premise that it can be very costly to acquire hardware and personnel to develop a successful data processing installation. Too often, the goals are not met; the expenses are higher than anticipated and management becomes disenchanted with computers. The turnkey systems approach can offer fixed expenses and realistic, achievable goals to the first-time computer user.

However, there are advantages to in-house development. For example, it can be difficult to locate software packages or turnkey systems that will perform to the precise definition of the task to be automated. Software packages and turnkey systems are developed to sell to as many users in an industry as possible. Therefore, the software must take a universal approach to solving a task. Frequently, a user wants or needs a more specific solution. In this case, the user needs an in-house development approach. The user will analyze his needs, design the specific programs that will meet those needs, and write the programs for use on his own computer installation.

Because the options are many and complicated, the decision to use computerized data processing must be thoroughly researched before a decision is made. The available alternatives must be carefully analyzed in terms of costs and potential benefits.

A computer installation will not necessarily displace sufficient costs to justify it on that basis alone. Therefore, it becomes important to know, and if possible to quantify, the intangible benefits. It is difficult to place a value on timeliness and accuracy of information, but it must be calculated if the worth of a computer installation is to be measured.

Planning the System

The decision to automate should come after a careful analysis of the needs to be addressed. The analysis should consider several key points before arriving at a conclusion. Many data processing installations have fallen short of the original goals, in part because the key points and goals were not well defined.

The following points are to be researched or considered:

Accessibility of Data

Where are the data? Are they readily available and are they in usable form? What changes can be made in the data to make them usable in a computerized environment? For example, suppose a task to be computerized is an accounts payable system with the objective of making disbursements automatically in an effort to control cash flow, eliminate errors in over- and underpayment, and establish better vendor relations by more regular payments.

The basic data are invoices from vendors. Each invoice has vendor's name and address, invoice date, due date, payment terms, description of items delivered, and amount due. Therefore, the basic data for a disbursement system are available from invoices and are in usable form. To put them on the computer, a program that permits entry of the data will be written. The program must allow an operator to read the invoice and enter the computer data from that source.

In this example, the basic questions were readily answered and the analysis could easily conclude that this data will be effectively put on a computer.

As another example, suppose the task to be performed is a sales analysis by menu item, showing gross daily sales by meal period for each menu item.

The basic data are the guest checks after settlement. Investigation reveals that the items on the checks are hand-written by the waiters. The waiters, in writing the item ordered by the guests, typically write rapidly and only an abbreviated description of the item.

Therefore, it can be concluded that the basic data are not readily usable and another approach will have to be discovered. The conclusion should be to improve the menu descriptions on the checks by preprinting or by asking the waiters to write a menu number.

In this example, the basic questions were not answered and the final analysis may reveal that these data, in their present form, cannot be computerized.

Report Requirements

After analyzing the basic data available and reconciling the input requirements, the information to be included and the uses of the reports must be defined.

In the case of the accounts payable example previously mentioned, the answers to these questions are relatively simple—the reports needed are checks to be mailed to the vendors, including the basic disbursement data. For control purposes, a trial balance and cash requirements report will also be needed.

However, in the second example, some research is again required. Should the sales report have comparative figures? If so, how will they be put in the computer? Should the sales report have any subtotals? For instance, should there be a subtotal for appetizers, entrées, desserts, beverages and so on? To discover this, management will need to define what they wish to use the report for and with what frequency and over what reporting period.

Future Needs of the User

When analyzing the task in this manner, also analyze what more can be done with the data in the future. Interview the management personnel to determine what information they could use but do not currently have. Include this information in the planning for the computerization. In this way, the future needs can be accommodated without costly reprogramming.

Reviewing the Alternatives

Earlier in this chapter we mentioned the many types of automated data processing equipment available. After carefully analyzing the availability of input data, the report requirements, and the future needs of the computer, an attempt must be made to match this analysis with the equipment available to find the best for the purpose.

Choosing the System

For the purpose of defining the data processing alternatives that should be reviewed, consider the following:

General Purpose Systems

These are computers provided by a vendor with no software. The user is expected to hire a programming staff and have them implement the software required. This approach is very costly, and typically a new system will require an analysis and programming time of six months or more for comprehensive software. This approach is effective for a large, high-volume operation able to show significant displacement costs.

Business Minicomputers

These are computers provided by vendors with no associated software. However, they do provide programming capabilities that are easily learned. The full-scale systems usually require that a computer specialist be hired; the business minicomputer can be programmed by an in-house staff member who has been trained by the vendor. The key is simplicity; these computers are designed to be simple to use, simple to program, and simple to justify. The limitation of this equipment is that they cannot handle as high a volume of data as the full-scale system. This approach is very cost effective for the small to medium-size user with well-defined needs.

Time-Sharing Services

These are massive computer centers that offer remote capability to a small user. The end user will usually have only a small printer, a teletype, and a card reader at his site. This means that he has only the capability to put data into the system or print reports. The programs to perform the tasks required are provided by the time-sharing service for a fee. The user will pay for the actual time he uses the service. This approach can be very effective for a low-volume operation that requires very few permanent files on the computer. Time sharing is less satisfactory when voluminous files must be maintained. The costs of doing so are high and may nullify any potential savings anticipated by this approach.

Time-sharing services do offer a "library" of statistical programs for their users. Frequently, a manager can find certain statistical programs useful to the point of justifying the service on that basis alone.

Service Bureaus

These are computer center that take data from their users to their own center, process it, and return it to the user. This approach can be very effective for the small to medium-size data processing user. One major service bureau has grown up providing primarily a payroll service to the point where it is more economical to use their service than any other alternative. Most service bureaus will provide programming services to their clients, thereby assuring that the programs will perform to the exact specifications. The only disadvantage to a service bureau for a small user is the costs. Start-up and conversion costs can be high. It is wise to solicit proposals from several service bureaus before taking this route.

Shared Systems

The hospital industry and the banking industry have made extensive use of this concept. Basically, a group of data processing users in the same industry will organize an entity for the purpose of establishing a computer center. The costs will be shared, and the programming development will be undertaken as an effort to satisfy the needs of all the users. The major drawback is in the control of confidential information. Frequently, there will be great concern about competitors' gaining access to this information by means of the computer. If these issues can be resolved, this approach can be most effective. Typically, the group will acquire a much larger, more powerful computer than any individual user could afford. The users can therefore expand their data processing uses beyond what is justifiable as an individual.

Turnkey System

The future of data processing for the small user will see much more of the turnkey approach. The system relieves the user of the burden of acquiring a data processing staff and managing it, while providing the computer power he needs. The disadvantage of these systems, as they are available today, is that the vendors are reluctant to modify their basic products to suit an individual client's needs. As a result, some clients are forced to change their methods to conform more closely to the computer's requirements.

Cost Considerations

There are many costs associated with a data processing installation over and above the cost of the hardware. The important ones are the following:

- Data processing staff salaries including data processing managers, programmers, and data input personnel whose function is to enter the basic data to the computer system.
- Forms and paper cost. The computer will use continuous-feed forms on its report printer, which are usually more expensive than the forms replaced from the manual system.
- Computer maintenance by a technician for both monthly preventive maintenance and for emergency repair service. The vendor will always be able to provide this service, but in recent years, third-party organizations have been able to offer maintenance service at lower prices. Research into this question may save several hundred dollars per month for a typical installation.
- Site preparation cost. Some equipment requires additional electrical power, additional air conditioning, and additional dehumidifying in the area where the computer is located.
- Conversion costs. At the time the conversion is made, the user should anticipate overtime expense on the part of his operating staff while they attempt to perform a task both manually and on the computer.

Careful planning is necessary if the organization is to select the equipment and system best suited to its needs from the vast range of types and models available today. Although the addition of computerization to an existing food service operation can be beneficial, the best time to introduce computerization is in the planning of a new operation. If you are thinking of a new, expanded, or remodeled operation, the investment in a computerized management information system is probably a sound investment. Either way, there are good reasons for taking the step. Computer processing costs have declined steadily since the early 1950s, but wages have gone up. Computerized information systems can be a hedge against inflation.

Making the right decisions depends on a plan that includes the following steps:

1. Development of a realistic definition of the information requirements in all phases of an organization's operations and management.
2. Exhaustive review of the wide variety of equipment and services now becoming available to the industry.
3. Careful matching of the available approaches to the requirements criteria established.
4. Painstaking quantification of the associated costs, the intangible benefits, and the value of controls to be applied.
5. Planning and scheduling of the conversion and implementation of a data processing system.

14

Energy Management

Until mid-1973, any combination of the words "energy," "cost," and "control" would have been the inspiration for extreme ennui. After all, we had long since come to believe not only that energy was cheap but also that its supply was endless.

Power companies exhorted their customers with such messages as "The more electricity you use, the less it costs" and "Live Better Electrically." Millions of miles of "adequate wiring" were installed to enable consumers, commercial and residential alike, to utilize more and more power-consuming devices capable of performing just about every menial task known to man. This was particularly true of kitchen facilities. The concept of a "power center" (a commercial concept) provided the ultimate symbol of affluence in the modern kitchen at home as well as in restaurants.

It is no surprise, in retrospect, that the discovery that our energy sources were in fact finite was so jarring. Worse that that, we were suddenly told that we were near the limit of our energy resources. In fact, it was no surprise at all to those who had been preaching energy responsibility and conservation since World War II.

One of the few economic concepts generally agreed to is the relationship of supply and demand. A good example of the effect of distortions in supply and demand has been the incredible increase in the cost of energy supplies since 1972. This increase was brought on primarily by the shortage of supply from traditional sources and has in turn made us realize the need to study, understand, and control the use of energy in all its forms. A whole new school of knowledge has had to be developed, and language and concepts heretofore the domain of engineers and technicians have had to be made intelligible to the energy "laity."

The intention of this chapter is to provide guidelines that will enable management to monitor and control energy costs in the food

---

This chapter was contributed by Richard H. Lorson, President, N.Y. Supply & Inspection Co., President, LORTEC Energy Conservation Service.

service business—costs that in a few years have grown from a rather small percentage of sales to over 5 percent in many cases and are capable of doubling by 1986.

The Basis of Energy

It is not always understood that most energy forms are produced by, or used for, processes involving heat. Electricity is generated by the burning of a fossil fuel such as coal, oil, or gas or by the development of steam to drive steam turbines using the heat generated by an atomic reactor or a solar heat collector. Except for the use of water or wind power, which contributes only a small part of our needs for electric power, a heat source is always required. Furthermore, when man is not developing power through a heat process or developing heat for direct use, he is busy removing heat for refrigeration, ice-making, or air-conditioning purposes.

It is clear, then, that when we talk of energy conservation we are really discussing the conservation or efficient use of heat. Nowhere is this principle better illustrated than in a commercial or institutional food service operation.

Conservation and Cost Control

One can look back today and realize that many food service plants have been designed with every facet of efficiency of use and movement considered *except* that of energy use. If power costs were considered at all, their consideration was at the bottom of a long list of other "more important" design criteria, and they were generally made to fit into the overall plan.

Of course, the availability of fuel or energy in its various forms had to be considered in the local framework. In 1965 one planned to use natural gas for cooking purposes in Louisiana and electricity for the same purposes in Tennessee because these energy forms were at low cost in those areas. But in the main, the most important consideration given to energy-consuming devices during the planning of a facility was the *first cost*—the cost of design and construction. If a plant of such vintage is an efficient operation in its use of energy *now*, it is efficient only because the design of its time happened accidentally to prepare for today's conditions, or present management has made the necessary adjustments in *operation and maintenance* that are requisite to sensible energy control under today's conditions.

Control requires a system of gauges so that its value can be measured against a valid frame of reference that will enable management to make sound decisions concerning its costs and operational status. Some of these gauges are real gauges, that is, electric, steam, water, and gas meters; thermostatic, pressure, and temperature controls; and the like. As in a laboratory, these gauges must be kept calibrated and in good working condition. But the more significant gauges, which have been activated since 1973, are those that measure, record, and analyze an operation's purchase, use, and waste of required energy forms.

To control energy use, someone in top management must become familiar with the required equipment and its use. If management does not already have the expertise, it must gain it, or at least obtain it from consultants and maintenance experts.

The fear and awe that most consumers feel toward the huge utility company must be overcome. The public utilities that provide electric, gas, and sometimes steam service, as well as the municipality that supplies water, have developed public images of being all-powerful, immutable giants with absolute authority to impose their wills on the consuming public. This chimera, although deserved in some cases, is not a true representation of the user's real position vis-à-vis the energy suppliers. The problem here, as in so many other energy-related matters, is that the need to know was slight in the 60 or so years of "cheap" energy.

The Control System—External

The first item of consideration in the systematic control of energy costs is the basis of purchase. Few know, and fewer believe, that many options exist in the rates at which one may purchase energy from suppliers. There are three basic types of supplier:

1. Public utilities (franchised electric, gas, water or steam companies)
2. Municipalities (government-supplied water and sometimes electricity and gas)
3. Private corporations or persons (sellers of oil, coal, bottled gas, or sometimes—surprisingly—the landlord)

Public Utilities

Most public utilities are controlled in one way or another by a government authority. This is usually a state-legislated body, but sometimes it can be municipal, and in some cases it is federal. All the rates, rules, and regulations of such public utilities are a matter of public record and hence are available for inspection and interpretation, a study that can require a para-legal expertise. In any case, it is the exception when there is only one rate classification available in a utility tariff for a given energy service. A prospective customer of a utility will be told by its representative that a given rate applies to his specific service requirement. However, an examination of the entire tariff might reveal that there are several different rates available. At this point, professional advice is usually required. A coordination must be made between the consumer's use of energy and the various utility rates available, rates that usually differ by type of user and time of use.

For example, suppose we have a restaurant that will operate only at night. Suppose further that the utility involved is one of those that have night-use discount rates. The utility representative in this case might assume—unless he was specifically informed otherwise—that the restaurant was going to operate both day and night and thus never consider the applicability of the night discount rate.

It is essential to remember that *it is not the responsibility of the utility to inform the customer of the most advantageous rate available.* It falls to the customer—and more often his qualified consultant—to ferret out the needed rate information.

Another surprise lies in the negotiability of rates in some areas. It is quite common nationally to find electric and gas rates that have been specially designed and agreed to by the utility for customers with unusual quantity or use requirements. Any utility can negotiate such a rate, although they must usually justify such a move to the public commission having jurisdiction. Special rates are most often found available or negotiable for public and quasi-public institutions where processes involving the public interest are involved. Here again, some professional assistance can be quite valuable.

Another point to remember is that utility rates are discriminatory and are intended to be. But the line of demarcation between fair and unfair utility rates is whether they are *unduly* discriminatory. It is beyond that point that special rates cannot be set.

A final point to remember about utility rates is that generally a customer is not locked into a given rate forever. It is true that some utility service classifications contain a clause that sets forth a minimum or maximum term during which the service agreement cannot be cancelled without penalty. This is rare, however, and it is the general rule that should a better rate become available (or be discovered to have existed all along) conversion to the preferred rate is relatively easy through conforming to the requirements that the tariff may set forth.

Municipalities

Municipalities are probably the most inflexible sellers of energy because they approach the matter of providing service on a civic/political basis. Because of their tax-free status, among other things, they can and sometimes do provide energy forms at a very low cost. This subject is the basis of the continuing national debate on public versus private power.

In most areas, municipalities confine their utility function to the service of water. This alone is a major undertaking, especially in the densely populated areas where there is increasing concern over the future availability of potable water in quantities that future generations will require.

Whereas one will usually find only a single supplier of electricity, gas, or steam in a given area, it is not unknown to find water available from more than one source—especially on or near the border between two or more municipalities—and it is advisable to examine this possibility during a site location examination. And, of course, there are still areas where one can drill for an adequate supply of healthy water.

The Private Energy Supplier

This category includes the oil supplier, the coal man, or any other nonpublic utility or nonmunicipal supplier of energy. Also included is the landlord of a property where the energy needs are supplied as a service included in the rent. This particular service is so complex, however, that it is treated separately at the end of the chapter.

There is a little more competition in the private energy sector. Where oil is to be used for space heating or bottled gas for cooking, there is usually more than one supplier available. Rates are a little different, also, especially in that they reflect current market conditions a lot faster than do public utility or municipal rates. In the past, term contracts, particularly for the supply of oil or coal, were common. More recently, however, with the many influences on the cost of oil, it is increasingly rare to find a supplier who is willing to be tied to a fixed price for very long.

The Real Area of Control—Internal

No negotiation for the supply of energy will be as susceptible to success as the establishment of a real, systematic control of energy use (and thus energy cost) *within* the facility. For, once it is established that the energy is being brought into the premises under the proper conditions (adequate and continuous supply under the best possible rate), *the entire matter of energy is under the purview of management and no one else.* Cost control begins with the choice of the energy source itself, followed by control of the use of the energy.

In outline, an internal program must consider:

1. Selection of the best energy form

2. Prescription of the use of energy within the operation
3. Analysis of the limits of use within the food and beverage service operation
4. Comparison of use and cost as against use and cost of other systems with same or similar functions.
5. Systematic maintenance and replacement of equipment at the optimal time
6. Computerization of critical data with continuing analysis
7. Evaluation of personnel attitudes and their correction where necessary and possible
8. Involvement of all phases of management, both operating and administrative, in energy knowledge and the decision-making process based on such knowledge
9. Sharing of the rewards
10. Evaluation of rents that include utilities

Selection of the Best Energy Form

It is, of course, easier to design a new facility with an eye to applying the best energy source for each function than it is to convert an existing facility to correct a misapplication. When planning a new facility, an analysis should be made of the current availability of the various energy forms together with the current pricing structure. Following that analysis, the future availability of the forms selected and the condition of reserves that will bear on future pricing should be studied.

It may be found that the present most advantageous energy costs obtained from one form of energy—say, gas—will be less advantageous than another form—say, nuclear-generated electricity—in the future. Here, as in many other phases of decision making, the services of a consultant familiar with local conditions can be invaluable in determining whether (1) the presently favorable source should be used indefinitely, (2) the installation should be designed for an economically feasible changeover after a given period of time, or (3) the utilizing of the presently higher cost energy form is feasible from the start.

With each passing year, both design and efficiency experts have more knowledge of equipment that has shown a better history of durability and cost of maintenance. These factors are treated elsewhere and must be considered in depth before the final decision on equipment selection is made.

Prescription of Use

It is one thing to choose the right equipment using the right energy form for optimal efficiency and least possible cost; it is quite another thing to see to it that the equipment is used in the manner intended. It is perhaps here that having the right personnel in the right job shows most clearly. If it is not practical to replace wrong equipment, it may be particularly difficult to retain personnel to use it efficiently. Established methods have already been ingrained, for better or for worse. It is in this area that the most attention to daily detail is required.

Each chef has his own methods. The classic case is the one in which the first thing the chef did on arrival in the morning was to turn on *all* gas jets for *all* stoves, ovens, and grills at 7:30 A.M. even though food service to the public did not start until noon and more than half of the gas used before 10:00 A.M. was not needed. It may seem close to impossible at first to change such patterns, and even when corrective measures appear to be taking hold, constant follow-up may be needed.

It has been fairly well demonstrated by now that the establishment of new energy-use habits is going to take a long time. Major corporations, faced with blackouts due to shortages of electricity in New York City in 1972 and 1973, established reduced-use programs that were extremely successful—for about one year. As soon as the power shortage appeared to be less critical, load and use patterns started to revert to earlier levels. Then, when the cost factor became a major one due to the oil embargo, it was found that the only way to ensure continued reduction in use was to disconnect a certain amount of lighting and put physical (sometimes computerized) limitations on the use of certain electric equipment. It simply was not possible to get people to reduce electricity use voluntarily on a permanent basis. True, it came to light that many installations were badly designed in the first place. Too much lighting had been installed, and the design itself sometimes called for an excessive use of air-conditioning equipment. Nevertheless, the installations were there and people used them. Such situations underline the need for careful design. Even so, part of management's continuing control program is the essential on-site follow-up of efficiency procedures.

Analysis of Use

It is in the area of energy use that measurement is invaluable. Management cannot effectively correct a cost problem if it is not aware of the basic cause. Energy cost problems are generally classed in two ways: energy waste and unknown loss. These two terms may appear to be the same, but they are not. Energy waste is defined as the energy consumed under conditions in which maximum possible efficiency is not achieved. Unknown loss, on the other hand, has to do with actual leakage of the energy form somewhere in the system without its ever having been used in any productive form.

This second item accounts for an amazing quantity of energy loss. The largest loss occurring in food service operations is in steam use. Faulty steam valves and traps have been known to waste millions of pounds of steam. In a busy kitchen, not a silent place at best, one has a tendency to dismiss the hissing sound of a faulty steam connection as a normal ambient condition. How would one know to look for such a condition? If the steam-consuming devices in the facility were subjected to a total steam-use expectancy analysis and if monthly steam consumption were metered at the source, the discrepancy would be noticed quickly.

This problem brings up a number of questions that are asked frequently.

Q. Are all forms of energy use subject to unknown loss?
A. Yes, but the worst offenders are steam and water because gas leaks are usually observed and repaired quickly and an electric "leak"—a short circuit—will blow a fuse or a circuit breaker instantly and thus provide discovery. But if water or steam is escaping through a valve directly into a drain somewhere in the system or into the ground, it is likely to go undiscovered for a considerable period of time.
Q. Can a use-expectancy analysis be made for all energy forms?
A. Yes, and it should be. The easiest energy use to predict is electricity. It is the least subject to undisclosed loss except in the unusual situation where another consumer's circuits are connected at some point on the customer's side of the utility meter. This situation rarely happens, but it is more likely to occur in ground-floor restaurant operations than, say, a sixteenth floor office. In complex urban locations where, for example, steam is purchased from a public utility and thereafter used, in addition to normal food service operations, to superheat water for dishwashing purposes, the potential for loss is great. It is in such situations that metering is almost essential.
Q. Is metering meant to include an installation of meters in addition to those of the utility?
A. Yes. No utility has any objection to a consumer's installing meters in his own premises strictly for the purpose of monitoring his use for cost-accounting purposes. Such an installation must, of course, be made by a qualified electrician or plumber and is subject to inspection by authorities having jurisdiction. The only time a public utility would have objection to the installation of a meter would be when the power so metered would be used by another consumer and the meter so installed would be used to charge that other consumer (such as a store next door or a subtenant to which the operation had sublet some space).

Q. When is it feasible to install special meters?
A. When it is clear that the use of the energy form varies more than 15 percent from the use-expectancy analysis. Although local installation costs vary, the two items involved in metering are (1) the cost of the meter, and (2) its installation cost. These are certainly justified costs when energy loss varies as stated above. One problem should be pointed out with respect to metering, that is, the ease with which meters can be *misread*. Reading instructions should be provided for members of the staff who are to read the meters regularly.
Q. How are the meter readings used in cost control?
A. In a number of ways. First, in each area in which a submeter is installed, the consumption can be seen and compared with the total use of the operation. If, for instance, a marked increase in gas consumption is shown and there is no known reason for the extra usage, one immediately looks for (1) unknown loss, (2) equipment deterioration, or (3) undisclosed use pattern changes. On the other hand, after installing an efficiency program, reduction in consumption should be quickly noted. It is also important to note that the basic utility metering data, usually shown on the invoice monthly, is of great use. It is this source of information that is the basis of control.
Q. In other words, submetering is useful in evaluating problems, but the utility metering provides the total control?
A. Correct. The utility metering shows the total use patterns and provides sufficient data from which appraisals can be made of operational gains or losses.
Q. Are there any other sources of information that bear on the analysis of use?
A. Yes, particularly with respect to the heating and air conditioning of the operation's premises. Many utilities provide a weather analysis each month which makes it possible to determine how much of an energy use variance is due to changes of weather from the local area norm. This can be quite helpful in keeping use in proper perspective. In an unusual hot spell, considerably more electric use may be required by air-conditioning compressors than normally. Here again, submetering on the air-conditioning system would be helpful, but the utility weather analysis can help to quantify the energy use without such submeters.
Q. How is the energy cost related to the total cost of the facility?
A. A number of useful guidelines can be developed. For example, energy use can be related to the number of persons served in a given month. It can be related to the total cost, to

profit, to maximum possible service, and so forth. A computer analysis program can be set up with relative ease to show these parameters each month and to compare them with the same parameters from previous months or years. All the various data sources should be made to fit into a total energy control report. This report should show all the sources of energy cost and then proceed to break them down into categories of use, relating them to production and ending up with an evaluation of efficiency and contribution to profit.

Q. Are such computerized systems available?

A. Yes. As a matter of fact, it is a field that is growing rapidly. However, great care should be taken in the selection of a system. Consultants specializing in the subject may be helpful in avoiding wrong decisions.

Comparison with Similar Facilities

One very helpful device in monitoring performance is comparison of results against those of an identical or similar operation. Consumption patterns may be used if the operations have similar characteristics but different billing rates for their utilities. Such comparisons can be used in the evaluation of management. In a chain operation, this sort of comparison is surely justified if not essential. Care must be taken in such evaluations that the two compared facilities are indeed alike, right down to the types of equipment and even to the equipment manufacturer. The greater detail that is observed in setting up any energy comparative analysis, the greater the benefits that will be obtained.

Maintenance and Replacement of Equipment

Although maintenance and equipment repair are covered in detail elsewhere, it must be clearly understood here that one of the prime offenders against cost-careful energy management has been a rather careless attitude toward any equipment maintenance except that demanded by dramatic events. Most manufacturers publish efficiency rating curves that purport to relate life expectancy and efficiency. Few, however, show recorded curves of actual experience under studied conditions. Only now are serious studies beginning to reveal how far from the anticipated curve some equipment has strayed. To the manufacturers' credit, it must be stressed that anticipated performance curves are based on *proper service and maintenance.* Many, if not most, managers skimp on this expense, and subsequently they or their successors must face the desperate struggle to "catch up"—usually a losing battle—or face replacement costs at a level much higher than the original investment.

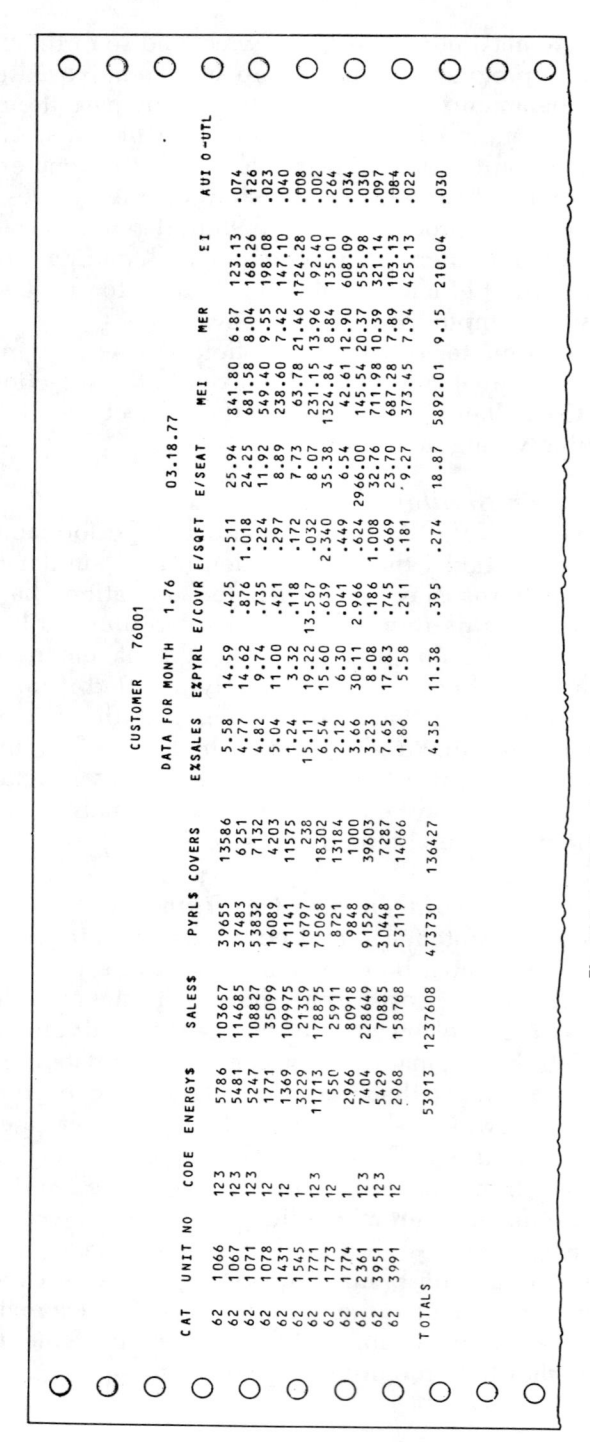

```
                          CUSTOMER  76001
                          DATA FOR MONTH  1.76        03.18.77

CAT UNIT NO CODE ENERGY$  SALES$   PYRL$  COVERS  EXSALES EXPYRL E/COVR E/SQFT E/SEAT   MEI    MER     EI   AUI O-UTL
 62  1066   123   5786   103657   39655   13586    5.58   14.59   .425   .511   25.94  841.80   6.87  123.13     .074
 62  1067   123   5481   114685   37483    6251    4.77   14.62   .876  1.018   24.25  681.58   8.04  168.26     .126
 62  1071   123   5247   108827   53832    7132    4.82    9.74   .735   .224   11.92  549.40   9.55  198.08     .023
 62  1078   12    1771    35099   16089    4203    5.04   11.00   .421   .297    8.89  238.60   7.42  147.10     .040
 62  1431   12    1369   109975   41141   11575    1.24    3.32   .118   .172    7.73   63.78  21.46 1724.28     .008
 62  1545    1    3229    21359   16797     238   15.11   19.22 13.567  -.032    8.07  231.15  13.96   92.40     .002
 62  1771   123  11713   178875   75068   18302    6.54   15.60   .639  2.340   35.38 1324.84   8.84  135.01     .264
 62  1773   12     550    25911    8721   13184    2.12    6.30   .041   .449    6.54   42.61  12.90  608.09     .034
 62  1774    1    2966    80918    9848    1000    3.66   30.11  2.966  -.624    6.54  145.54  20.37  555.98     .030
 62  2361   123   7404   228649   91529   39603    8.08    8.08   .186  1.008   32.76  711.98  10.39  321.14     .097
 62  3951   123   5429    70885   30448    7287    7.65   17.83   .745   .669   23.70  687.28   7.89  103.13     .084
 62  3991   12    2968   158768   53119   14066    1.86    5.58   .211   .181    9.27  373.45   7.94  425.13     .022

TOTALS            53913  1237608  473730  136427    4.35   11.38   .395   .274   18.87 5892.01   9.15  210.04     .030
```

Fig. 14-1. A sample printout for a multilocation restaurant corporation.

It is now essential that equipment be monitored in terms of its energy use. This practice is somewhat easier said than performed since there are few operations that can afford the cost of a meter for every piece of equipment. However, at least for electrical devices, there are temporary metering devices that can keep track of energy use, and maintenance personnel can be easily trained to use them, and should be.

Here again, reputable maintenance firms are available for service or for training of in-house personnel and should be utilized for one of these two purposes.

Computerization Techniques

A computer can be a marvel, or it can be a monster. It is well understood now that the computer is nothing more or less than an extension of man's ability to make mistakes. But properly applied a computer can provide instant evaluation of an energy conservation program.

Many food service institutions and companies have their own in-house computer operations. Few who now have them could survive without them. Some, however, are making only partial use of their computers' potentialities. Time and need will improve their situations, however. In the meantime, there are a few firms with the foresight and expertise to provide a format of computer evaluation of food service energy data.

A sample printout of one such firm is illustrated in Fig. 14–1. Here, the parameters required by the management of a multilocation restaurant corporation are all provided, monthly, after the utility data have been entered and analyzed. One can see any aberrations at a glance by reference to the several indexes utilized.

In short, the ultimate in data evaluation—the computer—is essential in making current operating information available for decision making on the shortest possible notice.

Evaluation of Attitudes

It has been stated, at least orally, that outside of the performing and visual arts, there are no more "artistic" temperaments to be found than in the gastronomic arts. The stereotype of the volcanic chef is well known, and legion are the restaurant owners and managers who treat their chefs with Toscanini-like deference. And well may this be justified, for the preparation of food in a manner sufficient to attract a clientele to spend heavily for its enjoyment is indeed an art. Such personalities may need careful handling if their cooperation in energy saving is to be achieved.

When less artistic personalities are involved, it is possible to utilize such operational "gimmicks" as color coding on switches and valves whereby colors are related to times of day for use and a sort of "game" made of the process. Here again, follow-up is indicated, together with some reward, the latter concept being discussed later.

Management Involvement

The time is now well past when energy management can be left to middle to lower-middle management. Management at the decision-making level must be aware of the cost/profit implications of energy use. This domain extends now to the legal sector, in which the question of utility and municipal contracts have become involved.

Particular concern may arise when an energy service is to be provided by a municipality that has, or threatens to have, a budget crisis. Such entities are being forced into reorganizing their income/expense procedures with the result that pricing structures for utility services may be reassessed. Future costs are not predictable.

For the best possible control, at least one member of top management should be more than casually familiar with the problems attendant on energy use. This will require a period of training in many cases and probably some diversion of executive time from other profitable corporate pursuits. However, the savings will compensate for it.

Sharing the Rewards

Incentive programs have been with us for years. In many institutional facilities, they have been impossible to establish, at least in a direct monetary way. But if one is to expect employees who perceive no direct financial benefit to perform any more than their basic duties, some reward is likely to be helpful. This can be either in the form of bonuses or special recognition, but in any case it must be established on a permanent basis.

Rents That Include Utilities

When the food and beverage facility is located in rented premises and some or all of the energy requirements are provided by the landlord, energy savings may be particularly difficult to achieve. Such an arrangement is called *rent inclusion* of energy charges. Rent-included energy is usually restricted to electricity, but sometimes gas and steam are also included. The problems that arise are many, but the greatest problem is that the service is almost never metered.

In many locations, the utility prohibits the landlord from remetering the energy form it purchases on the grounds that such remetering and reselling is parasitic and deprives the utility of revenue it would otherwise obtain directly from the ultimate consumer. It matters little in such reasoning that the landlord is paying the utility for such energy and sometimes at rates higher than those the facility/tenant would have been able to enjoy on a direct purchase basis. That is exactly where the problem arises. The landlord, now in the capacity of an unregulated private utility, must include in or add to the rental a certain amount of money for the energy to be provided. Let us examine a case in which electricity is provided to a restaurant.

Let us say that the ABC Restaurant Company has rented a store location in a building owned by the XYZ Realty Corporation. All terms of the lease have been negotiated and agreed on. At the end, the landlord, XYZ, states that when the restaurant facility is installed and in operation, he will have a survey made to determine the value of the electricity to be provided. At that time, the survey result in dollars will be added to the rent to repay XYZ for the electricity provided. Until that time, ABC will pay a flat $1.00 per annum per square foot of space rented, and the amount paid until the survey results are submitted will be credited by the landlord to ABC against the surveyed electric valuation.

Nowhere has ABC been informed as to the basis on which the survey will be made, or what rate, if any, is to be used in computing the charges. ABC has assumed that the landlord will not charge the restaurant any more for electricity than would the local electric company.

One must remember at this point that XYZ Corporation, the landlord, is in the business of building and renting space in its own building. That is its function. It is not versed in utility procedures or utility pricing. It has, therefore, retained a utility consultant to prepare the evaluation.

A survey is made and a report prepared. XYZ submits the report to ABC Restaurant and asks for their approval. ABC reviews the report and finds that it cannot make head or tail of it, but since the dollar valuation doesn't look too far out of line, the report is approved. Shortly thereafter, ABC receives a very legal (and binding) document that amends the lease between the parties to increase the rental by the amount of the electric evaluation (in dollars) set forth in the report. The agreement also contains the provision that the evaluation is subject to automatic increase if the utility should increase the rate under which the landlord is purchasing power. Having agreed to the evaluation, ABC executes the lease amendment document, XYZ renders a bill, and all accounts seem settled.

Without the services of a consultant of its own, ABC does not really know whether it is paying more to landlord XYZ than it would to the local utility. As it turns out in so many such situations, ABC Restaurant winds up paying considerably more than it would to the utility, and this difference is compounded with every rate increase charged to XYZ.

What should ABC have done? The answers are fairly simple to explain but quite difficult to negotiate, especially after the fact.

First of all, the restaurant would have been most wise to insist that it be enabled to purchase its electricity directly from the utility company. This step would have eliminated the need for any surveys and the further complications that can arise. Short of being permitted to make such a direct utility purchase, ABC should have secured expert advice prior to making any agreement under the lease. The main point to be made in this connection is that extreme care must be taken in such rent-inclusion situations.

In the case of the preexisting rent-inclusion situation, that is, where the arrangement already exists, there are sometimes remedies that can be taken either by legal counsel or a qualified consultant familiar with the rent-inclusion problems locally.

The National Restaurant Association and the Midwest Research Institute have developed an excellent practical check list for restaurant operators. It is reproduced below.

National Restaurant Association Checklist for Energy Control and Conservation[*]

These guidelines should be given to the person(s) responsible for energy management for the restaurant. Each item should be evaluated for its energy-saving potential. Place a check mark or date beside each guideline after disposition.

Energy Conservation Guidelines

Food Preparation

1. Determine a schedule of preheating times for ovens, steam tables, grills, broilers, fryers, etc. Generally, 10 to 30 minutes (depending on appliance) is adequate.
2. Stagger turn-on times for heavy duty electrical equipment so that 30-minute intervals can be achieved. This should reduce the demand load.
3. Use additional fry unit, broiler, oven, etc., only for peak business hours. Develop a schedule showing the hours and day when additional units are required.
4. When preheating ovens, set the thermostat at the desired

---

[*]Developed by the National Restaurant Association and The Midwest Research Institute.

temperature; it will preheat no faster and waste energy if you dial higher.
5. Calibrate oven thermostats to assure correct cooking temperature and maximum efficiency.
6. Determine the cooking capacity of ovens. Use the smaller or more energy efficient oven when possible.
7. Load and unload ovens quickly to avoid unnecessary heat loss. Every second an oven is open, it loses about 1 percent of its heat.
8. Use correct size hoods to capture grease-laden vapors.
9. Use proper blend of makeup air in exhaust hoods.
10. Install twist-on timers or individual switches on food warming infrared heat lamps.
11. Turn off cooking and heating units that are not needed.
12. Have serviceman check the fuel–air ratio on all gas burners and adjust to the most efficient mixture.
13. Consult your local gas utility company about the use of pilot lights. Adjustments made by persons not thoroughly familiar with the equipment could be dangerous.
14. Begin cooking food while oven is warming up (the exception being for food which will dry out or over cook).
15. Cook meat slowly at low temperatures. Cooking a roast for 5 hours at 250° F (121° C) could save 25 to 50 percent of the energy that would be used in cooking for 3 hours at 350° F (177° C).
16. Schedule baking or roasting so that oven capacity can be fully utilized, thereby reducing operating hours.
17. Aluminum foil retards the baking of a potato. If foil is necessary, wrap after potato is baked.
18. Oven should not be opened during operation. Food will cook faster and lose less moisture if door is opened at scheduled times.
19. Whenever possible, huddle food on griddle close together and heat only the portion of griddle being cooked on.
20. Placing weight on bacon and sausage quickens their cooking time but may alter the characteristics of the product.
21. Frozen food should be thawed in refrigerator. Food will thaw easily and help reduce power demand for refrigerator. Thaw all foods before cooking, unless product characteristics prohibit.
22. Use only the size of oven that is needed for the job. Heating extra space results in wasted energy.
23. Always turn char-broiler heat to medium after briquets are hot. Keep briquets clean.

24. When using a gas range for full heat conditions, the tip of the flame should just touch the bottom of pan or kettle.
25. Foods will cook faster when covered with lids.
26. Placing foil under range burners and griddles will improve the operation efficiency and make equipment easier to clean.
27. Griddles should be cleaned frequently. Remove deposits, being careful to prevent loose deposits from falling on hot area and forming air pollution by thermal degradation.
28. Fryers need to be cleaned and the oil filtered at least once a day.
29. Heating equipment should be clustered together and away from cooling equipment.
30. Develop a schedule for equipment use. Equipment should be turned on at a specific time, to a specific temperature, and turned off at the designated time.
31. Installation of an in-the-meat thermometer, with gauge outside the oven, will reduce heat loss from opening the oven to check roasting progress.
32. Install timers for kitchen equipment, to automatically control cooking time.
33. Electric range burners should always be smaller than the kettles or pots placed on them.
34. Place kettles and pots close together on range tops to decrease heat loss.
35. Have serviceman check gas pressure to appliances to assure that adequate pressure is available from supplier.
36. Turn on food warmers and hot plates only as needed; don't let them run when not in use. Also, run at the lowest temperature permissible for safe food handling.

Heating, Ventilation, and Air Conditioning

1. When heating is required, set the thermostat to 68° F (20° C). For cooling, set thermostat at 78° F (26° C). After closing, the thermostat can be set for 55° F (13° C) to 60° F (16° C) during the winter, and 80° F (27° C) to 82° F (28° C) during the summer.
   When cooling, each degree Fahrenheit the thermostat is raised will result in about 5 percent reduction in electrical consumption. When heating, each degree lower will result in about 3 percent reduction in energy consumption. If you anticipate a room to be vacant for more than two days during the summer months, cut the air conditioning off. In some areas of the country high humidity would prevent this practice.

Energy Management 265

2. Stagger start-up times of equipment to avoid heavy electrical demand at one time.
  This could save money on the electric bill. Most utility companies charge according to peak demand for each half hour, and total power usage.
3. Balance registers properly for best heat distribution between kitchen and dining room.
4. Inspect and clean all HVAC system filters at least monthly (remember to inspect makeup air units).
  The National Bureau of Standards estimates that a general energy reduction of 10 percent can be realized if a cooling system is kept clean and in good operating condition.
5. Inspect all heating and cooling air ducts for cleanliness, proper insulation, and leaks.
6. Keep all doors and windows closed.
  Perhaps in parts of the country, ambient air can be used instead of conditioned air. In these cases, windows can be opened and air movement accomplished with exhaust fans.
7. Vestibules should be installed at entrance doorways. Delivery doors should have adequate weather stripping.
8. All pipes and vents where thermal control is important (hot water, steam, air conditioning, etc.) should have adequate insulation.
9. Check the accuracy of HVAC system thermostats.
10. Compressors should not be located near heating units.
11. Check size and speed of exhaust fans and limit to actual needs.
12. Check doors, windows, openings, and walls for tightness. Replace insulation or caulk where necessary.
13. Ceiling and walls should have adequate insulation. Concrete block walls should be covered with insulation board.
14. Attic areas should be ventilated during hot weather.
15. Fresh air dampers installed in HVAC return air duct could eliminate the operation of the air conditioning (except fan) during off-peak seasons.
16. Fresh air makeup units should be designed so that the damper is closed when the unit is shut down.
17. Drop panel screening should be installed to reduce solar heat gain through glass windows and walls.
18. Operations that heat with fuel oil should check size of oil nozzle in use.
19. Close the damper on unused fireplaces to prevent room heat loss.
20. Maintain adequate humidity to eliminate the extra heat needed to ensure customer comfort.

21. Install water treatment system on hot water and steam systems if needed. Chemical deposits in piping reduce heating or cooking efficiency.
22. Balance ventilation and exhaust systems to maintain the rate of air turnover at the lowest number consistent with adequate ventilation and safety.
23. Close off dining areas not in use and turn off their heating or cooling systems (high humidity areas may require some air treatment).
24. During cold weather, draperies should be open during daylight hours to allow increased light and absorption of heat. They should be closed during the night hours to conserve heat.

Sanitation

1. Turn water heater down to 75° F (24° C) on closing, and turn back up two hours before opening. (Adjust warmup time to fit the particular units.)
2. Drain water heater every six months.
3. Shut off electric booster heaters on dishwashers when the kitchen is closed.
4. Use hot water only when necessary.
5. Do not use dishwashing machine for a small number of dishes. Wait until a full load is available before running.
6. Keep heater coils free from lime accumulations.
7. When the main dishwashing rush is over, turn off equipment booster heaters and accumulate dishes until the next rush period.
8. Dripping water faucets are costly in water and energy use. All leaky faucets should have washers replaced immediately.
9. Install water pressure regulators for hot water line to dishwasher to reduce wasted hot water. Set regulator to the operating pressure required by the machine.
10. Make sure power rinse on dishwasher is turning off automatically when tray has gone through machine.
11. Insulate hot water lines.
12. Limit general-use hot water to 110° F (43° C).
13. Cleaning should be done during daylight hours if possible.
14. Mop from bucket to conserve hot water.
15. Accumulate trash for full load-burning frequencies when incinerators are used.

Lighting

1. Standard life lamps save energy when compared with extended life lamps.

2. Parabolic floodlights give the same lighting as reflector floodlights but use about half the wattage.
3. High efficiency fluorescent lights will use about 14 percent less energy than older models.
4. Incandescent lamps, high intensity discharge lamps and some types of fluorescents can be switched off and on as needed without serious loss of lamp life or performance.
5. Relamp to lower wattage where possible.
6. For lighting design, use the ESI (equivalent spherical illumination) concept in selecting equipment and layout.
7. Metallic additive lamps and high pressure sodium lamps are two of the most efficient lamps.
8. The energy requirements for office lighting can be reduced around 30 percent by turning off lights in vacant offices, reducing lighting during noon hours, and using minimum lighting for after-hours cleanup.
9. The lumens per watt available from various lamps are:

Lamp	Lumens per Watt
Incandescent	17 to 22
Mercury	56 to 63
Fluorescent	67 to 83
Multivapor	85 to 100
Sodium	105 to 130

10. Obtain a computer analysis of lighting cost for planned and established restaurants. The analysis will provide information on lamp types, operating hours, and costs.
11. Consider time clocks or photocells that automatically turn power on and off for (a) signs; (b) exterior lights, fountains, waterfalls, etc., on grounds; (c) exterior lights on building.
12. Replace resistance-type dimmers with transformer type.
13. Investigate the feasibility of short-time (twist-on) timers for controlling lights in storerooms and walk-in boxes or other time-use areas where light is apt to be left on indefinitely.
14. Have local contractor measure lighting output in your kitchen. FEA's lighting guidelines generally call for 50 foot candles at desks, 30 foot candles in rooms and work areas, and 10 foot candles in halls, corridors, etc. Check with your local public health office for lighting requirements in food preparation, storage, and serving areas.
15. Turn off individual office lights when leaving for the day.
16. Install individual electric switches to improve control of lighting in specific areas.

17. Apply light finishes to walls, ceilings, floors, and furnishings to reduce lighting requirements.

Refrigeration

1. Close doors immediately after items have been removed from refrigerator. Do not use a walk-in cooler, which requires opening the door every time a customer is served, to store individual portions of products such as salads, beer glasses, etc.
2. Keep all gaskets and seals in good condition.
3. Keep blower coil free of ice build-up.
4. Do not store products in front of coils in a manner that would restrict air flow.
5. Replace refrigerator compressor belts that are worn or damaged.
6. Inspect and service all electric motors.
7. Plan ahead so that when a worker enters the walk-in refrigerator, he can fill many needs at one time. Prepare a schedule for use.
8. Turn off lights in walk-in cooler when leaving. Units should have pilot lights on light switches to warn if lights were left on.
9. Hot food should not be placed directly in refrigerator but allowed to cool for a few minutes.
10. Check refrigerators for short cycling and loss of temperature control. Check refrigerant level if abnormal operation exists.
11. Compressors need to have open space to give off the heat removed from the unit. Keep coils free of dust and do not store anything within four feet of the compressor.
12. Compressors should be placed in cool areas rather than located near heating units.
13. Refrigerator and freezer fan cleaning and compressor checkup should be scheduled as regular maintenance items.
14. Consolidate refrigerated and freezer storage when possible.
15. Schedule food deliveries, when possible, to avoid overloading refrigeration facilities.
16. Expedite receiving and prompt refrigeration of frozen and perishable foods.
17. Defrost freezers frequently. Ice should not be allowed to build up more than ⅛ inch on the walls and shelves.

Transportation

1. Drivers should not exceed a speed of 50 miles per hour. In most cases, speeds from 45 to 50 miles per hour are the most efficient.

2. Maintain steady speeds whenever possible. One speed change per mile can increase fuel consumption up to 25 percent.
3. Avoid fast starts. Conservative driving in city traffic can save 10 to 20 percent in fuel consumption.
4. Slowing down on grades is recommended. It takes 55 percent more fuel to maintain 50 miles per hour on a 17 percent grade than on a flat road. A 17 percent grade is the steepest allowed on any of our interstate road systems.
5. Keep the vehicle in good operating condition. A tuned engine can save from 6 to 20 percent in fuel.
6. Keep tires inflated on the high side recommended by the manufacturer. Vehicles with radial ply tires use 3 percent less fuel than if equipped with conventional bias ply tires.
7. Eliminate all engine idling time. A rule of thumb cost figure is $1.50 for every hour a vehicle engine is idling.
8. Curtail use of company vehicles, especially for employees taking vehicle home at night. Investigate a possibility of car pools in this type of situation.
9. Investigate possibility of obtaining in-plant storage, thus reducing the need for vehicles that are primarily used as storage units.
10. Reduce nonessential loads carried in vehicles. Even 400 pounds added to the vehicle weight can cut mileage by 10 percent.
11. Change oil filter according to manufacturer's suggestion. A dirty filter can reduce mileage by 10 percent.
12. Encourage employee car pools.
13. Use the telephone rather than a car when possible.
14. Consolidate food delivery schedules.
15. Avoid engine warm-up. Simply drive slowly for a few minutes until engine is warm.
16. Consider exchanging full-size cars for economy cars. The fuel savings will amount to at least 35 percent with compacts and more with subcompacts.
17. Use air conditioning only when necessary. A full size V-8 will lose about 2 miles per gallon and a compact six cylinder will lose 2.6 miles per gallon with the air conditioner running.
18. Tests using gas catalysts have resulted in about 23 percent better mileage when used with compact size cars.
19. Buy slightly less than a full tank of fuel. This will eliminate wasteful overflow, allowing room for fuel expansion, especially in hot weather.
20. If you have a sudden drop in gasoline mileage, you may have

mechanical trouble. Repair as soon as possible to save fuel consumption.
21. Check and adjust the wheel alignment to the manufacturer's specifications so the car's rolling resistance will be minimized.
22. Travel during off-peak traffic whenever possible and use routes with a minimum number of traffic lights and stop signs.

Miscellaneous (Heat Recovery, Pollution Control, General Observation)

Pollution control in the restaurant industry is becoming increasingly important. Local ordinances generally require that the vent gas be no more than 20 percent opaque or register no higher than Number 1 on the Ringleman scale. In a recent survey conducted by pollution control officials in Kansas City, it was found that ordinances that limit visible emissions in restaurant vent gases are common throughout the United States. Most of the cities also enforce the ordinance.

Visual emission codes can generally be met by the following alternatives:

1. Install an afterburner to reduce visible emissions. A restaurant may have an average natural gas bill of $75 per month (based on cost of gas at $0.80 per thousand cubic feet) for operation of the unit. The average cost is 50 to 60 cents per hour of operation. The cost for the equipment and installation will be approximately $3,500 to $8,000. The blower fan is generally rated at 3 to 5 horsepower and exhausts 3,000 to 6,000 cubic feet of air per minute. The efficiency is usually greater than 98 percent.
2. Install an Electrostatic Precipitator to trap the grease and smoke particles. The power consumption of a typical unit is 2.6 kilowatt-hours (0.1 for ESP unit and 2.5 for fan) for 3,000 to 6,000 cubic feet per minute of exhaust volume. The efficiency of the units is generally 90 to 95 percent. The units need an automatic detergent rinse cycle for best operation. Several companies now have many ESP units in operation across the country. The cost of equipment plus installation can run from around $8,000 to around $30,000. Many companies are still in the development stage of producing a satisfactory unit for a reasonable price.
3. Consider the replacement of equipment causing excessive air pollution. For example, a char-broiler could be replaced with units that do not have the problems of grease dripping on open flames. Some suggestions are:

a. *Serrated grill.* A steel plate installed with a 15-degree slant that allows the grease to run off into reservoirs.
b. *Overfired broiler.* The flame is above the meat, which prevents grease from falling into the flame.
c. *Sealed cabinet.* Unit that allows no smoke to escape during cooking.

Restaurants that must meet local ordinances within a short period will have a difficult choice to make regarding whether to choose an afterburner, an electrostatic precipitator, or to change methods of cooking. Natural gas supplies are limited. In some areas of the country, new services are not being granted. The afterburner would probably use between 1,500 and 5,000 cubic feet of gas per day, with costs varying between $30 to $120 per month (at 80 cents per thousand cubic feet of gas.) The electrostatic precipitator would cost less than 5 cents per day for electricity (to operate 12 hours per day at 0.1 kilowatt per hour), however, the capital costs could vary from $8,000 to $30,000 for equipment that has had only a few years to establish a record for reliability. Switching to other cooking methods may reduce the business volume for many restaurants.

4. Heat recovery units are not in general use at the present time. The units could be applied to afterburner exhaust, water heater exhausts, and possibly other equipment, if the heat loss is sufficiently high. The efficiency of the recovery units would probably be around 50 percent.

15

Advertising and Sales Promotion

Advertising is only one facet of the total marketing activity of a business enterprise. In other chapters of this book, many aspects of the total marketing approach are discussed. The market research and analyses made in planning a new restaurant operation are the basis of the initial marketing policy, but this fundamental market research and analysis must be ongoing, because people's tastes and habits change as time passes. Restaurant operators, like other retailers, frequently find themselves losing their traditional customers and must constantly be thinking of new advertising and promotional approaches.

The marketing, advertising, and promotion effort for a restaurant covers all the following activities:

1. Research and analysis
2. Advertising (newspapers, radio, direct mail, etc.)
3. Publicity and public affairs
4. Internal promotion
5. Special promotions
6. The sales department

Linking all these activities is the budget. The advertising program should, of course, produce a benefit substantially greater than its cost, but in practice it is usually extremely difficult to measure the results and effectiveness of promotional expenditures.

Advertising and Promotion Budgeting

In the absence of an objective measure of benefit received, several methods are commonly used in determining how much to spend for an advertising campaign. These include the following:

1. A percentage of the previous year's sales
2. A percentage of the estimated year's sales

3. A combination of the two
4. A fixed dollar amount

Expenditures for food service advertising range from 2 to 5 percent of sales according to the best available industry-wide statistics. Some operations with a very high degree of repeat clientele may spend as little as 1 percent of total sales. Profit margins in food service generally do not warrant an expenditure much above 5 percent of revenues.

The actual dollar expenditures for advertising may sometimes exceed or fall somewhat below these guidelines for common sense reasons. For example, a particular hotel restaurant operation with $5 million in sales may not need to spend more than $50,000 (or 1 percent) for advertising, whereas a smaller restaurant might have to exceed 5 percent of its annual sales volume in order to have a sufficient dollar amount to purchase adequate advertising space. The advisability of such a budget would be questionable, however.

Additionally, the timing of the advertising campaign in relation to the operation's economic life cycle is important. Specifically, most operations may have to spend a proportionately larger amount of money for advertising in their initial years of operation in order to become known and to build up a clientele. Conversely, a good quality, well-established operation with a strong repeat clientele should be able to spend a proportionately lesser amount of its revenues on advertising.

One important factor that should not be overlooked, however, is "continuity." Once an advertising program has been adopted and is successful, it should be maintained and continually improved on in order to ensure continued market identification and penetration.

Advertising Objectives

Until the restaurant business became highly developed by major chains, the marketing and advertising programs of the industry were generally at a very unsophisticated level, largely because of budget restraints. The recent development of extensive television, radio, and other media advertising by major chains has shown how important the total packaging can be.

The growth of consumerism has shown the importance of truth in advertising, and it must be recognized that many food service establishments are vulnerable to charges of false advertising. It is bad business and illegal to advertise a product that is not in fact provided. Advertising "gourmet" delights that the kitchen cannot prepare or fine wines that the waitress does not know how to identify or serve disappoints the consumer. Needless to say, a failure of a food service operation because of poor products will not be remedied by an advertising program unless the product defects themselves have been corrected.

The goal of advertising is to inform, usually (but not always) for the purpose of promoting sales. Advertising for a restaurant or other food service enterprise can range from a simple announcement of its business activity for the purpose of keeping its name before the public to a special-purpose campaign. All restaurant advertising must seek to induce prospective customers to eat out rather than stay at home. A major aim of advertising is to stimulate interest and encourage discretionary spending on one's own product rather than on someones else's, but whatever the program, the objective of the advertising should be clearly established.

An initial advertising campaign is usually designed to identify the restaurant in the minds of the public and to attract patrons. Subsequent advertising campaigns, however, can be designed to optimize sales potential at some particular time or to attract some particular market. For example, an analysis of sales and seat turnover might indicate that an operation is achieving a very good level of success on specific days of the week and for certain meal periods but that opportunities exist to increase overall revenue and staff utilization by increasing the sales volume during other meal periods or days. If dinner business is concentrated from 8:00 P.M. to 10:00 P.M. and is slack at earlier hours, pretheater dinners at a special price may be promoted from 6:00 P.M. to 8:00 P.M. to utilize otherwise lost staff time. It could be counterproductive to promote business during the busy periods because more idle time might be generated at slack periods.

It should be emphasized that the most successful advertising campaigns for restaurants are those that do not have to be carried out on a continually broad scale. A sound operation with a good price value should need heavy advertising only during its start-up period. If a market exists for the product being sold and the product is a good one, word-of-mouth advertising can lead to continued success.

Market Identification

Most frequently, a combination of sound research and perceptive observations will lead to a thorough knowledge of the markets available to a food service operation. Naturally, the markets available to the operation will vary depending on its location, quality, price level, and image. Before entering into an advertising campaign, the operator should ascertain whether his primary markets are local residents or businessmen who could be encouraged to frequent the restaurant on a regular basis or tourists or other out-of-town visitors who must be encouraged primarily by advertising to utilize his facilities. This basic research was discussed in earlier chapters.

After the product and the market have been defined, management must determine:

1. What type of advertising campaign will attract the attention of potential customers?
2. Once the attention of potential customers has been attracted, how can they be convinced to patronize the facility?
3. Will the advertising be profitable in relation to its cost?

Promotion may make use of media advertising, direct mail campaigns, outdoor advertising on billboards, publicity brochures, or internal promotions. Once the types of promotional activity have been selected, financial and managerial resources must be allocated among them. Regardless of the media used, a theme should unite the promotional effort.

Advertising agencies can play an important role in developing a campaign, although an operator may decide to handle it in house. There are advantages and disadvantages to both approaches.

The Advertising Agency

The advertising agency performs an important and valuable function in the modern business world. Its highly professional experts can enable an advertiser to sell his product or service in the most efficient manner.

The important advantages of an advertising agency include the following:

1. The operator is relieved of the burden of creating, administering, and executing the advertising campaign and is thus able to concentrate on his primary function of operating his place of business with the maximum degree of efficiency.
2. With proper agency selection, the operator is assured of a group of experts whose sole task is to identify, merchandise, and sell a product.
3. The operator is usually able to obtain the best possible results from his advertising dollars.

For many operators, the major disadvantage in using an advertising agency is cost. Usual agency commissions approximate 15 to 20 percent of the total media budget, although some firms work on the basis of a flat monthly fee in addition to a percentage of a media budget. Another disadvantage is that some agencies may be more sophisticated than an operator requires or, alternatively, the operator may be located in an area removed from a major metropolitan area, and a highly professional advertising agency is thus not readily accessible. In such cases, the operator may be better advised to administer his own advertising program.

Media Selection

As part of its function, an advertising agency will select or recommend the media to be used. In a self-administered program, the choice must be made by management.

The various forms of media used in advertising include newspapers, which provide repeated, quick, and timely advertising, usually at a relatively low cost per exposure compared to other forms of media. Newspapers are especially useful for advertising operations whose markets are extremely localized. Consumer and specialized magazines are also widely used. The consumer magazines have a longer reading life than newspapers, generally a greater number of readers per issue, and a wider geographic exposure. Advertisers using such publications should keep these features in mind. Specialized magazines such as *Gourmet* have longer lives than do consumer-oriented magazines but often have a far smaller circulation base. They are especially well suited for unusual or very high-quality operations.

In almost all large cities and resort areas, visitor and tourist guides are widely used for restaurant advertising. These publications have a large circulation in hotels where they reach out-of-town visitors at modest cost to the advertiser. Billboard, taxi, and public transportation car posters are also useful if visitors to an area form a large part of its available market. Listings in credit card company booklets and the telephone directory yellow pages are helpful and readily available.

Radio advertising, possibly more than any medium except television, has the ability to present ideas in a setting that enables the mind to dwell on them. Television adds the visual image to the oral presentation, thus amplifying the product image. Both radio and television have the ability to capture the potential customers' attention totally and focus it on the item being advertised. Television, however, is too expensive for operations other than a large chain operation.

Media Effectiveness

There are several ways to judge the effectiveness of the media being considered for use. Several organizations can provide information about the potential exposure to be garnered from any specific media. Included are the following.

Audit Bureau of Circulation (ABC): The ABC is a nonprofit association of advertisers and advertising agencies and publishers that audits the circulation of the membership, including newspapers, magazines, and business and trade publications. Included in the information supplied in an ABC report are the following:

1. Total circulation
2. Percentage of circulation paid and unpaid
3. Prices at which the respective publications are sold
4. Special inducements granted to subscribers
5. The way in which subscriptions are obtained

Controlled Circulation Audit Bureau (CCA): The CCA audits, in a similar fashion to the ABC, the circulation of professional publications.

Standard Rate and Data: *Standard Rate and Data* is a monthly publication issued in two parts and giving the following information:

1. Rates for advertising
2. Technical requirements
3. Publication dates
4. Closing dates for submission of advertising copy
5. National representatives
6. Personnel of the publications

This information is supplied for newspapers, consumer magazines, business papers, radio, television, transportation advertising, and Canadian and Mexican markets. Finally, it also indicates what type of readership each media reaches.

Publicity

Restaurants and hotels receive a surprisingly large amount of publicity, some good and some bad, in newspaper gossip columns, restaurant reviews, and travel publications of all varieties. The importance attached to a good rating in the *Michelin Guide, Holiday Magazine,* or the *Mobil Guide,* for example, is well known, and a good review in a local newspaper can assist a new or restyled operation to get a good start.

Newspapers and magazines should be informed of new ventures, but since serious restaurant critics on the staffs of these publications try to remain incognito, an operator will not usually have an opportunity to make a special effort for them. The operator must be prepared to be judged by the product available to the general public.

Internal Promotion

In any kind of lodging facility where a food or cocktail service operation exists, internal promotion may be used to sell this operation to resident guests. Informative and attractive promotional literature should be provided in all guest rooms, and maids should be instructed to replenish the literature when necessary. Attractive signs in elevators and public corridors and walkways should also be utilized. All promotional literature for any facility in the operation should convey the character of the operation, the level of formality, the type of food or beverage served, hours of operation, whether reservations are required, and the type of entertainment offered, if any.

The use of attractive table tent cards and menu inserts should be utilized wherever possible. Table tent cards, which can be printed in small quantities, can be utilized to promote impulse items such as wine, desserts, appetizers or specialty side dishes. Table tent cards and all other promotional material should be attractively designed and printed, easily readable, and compatible in color of stock, printing, and overall appearance with the menu, decor, and image of the restaurant.

Promotional displays, such as attractive dessert carts at the entrance to the restaurant or the use of wine racks either at the entrance or within the restaurant, bring such items to the attention of diners and should be incorporated into the overall decor of the restaurant.

Naturally, an important feature of promotion is creative selling by captains, waiters, and waitresses. Sales campaigns can be used to motivate service personnel to increase sales both for the benefit of the business and to increase their own tip income. Most diners compute tips on the basis of a percentage of the total check; therefore, the larger the check, the larger the earnings of the service personnel. Additionally, incentive campaigns may be undertaken in which additional rewards may be given to service personnel who achieve sales goals over a specific period.

To enable service personnel to increase their creative selling ability, training sessions should be undertaken. Servers should be taught the proper timing and wording of their approach to a guest. Additionally, and most important, service personnel should be instructed in the details of proper service and the appearance, taste, and quality of all the items they are selling. Wine-tasting sessions may be conducted on a periodic basis so that servers will be familiar with all the wines offered on the menu, the proper pronunciation of their names, their taste, and the type of food items they best complement. Service personnel should be instructed in the ingredients, taste, and character of all appetizers and desserts offered. Periodic tasting sessions of such items should also be conducted.

Special Promotions

There is no limit to the ingenuity with which restaurant operators can publicize their restaurants and stimulate interest through special promotions. It is usually helpful for restaurant owners and managers to be involved in public affairs locally. The monthly meetings of the Rotarians and similar organizations provide a steady business to many restaurants. Local bridge clubs, political groups, taxpayers associations, and so forth can be relied on to organize luncheons and dinners, particularly if contacts are cultivated with them. Some operators follow announcements of weddings, baptisms, and birthdays for the purpose of building up a mailing list or for specific promotional efforts. Mother's Day, Thanksgiving, Easter, and Christmas are promoted by restaurants with special holiday menus. For many operations, Mother's Day can be the biggest sales day of the year. To attract this business, local newspaper advertising and direct mail may be used to advantage.

With the growing interest of many Americans in fine food, it is possible to organize special promotions of French, Italian, or other ethnic cuisine. Foreign chefs may be invited, and in some cases the chefs will even bring the food supply with them so that the most authentic taste can be provided. Such promotions are frequently tied in with special wine promotions subsidized by liquor dealers and wine merchants. Along these lines, the promotion of special dinners that must be reserved in advance, rather as if they were mini-banquets, has a promising future. Many patrons are willing to pay premium prices for a well-organized private party for four or more persons. The advantage of this type of arrangement in a restaurant is similar to the advantages that accrue from banquet business. In all these special promotions, the key factor is that the restaurant is not merely selling food but also an experience.

The Sales Department

Although only large restaurants and catering establishments have need of a structured sales department such as that described in the chapter on banqueting (Volume II), other group and party business may offer sufficient potential for relatively small operators to warrant some specialized sales personnel. Tour operators, theatre party organizers, and land sale agencies, for example, often have groups who can be served at off-peak hours. A sales kit showing menus, table settings, price ranges, and conditions should be prepared for mailing or direct solicitation if this type of business is desired.

Menu Merchandising

For many restaurant operations, the major internal promotion is the menu itself. The growing custom of posting menus on the outside of restaurants, as is done by law in France, is perhaps the least expensive and the most effective advertising that a restaurant can offer. Menus can be used to interest and stimulate the appetite of the passerby. Once the patron is in the restaurant, the eye appeal of the menu and the selections offered form the major selling tool. Because of the importance of menu merchandising and its applicability to almost all food service operations, the following sections are particularly important.

Stock and Typeface

Most menus begin as a sheet of paper. Printing houses, menu designers, and artists can advise which stock to select. If the menus are for long-term use, the stock should be sturdy and soil-resistant. Coatings or laminates can be applied so that the menus can be wiped clean. The stock should take inks well and be of a character in keeping with the atmosphere of the restaurant. If the menu is to be folded, the stock should wear well at the folds and not crack or tear.

If colored stock is used, it should harmonize with the color scheme of the restaurant, but more important, the color should not interfere with readability. Light inks on dark backgrounds are difficult to read with normal lighting, and when the lighting is subdued, as it often is in a restaurant, they may be completely illegible. The colors selected for the paper and ink should complement each other and provide sufficient contrast for readability.

Many restaurateurs decide to use a lightweight insert in a decorative, durable cover. Such a menu can be changed quickly and inexpensively by reprinting the insert. This format is also very adaptable to the requirements of cycle menus.

The size and style of the type face and the way in which the type is set also affect readability. Type is measured in "points." There are 72 points to the inch. Type size of menus should be at least 12 points.

The space between lines of type is called "leading." Leading is also measured in points. Two-point leading makes for better readability than one-point leading. Blocks of type should not be more than about 40 characters wide (including spacing). When lines of type are very long, the eye tends to "swim" or to jump to the line above or below. Since the eye is trained to read from left to right, type set vertically or diagonally is difficult to read.

The style of type can indicate certain qualities of a restaurant. Thickness of lines, light or bold, extent of slant, style and amount of embellishment, extended or condensed, all such features denote qualities such as formal, casual, elegant, graceful, feminine, masculine, fancy, plain, modern, or antique. Ordinarily, no more than two styles of type should be used, one for headings and another for the list and descriptions of the menu items.

Copy

The nature of an operation determines to some degree how much menu copy is required. A fast-food operation with its limited menu pasted on illuminated signs has no room for menu copy, and the items offered are so well known that they do not have to be explained. At the other end of the spectrum, the *haute cuisine* restaurant with a knowledgeable, sophisticated clientele also probably has little need for descriptive copy. For it to have detailed explanations on the menu would be an affront to the customers and to the service staff who are available for consultation on the selection of the meal. Most operations, however, benefit from having some descriptive copy on the menu.

The item must first be listed, and the name given should be descriptive of the dish. In most restaurants, patrons would be puzzled by such terms as "Breast of capon, Eugenie," "Paupiette of veal, Toscanini," "Noisette of lamb, Pollard." Names like these do not indicate whether the food is broiled, boiled, braised, or fried, and there is no way of knowing whether it will arrive on a plate under glass, on a skewer, or in a casserole dish. Some patrons will avoid such dishes because they hesitate to ask the waiter for descriptions.

It usually does not belittle the knowledge of patrons to indicate the composition of a dish or how it is prepared. They like to know what they are getting. A menu containing many foreign phrases will not sell as much food as one that includes clear descriptions of the dishes. If desired, the traditional foreign names may be used with English descriptions telling the patrons what to expect.

"Mystery" listings, then, should generally be avoided. Often, however, there are some special dishes that may be featured as a house specialty and given a name. Such dishes have tremendous merchandising value, but the listing should carry a complete description of the item. The copy should indicate what is in the dish, how it is prepared and served, and what (if anything) goes with it, if the name itself is not self-explanatory. This dictum is true for all dishes whether or not they are featured. For example, consider the following menu entries:

Fruits of the Sea, Old English Style

Selected Shrimp, Scallops, Oysters, Filet of Sole from the Buttery, Imperial Crab, and Lobster Tail from the Grill. Served with Crisp Potatoes and Coleslaw.

Roast Prime Ribs of Beef, Au Jus
A Thick Slice of Prime Ribs, Cut to Your Preference: Rare, Medium or Well-Done. Served with a Stuffed Baked Idaho Potato and Crisp Garden Salad.

Princess Salad
Chilled Crisp Leaves of Romaine with Sliced Tomatoes, Hard Cooked Egg and White Asparagus Spears. French Oil–Vinegar Dressing.

Qualifying adjectives such as those indicating type or brand, condition (fresh or frozen), source or location, or quality must be factual and must avoid misrepresentation for legal as well as ethical reasons.

Flavor is added to the menu by words such as "sugar cured," "honey cured," "candied," or "hickory smoked" with regard to ham. Almost all menu readers are hungry, and words like "savory" or "flavorsome" can whet an appetite and build sales volume. A chef, in describing the dishes he makes, will often use phrases that, in print, appeal to the appetite. Trade names may have merchandising appeal if they are well known.

Another way of merchandising is to have descriptive headings. Instead of merely listing "appetizers," "fish," "entrées," "salads," "desserts," try headings such as "From the Seacoast" "Salad Suggestions," or "Broiled to Your Order." Many operators have also increased wine and liquor sales substantially through menu promotion.

In addition to selling food and drink, menu copy may sell other things. What is known as "institutional copy" sells the restaurant as a whole. It may provide background information about the decor or theme, give the history of the restaurant or the area, biographical information about the owner or manager, or information about the community or locale.

Other aspects of the business may be promoted, such as a gift shop, party rooms, catering service, cocktail lounge, or take-out service, affiliated hotel or motel, and other restaurants.

Copy need not be staid and formal but should be in keeping with the tone of the establishment. Humor in good taste can prove to be very effective merchandising.

Dessert sales can sometimes be increased by the use of a separate dessert menu that is kept on the table to assure the guest's awareness of the dessert selection. The dessert menu can list after-dinner drinks as well as desserts. Other beverages, such as special coffees, and cigars can also be promoted in this way.

Layout

The theme or decor of the restaurant may indicate a certain shape or layout. For example, a round, revolving restaurant on the top of a tall building may use a round menu and relate the items listed to visible landmarks. A nautical restaurant could use a menu in the shape of a ship's wheel or a sailboat.

The number of listings and amount of copy also help to determine the size and shape of the menu. Since custom-cutting of a sheet of paper adds to the cost, most menus are printed on standard-sized sheets. If desired, however, unusual shapes can be die-cut.

The number of folds in the paper determines the number of panels in the layout. Figure 15–1 shows some of the folds possible with the average printer's equipment.

On a single vertical card menu, the eye scans from left to right, top to bottom, whereas with a single-fold sheet the right side is usually the first to be read, as with a folded greeting card. When there is a vertical double fold, the center panel will receive first attention. A multipage menu is read front to back like a book. A single-page menu with numerous attention-getting elements can be designed to be scanned clockwise, starting in the upper left-hand corner.

The arrangement of the headings and listings on the menu panels or pages can exert considerable influence on the sales of the various items. The menu layout should follow the sequence of the meal. It should also be attractive and readable. The arrangement of the headings, listings, descriptive copy, and illustrations should lead the reader's eye to the items being promoted. The placement of these elements should be balanced but not necessarily symmetrical.

Numerous menu studies have shown that if an item is listed first in any category, its position will give it an advantage in salability over the others. Therefore, the items listed first should be those that are not only the most profitable and known to be popular but also the easiest to produce in volume.

A number of other techniques can be used to increase the sales of special items. A border can be placed around the item to be featured; an ink and type face can be used that are different from the ink and type faces used for the rest of the menu. Special literature material can be employed to focus attention on the featured item. Each featured item then becomes a separate "element" in the overall layout. Care must be taken, however, not to have so many special features that the layout has a jumbled appearance.

Figures 15–2 and 15–3 show how a menu was made much more readable by an improvement in layout. Originally, the entrées were lost at the bottom of the left-hand side of the menu, with most of

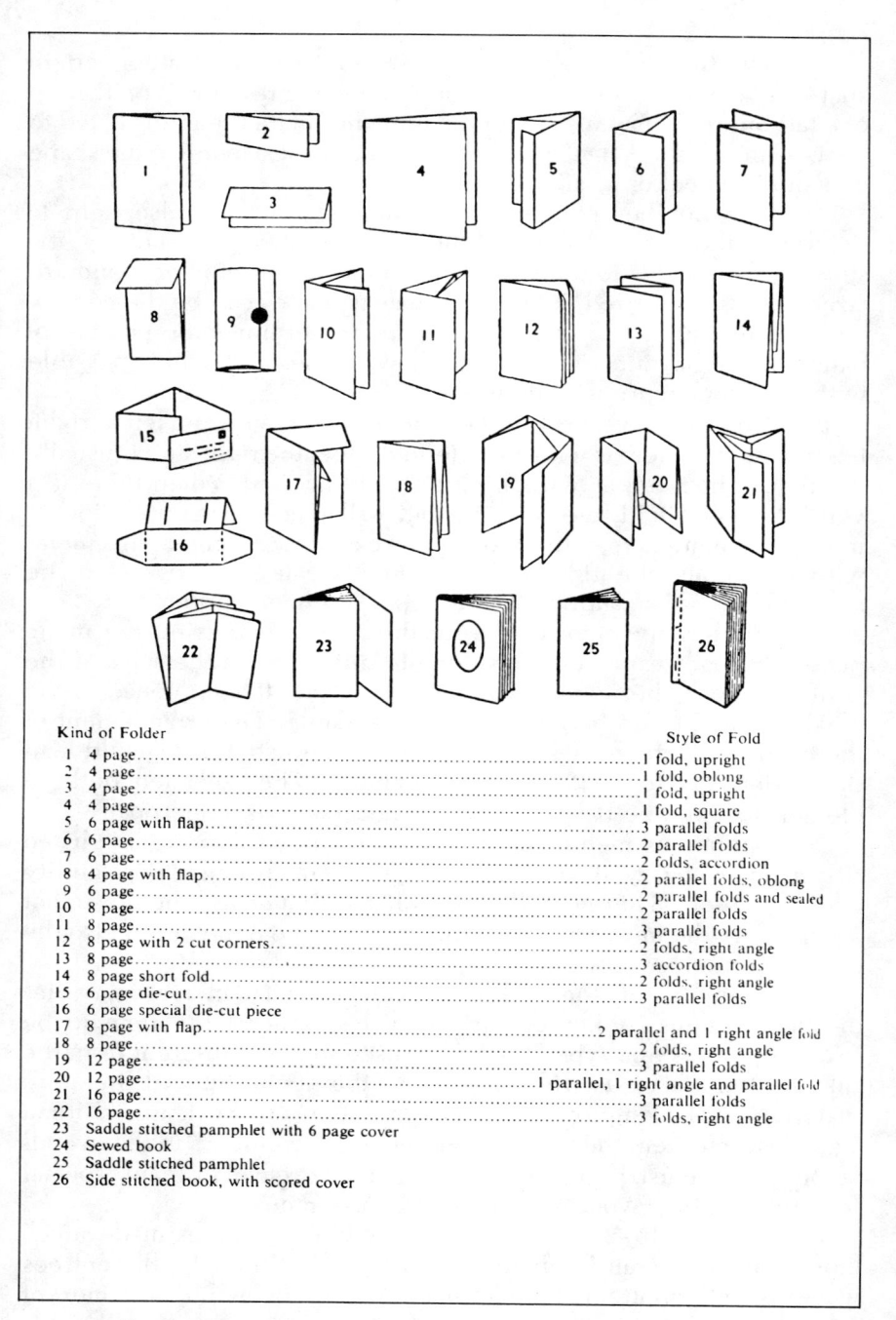

284 *Profitable Food and Beverage Management: Planning*

Kind of Folder		Style of Fold
1	4 page	1 fold, upright
2	4 page	1 fold, oblong
3	4 page	1 fold, upright
4	4 page	1 fold, square
5	6 page with flap	3 parallel folds
6	6 page	2 parallel folds
7	6 page	2 folds, accordion
8	4 page with flap	2 parallel folds, oblong
9	6 page	2 parallel folds and sealed
10	8 page	2 parallel folds
11	8 page	3 parallel folds
12	8 page with 2 cut corners	2 folds, right angle
13	8 page	3 accordion folds
14	8 page short fold	2 folds, right angle
15	6 page die-cut	3 parallel folds
16	6 page special die-cut piece	
17	8 page with flap	2 parallel and 1 right angle fold
18	8 page	2 folds, right angle
19	12 page	3 parallel folds
20	12 page	1 parallel, 1 right angle and parallel fold
21	16 page	3 parallel folds
22	16 page	3 folds, right angle
23	Saddle stitched pamphlet with 6 page cover	
24	Sewed book	
25	Saddle stitched pamphlet	
26	Side stitched book, with scored cover	

Fig. 15-1. Some shapes and folds commonly used for menus or promotional pieces.

Appetizers

Native Oysters on the Half Shell   Hot Spiced Shrimp Cocktail, Christiana
Shrimp Cocktail, Williamsburg or Cocktail Sauce   Clam Juice Cocktail
Chesapeake Bay Clams on the Half Shell   Tomato Juice Cocktail
Hampton Crab-meat Cocktail,

Soups and Chowders

Oyster Stew with Milk, Bowl   Clam Broth, Cup
with Half Cream, Bowl   Bowl
Captain Rasmusen's Clam Chowder, Cup   French Onion Soup, Cup
Bowl   Bowl
James Island Fish Chowder, Cup

Salads

Shrimp   Lobster
Crab Ravigote

Breads

(Served with all Meals)

Corn Sticks   Corn Bread   Spoon Bread

Entrees

(Cole Slaw or Green Salad served with Entrée)

Hampton Crab Imperial   Shad Roe with Country Bacon

Chunks of back fin meat from giant Blue crabs, fresh caught in Back River, diced fresh green pepper, capers, and diced pimiento, mixed in a piquant cream sauce of egg yolk, mustard, Worcestershire sauce, and tabasco.

Buttered roe from the shad, which migrates each year up the James and York rivers with the coming of spring. Sliced, hickory-smoked bacon from Surry served over each order.

Sweetbread and Oyster Pie   Individual Sea Food Pie

Fresh, firm Chincoteague oysters and delicate sweetbreads in a savory cream sauce with Sherry wine to taste, served piping hot in a potpie dish topped with light, flaky pastry crust.

Chesapeake Bay oysters, New England scallops, Maine lobster, and Florida shrimp — all together in a finely seasoned sauce — baked between two layers of light pastry and served steaming hot.

The Furnishings of Mrs. Campbell's Coffee House

MRS. Campbell's Coffee House is furnished in simple fashion, typical of taverns in the latter half of the eighteenth century. There is a mixture of many styles of utilitarian pieces such as Mrs. Campbell undoubtedly used—round tables, square tables, oval tables, sawbuck tables, and English tavern-type chairs, American Windsor chairs, ladderback chairs, and English Windsor types. All are reproductions of English and American antiques in the Williamsburg collection.

The case pieces, on the other hand—the corner cupboards, the serving table, and dresser, for example—are original eighteenth-century antiques. So are the decorative pieces of pewter, the prints, and ceramics, which include Delft, Whieldon, Creamware, Slipware, and German Stoneware made for the English market.

The candle holders on the bare tables are reproductions of eighteenth-century wine bottles, taken from contemporary prints, and pewter and hog-scraper candlesticks. The side lighting is provided by reproductions of two-armed wooden candle standards, and tin sconces. Overhead hang two American wood-and-tin chandeliers of the eighteenth century.

For the tableware, two outstanding pieces of English Lambeth Delft in the Williamsburg collection were reproduced. One pattern is taken from a plate showing caricatures of King William and Queen Mary, the other is the well-known dolphin pattern. The two antique originals are displayed in a corner cupboard. The glassware duplicates examples uncovered in the archeological exploration of Williamsburg in the early stages of the restoration.

Platter of Assorted Sea Food

A taste-tantalizing variety of choice sea food — such delicacies as fried Florida shrimp, Chincoteague oysters, crab Imperial, Wisconsin smelt — served in appetizing fashion with French fried potatoes. If you like sea food, you will like this ever-changing selection of the best dishes the sea has to offer.

Lobster Newburg

Large pieces of delicately flavored lobster, fresh out of frigid Maine waters, served, en casserole, in rich Newburg sauce made with fine Sherry wine.

Entrees, CONTINUED

Blow Fish

The firm flesh of the colorful blow fish, puffing "sea squab" of the York, James, and Rappahannock rivers and Mobjack and Chesapeake bays. Three pieces of solid white meat (only one center bone in each) lightly dredged in Chuckatuck corn meal, cooked to order, and served with almond-butter sauce.

Fried Florida Shrimp

Pink fisherman's gold from the Gulf of Mexico, the jumbo shrimp, lightly fried in deep fat and served with a tangy, mustard-butter sauce.

Prime Steaks

(French fried potatoes served with steak)

8-ounce Sirloin Steak, Minute Sauce
10-ounce Charcoal-Broiled Tenderloin Steak
12-ounce Charcoal-Broiled Sirloin Steak
20-ounce Charcoal-Broiled Sirloin Steak for Two People,

Desserts

Vanilla, Chocolate, Coffee, or Fig Ice Cream

Deep Dish Apple Pie

Cheesecake with Strawberry Sauce

Camembert, Gruyere, Liederkranz or Bleu Cheese
with Crackers

Rum Cream Pie

Beverages

Tea   Milk

Choice of Coffee

American, Sanka,   or Italian Espresso,
Coffee Vienna (black coffee topped with whipped cream)

Coffee Mocha (black coffee, scalded milk, with chocolate)

Coffee Cappuccino (black coffee, scalded milk,
with cinnamon)

Fig. 15-2. The original menu layout. The appearance is poor, and the menu is difficult to read. Low-priced and nonrevenue-producing items are given prominence, while entrées, and especially high-priced items, are deemphasized. Institutional copy is squeezed into the most prominent space on the menu.

CHRISTIANA Campbell's Tavern is furnished in simple fashion, typical of taverns in the latter half of the eighteenth century. The utilitarian pieces, such as Mrs. Campbell undoubtedly used, are a mixture of many styles and woods — round tables, square tables, oval tables, sawbuck tables and English tavern-type chairs, American Windsor chairs, ladderback chairs, and English Windsor types. All are inspired by English and American antiques in the Williamsburg collection.

The case pieces, on the other hand — the corner cupboards, the serving table, the dresser, for example — are original eighteenth-century antiques. So are the maps, the prints, the decorative pieces of pewter, and the ceramics, which include delft, Whieldon, creamware, slipware, and German stoneware made for the English market.

The candleholders on the tables are reproductions of eighteenth-century brass, pewter, and tin candlesticks. Reproduction wine bottles are also used as candleholders. Their use in such a manner is taken from prints of the period. The sidelighting is provided by reproductions of two-armed wooden candle standards and tin sconces. Two American wood-and-tin chandeliers of the eighteenth century furnish additional light in the first-floor rooms.

For the tableware, the decorations of two outstanding pieces of English Lambeth delft in the Williamsburg collection were adapted. One pattern is taken from a plate showing caricatures of King William and Queen Mary; the other is the rare dolphin pattern. The two antique originals are displayed in a corner cupboard.

Fig. 15-3. A revised layout. The number of selections has been reduced, based on the sales history. The remaining selections are shown in a balanced layout which emphasizes the main items. The menu has also been made more readable by a reduction of descriptive copy and increased white space. *(Courtesy of Colonial Williamsburg)*

Bill of FARE

Fresh Melon with Surry County Ham

Clams from the Eastern Shore

Chesapeake Bay Oysters (in season)

Tomato Juice Cocktail

Captain Rasmussen's Clam Chowder

French Onion Soup with Croutons

Shrimp Cocktail

* * * * * * *

A Made Dish of Shrimp and Lobster

A Casserole of Shrimp and Lobster combined with Fresh Mushrooms, Tomatoes, Green Pepper, Onion, and Sherry. Served with Blended Wild Rice.

Platter of Assorted Seafoods

Fried Chesapeake Bay Oysters, Carolina Shrimp, and Scallops combined with Virginia Fish and Crab Imperial. Fried Potatoes.

Hampton Crab Imperial

Freshly Picked Lump Crabmeat seasoned and baked in the Natural Shell. Fried Potatoes.

Fresh Fish from Virginia Waters

Broiled to Your Liking. Fried Potatoes.

Boneless Rib Eye Steak

Garnished with Fresh Braised Mushrooms and Fried Potatoes.

Roast Young Urbanna Duckling

Seasoned with Apples and Onions and served with Blended Wild Rice.

Colonial Game Pie

Braised Venison, Duck, and Rabbit with Fresh Mushrooms, Bacon Lardoons and Currant Jelly. Blended Wild Rice.

(Cole Slaw or Mixed Green Salad served with Entree)

* * * * * * *

Corn Sticks   *Biscuits*   *Spoon Bread*

* * * * * * *

Campbell's Fig Ice Cream

Vanilla or Chocolate Ice Cream   *Rum Cream Pie—Chocolate Curls*

Warm Apple Dumpling with Nutmeg Sauce   *Tipsy Squire with Whipped Cream and Almonds*

Raspberry Sherbet

* * * * * * *

Tea   *Coffee*   *Milk*

Fig. 15-3. A revised layout. The number of selections has been reduced, based on the sales history. The remaining selections are shown in a balanced layout which emphasizes the main items. The menu has also been made more readable by a reduction of descriptive copy and increased white space. *(Courtesy of Colonial Williamsburg)* (Cont'd.)

the space being occupied by the listings of soups, salads, and breads. In the revised version, the entrées are given a much better position. Menu clip-ons and rider cards can be used to advantage, but not if they hide the listings underneath. Patrons seldom lift a rider card to read the hidden part of the menu. When clip-ons are a regular feature, space should be provided for them. Institutional copy can be placed on that portion of the menu card over which the clip-on goes to fill the space when the clip-on is not used. One way of distributing rider cards without hiding any portion of the menu is to equip the menu with pockets into which the special cards are inserted. Illustrative material can be employed to guide the attention of patrons to the pockets.

Color

Advertisers are very aware of the effectiveness of color in increasing the readership of their copy. In restaurants, color is an important merchandising tool. On a restaurant menu, it can be used to illustrate, to decorate, or to emphasize. Color used to decorate should harmonize with the color scheme of the restaurant.

The most effective illustration is the color photograph, but it is also the most costly to produce. Food photography requires a particular skill and technique and is best left to experts. Colors must be reproduced truly, both in the original photograph and in the printing process, or else the picture will not whet the patron's appetite. If the menu is used in a number of outlets, the expense of four-color printing is less burdensome.

Color may be used for emphasis. For example, the headings on a menu may be in a different color from the rest of the type. Another technique is the "tint block," or the setting of type all in one color over background blocks that are different in color from the background of the rest of the menu.

The use of color on the menu adds to the cost, because printers usually charge least for putting black ink on white stock. The use of a stock that is not white or ink of a color other than black for all of the type is usually the most inexpensive way to introduce color. When an ink of a color other than black is used in addition to black ink, the result is a two-color job, for which an extra charge is made. The four-color process, required to reproduce photographs in full color, is the most expensive.

Other Forms of Presentation

Self-service operations invariably have their menus posted on signs. One commonly used type of menu board uses individual letters inserted into a grooved, felt-covered background. These boards have several disadvantages. If the menu is changed daily, changing the letters is a tedious, time-consuming chore. There is also opportunity for errors in pricing and spelling. With set menus, boards tend to become dusty and faded if they are not maintained. This type of menu board also has the disadvantage of not being decorative and not lending itself to individuality.

Another widely used type of menu board has a background of translucent plastic against which individual letters or strips of lettering are displayed. These boards often include advertising messages for brands of soft drinks or beer and are provided by the distributors of those products.

Specialty operations may have custom-designed menu boards. Fast-food operators have developed the menu board into an effective merchandising tool, using graphics, including decorative lettering, and photographs in color.

Blackboards have been used in all types of operations from snack bars to fine French restaurants. Messages can be written quickly on them and erased very easily. The principal drawback is that the menu listings may not be legible at a distance.

Souvenir Menus

A menu requested as a souvenir becomes an "outside salesman." It automatically indicates that a favorable impression has been created. Restaurants that get frequent requests for menus may have special souvenir menus printed to avoid giving away expensive originals. The souvenir menus are often miniature facsimiles printed at only a fraction of the cost of the original. The restaurant's complete name and address, hours of operation, and other pertinent data should be included on the souvenir menus, even though they may not appear on the original menus. Some even include driving directions. One thing that should not be included is the prices. This is to eliminate the need to reprint the souvenirs every time the prices are changed and to reduce the impact of a price increase on the guest who may have an old menu at home.

Another approach to the souvenir menu is to print the regular menu on inexpensive stock. In this case, all the pertinent selling data must be included on the regular menu.

For the menu to be a good souvenir, it must offer the guest some reason to want to keep it. An ordinary menu from an ordinary restaurant offers no appeal. Good souvenirs may include humorous or informative copy which the guest may read at his leisure. Topics may include a history or description of the restaurant or the area or information concerning the types of foods and drinks offered. Attractive or unusual decoration may also provide appeal.

The menus shown in Figs. 15-4 through 15-6 illustrate some of the points made in the preceding pages. In carrying out its railroad

290   *Profitable Food and Beverage Management: Planning*

motif, The Summerdale Junction uses a railroad poster (Fig. 15–4a and 15–4b) for its dinner menu. The poster measures 10 inches by 29 inches. Railroad terminology is used throughout, and ingredients and

Fig. 15-4A. Summerdale Junction lunch and dinner menus. *(Courtesy of Summerdale Junction, Summerdale, Pa., and Design Unlimited Menu Consultants, Hempstead, N.Y.)*

THE MAIN LINE

NOTICE TO ALL PASSENGERS: Entrees are served with choice of baked, home fried or French fried potatoes or buttered egg noodles, Bountiful Baggage Salad Cart and assorted fresh breads and butter

ROAST PRIME RIB OF BEEF, au jus	
The Stationmaster's Specialty! Medium rare honors its flavor best, but order it your favorite way.	
The Engineer's 12 oz. cut 7.75	
The Fireman's cut 6.25	

BONELESS NEW YORK CUT SIRLOIN STRIP STEAK
Prepared to your liking, and touched with Chef's butter
    Main line size 7.75   Branch line size 6.50

BROILED PRIME THICK CUT FILET MIGNON
The brass hat of all steaks. Served with a savory mushroom sauce   Station Master 7.95   Station Mistress 6.75

BROILED HICKORY SMOKED HAM STEAK ON A FLAT CAR
Served on a plank with potato border, and two of today's vegetables   5.50

BROILED DELMONICO STEAK, Tender and flavorful.
Served with sauteed mushrooms   6.25

VEAL CORDON BLEU	
Milkfed Veal filled with Ham and Cheese crusted with a lightly seasoned breading and sauteed. 5.85	

KEYSTONE PLATTER OVER RICE PILAF
Tender beef tips, and vegetables, broiled on a skewer   6.25

ROAST DUCKLING ON A FLAT CAR Cherry glaze, potato border and two of today's vegetables   6.50

† **VEAL PARMIGIAN,** Tangy tomato sauce, melted cheese, and spaghetti instead of potato, if desired   5.75

† **BONELESS BREAST OF CHICKEN, ENOLA** With a full lading of tender ham and mellow Swiss cheese within   4.95

12 oz. BROILED CHOPPED SIRLOIN OF BEEF With sherry mushroom sauce or plain 4.75

THE SEA COAST ROUTE

MOUNTAIN BROOK TROUT, Oven broiled or pan sauteed.
Served with slivered almonds or tidbits of shrimp and crabmeat   4.95

OUR TWIN COQUILLE ST. JACQUES, A blend of scallops, shrimp, clams and mushrooms baked on cheese crust   5.50

BROILED TWIN FILLETS OF FLOUNDER, Stuffed with crabmeat Basted in lemon butter with herbs   5.25

† **BAKED STUFFED JUMBO SHRIMP,** Stuffed with crabmeat.
Served with drawn butter and fresh lemon   5.40

FRIED JUMBO SHRIMP, Dipped in buttermilk batter   5.75

SAUTEED FILLET OF FLOUNDER
Dipped in almond breading and topped with lemon butter   4.75

JUNCTION SPECIAL
SURF & TURF ON A FLAT CAR. Single Coquille St. Jacques & filet mignon, potato border and todays vegetable 8.95

FROM THE REEFER

Served with assorted fresh breads, butter and beverage

BOUNTIFUL BAGGAGE CART SELECTION
Served with assorted breads, butter and beverage   3.25

CHEF DE RAILROAD'S SALAD Julienne of white meat turkey, hickory smoked ham and cheese, atop a ballast of crisp garden greens, with choice of dressing   2.85

HORSESHOE CURVE A small mountain of cottage cheese, encircled by fresh cut in-season fruits, with a frosty sherbet garnish   2.50

ANTIPASTO "2-8-0" A delicious "consolidation" of Genoa Salami, cheese, anchovy, ripe and green olives, tomato, and seasoned peppers, with olive oil and vinegar dressing. Bread, butter and beverage   3.45

SIDE ORDERS:
Buttermilk onion rings .85
Sauteed mushrooms .95

REFERENCE NOTES:

● ALL PASSENGERS are invited to take this menu as a souvenir of their trip, and as a reminder to book a return trip in the near future.

▲ DINNER is served Monday thru Thursday 5:00 to 10:00 PM, Friday and Saturday 5:00 to 11:00 PM

L LUNCHEON is served in the Keystone Lounge from 11:30 AM to 2:30 PM Mon.-Fri.
**Does not run Sundays before noon, or Election Day.

✻ SLEEPING CAR ACCOMMODATIONS are available at our 72 unit Quality Inn, adjoining the restaurant. For reservations, call (717) 732-0785.

† In junior section under eight years of age may order items marked † in junior portions for 2.50, including milk and ice cream or pie.

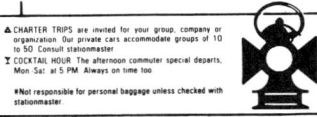

△ CHARTER TRIPS are invited for your group, company or organization. Our private cars accommodate groups of 10 to 50. Consult stationmaster

Y COCKTAIL HOUR The afternoon commuter special departs, Mon.-Sat. at 5 PM. Always on time too

Not responsible for personal baggage unless checked with stationmaster.

Fig. 15-4B. Sections of Summerdale Junction dinner menu. *(Courtesy of Summerdale Junction, Summerdale, Pa., and Design Unlimited Menu Consultants, Hempstead, N.Y.)*

Fig. 15-5. Front page of the menu used in The Back Room at Nathan's Famous Times Square restaurant in New York City. *(Courtesy of Nathan's Famous, Inc., New York, N.Y., and Design Unlimited Menu Consultants, Hempstead, N.Y.)*

If you think the hot dog is a purely American dish, think again. The hot dog traces its ancestors as far back as 1500 BC, to the ancient Babylonians, the Greeks picked it up from the Babylonians, and the Romans got it from them. Some time during the Roman empire, it picked up the name of sausage.

It came close to its present form in Frankfort, Germany many centuries later.

The modern hot dog—the hot dog on a roll—is an American invention. In 1857, Charles Feltman, who drove a pie wagon in Coney Island, noticed that two new inns had opened, featuring hot sandwiches. To compete, he felt he needed a hot sandwich of his own, and came up with the idea of putting a hot sausage in a roll. He subsequently opened Feltman's Restaurant in Coney, which sold hot dogs for a dime.

Although the term "hot dog" was used in the early days, it was popularized nationally by Ted Dorgan, a New York newspaper cartoonist who saw franks being served for the first time in the New York Polo Grounds in the early 1900's.

CELEBRITY TALK AT NATHAN'S

Many marriages have been proposed... and even accepted... at Nathan's. Not the least famous is that of actor *Alan Arkin* to actress *Barbara Dana*, while they were at the clam bar at Nathan's at Coney. Guess who catered the wedding? Right!

Many of the famous and beautiful people are fans of Nathan's... *Queen Mother Elizabeth of Britain, Princess Grace of Monaco, Svetlana (Stalin) Allilueva* are just a few.

And New York's former Governor Rockefeller has said that "No candidate can hope to carry New York State without being photographed eating a hot dog at Nathan's Famous." Look out during election years... it's a job elbowing your way through all the mayoral candidates to place your order.

The Rockefeller's, the Kennedy's, the Harriman's, the Lodge's and the Onassis' have all made the pilgrimage. And FDR, while President, served Nathan's hot dogs to the King & Queen of England at his Hyde Park estate.

And let's not forget Brooklyn born Barbra Streisand... a Nathan's regular... and Cary Grant who, as a Coney Island stilt-walker, was advised by Nathan Handwerker. "You can't sing, dance, or tell jokes. Forget Hollywood. You'd better keep your job here."

WE HAVE PREPARED OUR MENU AS A TRIBUTE TO CONEY ISLAND, THE HOT DOG, AND NATHAN HANDWERKER. WE WOULD BE PLEASED IF YOU WOULD CONSIDER IT A

SOUVENIR

OF YOUR VISIT

...and a reminder to visit one of the many Nathan's locations again soon.

Souvenir copies available at cashier's counter.

When Nathan's first opened, believe it or not, it was nameless. It was the popularity of this hit song of 1916 which convinced Nathan Handwerker to use his own first name on the signboard.

Fig. 15-5. Front page of the menu used in The Back Room at Nathan's Famous Times Square restaurant in New York City. *(Courtesy of Nathan's Famous, Inc. New York, N.Y., and Design Unlimited Menu Consultants, Hempstead, N.Y.)* (Cont'd.)

Fig. 15-6. Menu board as seen at "Skydive," a self-service restaurant at the World Trade Center in New York City. *(Courtesy of The Joseph Baum Company, Inc., New York, N.Y.)*

methods of preparation are stated in descriptive copy. Profitable items and house specialties are promoted in tint blocks. The entire menu is organized in the order of the meals, but entrées are emphasized by the "Main Line" heading in 72-point bold type. Specialty cocktails are promoted at the top of the menu ("Lubrication"). "Reference Notes" at the bottom of the menus promote related business, although in very small print.

Nathan's Famous, Inc. uses a newspaper menu format for the Back Room of the Times Square operation (Fig. 15-5). The outside of the single-fold menu is devoted to institutional copy stressing Nathan's Coney Island, turn-of-the-century atmosphere. Articles about the history of the company, its founders, Coney Island, and hotdogs make it an appealing souvenir that the customer will want to take away. The menu is printed on newsprint and has a place on the back for a mailing address.

Figure 15-6 shows a menu board for Skydive, a self-service operation in the sky lobby of the World Trade Center, New York City. The "sky" theme is carried out in blue and white signs, magnetized plastic strips on which the menu items are printed. The strips are washable and can be changed very easily during service. Prices are separate from item names. New strips can be made in-house for changes in menu items or prices.

Printing

It is not usually desirable to have a large supply of menus printed at one time. The operator who tries to reduce printing costs by ordering menus in quantity will often find that he soon has an out-of-date menu because of changes in food supply, customer preferences, and food costs. There is also a temptation to scratch off items or to write over the printing to show increases in prices. Menus revised in that way present a very poor appearance and may well antagonize a cost-conscious guest.

For a quality or atmosphere restaurant, having an attractive, well-designed menu is essential to merchandise the theme of the operation. Such a menu usually is custom designed by a professional menu designer. Less unusual restaurants may find that a stock menu cover or "clip art" from a menu printing firm will suit their operation. Small operations such as coffee shops, lunch counters, and taverns can reduce their printing costs by using menus supplied by major food and soft-drink manufacturers, distillers, or breweries. Of course, the supplier's products and logo are featured on such menus. A wide variety of promotional aids such as signs, table tents, menus, and menu clip-ons are available from food producers and processors and also from trade associations. Some fast-food operations print their menus on place mats to reduce menu printing costs and to facilitate service.

Reusable clip-ons or inserts in a set menu can eliminate the need for daily printing and, in that way, reduce costs. If the inserts are used cyclically, costs are reduced even more. Clip-ons can be used for messages other than menu listings.

Even if not professionally designed, printed menus are the most desirable. Typewritten or mimeographed menus should be avoided. Too often they are carelessly typed with misspelled words and smeared carbon. They are cheap, and they look it. If the operation does not warrant the expense of printed menus, the restaurant should have a good typist type one clear black copy and have it duplicated by the offset process. Most offset houses have their own electric typewriters and will make their own original copies. In this way, a very creditable menu may be turned out at relatively small expense.

Before deciding in favor of an offset process, however, bids for printing the menus should be obtained. Printers often charge a very fair price for work they can expect on a regular basis. When menus are printed daily, they should include the day, date, and only those items available on that day. This rule seems self-evident, but one often sees listings such as "prime ribs—Friday only" on a menu dated Monday or "berries—in season" on a winter menu.

All menus have a limited definite life span and should be replaced as soon as they become soiled or worn. Offering a patron a menu that is dirty and torn may cause him to form a bad opinion of the restaurant before he is served any food. A soiled menu is an unattractive menu, no matter how much planning and effort went into its design.

16

LAWS AFFECTING FOOD AND BEVERAGE OPERATIONS

No book on profitable food and beverage operations would be complete without some attention being given to the laws affecting such operations. The applicable laws have a profound impact on what the bottom line figure will be in that these laws sometimes tell you whom you may hire, how much you must pay them, and even what you may sell, as in the case of alcoholic beverages where the law may require different licenses to sell beer only, wine and beer, or any type of alcoholic beverage.

It is not possible in a book of this nature to discuss all the laws applicable to food and beverage operations in detail, for such a work would require many volumes. We do, however, outline briefly here some of the more important laws that have an impact on the food service industry and call attention to some problems shown by experience to occur with some degree of regularity and to have a possible monetary impact on operations. This should be of practical value to the owner, tending to make him aware of pitfalls in his occupation and enabling him to recognize potential problem areas before he finds himself enmeshed in legal difficulties. Litigation in the courts is expensive both in the time spent in defending yourself and in fees paid to lawyers to protect your interest. All these expenditures find their way into your income statement.

At the outset it is important to note that, in general, we are dealing with three levels of government: federal, state, and local (i.e., county, city, town or village) and all these governmental branches are empowered to enact statutes or ordinances that may affect operations. We must keep in mind, too, that the laws on the various matters discussed here will vary from locality to locality. What is good law in one community may be a violation in another. You must, therefore, be cognizant of the law in your community, and if you move your business, you must adjust to laws of the new location.

The law is dynamic and constantly in a state of change because of new legislation, new regulations, new interpretations of government authorities, and new decisions by the courts. In recent years, for example, the courts have held the innkeepers' lien laws to be unconstitutional, notwithstanding the fact that this legal concept originated in medieval times in England, became part of the English common law, and has been part of the law of this country since colonial times.

It will be helpful if we understand exactly what constitutes the law. In general, the law is the statutory enactments of the legislative bodies (the Congress, the state legislatures, the city or town councils), the regulations issued by the various government agencies entrusted with the enforcement of a particular law and interpretations issued by such agencies, and decisional law of the courts handed down over the years. The statutes are generally written in broad terms, and the enforcing agencies are generally empowered to supplement their terms and flesh them out with regulations that have the force of law and with interpretations. The regulations, of course, must be within the general scope of the statute under which they are issued in order to be valid.

In operating under these conditions, then, the efficient operator will of necessity find it advisable to keep abreast of legal developments to be sure they do not adversely affect his operation. He cannot do this by himself, but his trade association, which generally follows all these matters, will be of immeasurable assistance to him in this regard. These associations watch legislative and other developments and issue frequent bulletins advising their members of matters of interest to them on law as well as operational problems. In the food service field, these functions are undertaken by the National Restaurant Association, the American Hotel and Motel Association, the American Hospital Association, and the various state associations affiliated with these organizations.

Common Law

The first principles of law that became applicable to the food and beverage industry in this country are those derived from the English common law brought to this country by the early settlers and made part of our body of law after the War of Independence. The common law is that body of court decisions and customs of the realm that became embodied in the law. As the late Oliver Wendell Holmes expressed it: "The life of the law has not been logic: it has been experience."

Innkeepers' Liability

In medieval England, for example, there was a considerable amount of travel, and at night the weary traveler had to rest his faith and safety in the integrity of the innkeeper who put him up for the night and furnished him with food and lodging. Because the traveler was peculiarly without remedy in the event his property was stolen while he slept and any witnesses to whom he might resort were generally in the employ of the innkeeper, the law imposed on the innkeeper an absolute liability as an insurer for the safety of the property his guest might bring on his premises, including the property of a guest in the inn's restaurant. That insurer's liability continues in this country today except insofar as it has been limited by statute. Some of these statutes have continued the insurer's liability but limited the amount the guest could recover; others have changed the basis of liability from that of an insurer to the liability applicable to a bailment where the degree of responsibility is not so great. In the case of absolute insurer's liability, all the guest must prove is that he brought the property on the premises of the innkeeper and that it disappeared. In the case of bailment, the guest usually must prove that he gave physical possession of the property to the innkeeper, who failed to return it on demand. The bailment theory of liability is generally applicable to restaurants other than those in hotels.

Some states have requirements that the innkeeper post copies of the statutes limiting liability in certain places about the hotel premises in order to obtain the benefit of the limitation of liability. Such requirements must be literally adhered to. Some states also require the posting of the price range for meals. The state hotel associations have prepared the proper card for posting and make such cards available to their members.

Duty to Receive Guest and Lien

Under the English common law, an innkeeper was also required to receive every proper person who presented himself requesting food and lodging. Because of the imposition of this duty on the innkeeper, the law gave the innkeeper a lien for his charges on the property the guest brought on the premises: The innkeeper had the right to detain the baggage of the guest for the payment of his proper charges, including restaurant charges. The courts in four states have now held these laws, which have been in existence since colonial times, to be unconstitutional as violative of procedural due process. Many states have so-called hotel frauds statutes making it a penal offense willfully to fail to pay for food and lodging. Some states have theft of services statutes that make it a crime to walk out without paying the restaurant its charges, although such statutes are not part of the common law.

Distinction between Guest and Tenant

It is important that you know the difference between a guest and a tenant. If a person is a guest, the absolute insurer's liability principle may apply to him, and the hotel becomes an insurer of his property. If the person is a tenant, that liability would not apply to him. In general, it may be said that a guest is a traveler. A tenant is one whose stay is of a longer and more permanent nature, that is, one who intends to make the hotel his home. It is a factual question that can be resolved only after careful consideration of all the facts.

Lockout and Dispossess

In some states, a hotel may lock out a guest who fails to pay its charges, including meal charges, by plugging the lock of the door of the guest room, but it can terminate a tenancy only by dispossessing the tenant in a court proceeding. There is also the danger of an action for damages in these states for wrongful eviction if the hotel wrongfully locks out a tenant.

Contracts

The law of contracts is also an outgrowth of the English common law. A contract is an "agreement" between the parties to it. It is usually created by one party's making an offer and the other party's accepting it. The offer must be definite; otherwise, at a later date the courts may have to be called on to determine whether the performance is in compliance with the terms of the offer. In other words, there must be a meeting of minds. Generally, too, there must be consideration: a detriment to the promisee and a benefit to the promisor. Certain contracts are also required to be in writing. In any situation in which a contract calls for payment of a substantial sum or the assumption of a substantial obligation or liability, you should consult with your attorney before acting.

Negligence

Negligence is also a development of the common law, but we will not discuss it here because it is generally covered by insurance, which is discussed in Chapter 18 of this book. Suffice it to say that negligence is the failure to do that which a reasonably prudent man would do in a given situation, or the doing of some act detrimental to another in some way in which an ordinary, prudent man would not have done it.

Federal Laws

The operation of food and beverage establishments was a relatively uncomplicated occupation for many years, almost down to the third decade of the present century, at which time a flood of tax laws and social legislation such as wage and hour, unemployment insurance, anti-discrimination, alcoholic beverage control, Social Security, income tax, and sales tax laws were enacted. These laws have had an especially heavy impact on food and beverage operators because their situation is complicated by the fact that a large portion of the compensation their employees receive is in the form of tips from the patrons and free meals and lodging. Consequently, these items require different treatment. Although most of these statutes are now 50 to 60 years old, the battle is still being fought as to the proper treatment of such items as tips. Efforts are underway in Congress now to eliminate the tip credit under the Federal Fair Labor Standards Act.

Federal Fair Labor Standards Act

Among the pieces of social legislation at the federal level having a profound impact on food service industry was the Federal Fair Labor Standards Act, also known as the Federal Wage and Hour Law. At the time this is written, this statute requires that an employee be paid $2.30 per hour with time and a half for overtime, generally after 40 hours, and after 46 hours with respect to certain hotels, motels, and restaurants. The overtime under the federal law must be computed on the actual wage paid the employee, not the theoretical wage as computed under some of the state minimum wage laws discussed below. Executive, administrative and professional employees are generally not subject to the provisions of this law. However, in recent years there has been considerable litigation as to whether, for example, the manager of a motel in a small operation who also performs nonsupervisory duties is, in fact, an exempt supervisory employee. The U.S. Department of Labor in some instances has ruled that such a manager is not an exempt supervisory employee and has held that the act is applicable to such an employee. In these cases the department has assessed a deficiency against the proprietor retroactively for several years. There are numerous difficult problems of interpretation under the law, and *Interpretative Bulletins* are issued by the Wage and Hour Division of the U.S. Department of Labor from time to time which state the position that will be taken by the department on a particular problem. These bulletins can be obtained by writing to the U.S. Department of Labor, 200 Constitution Avenue, Washington, D.C. 20210, or to your regional Employment Standards Administration office of the U.S. Department of Labor.

The Fair Labor Standards Act provides that when a state or municipal ordinance provides for a higher minimum wage, then such higher wage may be paid. The state statutes are discussed below under the heading State Laws. The Fair Labor Standards Act prohibits interstate commerce of any goods on which oppressive child labor, as defined in the act, was employed.

Social Security Taxes

The taxes under the Social Security program are assessed under two separate statutes. The first of these is the Federal Insurance Contribution Act (FICA), and the second is the Federal Unemployment Tax Act (FUTA). The FICA tax is assessed for the purpose of paying retirement benefits; the FUTA tax is to provide unemployment benefits. The FICA tax is assessed against both the employer and the employee; at present the tax rate is 5.85 percent on each, or a total of 11.7 percent of the first $16,500 of wages paid to each employee. The returns are required to be filed on a quarterly basis by the end of the month following the last day of the quarter.

The FUTA tax is due on an annual basis by the employer on or before January 31 of any year, but for deposit purposes, the FUTA tax may be required to be paid on a quarterly basis in certain cases in which the amount subject to deposit is more than $100. The present tax rate for FUTA purposes is 3.4 percent up to $4,200 a year of remuneration ($6,000 effective January 1, 1978), but a credit of 2.7 percent is allowed against such tax for amounts paid to the state for unemployment insurance purposes.

The Social Security laws are generally administered by the Social Security Administration, 6401 Security Boulevard, Baltimore, Maryland 21235. The taxes, however, are collected by the Internal Revenue Service.

The Internal Revenue Service has published in pamphlet form instructions in simplified language which may be obtained on request from the District Director in your locality. It is known as *Circular E—Employer's Tax Guide*. Every operator should have a copy of *Circular E*.

The benefits paid to employees will not be discussed here since this book is written to provide information for the guidance of the employer. However, such information can be obtained from your local Social Security office. The state aspect of the unemployment insurance will be discussed later under the heading State Laws.

As noted above, the problem areas for the food service industry under the Social Security and employment tax laws are generally those relating to gratuities, meals, and lodging. Again, helpful information in summary form will be found in *Circular E*. The federal authorities have made it a practice in the past to accept the value fixed by the state authorities for meals and lodging. Recently, however, instead of accepting state values, the Internal Revenue Service has been seeking a valuation of anywhere from $1.25 to $2.00 for such a meal, as well as increased values for lodging. The question of the proper value is being litigated at the time this is written.

Income Withholding Tax

Income withholding tax is another employment tax. Again, *Circular E* of the Internal Revenue Service will be helpful to you in determining how much you should withhold and what to withhold on. Once again we find gratuities, meals, and lodging to be the difficult problem for the food service industry. Tips must be reported to the employer by the employee by the tenth day of the month following the month in which they were received. The employer must collect both employee Social Security taxes and income tax on tips reported to him by the employee on Form 4070, or a statement showing (1) the employee's name, address, and Social Security number, (2) the employer's name and address, (3) the calendar month or period the statement covers, and (4) the total tips.

Meals and lodging under Section 119 of the Internal Revenue Code furnished for the "convenience of the employer" are excludable from gross income and therefore are not taxable for income tax purposes, but only if: (1) in the case of meals, the meals are furnished on the business premises of the employer, or (2) in the case of lodging, the employee is required to accept such lodging on the business premises of his employer as a condition of employment. However, it has been ruled that the "convenience of the employer" rule does not apply to FUTA and FICA taxes. The Internal Revenue Service has issued detailed regulations on this subject explaining its application in numerous situations [Reg. § 1.119-1(a)(1)].

Corporate Taxes

With respect to corporate taxes, there is nothing particularly unique to the food service industry. The operator should consult his accountant on these tax matters and his attorney on matters of corporate law.

Pensions

In 1974 the Pension Reform Act was passed by the Congress, and this was the most far-reaching revision of pension and employee rules in history. The Congress took note of the problems arising under then existing law and enacted a vast body of new law, including provisions relating to employee participation, vesting of benefits, funding of plans, and a number of rules governing the conduct of fiduciaries. A number of strict standards governing plan administrators and trustees were also adopted. The U.S. Treasury Department and the U.S. Department of Labor both administer this law.

Civil Rights

Under the Federal Civil Rights Act of 1964, neither a hotel with more than five rooms for hire, nor its concessionaire, nor any restaurant can discriminate against a guest or patron nor segregate them on the basis of race, color, religion, or national origin. The law is administered by the U.S. Department of Justice, Constitution Avenue and Tenth Street, Washington, D.C. 20530, and inquiries can be addressed to that department. The Department of Justice also has regional offices throughout the country.

Some states also had civil rights laws for many years prior to the federal enactment, and such local laws remain in effect with the exception of conflicting provisions.

Alcoholic Beverages

Alcoholic beverages are under strict controls from their source right down to the ultimate consumer. The U.S. Treasury Department, through its Bureau of Alcohol, Tobacco, and Firearms, regulates the distillers and breweries, whereas the state agencies in general concern themselves with licensing the wholesalers and retailers as discussed hereafter, although there is considerable overlapping of regulations. The Treasury Department is also engaged in a much-publicized campaign of cracking down on "moonshiners" and bootleggers of alcoholic beverages. Insofar as the retailer is concerned, the Bureau of Alcohol, Tobacco, and Firearms is concerned that the quality of the brand sold meet proper standards and that the liquor is not diluted with water or otherwise adulterated. In some instances where a retailer mixes large quantities of mixed drinks in advance of a sale, the bureau may require the retailer to obtain a rectifier's license. The bureau has regional offices throughout the country where copies of its regulations and rulings may be obtained.

Copyright

The federal copyright law grants to the copyright owner of music the exclusive right to perform his work publicly for profit and subjects any infringer of that right to damages. The owners of music frequently assign their performance rights to organizations that police the use of music and collect the copyright royalties due the composers. The principal licensing organizations in this field are the American Society of Composers, Authors, and Publishers (ASCAP), Broadcast Music, Inc. (BMI), and the Society of European Stage Authors and Composers (SESAC), all of which have their principal offices in New York City.

An entirely new copyright law became effective on January 1, 1978.

National Labor Relations Board

Any employer subject to the National Labor Relations Act is restricted in his conduct with respect to his employees and to unions generally. If he engages in certain proscribed unfair labor practices, he can be ordered to stop them. The administrative body is the National Labor Relations Board, which has its main office at 1717 Pennsylvania Avenue, N.W., Washington, D.C., with regional offices throughout the country to which inquiries can be addressed.

Federal Food and Drug Administration

The Federal Food and Drug Administration (FFDA) issues model sanitary regulations that it encourages state and local sanitation authorities to adopt and enforce. Approximately 30 states have now adopted these regulations. The FFDA does not, however, attempt to enforce such sanitary regulations.

The principal office of the Federal Food and Drug Administration is located at 5600 Fishers Lane, Rockville, Maryland, and it also has regional offices throughout the country.

Occupational Safety and Health Act

In 1970 Congress enacted the Occupational Safety and Health Act under which the Occupational Safety and Health Administration (OSHA) was created within the Department of Labor to:

> Encourage employers and employees to reduce hazards in the workplace and to implement new or improve existing safety and health programs;
>
> Establish "separate but dependent responsibilities and rights" for employers and employees for the achievement of better safety and health conditions;
>
> Establish reporting and recordkeeping procedures to monitor job-related injuries and illnesses;
>
> Develop mandatory job safety and health standards and enforce them;
>
> Encourage the states to assume the fullest responsibility for establishing and administering their own occupational safety and health programs, which must be "at least as effective as" the federal program.

Although OSHA continually reviews and redefines specific standards and practices, its basic purposes remain constant. OSHA strives to implement its congressional mandate fully. In all its procedures, from standards development through implementation and enforcement, OSHA guarantees employers and employees the right to be fully informed, to participate actively, and to appeal its actions.

The Department of Labor has issued a pamphlet entitled *All About OSHA*, which may be obtained by writing the Department, 200 Constitution Avenue, N.W., Washington, D.C. 20210.

Record Keeping

Under nearly all the statutes discussed above, there are requirements for the maintenance of records in order to establish compliance with the requirements of the various laws. Failure to maintain the required records for the prescribed periods can be costly in both time and money if a question is raised. In addition, every food service operator should know the period of the general contract statute of limitations in his particular state, and when there is any likelihood of litigation being commenced against him, he should retain records for that period of time for his own protection, even when not otherwise required to by law.

Trade associations sometimes prepare comprehensive bulletins that list all record-keeping requirements helpful to the food service operator. The Federal Register also has published a compilation of such requirements under federal laws entitled *Guide to Record Retention Requirements*, and copies can be obtained by writing the Superintendent of Documents, Washington, D.C. 20402.

The U.S. Department of Labor, Occupational Safety and Health Administration has issued a pamphlet entitled *Recordkeeping Requirements under the Williams–Steiger Occupational Safety and Health Act of 1970*, copies of which can be obtained from the Department at 200 Constitution Avenue, N.W., Washington, D.C. 20210.

State Laws

In many instances the individual states enacted laws concerning labor and wages and hours before the federal government moved into these areas. For many years, these matters were considered only of local concern. In recent years, however, the Congress has enacted statutes in some ways similar to the previously existing state statutes, so now we find that the federal statutes in some areas have preempted the field. In other cases, we find concurrent federal and state jurisdiction, and in still others, we find the matter has been left to the jurisdiction of the individual states by way of an exception in the particular federal law.

Minimum Wage

A number of the states had enacted minimum wage laws long before the passage of the federal Fair Labor Standards Act, and these state statutes regulate a number of practices in the food service industries, such as meals, uniform maintenance, and others, which have a bearing on the employees' wage as well as the cash wage itself.

The Federal Fair Labor Standards Act permits states and municipalities to enact minimum wage laws providing for the payment of wages higher than those required by the federal act. In some states, then, you may find that your operation is subject to the state minimum wage law and also subject to the federal Fair Labor Standards Act.

The minimum wage is sometimes established by tripartite boards that fix the wage after hearings in which they ascertain the basic information. In other instances, the wage is fixed by a statutory enactment. A wage order is frequently issued for a particular industry to permit allowances against the cash wage for tips, meals, and lodging. Some of the states require the payment of overtime at time and a half the basic minimum rate, unlike the Federal Fair Labor Standards Act, which requires that the overtime be computed at one and a half times the actual rate being paid an employee. This is an important distinction. The regulations generally cover a number of different items having a relationship to the minimum wage, such as detailed records, statements to the employees, posting of requirements, prohibitions against deductions from wages, and diversified employment that might result in different wage payment requirements.

Copies of the appropriate wage orders can be obtained from your state labor department, and also when posting is required, the posters can give you helpful information.

Unemployment Insurance

We discussed the general pattern of this subject above under the heading of Social Security taxes and the Federal Unemployment Tax Act. The state unemployment insurance laws are integrated with the federal act and are financed by the credit allowed the states by that act. The state programs are required to be approved by the U.S. Department of Labor.

Some states have some form of experience-rating formula in their laws so as to reward employers with stable employment and penalize those with a large labor turnover. It is important, then, that you keep your turnover to a minimum and that a close watch be kept on employees to see that the program is not abused by employees applying for and receiving unwarranted benefits. Such benefits will be charged against your account, and your contributions for unemployment insurance will be increased the following year.

Most states have a division of employment in their labor department which publishes handbooks for employers to guide them in the operation of the program. You should check and obtain such handbooks when they are available.

Workmen's Compensation

Most states have some form of workmen's compensation to lessen the burdens of an employee injured on the job. This is one of the earliest pieces of state social legislation, being first enacted in the early part of this century. It is a form of no-fault insurance with the employee receiving benefits depending on the type and severity of his injury. The program was intended to be simple and to be administered without involving the formal complex requirements of a court system of law, but, unfortunately, it did not work out that way. Here, again, the employer should take steps to see that injuries do not occur by giving his employees a safe place to work in and by making them safety conscious. The laws generally require the employer to obtain coverage from an insurance company or a state fund, or to qualify as a self-insurer. The employer's premium is generally calculated on his individual experience. It pays, therefore, to have a good safety record.

This program is usually operated by a division of your state labor department from whom you can obtain information and publications.

Disability Benefits Laws

Some states have programs to provide supplemental benefits to employees in the form of disability benefits. Workmen's compensation awards benefits to workers injured on the job. Disability benefits are awarded to a person suffering an injury while not engaged on his job; they are nonoccupational benefits. Here, again, claims must be carefully scrutinized to prevent unwarranted payments of benefits. You should check with your state department of labor and obtain any literature that is available for the guidance of employers.

Civil Rights

Many states have statutes prohibiting discrimination based on race, creed, color, or national origin in places of public accommodation, such as hotels or restaurants. Other states have set up a so-called Human Rights Division in the executive branches of their governments and make it an unlawful labor practice to deny to or withhold from any person employment on account of sex or age, as well as race, creed, color, or national origin. Some of these statutes provide for criminal as well as monetary damages for their violation.

Many of these agencies have issued pamphlets describing in summary form what is and what is not permissible, and the food service operator should obtain copies of these for his guidance.

Alcoholic Beverages

We have discussed the operations of the Bureau of Alcohol, Tobacco, and Firearms and noted that liquor is strictly controlled from the manufacturer right down to the ultimate consumer with the federal government, in general, regulating the manufacture and the interstate and foreign shipment of liquor. The retail operations are licensed by the individual states with equally strict regulations governing such items as hours of sale, gambling on the premises, adulteration of liquor, sales to minors, advertising, visibility into the premises, record-keeping requirements, credit sales, restrictions on employment of certain persons, such as minors, and sales to intoxicated persons. The state control agencies issue the licenses and may have different types of licenses with varying fees for hotel, restaurant, tavern, and club licenses. Most of these state agencies publish pamphlets describing the requirements of the law for the guidance of the licensees. Some also publish small booklets highlighting the more common violations that occur under the law. The careful food service operator will obtain and study these releases because in his business, the most valuable asset he has may be his liquor license.

Dram Shop Laws

The dram shop statutes are a vestige of the Prohibition era but have been continued on the statute books of many states even after the repeal of Prohibition. They create a cause of action in favor of a person who might be injured by a person intoxicated as a result of an unlawful sale of liquor to such a person. For example, if in violation of the state statute the licensee sells liquor to an individual who is drunk and the drunken party injures another person while driving home, then the injured party can sue for damages the one making such sale. You may wish to consider taking out insurance against this type of liability. This aspect of the matter is discussed in Chapter 18 on the subject of insurance.

If you are confronted with a dram shop claim, you should consult your attorney.

Labor Laws

Many states have labor laws and regulations covering a wide variety of subjects, and the food service operator should familiarize himself with these matters by obtaining labor department literature on these matters which may include:

1. Issuance of employment certificates to minors
2. General prohibition of certain types of work by minors
3. Hours of employment of minors during school year
4. Prohibited hours of employment
5. Restrictions on hours and type of work for women
6. Sanitation
7. Window cleaning
8. Time off for meals
9. Regulations relating to safety in places of public assembly

Fire Laws

Some states and municipalities have building codes that have special provisions dealing with safety and fire prevention. Many of these provisions are particularly concerned with hotels, hospitals, and restaurants where a fire may be the cause of the loss of a large number of lives. Some of our worst fires with high numbers of fatalities have occurred in these operations. The careful food operator will familiarize himself with these building codes to protect his patrons as well as to protect himself from liability. In the event of a loss of life in his building, if the building is subsequently found to be in violation of the building code and if such violation was a contributing factor to the loss, he may be subject to heavy damages.

Your local building department or town clerk can advise you where you can get information on such building codes.

Local Laws

We have discussed the pertinent laws affecting food and beverage operations at the federal and state levels of government. The third level of government with the power to enact laws is in the local municipal, county, town or village governing body. In general, these bodies legislate in the area we might call the housekeeping field. They are concerned with numerous problems of local interest such as police protection, fire regulations, building codes, electricity, gas, health, hospitals, licenses, sanitation, real estate and sales taxes, water, zoning, and countless other problems of interest to the particular community, problems almost too numerous even to attempt to list. However, if a food service operator is in need of information on any subject regulated at the local level, he should turn to the city, town, or village clerk for guidance as to where he should address his inquiry. If your problem involves a matter of concern to one of your local departments, for example, the police department, you should, of course, turn to that department for guidance.

The laws listed and discussed above are some of the more important ones relating to food and beverage operations, but they are by no means all of them. However, this list will give you some standard to guide you in your day-to-day operations and alert you to some of the problems that may arise from time to time. The laws are discussed in general language. If you need more detailed information, you should contact the agency charged with the enforcement of the law or your own attorney.

17

Unions and Contract Negotiations

Historical Highlights

There is disagreement among labor historians regarding the beginning of labor unionism in the United States. It appears, however, that unions grew out of the old guilds, originating with a type of journeymen's association among shoemakers in Philadelphia in 1792.

In the 1830s, small local unions and other worker groups emerged; some of these groups banded together to form the first, loosely knit, National Trades Union. In the business crash of 1837, the National Trades Union and its locals vanished. The then-prevailing attitude regarding unions was that they were criminal conspiracies. Employers fought them by every means.

By 1933 union development in the United States had passed through periods of growth, decline and stagnation. The severe depression had cut back union membership to a level that had existed prior to World War I.

In 1935 there were two definite boosts for organized labor. First there was the enactment of the National Labor Relations Act (NLRA), commonly known as the Wagner Act, which detailed the rights of workers, greatly increased labor's powers, forbade the employers' antiunion practices then prevalent, and put teeth into the unions' power to bargain collectively. Unions were guaranteed recognition if they won a majority vote among the workers. A National Labor Relations Board, which consisted of three members, was established. These members were not affiliated with either labor or industry, and their mission was to administer the provisions of the NLRA.

The second significant occurrence, although nonlegislative in nature, was the separation in the ranks of organized labor. A group called the Congress of Industrial Organization (CIO) splintered off from the American Federation of Labor (AFL). The CIO's activities resulted in the eventual unionization of the mass production industries.

As time passed, there were many who felt that the Wagner Act had gone too far in trying to change a situation that had been more favorable to management than to labor. In 1947 the Taft–Hartley Act (National Management Relations Act) was enacted. Its preamble stated that this was "an act to amend the National Labor Relations Act, to provide additional facilities for the mediation of labor disputes affecting commerce, to equalize legal responsibilities of labor organizations and employers, and for other purposes." Under its terms, the provisions of the NLRA that were not amended or repealed remained in force.

In 1959 the National Labor Relations Board (NLRB) asserted jurisdiction over the lodging industry, indicating that it would enforce the National Labor Management Relations Act in any hotel–motel establishment with annual gross receipts in excess of $500,000. Following shortly in 1961, amendments to the Fair Labor Standards Act made the law applicable to any retail or service establishment with an annual gross income of $1 million or more.

During the middle 1950s, the service segment of our national economy accounted for 50 percent of total national employment. By 1965 the distribution of the members of the nonagricultural national work force of about 61 million persons was 21.8 million in goods-producing industries and 38.9 million in service-producing industries.

If the trend toward greater employment in the service-producing industries continues (and all indications are that it will), it is estimated that by 1980 the goods-producing segment of the non-agricultural work force will be 27 million and the service-producing segment will be 59.5 million.

A significant segment of the service portion of the work force is employed by the food service industry, which now has upward of 2.7 million workers in establishments with total annual sales of over $30 billion. The zeal with which unions sought membership of workers in the manufacturing segment of the economy is now also evident in membership drives in the service sector.

According to a table appearing in the *Statistical Abstract of the United States 1972*, the hotel and restaurant union (which is affiliated with the AFL-CIO) had 445,000 members in 1965, and 461,000 members in 1970. If the work force in the food service industry increases to 3 million by 1980, as forecast, it is reasonable to suppose that unionization efforts will continue to be very strong. Consequently, collective bargaining in the food service industry will be more extensive.

Negotiating a Union Contract

Negotiating a collective bargaining agreement (union contract) requires a considerable amount of skill and knowledge. When negotiation by an individual food service operator is being considered, it is advisable that the services of an experienced labor counsel be secured. In essence, the collective bargaining agreement is a binding legal contract. It establishes the terms and conditions for that part of a work force that will be covered by the document, and it also describes certain basic contractual relationships that will exist between labor and management.

The practice of having negotiations conducted with a group of employers instead of an individual employer has been accepted as a means of establishing collective bargaining agreements. Whether the individual owner believes it necessary to align himself with the group and not negotiate individually is a policy matter that should be carefully considered. Once an affiliation with a group is established, it is difficult to break away and negotiate a contract individually again.

The NLRB has had to establish certain rules regarding withdrawals from multiemployer bargaining units. Such a situation manifested itself in the 1972 strike against restaurants in New York City, when there was a splintering off of individual establishments from the negotiating group in order to try to reach separate union agreements. In its ruling on that occasion, the NLRB stated that "under certain conditions an employer could withdraw from a multiemployer group and not be bound by the agreement eventually reached with the union." The NLRB also ruled that this same right of withdrawal should be given to the unions. In so ruling, the NLRB performed its primary function, namely, maintaining a balance between the interests and rights of labor and management.

Preparing for Negotiation

Once the plan of negotiation has been determined—either negotiating individually or joining a group of employers—it is then time to begin preparation for the bargaining with the union so that its claims and demands can be met with facts. Since the life of the collective bargaining agreement is usually several years, it is imperative that union demands receive the time and study required to enable a food service operator to negotiate a viable agreement. There are several important areas that should be covered prior to the beginning of actual contract negotiations.

To prepare properly for the claims and demands of the union, management must know what they will be. Any manager who keeps in close touch with his business and the industry will know the direction of the demands that will be made, even though he may not know the extent of them. A review of the trend of wages and benefits in the industry in nearby areas will provide guidelines regarding the probable extent of the monetary wage and benefit demands of the union. This knowledge can be used to determine not only whether the union demands are in line but also the viability of the demands based on the status of the labor market, the local economy, and the probable reaction of the market to increases in menu prices, which may be necessary to meet the prospective higher labor cost.

Familiarity with recent trends in the cost of living index, such as that prepared by the Department of Labor, will be of value in the negotiations, especially in the evaluation of the demands made by the union. It is also important to gain some information about the overall philosophy of the union, its approach to bargaining, and the terms of agreements reached with it by other employers in the industry, individually or in groups.

When the time approaches for renegotiation of the contract, knowledge of what grievances have been filed and what problems line supervisors may have experienced with the present contract should be sought. Conferences should be held with supervisors to acquire an understanding and appreciation of problems on the operating level. Evaluation of the economic aspects of the union's demands is vital, but the noneconomic demands are also extremely important and should be reviewed in light of their potential impact on operations.

An attempt should be made to determine which of the contract demands are relatively unimportant and were tacked on for bargaining purposes. It is those demands that are quickly compromised once negotiations begin. Care must be taken to identify the demands that the union does not expect to be met in current negotiations but that it hopes will have a better chance in the future. Preliminary positions should be established by the employer regarding which of the demands are acceptable, which are unacceptable, and which might be acceptable if they were modified.

Some thought should be given ahead of time to employer demands, the existence of which is a normal part of the collective bargaining process. If the negotiating team makes a concession favorable to labor, it should seek something favorable to management in return.

Contracts and Some of Their Important Clauses

Ideally, the union contract should be clearly written so there is no doubt as to its meaning. History shows that there are flaws in most collective bargaining agreements. That applies to agreements not only in the food service industry but in other fields as well. Improper drafting of agreements can result in costly disputes and possible limitations in employee control. It is not possible to identify every area where problems can occur, but labor negotiators agree that the following suggestions, if followed, can help to avoid some of the more common problems that arise after agreements become operative:

1. A contract proposal should never be accepted without first directing some effort to ascertaining the reason for its having been submitted.
2. A contract should include a clause stating that the contract terms as written constitute the total agreement between the parties.
3. It is generally accepted that contract language and phraseology are to be interpreted in their usually accepted meaning. Therefore, a meaning other than that written should be spelled out.
4. Administrative, executive, and supervisory employees should be specifically excluded from the union contract by the recognition clause in labor contracts.

It is not uncommon for unions in the food service industry to insist on recognition of past practices in the contract.

If a clause is inserted like the one in suggestion two above, past practices do not present a major problem. This clause is a particularly important consideration if the past practices in question existed prior to the recognition of a union and were favorable to the employees. In such a circumstance, the union understandably vigorously attempts to maintain a "status quo." If any of the past benefits are lost, it is difficult indeed for the union to justify to new members its failure to obtain the rights and privileges they were entitled to prior to the advent of the union.

Grievances

The absence of a well-defined system to provide the employee with a means of getting a hearing if he has a grievance is often considered a major reason for the spread of unionization. In negotiating a contract, considerable care must be exercised to provide a fair and workable system for hearing grievances. More important, there should be a clear understanding of what constitutes a grievance under the terms of the contract.

The procedure for handling grievances should be developed around the relationship between the worker and his immediate supervisor. The first-line supervisor in most organizations is the management employee closest to the scene. Accordingly, when a problem develops, a well-trained supervisor with some understanding of human relations may quickly step in, investigate the situation, and often solve it before the complaint is put in writing. Regardless of the validity of the complaint, which would have to be established by some subsequent investigation, the fact that an employee made it presents management with a problem.

Depending on the size of the organization, the number of steps in the grievance procedure will vary. Most grievance procedures, however, begin at the first line, where the employee's shop steward and the employer's supervisor attempt to solve the problem.

The second and third steps in the grievance procedure may involve the supervisor and the unit manager. If a grievance progresses to this point, the complaint is probably now in writing, and the shop steward is joined by the union's business agent. It is usually the policy that once the grievance is put in writing, management's answer must also be in writing, within a stipulated period of time.

Union contracts provide for the arbitration of grievances that cannot be resolved through the various steps in the grievance procedure. The following paragraph was extracted from an existing union contract in a major city to show the language used and the intentions of both parties concerning arbitration:

> All matters in controversy or in dispute arising out of the interpretation or application of this agreement shall immediately be taken up for adjustment by employer and officials of the union. If unable to reach an agreement, the matter in dispute shall be submitted for determination to the American Arbitration Association. The expense of arbitration proceedings shall be borne equally between employer and union. The arbitrators shall not have the power to change any of the matters agreed upon herein, including, without limitations, wages, hours, overtime or vacations.

Productivity

Among the more serious issues confronting the nation today is the cost of labor, which is an important element in the determination of the selling prices of products manufactured in the United States. The problem is one of macroeconomics because consideration must be given to the best interests of the total economy, not just the food service industry, which is but one component of it. The inflationary trends experienced in our economy have manifested themselves in an upward spiral in the cost of products and services, often causing an imposition of government wage and price controls. Regardless of the cause, higher wages, salaries, and fringe benefits sought by employees must in the final analysis translate themselves into higher cost of products and services.

The term *productivity* generally refers to the amount of output per unit of input. It is meaningful only when it can be compared with some standard of reference. The need for improving productivity is now being discussed increasingly often, and it represents a controversial area in the negotiation of a union contract. In fact, it is not unusual for productivity to become a major issue as management attempts to hold the line on wages and fringe benefits.

Unions tend to oppose the establishment of productivity standards. Unions traditionally favor general wage increases applied across the board. This view stems in part from the union's policy of representing all the employees in the organization. The unions believe that wage increases should not be in recognition of any individual achievement. Undoubtedly, the issue of productivity will continue to be a major concern of management and labor in the future.

Right of Access

The right of access clause, which generally appears in most union contracts, recognizes the right of the union representatives to visit the employer's premises. Great care should be exercised in establishing the language in the contract so that it is clear that visits to the premises must be for legitimate reasons. The privilege of access should not be used by the union's representative for social gatherings or as means of searching for problem areas that often can be better resolved by a shop steward.

Consider the language of the following two paragraphs, the first of which is a clause extracted from an existing union contract and the second of which is a suggested revision by a prominent labor expert:

> Representatives of the union shall have the right to visit the establishment in order to investigate wages, hours, working conditions and grievances.

> A duly authorized officer or representative of the union shall have the right to visit the establishment's operation for the purpose of investigating grievances under the terms of this agreement. On any such visit the representative shall apply first at the establishment's office for permission. Such permission shall not arbitrarily be denied and such visits shall not be permitted to be disruptive to normal operations.

The suggested revision restricts the privilege of entry to investigation of grievances only.

Established Wage Rates

Most union contracts include a scale of contractual wage rates and agreed-on increases to cover the life of the agreement. In general, the various job categories are listed, and the negotiated annual increases are spelled out. These wages represent the contract wage agreed on, and no employee in the category can be paid less than that wage.

For some time, skilled cooks and, in some instances, other food industry employees have been in short supply, which has often caused food service operators to pay wages above the contract wages with adverse results in future union contract negotiations. Subsequent negotiated increases during the life of the contract are added to the above-scale wage rather than to the contractual rates. So widespread is this practice that some union contract negotiators recognize it and seek appropriate language to protect employees from receiving less than the above-scale wages they are receiving. The danger in this is simply that the above-scale wage will ultimately become the accepted wage. Therefore, management should first explore every possible alternative action and all likely reaction before making an upward adjustment in the contract wage.

Contract Negotiation in the Future

As previously stated, employment in the food service industry is expected to reach 3 million persons by 1980. To attain that figure, it will probably be necessary for growth to occur throughout the industry—in fast-food establishments, cafeterias, table service restaurants, and hotels. The efforts of unions to organize and represent employees in these establishments will receive impetus in proportion to the growth of the industry.

Greater concentration of food facilities offering a wide variety of food service is expected to accompany the increased growth in major office complexes with substantial resident populations and a large number of visitors each day. Such multiunit food service systems located under one roof have become attractive to large food service operators who are willing to accept the challenge of providing management for many different types of food outlets. In such a situation, the operator would logically be interested in negotiating a master agreement that would assure maximum flexibility in the utilization of employees. Agreements of this type will undoubtedly be developed further because of the growth in major office complexes, and that development probably will create some challenging situations in the contract negotiation process.

18

INSURANCE

In addition to the legal obligations of his business, the food service operator should be certain that he has adequate insurance coverage to protect the business against a variety of risks. It is wise for the operator to contact a reputable insurance agent or broker prior to the construction or purchase of a food service operation. The agent or broker can assist the operator in tailoring insurance coverage to suit his needs and special requirements. Although the basic principles of insurance apply to all businesses, the food service business is unique in several ways regarding insurance risks. Each operation has its own special insurance requirements.

Basically, the food service operator should provide for several types of insurance coverage: *property insurance* to protect against losses such as fire, theft, vandalism, windstorm, robbery, burglary, and similar risks; *employee dishonesty insurance* to protect against losses from within the business; *liability insurance* to protect against a number of forms of liability encountered by innkeepers and all businessmen; *accident, health, and disability insurance* to protect the employees and principals of the business against those risks; *life insurance* on key employees whose presence is vital to the enterprise; and *workmen's compensation insurance* as required by law to protect employees from losses associated with on-the-job injuries or illnesses.

Property Insurance

The food service operator should obtain insurance coverages against damage or loss of property from a variety of perils. Some of the property insurance policy coverage the operator should discuss with his insurance advisor are discussed in the following paragraphs.

Fire Insurance

Fire insurance should cover against loss from fire and lightning on building, contents, leasehold improvements, and personal property. It should also include mortgage insurance for loss from fire. The operator can tailor the coverage to meet his needs, but he should be careful to know exactly what his co-insurance restrictions are. He should also be careful to increase his fire coverage periodically to reflect the inflated cost of repairing and replacing his property.

Additional Perils Coverage

Among the additional perils against which the operator can obtain insurance are windstorm, smoke and smudge, explosion, riot, vandalism, aircraft and vehicles damage, malicious mischief, water damage, steam or hot water systems damage, sprinkler system leakage, glass breakage, ice, snow, and sleet, freezing of plumbing, heating or air conditioning systems and appliances, fall of trees, collapse, hail, civil commotion, falling objects, burglar damage, and consequential loss. These are available as endorsements to the basic fire coverage in a variety of combinations.

Business Interruption Insurance

When a business is heavily damaged by fire, it may be covered against the physical property losses from that fire but not against the loss of the earnings that would accrue while the property is being repaired or rebuilt. This frequently results in the permanent closing of a food service operation because the earnings flow interruption cannot be covered by the owners. Business interruption insurance protects against this risk by continuing the earnings flow during the period the business is closed because of fire or additional perils against which there is property insurance. The operator may also wish to include accounts receivable coverage if there is a significant amount of receivables which the loss of records in a fire would make difficult to collect.

Burglary, Robbery, and Theft Insurance

A variety of insurance packages is available to provide coverage against the risks of burglary, robbery, and theft. These include open stock burglary insurance, mercantile safe burglary insurance, mercantile robbery insurance, paymaster robbery insurance, and money and securities insurance. These coverages can be purchased individually or in broad-form package policies providing protection against all these criminal risks.

Employee Dishonesty Insurance

The food service operator may also wish to protect himself against the potential dishonesty of his own employees. This protection is usually in the form of a fidelity bond. Essentially, the fidelity bond guarantees the *honest* performance of the employee. When an employee theft, embezzlement, willful misapplication, forgery, or any act of fraud or dishonesty occurs, the bonding company guarantees restitution to the employer. If the bonding company cannot recover from the dishonest employee, it must cover the losses itself. It is important to note that there must have been *dishonest intent* on the part of the employee. The bond does not cover losses due to employee mistakes or lack of judgment when there was no intent to commit fraud.

Liability Insurance

Like any other businessman, the food service operator is liable for his actions and those of his employees. In a business in which the general public is invited to partake of the products and services of the enterprise, the risk of liability claims is even higher. Therefore, every food service operator should provide adequate insurance coverage against the various forms of liability he may incur. Liability to another person for one's acts or omissions may result from a statute governing liability, from the common law, or from having undertaken a contractual obligation. Therefore, the operator must fully inform his insurance advisor of all his legal obligations to others and of the specific aspects of his business for which liability protection is required.

Most liability policies are divided into two main sections: bodily injury liability and property damage liability. Bodily injury or property damage can result in a number of ways. For example, a guest can be injured by a fall on the stairs in a restaurant. A guest's automobile can be damaged by an accident in the restaurant's attended parking lot. Liability can arise as a result of a guest's becoming ill after eating allegedly contaminated food. If covered by the proper liability insurance, the operator is provided with defense by his insurance company against any claims, even if the claim is false or groundless. The insurance company pays all costs of defense against claims for which there is insurance coverage.

Liability policies may be endorsed to provide coverage for medical payments to persons incurring medical expenses as the result of an accident on the insured's premises. The comprehensive general liability policy can offer this type of protection as well as product liability and contractual liability coverages. The food service operator should discuss these policies in detail with his insurance advisor who will tailor the policy to suit special needs. For example, the operator may need to include elevator liability coverage and sprinkler leakage liability coverage but may not need other types of endorsements.

If there are motor vehicles associated with the food service operation, liability insurance must be provided for these vehicles. Automobile coverage can be included as a part of a comprehensive general liability policy or as a separate policy.

If the operation serves alcoholic beverages, the operator may also require dram shop insurance. In those states with dram shop laws, the operator serving alcoholic beverages may be held liable for the actions of his customers if they are served liquor *illegally*. For example, in most states, it is illegal to serve alcohol to a person who is already inebriated. If the bartender fails adequately to observe this condition and serves liquor to such a person who subsequently commits an act creating a liability, the operator may be held liable for the act committed under the influence of alcohol. Dram shop insurance is intended to protect the operator against claims arising from these circumstances.

Failure by the food service operator to insure his business adequately against the various forms of liability is as dangerous as failure to provide proper fire insurance. It can result in the permanent closing of an otherwise successful enterprise by forcing the owners to liquidate assets to satisfy a legitimate liability claim. The intelligent operator will inform himself as to the various types of liability coverage through consultation with qualified insurance advisors and purchase that insurance required to protect the future of his business against any potential claims.

Accident, Health, and Disability Insurance

We have seen how the food service operator can protect himself against losses of property from a variety of perils and against liability claims against his business. But these insurance policies are not designed to protect one of the operator's most important assets— the people who make the business run. Without the people, the food service operation is simply bricks, mortar, and sticks of furniture. The management and employees are the assets that make the enterprise a success; they bring the customers in and make the business profitable. The enlightened employer realizes that good employees are difficult to find and harder to keep. He understands that to attract and hold top-notch peole, they must be provided with a series of benefits in addition to competitive wages. He also realizes that it is in *his* best interests if these people are provided with adequate health, accident, and disability insurance coverage.

Provision for protection of people-assets against the perils of illness, injury, and long-term disability has been part of organized collective bargaining since the labor movement began. Many union contracts now provide for employer contributions to accident, health, and disability plans as part of the overall agreement. If the food service operation is covered by such a union agreement, the operator may not need to provide additional insurance coverage against these risks for his hourly employees. However, in union shops, these plans make no provision for protection of key management personnel. And in nonunion shops there is often no protection for any category of employee against illness, injury, or disability. Insurance coverage against these perils commonly takes several forms: group accident and health insurance, major medical expense insurance, and disability insurance. Some companies and unions are now also providing for dental care insurance for their employees and members.

Group Accident and Health Insurance

Group accident and health insurance is designed to provide payment to those persons covered for expenses of medical care, hospitalization, and surgery. The premiums for this coverage may be paid entirely by the employer, or he may require employees to contribute to the cost of this insurance. Generally, group policies require that a certain percentage of employees participate in the plan in order for the group to qualify for the lower group premium role.

A wide variety of health and hospitalization plans is available, and the operator must consult his insurance advisors as to the type of coverage most suitable to his needs, and those of his employees. Most of these policies have deductible provisions under which the employee pays medical expenses up to a certain amount, with amounts over the deductible amount covered by insurance. Most hospitalization and surgery benefits are set up as a schedule of payments for specific treatments.

Major Medical Expense Insurance

Major medical expense insurance is designed to provide protection against those large medical expenses exceeding the coverage in most group accident and health plans. These policies typically make payments to the person covered for expenses above a relatively large deductible amount. In addition, almost all major medical policies provide for some participation of the insured in the medical expenses incurred above the deductible amount. These policies generally cover all medical expenses in or out of the hospital without any specific limitation on such charges. The policy also includes expenses for ambulance, nursing care, drugs and medicines, and similar charges. Policies may vary on limitations of coverage, and the operator is wise carefully to read and evaluate any such plan presented to him by his insurance advisor.

Disability Insurance

Insurance coverage against short-term disability is law in many states, often as part of workmen's compensation coverage for on-the-job disability. However, these plans may offer no protection for off-the-job disabilities, and many employers and trade unions offer this insurance as a fringe benefit. The food service operator is advised to consult his attorney and insurance advisors regarding his legal obligations as to disability insurance coverage for employees in his state. All disability insurance is designed to protect the earning power of the insured when he is unable to work because of an injury or illness. Benefits vary widely, and the employer may wish to increase the coverage mandated by law with supplemental disability insurance. In addition to short-term disability coverage, the employer should investigate long-term disability insurance for both management and hourly employees. This insurance is designed to pick up where short-term insurance coverage terminates, providing earnings protection against long-term disability. Long-term disability plans are frequently arranged with contributions by employees to cover the premium costs, with this additional protection being optional on the part of each employee.

Group Life Insurance

Another fringe benefit often provided by employers or trade unions is group life insurance. Under the terms of group life insurance, an employee selects a beneficiary to receive a cash payment upon the death of the employee. As with medical and supplemental disability insurance, the employer may require the employee to pay some or all of the life insurance premium. Group life policies are usually term insurance rather than whole life coverage. Under term insurance, no cash value builds up for each specific member of the plan. Death benefits may be paid out either as a lump sum or as an annuity over a period of time, according to the wishes of the employee and to the terms of the plan.

Workmen's Compensation Insurance

Every state has laws on its books to provide immediate medical assistance to employees injured in occupational accidents. In addition, these laws provide financial assistance to compensate for loss of earnings to employees disabled by occupational injuries and death benefits to widows and children of employees if injuries are fatal. Most states also include coverage for occupational illnesses and diseases incurred as a result of work-related activity. The cost of this protection is not borne by the employee. Employees are eligible for benefits whether or not the employer is guilty of negligence. However, there are usually some limitations in which injuries are not compensable, such as intoxication, instigation of horseplay, or illegal employment. The workmen's compensation statutes limit the liability of the employer to those benefits payable under the law for injuries or illnesses covered by the Workmen's Compensation Law. However, the employee does have the right to sue for damages incurred as a result of a situation not covered by the applicable law.

The method of compliance with the Workmen's Compensation Law usually is to provide a standard workmen's compensation insurance policy with an approved insurance carrier. Some states have state-managed insurance funds in competition with or in lieu of private insurers. In some states, the employer is permitted to be a self-insurer but must comply with defined financial requirements set by law. Usually, only very large corporations with a large number of employees are eligible to be self-insurers. *Failure to comply with Workmen's Compensation Laws is punishable by fines and/or imprisonment.* In addition, the employer who fails to provide the mandated workmen's compensation coverage is liable for suit by his employees for damages incurred in an occupational accident or illness.

Workmen's compensation insurance generally provides for several forms of coverage: (1) The employer is covered for his legal obligations under the applicable statute for situations specifically covered in the law, (2) the employer is provided with liability coverage up to a specified limit for situations not covered by the applicable workmen's compensation statute, and (3) the insurance carrier defends the employer against any suits brought by an employee for damages resulting from an occupational injury or accident.

The benefits provided by this insurance include medical benefits to injured employees, surgical care, hospitalization, nursing care, drugs and medicines, and all related expenses. Benefits vary from state to state for specific situations covered by the applicable law, and there are usually limits of coverage for situations not covered by the statute. In addition to medical care, disability benefits are made a part of workmen's compensation insurance. In most states, some waiting period is required before disability benefits are paid, and most states specify both a maximum period and amount in the law. In the majority of states, an employee permanently disabled by an occupational injury or illness is entitled to get disability benefits for life.

In addition to providing adequate workmen's compensation insurance, all states and the federal government require employers to report occupational injuries, but these reporting requirements vary. The employer is required to keep a set of accident records as well.

The food service operator must be certain that his workmen's compensation insurance is in force at all times and that he is complying with the law in every respect. The very nature of the food service industry is such that occupational injuries occur from time to time. Failure to provide workmen's compensation coverage is not only illegal; it can result in the permanent closing of a successful operation through a large fine, the imprisonment of the operator, or the awarding of a large liability claim to an injured employee. The operator must obtain this insurance before the first day of operation and maintain it in force at all times.

BIBLIOGRAPHY

Planning Management

**General Books on Commercial
and Noncommercial Food Service Management**

Cloyd, Frances (ed.). *Guide to Food Service Management.* Cahners Books, Boston, Mass., 1972
Coates, Dennis. *Industrial Catering Management.* Cahners Books, Boston, Mass., 1971.
Drive-In Management Magazine. *Drive-In Management Guidebook.* Harbrace Publications, New York, N.Y., 1970.
Eshbach, Charles. *Food Service Management.* Cahners Books, Boston, Mass., 1974.
──. *Food Service Trends.* Cahners Books, Boston, Mass., 1974.
Gardner, Jerry. *Contract Food Service/Vending.* Cahners Books, Boston, Mass., 1973.
Kahrl, William. *Food Service on a Budget for Schools, Senior Citizens, Colleges, Nursing Homes, Industrial, Correctional Institutions.* Cahners Books, Boston, Mass., 1974.
──. *The Food Service Productivity and Profit Idea Book.* Cahners Books, Boston, Mass., 1975.
──. *Meeting Challenges in Food Service.* Chain Store Age Books, New York, N.Y., 1974.
Keister, Douglas, and Wilson, Ralph. *Selected Readings for an Introduction to Hotel and Restaurant Management.* McCutchan Publishing, Berkeley, Calif., 1971.
Kotschevar, Lendal. *Food Service for the Extended Care Facility.* Cahners Books, Boston, Mass., 1973.
Miller, Edmund. *Food and Beverage Management and Service.* Educational Institute of the American Hotel & Motel Association, Kellogg Center, East Lansing, Mich., 1964.

Soloman, Kenneth, and Katz, Norman. *Profitable Restaurant Management.* Prentice-Hall, Inc., Englewood Cliffs, N.J., 1974.
Stokes, John W. *Food Service in Industry and Institutions.* Wm. C. Brown, Dubuque, Iowa, 1973.
———. *How to Manage a Restaurant or Institutional Food Service.* Wm. C. Brown, Dubuque, Iowa, 1974.
U.S. Department of Commerce. Small Business Administration. *Starting and Managing a Small Drive-in Restaurant.* U.S. Government Printing Office, Washington, D.C., 1972.
———. *Starting and Managing a Small Restaurant.* U.S. Government Printing Office, Washington, D.C., 1964.
Warner, Mickey. *Industrial Food Service and Cafeteria Management.* Cahners Books, Boston, Mass., 1973.
West, Bessie et al. *Food Service in Institutions.* John Wiley & Sons, New York, N.Y., 1966.
Zaccarelli, Herman, and Maggiore, Josephine. *Nursing Home Menu Planning, Food Purchasing and Management.* Cahners Books, Boston, Mass., 1972.

Restaurant and Food Service Industry

Lundberg, Donald E. *The Hotel and Restaurant Business.* Cahners Books, Boston, Mass., 1974.
Powers, Thomas F., and Swinton, John R. (eds). *The Future of Food Service: A Basis for Planning.* University Park: Pennsylvania State University, Food Service & Housing Administration, 1974.
Woodman, Julie. *The IFMA Encyclopedia of the Food Service Industry.* The International Food Service Manufacturers' Association. Chicago, Ill. 1975.

Marketing, Sales Promotion, and Advertising

American Hotel & Motel Association. *Outdoor Advertising for Hotels and Motels.* AH&MA, New York, N.Y., 1965.
Axler, Bruce. *Focus on: Increasing Lodging Revenues and Restaurant Checks.* ITT Educational Publishing Co., Indianapolis, Ind., 1974.
Campbell-Smith, Graham. *Marketing of the Meal Experience.* University of Surrey, England, 1967.
Club Managers' Association of America. *Promotion Handbook.* CMAA, Washington, D.C.
Coffman, C. Dewitt. *Marketing for a Full House.* School of Hotel Administration, Cornell University, Ithaca, N.Y., 1972.
Crissey, W. J. E. et al. *Marketing of Hospitality Services—Food, Lodging, Travel.* Educational Institute of the AH&MA, East Lansing, Mich. 1975.
Gallup Organization, Inc. *Gallup: Your Marketing Touchstone.* Vols. I-IV. Food Service Marketing Magazine, Madison, Wisconsin.
Hertzon, David. *Hotel-Motel Marketing.* ITT Educational Publishing Co., Inc., Indianapolis, Ind., 1972.
Kramer, Amihud. *Food and the Consumer.* Avi Publishing Co., Westport, Conn., 1973.

Laine, Steven, and Laine, Iris. *Promotion in Food Service.* McGraw-Hill Book Company, New York, N.Y., 1972.
McCarthy, E. Jerome. *Basic Marketing: A Managerial Approach* (4th ed.). Richard D. Irwin, Inc., Homewood, Ill., 1971.
Riso, Ovid. *Advertising Cost Control Handbook.* Van Nostrand Reinhold, New York, N.Y., 1973.
Rubel, Lavon G. *Away from Home Eating: Characteristics and Nutritional Analysis.* California State Polytechnic University, San Luis Obispo, Calif., 1972.
Schaffir, Kurt H., and Trentin, H. George. *Marketing Information Systems.* AMACOM, New York, N.Y., 1973.
Stein, Bob. *Marketing in Action for Hotels, Motels, and Restaurants.* Hayden Book Co., Rochelle Park, N.J., 1973.
Thompson, J. Walter, Co. *How to Promote Your Restaurant.* National Restaurant Association, Chicago, Ill., 1965.
Troelstrup, Arch W., *The Consumer in American Society.* McGraw-Hill Book Company, New York, N.Y., 1974.

Accounting, Internal Control, and Finance

Albers, Carl H. *Food and Beverage Controls.* Educational Institute of the American Hotel & Motel Association, Kellogg Center, East Lansing, Mich., 1964.
Dittmar, Paul. *Accounting Practices for Hotels, Motels and Restaurants.* ITT Educational Publishing Co., Indianapolis, Ind., 1972.
Dudick, Thomas S. *Profile for Profitability: Using Cost Control and Profitability Analysis.* John Wiley & Sons, New York. 1972.
Fay, Jr., Clifford T., Rhoads, Richard C., and Rosenblatt, Robert L. *Managerial Accounting for the Hospitality Service Industry.* Wm. C. Brown, Dubuque, Iowa, 1971.
Fay, Jr., Clifford T., and Tarr, Stanley B. *Basic Bookkeeping for the Hospitality Industry.* Educational Institute of the American Hotel & Motel Association, Kellogg Center, East Lansing, Mich., 1975.
Fisher, William. *Profitable Financial Management for Food Service Operators Through Profit Planning.* National Restaurant Association, Chicago, Ill., 1973.
Illich, John. *Restaurant Finance: A Handbook for Successful Management and Operation.* Chain Store Age Books, New York, N.Y., 1975.
Keiser, Ralph J., and Kallio, Elmer. *Controlling and Analyzing Costs in Food Service Operations.* John Wiley & Sons, New York, N.Y., 1974.
Keister, Douglas K. *How to Use the Uniform System of Accounts for Hotels and Restaurants.* National Restaurant Association, Chicago, Ill., 1971.
Laventhol, Krekstein, Horwath, & Horwath. *Uniform System of Accounts for Restaurants.* (Revised ed.). National Restaurant Association, Chicago, Ill., 1968.
Maizel, Bruno. *Food and Beverage Cost Controls.* ITT Educational Publishing Co., Indianapolis, Ind., 1972.
Merrill Lynch Pierce Fenner & Smith. *How to Read a Financial Report* (3rd ed.). Merrill Lynch Pierce Fenner & Smith, New York, N.Y., 1971.

Reynolds, Eban S. *Financial Management*, Educational Institute of the American Hotel & Motel Association, Kellogg Center, East Lansing, Mich., 1969.

Feasibility Studies and Site Selection

Applebaum, William et al. *Guide to Store Location Research.* Addison-Wesley Publishing Co., Reading, Mass., 1968.

Bohon, David T. *Complete Guide to Profitable Real Estate Leasing.* Prentice-Hall, Inc., Englewood Cliffs, N.J., 1969.

Goldstein, Charles A., and Arnold, Selma. *Real Estate Financing: Contemporary Techniques.* Practicing Law Institute, New York, N.Y., 1973.

Hanford, Lloyd D. *Feasibility Study Guidelines.* Institute of Real Estate Management, Chicago, Ill., 1972.

Mair, George. *Guide to Successful Real Estate Investing, Buying, Financing and Leasing.* Prentice-Hall, Inc., Englewood Cliffs, N.J., 1971.

Taylor, Arlie L. *Guide for the Development and Pre-Opening of a Motel.* Hospitality Media, Dallas, Tex., 1974.

Restaurant Planning and Design

Aloi, Giampiero. *Restoranti.* Heinman, New York, N.Y., 1972.

Dukas, Peter. *How to Plan and Operate a Restaurant.* Hayden Book Co., Rochelle Park, N.J., 1973.

Dyer, Dewey. *So You Want to Start a Restaurant?* Cahners Books, Boston, Mass., 1971.

Fengler, Max. *Restaurant Architecture and Design.* Universe Books, New York, N.Y., 1972.

Food Service Equipment Dealer Magazine. *Food Service Equipment Directory.* Cahners Publishing Co., Boston, Mass. (published annually).

Jernigan, Anna K., and Ross, Lynn N. *Food Service Equipment: Selection, Arrangement and Use.* Iowa State University Press, Ames, Iowa, 1974.

Kahrl, William. *Planning and Operating a Successful Food Service Operation.* Chain Store Age Books, New York, N.Y., 1973.

———. *Restaurant Planning for Efficiency and Profit.* Chain Store Age Books, New York, N.Y., 1973.

Kazarian, Edward A. *Food Service Facilities Planning.* Avi Publishing Co., Westport, Conn., 1975.

Kotschevar, Lendal H., and Terrell, Margaret E. *Food Service Planning: Layout and Equipment.* John Wiley & Sons, New York, N.Y., 1961.

Kuhne, Gunther. *New Restaurants: An International Survey.* Architectural Book Publishing Co., New York, N.Y., 1973.

Lawson, Fred. *Principles of Catering Design.* Architectural Press Ltd., London, 1973.

———. *Restaurant Planning and Design.* Architectural Press Ltd., London, 1973.

Lemoine, Franz K. *Profile of a Restaurant Organization,* National Restaurant Association, Chicago, Ill., 1970.

National Restaurant Association. *Hospitality Now!* National Restaurant Association. Chicago, Ill., 1972.

National Sanitation Foundation. *Food Service Equipment Standards. Sanitation Aspects of Installation of Food Service Equipment.* National Sanitation Foundation, Ann Arbor, Mich., 1976.

Wilkinson, Jule (ed.). *Anatomy of Food Service Design,* Vol. 1. Cahners Books, Boston, Mass., 1974.

———. *The Complete Book of Cooking Equipment.* Cahners Books, Boston, Mass., 1972.

———. *Special Atmosphere Themes for Food Service.* Cahners Books, Boston, Mass., 1972.

General Management and Administration

Anthony, Robert N., and Welsch, Glenn A. *Fundamentals of Management Accounting.* Richard D. Irwin, Inc., Homewood, Ill., 1974.

Brown, J. Douglas. *The Human Nature of Organizations.* American Management Association, New York, N.Y., 1973.

Drucker, Peter. *The Effective Executive.* Harper & Row, New York, N.Y., 1967.

———. *Managing for Results.* Harper & Row, New York, N.Y., 1964.

———. *The Practice of Management.* Harper & Row, New York, N.Y., 1954.

Hayes, W. Warren et al. *Management: Analysis, Concepts and Cases* (3rd ed.). Prentice-Hall Inc., Englewood Cliffs, N.J., 1975.

Hicks, Herbert G. *The Management of Organizations: A Systems and Human Resources Approach* (2nd ed.). McGraw-Hill Book Company, New York, N.Y., 1972.

Homa, Edna. *What Managers Do.* American Management Extension Institute, New York, N.Y. 1971.

Jucius, Michael et al. *Elements of Managerial Action* (3rd ed.). Richard D. Irwin, Inc., Homewood, Ill., 1973.

Litterer, Joseph A. *The Analysis of Organizations.* John Wiley & Sons, New York, N.Y., 1973.

Longenecker, Justin G. *Principles of Management and Organizational Behavior* (3rd ed.). Charles E. Merrill Publishing Co., Columbus, Ohio, 1973.

Law and Insurance

Anderson, Ronald A. *The Hotelman's Basic Law (1974 Supplement).* Littoral Development Co., Philadelphia, Pa., 1974.

Coccia, Michael. *Product Liability: Trends and Implications.* American Management Association, New York, N.Y., 1970.

Gordis, Philip. *Property and Casualty Insurance: Guidebook for Agents and Brokers* (22nd Ed.). Rough Notes, Inc., New York, N.Y., 1975.

Insurance Information Institute. *Insurance and Restaurant Fires.* Insurance Information Institute, New York, N.Y., 1970.

Kalt, Nathan. *Legal Aspects of Hotel, Motel and Restaurant Operation.* ITT Educational Publishing Co., Indianapolis, Ind., 1972.

National Restaurant Association. *Insurance Review.* Business and Technical Advisory Service No. 4. National Restaurant Association, Chicago, Ill., n.d.

Sherry, John. *The Laws of Innkeepers.* Cornell University Press, Ithaca, N.Y., 1972.

Information Systems and Electronic Data Processing

Burch, John G., Jr., and Strater, Felix R., Jr. *Information Systems: Theory and Practice.* Hamilton Publishing, Div. of John Wiley & Sons, Inc., Santa Barbara, Calif., 1974.

Casbergue, John P. *A Compilation of Information on Computer Applications in Nutrition and Food Service.* The Ohio State University, School of Allied Medical Professions, Columbus, Ohio, 1968.

Davis, Gordon B. *Computer Data Processing.* McGraw-Hill Book Company, New York, N.Y., 1973.

Hospitals Magazine. *Electronic Data Processing in Support of Hospital Dietary Services.* American Hospital Association, Chicago, Ill., 1969.

Sanitation, Safety, and Security

Axler, Bruce. *Focus on Kitchen Sanitation and Food Hygiene.* ITT Educational Publishing Co., Indianapolis, Ind., 1974.

———. *Focus on Security for Hotels, Motels and Restaurants.* ITT Educational Publishing Co., Indianapolis, Ind., 1974.

———. *Sanitation, Safety, and Maintenance Management.* ITT Educational Publishing Co., Indianapolis, Ind., 1974.

Burstein, Harvey. *Lodging Security and Safety.* Educational Institute of the American Hotel & Motel Association, East Lansing, Mich., 1974.

Chamber of Commerce of the United States. *White Collar Crime.* Chamber of Commerce of the United States, Washington, D.C., 1974.

Continental Bank. *A Businessman's Guide to Protection Against Crime.* Continental Bank, Chicago, Ill.

Correl, John. *Sanitation Now.* John Correl Co., Plymouth, Mich., 1972.

Curtis, Bob. *Food Service Security: Internal Control.* Chain Store Publishing, New York, 1975.

———. *Security Control: External Theft.* Chain Store Publishing, New York, N.Y., 1971.

———. *Security Control: Internal Theft.* Chain Store Publishing, New York, N.Y., 1973.

Guthrie, Rufus K. *Food Sanitation.* Avi Publishing Co., Westport, Conn., 1972.

Longree, Karla. *Quantity Food Sanitation.* John Wiley & Sons, New York, N.Y., 1972.

Longree, Karla, and Blaker, Gertrude G. *Sanitary Techniques in Food Service.* John Wiley & Sons, New York, N.Y., 1971.

Matwes, George, and Matwes, Helen. *Loss Control: A Safety Guidebook for Trades and Services.* Van Nostrand Reinhold, New York, N.Y., 1973.

National Fire Protection Institute. *Fire Protection Handbook.* National Fire Protection Institute, Boston, Mass. 1970.

National Institute for the Foodservice Industry. *Applied Foodservice Sanitation.* NIFI, Chicago, Ill., 1974.

National Restaurant Association. *OSHA: A Technical Bulletin about the Occupational Safety and Health Act.* NRA, Chicago, Ill., n.d.

———. *Pest Prevention Bulletin.* NRA, Chicago, Ill., 1970.

———. *A Safety Self-Inspection Program for Foodservice Operators.* NRA, Chicago, Ill., 1973.

———. *Self-Inspection Sanitation Program for Foodservice Operators.* NRA, Chicago, Ill., 1973.
National Sanitation Foundation. *Food Service Sanitation: A Reference Manual of Educational and Training Materials.* NSF, Ann Arbor, Mich., 1973.
Nuerge, William Jr. *Training Yourself to Efficiently Clean and Sanitize a Restroom.* Restaurant Hotel Aids, Minneapolis, Minn., 1973.
Occupational Safety and Health Review Commission. *Guide to the Procedures of the Occupational Safety and Health Review Commission.* The Commission, Washington, D.C.
Richardson, Treva M. *Sanitation for Food Service Workers.* Cahners Books, Boston, Mass., 1974.
Security World Publishing Co. *Restaurant and Bar Security: Front of the House,* and *Back of the House* (two vols.). Security World Publishing Co., Los Angeles, Calif., 1974.
Weber, Thad. *Think Like a Thief! Alarm Systems and Theft Prevention.* Security World Publishing Co., Los Angeles, Calif., 1973.

Energy
Fulweiler, John. *Profitable Energy Management for Retailers and Shopping Centers.* Chain Store Publishing Co., New York, N.Y., 1975.
Gatts, Robert et al. *Energy Conservation Program Guide for Industry and Commerce.* U.S. Government Printing Office, Washington, D.C., 1974.
Rickles, Robert N. *Energy in the City Environment.* Noyes Press, Park Ridge, N.J., 1973.

Maintenance, Housekeeping, and Property Management
Allphin, Willard. *Primer of Lamps and Lighting* (3rd ed.). Addison-Wesley, Reading, Mass., 1973.
Axler, Bruce. *Focus on: Building Care for Hospitality Operations.* ITT Educational Publishing Co., Indianapolis, Ind., 1974.
Berkeley, Bernard. *Floors and Floor Maintenance.* Cornell University. Ithaca, N.Y., 1967.
Berkeley, Bernard, and Kimball, Cyril. *The Selection and Maintenance of Commercial Carpets.* Cornell University, Ithaca, N.Y., 1970.
Borsenik, Frank. *Maintenance and Engineering for Lodging and Food Service Facilities.* Educational Institute of the American Hotel & Motel Association, Kellogg Center, East Lansing, Mich., 1975.
———. *Property Management.* Educational Institute of the American Hotel & Motel Association, Kellogg Center, East Lansing, Mich., 1974.
Bradley, L.A. *The Selection, Care and Laundering of Institutional Textiles.* Cornell University, Ithaca, N.Y., 1963.
Brigham, Grace H. *Housekeeping.* Hayden Book Co., Rochelle Park, N.J., 1962.
Feldman, Edwin B. *Housekeeping Handbook for Institutions, Businesses and Industry.* Fell Publishing Inc., New York, N.Y., 1973.
Gunther, Raymond C. *Refrigeration, Air Conditioning and Cold Storage,* (2nd ed.). Chilton Book Co., Philadelphia, Pa., 1969.

Johnson, Keith. *Dry Cleaning and Degreasing Chemicals and Processes.* Noyes Data Corp., Park Ridge, N.J., 1973.

Kotschevar, Lendal H. *How to Select and Care for Serviceware, Textiles, Cleaning Compounds, Laundry and Dry Cleaning Facilities.* Cahners Books, Boston, Mass., 1969.

Lewis, Bernard T. *Developing Maintenance Time Standards.* Cahners Books, Boston, Mass., 1967.

Lewis, Bernard T., and Pearson, William W. *Maintenance Management.* Hayden Book Co., Rochelle Park, N.J., 1963.

McLaughlin, Terence. *The Cleaning, Hygiene and Maintenance Handbook.* Prentice-Hall, Inc., Englewood Cliffs, N.J., 1973.

National Restaurant Association. *Equipment Service and Maintenance.* NRA, Chicago, Ill., 1964.

Perth, Don. *No-Iron Laundry Manual.* Cornell University School of Hotel Administration, Ithaca, N.Y., 1970.

Snell, Foster D., Inc. *Carpet Underlays: Performance Characteristics.* American Hotel & Motel Association, New York, N.Y., 1968.

Tucker, Gina. *The Science of Housekeeping* (2nd ed.). Cahners Books, Boston, Mass., 1973.

Index

INDEX

Accounting, 186-214
  and balance sheets, 199-214
    assets, 199-203
    liabilities, 203-204
    net worth, 204
    statement of income, 204-214
  banquet revenue, 196-199
    beverage service, 196-197
    billing, 197-198
    food service, 196-197
  bar revenue controls, 195-196
  basic financial statements, 185-186
  comparative statements, 186-188
  controls, 192-193
  fast-food and cafeteria controls, 194-195
  internal audits, 192-193
  management reports, 190-191
  other functions of, 191
  ratio indicators, 186-188
  revenue control procedures, 193-194
  uniform account systems, 189
Advertising, 272-296
  advertising agencies, 275-276
  internal promotion, 278
  market identification, 274-275
  media selection, 276
    effectiveness of, 276-277
  menu merchandising, 280-296
    color, 288
    copy, 281-282
    layout, 283-288
    other forms, 288-289
    printing, 295-296

Advertising, menu merchandising *(continued)*
    souvenir menus, 289-295
    stock, 280
    typeface, 280-281
  objectives, 273-274
  promotion budgeting, 272-273
  publicity, 277
  sales department, 179
  special promotions, 279
American Hotel and Motel Association, 12
Audit Bureau of Circulation, 277

Big business, suspicion of, 13
  countering, 13
Budgets, 215-226
  basic, 215-216
  operating, 217-225
    benefits of, 221-222
    capital budget, 225-226
    cash budget, 226
    control, 221
    direct operational costs, 223
    fixed operating costs, 223-225
    preparation, 220-221
    sales forecast, 222-223
    structure, 217-220
  organization and system, 216-217
  participatory, 217
  prerequisites, 216-217
  types of, 215

Business
  cycles in, 14
  Dun & Bradstreet, 10
  failures, 10
  organization of
    corporation, 36-37
    partnership, 36
    sole proprietorship, 36

Cafeteria layouts, 133-137
  cashiering, 136
  counters, 134-135
  hatch, 134
  kitchens and dishroom, 136
  queueing, 135-136
  shopping center, 133
  single-line, 133
Capital, requirement estimates, 40-43
  building, 41
  equipment, 42
    costs of, 42
  fixtures, 42
  furniture, 42
  land, 40-41
  leasehold improvements, 41-42
    depreciation, 41
    fixed installations, 41
    raw space, 41
    turnkey lease, 41
    vacated space, 41-42
  organization costs, 42-43
  preopening expenses, 42-43
  sale-leaseback, 40-41
  small equipment, 42
  working capital, 43
Capital, sources of, 37-39
  debt, 38-39
  debt/equity ratio, 37
  debt financing, 38
  equity, 38
  equity financing, 37-38
  government agencies, 39
  leasing, 39
  short vs. long-term financing, 38
  suppliers, 39
  taxes, 37
  venture, 39
Consumer demand, range of, 22
Consumerism, 12
Consumers
  behavior of, 20-21

Consumers *(continued)*
  class values, 20
  discretionary income, 21
  disposable income, 20-21
  reasons for, 20
Consumption
  and ecology, 14
  effect of technological change on, 14
  and food roles, 14
  patterns of, 13-14
  and weight consciousness, 14
Contracts, important clauses of, 314-319
  grievances, 315-316
  in future, 318
  productivity, 316-317
  right of access, 317
  wage rates, 318
Controlled Circulation Audit Bureau, 277

Data processing, 227-247
  accounting functions, 240
  applications of, 227-228
  choice of system, 244-246
    business minicomputers, 244-245
    general purpose system, 244
    service bureaus, 245
    shared systems, 245-246
    timesharing services, 245
    turnkey system, 246
  computer equipment, 240-242
    hardware, 241
    point-of-sale devices, 240-241
    prechecks, 241
    software, 241-242
  costs, 246-247
  management information, 228-229
    cost evaluation report, 229
    financial management reporting, 237
    inventory control, 228-229
    labor productivity, 236-237
    purchasing, 231-233
    sales analysis, 228, 233-236
  payrolls, 240
  planning of system, 242-243
    alternatives review, 244
    data accessibility, 243
    future needs, 244
    report requirements, 243-244
Design trends in kitchen, 126-129

Index

Energy, 248-271
  background, 248
  basis, 249
  conservation and cost control, 249-250
  external control system, 250-252
    municipal utilities, 251-252
    private supplier, 252
    public utilities, 250-251
  internal control, 252-262
    attitudes, 259-260
    best energy from, 253
    comparison with similar others, 257
    computerization, 259
    maintenance, 257-59
  mangement involvement, 260
  National Restaurant Association checklist, 262-271
    food preparation, 262-264
    heating, etc., 264-266
    lighting, 266-268
    miscellaneous, 270-271
    refrigeration, 268
    sanitation, 266
    transportation, 268-270
  prescription of use, 253-254
    analysis of, 254-257
  rents including utilities, 260-262
  replacement, 257-259
  reward sharing, 260
  shortages, 12-13
    effects of, 13
Environmental concerns, 12
  air pollution, 12
  litter, 12
  sewage disposal, 12
  teenagers, 12
  visual pollution, 12
Equipment selection, 122-124

Fast food, 10, 16-17
  convenience, 16-17
  low prices, 17
  speed of service, 17
Feasibility studies, 72-81
  general market area, 72-75
    area economics, 74
    employment, 74-75
    land uses, 75
    population characteristics, 73
    traffic, 75
    wages, 74-75

Feasibility studies (continued)
  sites, types of
    central business district, 75
    evaluation, 77-78
    highway, 76
    multiple-use complex, 76-77
    other, 77
    planned complexes, 77
    secondary business district, 76
    selection, nonmarketing factors in, 81-83
    shopping centers, 76
    trading area, 78-80
Food service management companies, 17-20
  agreements of, 18
  economies of scale, 18
  expertise of, 18
  marketing, 19
Franchising, 7
French restaurants, 22

Government activities, 13
  Equal Employment Opportunity Act, 13
  Occupational Safety and Health Act, 13
  National School Lunch Program, 13
Growth
  corporations in, 11
  educational institutions, 11-12
  of industry, 101-102
  reasons for, 11

Historical highlights, 311-318
  American Federation of Labor, 312
  Congress of Industrial Organizations, 311
  National Trades Union, 311
  negotiating union contract, 313-314
  preparing for, 313-314
  Taft-Hartley Act, 312

Institutions/Volume Feeding Chain Reports, 10
Institutions/Volume Feeding Magazine, 7
Insurance, 319-325
  accident, health, and disability, 322-324

Insurance *(continued)*
    and employee dishonesty, 320-321
        liability, 321-322
    group life, 324
    major medical expenses, 323
    property
        additional perils, 320
        business interruption, 320
        burglary, robbery, and theft, 320
        fire, 319
    workmens' compensation, 324-325
Interior design, 104-105
    case study, 110-119
        space allocation in, 112
    elements of, 106-107
    nonpublic areas, 109
    process of, 105-106
    public areas, 108-109
    seating, 108
    space allocation, 107-108
Internal Revenue Service, 2
Investment opportunity, 48-50
    cash flow, 49-50
    distinct from profit and loss, 49
    profitability, 48-49
    return on investment, 49

Kentucky Fried Chicken, 7
Kitchens, 129-130, 137-145
    commissaries, 130
    design, case study, 137-145
        availability of supplies, 138
        cost factors, 140-141
        garbage, 140
        health codes, 139
        lease vs. own, 139
        menu, 137
        number of meals, 138
        power, 138-39
        process of, 141-145
        space, 141
        type of service, 138
        union regulations, 139-140
    flight, 130
    hospital, 129
    kosher, 129-130

Labor costs, 10
Legal factors, 297-310
    alcoholic beverages, 8, 304, 308-309

Legal factors *(continued)*
    civil rights, 303-304, 308
    common law, 298
    copyrights, 304
    corporate taxes, 303
    disability benefit laws, 308
    dram shop laws, 309
    Food and Drug Administration, 305
    fire laws, 310
    income withholding tax, 303
    innkeepers' liability, 299
        bailment, 299
        changes in, 299
        contracts, 300
        dispossession, 300
        distinction between guest and tenant, 300
        duty to receive guest, 299
        innkeepers' lien, 299
        lockouts, 300
        negligence, 300
    labor laws, 309
    local laws, 310
    minimum wages, 306-307
    National Labor Relations Board, 304-305
    Occupational Safety and Health Act, 305
    pensions, 303
    record keeping, 306
    state laws, 306
    statutes, 300-305
        Federal Fair Labor Standards Act, 301
        Social Security taxes, 302
    unemployment insurance, 307
    workmen's compensation, 307-308

Management
    defined, 165
    history of, 165-166
    how it is done, 177-181
        decision making, 177-178
        motivation, 179-181
        styles of leadership, 178-179
    organization, 170-177
        authority, 170-171
        informal organization, 175-177
        principles of design, 170-172
        span of control, 171
        specialization, 170

Management, organization *(continued)*
    structure, 172-175
    unity of command, 171-172
  small business, 181-184
    difficulties of, 181-183
    in food service industry, 184
    other properties of family-owned business, 183-184
    research and development, 183
  traditional view of, 166-168
    control, 167-168
    implementation, 167
    in food service industry, 169
    operations research, 168-169
    planning, 166-167
    systems theory, 168
  types of, 45-48
    franchise, 47-48
    leasing, 47
    by others, 45-47
    by owner, 44
Market research, 22-23
  Bureau of Labor Statistics, 23
  college operations, 23
  National Restaurant Association, 23
  United States Department of Agriculture, 23
Marketing strategy, 23-27
  and grids, 25
  target market, 23-27
Maslow, Abraham, 20
McDonald's, 7
Menu planning, 119-120
Menu pricing, 152-159
  base cost method, 153-154
    example, 154-155
  markup on cost, 152-153
    determining, 153
  menu price structures, 155-157
    à la carte, 155
    determining, 157-159
    price fixe, 156-157
    table d'hôte, 155-156
  package plan, 157
  variants and combinations, 157
    determining, 157-159
Merchandising concept, 68-69
  differentiation, 68
  display, 68-69
  location, 71
    concentration, 71
  menu concepts, 69

Merchandising, concept *(continued)*
  operating policies, 69-71
    alcohol, 70
    hours and days, 70
    "make-or-buy," 70
    staffing, 71
    style of service, 70
    tableware, 70

National Restaurant Association, 2
New products, 15-16
  and dietetics, 15
  drive-in, 16
  fast-food, 15-16
  hot-dog stands, 16
  and restaurants, 15
  saloons, 16
  soda fountains, 15

Operating profitability
  cash flow, 65-66
  occupancy costs, 63-65
  return on investment, 65
  sensitivity analysis, 66-67
  systems approach, 67

Plan
  control, 131
    flexibility, 131-133
    materials, 131
    staffing, 131
    traffic flow, 130-131
    work stations, 133
  data gathering, 29
    inside organization, 29
    outside, 29
    research, 32
    visit rate, 32
  evaluation of, 130-133
    place, 27-28
    price, 28
    product, 27
    promotion, 27
  uncontrollable factors, 28-29
Pricing, 148-162
  based on cost, 148-149
  based on market, 149-150
  of beverages, 159

Pricing *(continued)*
  demand, nature of, 150-151
    competition, 151
    elasticity of, 150
  loss leaders, 160
  menu pricing, 152-159
  odd-cent pricing, 160-161
  raising of, 151-152
    and portions, 152
  sales pricing, 161
  to discourage sales, 160
Profitability, 8-10
  and type of restaurant, 8, 10
Pro forma estimates, 83-98
  cost of food and beverages, 86
  example of pro forma, 88-98
    controllables, 95-96
    cost of sales, 93-95
    description of restaurant, 89
    dinner, 91-92, 93
    luncheon, 91, 92
    operating expenses, 93
    profit, 97-98
    sales estimate, 89-90
  occupation costs, 88
  other controllables, 87-88
  payroll, 86-87
  sales forecast, 84-86
    and covers, 84-85
Purchase of existing operation, 34-35
  criteria of, 35
  financial planning, 35
  financial strategy, 35
  image, 34

Resorts, 161
Restaurants, types of
  coffee shop, 51-53
  family steak house, 50-51
  franchised fast-food restaurant, 54-55
  full-menu cafeteria, 53-54
  large specialty restaurant, 55-57

Restaurants, types of *(continued)*
  meaning of comparison, 61
  small luxury restaurant, 57-58
  traditional table service, 58-61

Safety and cleanliness, 124-126
Sales of restaurants, 2, 7-8
Specialists, roles of, 98-103
  architect, 98-99
  consulting engineers, 99
  contract food service companies, 102-103
  contract furnishing houses, 101
  equipment manufacturers, 102
  fees, 103-104
  food facility designers, 100-101
  interior decorator, 100
  interior designer, 99-100
  kitchen equipment dealer, 101-102
Specialty restaurant, 32-33
  appeal of, 33
Standard Rate and Data, 277
Subsidized operations, 161-162
Suburbia, 21

United States Department of Commerce, 2, 7

Vanity project, 33
  owners of, 33-34
  as prestige or hobby, 33

Work stations, 120
  design of, 120-122

Youth market, 21
  and evolution of fast food, 21